RHETORICAL
HERMENEUTICS

SUNY Series in Speech Communication
Dudley D. Cahn Jr., Editor

RHETORICAL HERMENEUTICS

Invention and Interpretation
in the
Age of Science

Alan G. Gross and
William M. Keith, Editors

STATE UNIVERSITY OF NEW YORK PRESS

Published by
State University of New York Press, Albany

© 1997 State University of New York

For information, address State University of New York
Press, State University Plaza, Albany, N.Y. 12246

Production by E. Moore
Marketing by Bernadette LaManna

Library of Congress Cataloging-in-Publication Data

Rhetorical hermeneutics : invention and interpretation in the age of
  science / Alan G. Gross and William M. Keith, editors.
       p.   cm.
    Includes bibliographical references and index.
    ISBN 0-7914-3109-6 (alk. paper). — ISBN 0-7914-3110-X (pbk. :
alk. paper)
    1. Rhetoric—Philosophy. 2. Rhetorical criticism.
3. Hermeneutics. 4. Science—Language. I. Gross, Alan G., 1936
II. Keith, William M., 1959-
P301.R4718   1997
808'.001—dc20   95-52683
                                                                      CIP

10 9 8 7 6 5 4 3 2 1

CONTENTS

ACKNOWLEDGMENTS

AGG:

I would like to thank the Minnesota Agricultural Extension Service, the Rhetoric Department at the University of Minnesota, and its head, Billie Wahlstrom, for their support. I would also like to thank Michael Tiffany, of the Classics Department at the University of Minnesota, for unearthing the ancient and beautiful photograph of the Rosetta Stone that is the centerpiece of our dust jacket.

I would like to dedicate this volume to my wife, Suzanne, without whom my scholarly career, and daily life, would be impossible.

WMK:

I would like to thank the *Southern Communication Journal* for permission to reprint several pieces in this volume, and particularly Keith Erickson for taking a chance on an essay that had not yet been written and an editor without experience. Substantial portions of the essays by Gross, Campbell, Leff, Fuller and Gaonkar are reprinted from the *Southern Communication Journal*, 58, 1993. The Oregon State University Communication Department deserves thanks for supporting this project. Our editors at SUNY, Priscilla Ross and Elizabeth Moore, have been patient and helpful beyond the call of duty.

The authors merit both thanks and praise, every one, for their contributions to an excellent, but probably controversial, volume; I could not have foreseen how very *interesting* this project would become.

Special thanks go to Dilip Gaonkar, for charting a steady course into provocative waters and never wavering; to Steve Fuller, for his constant support, and for making the world a safer place to talk about rhetoric and science; to Danny Maron, Brian Chaney and other students compelled by me to read and discuss these essays, much to my profit; and to Alan Gross, whose enthusiasm and experience were seemingly boundless.

But, most of all, I want to thank my wife Kari, in inexpressible and innumerable ways, for her patience and support, and I dedicate this book to her.

INTRODUCTION

Alan G. Gross
William M. Keith

Can a rhetorical hermeneutic, or way of reading texts as rhetoric, be anchored in coherent and enabling theory? In the lead essay in this volume, "The Idea of Rhetoric in the Rhetoric of Science," Dilip Gaonkar raises this fundamental issue. This issue cannot be addressed abstractly; only a close examination of current critical practice will do. Gaonkar intends to test the assumptions underlying rhetorical theory and criticism for coherence, and so his best choice will be a interpretive practice confined to a single disciplinary community; such a practice is one most likely to share a common theoretical/interpretive tradition. Since he also intends to test the scope and depth of these assumptions, a critical practice at the vanguard of this discipline will be necessary; such a practice is most likely to put the greatest strain on its underlying theses, forcing the underlying assumptive cracks to appear. In a reversal of the usual *topos*, Gaonkar does not attempt to question whether the rhetoric of science has understood *science* properly, but whether it has sufficiently comprehended *rhetoric*. These considerations account for the site of Gaonkar's critique of contemporary rhetorical theory and criticism: the rhetoric of science literature.

As a consequence of its more encompassing purpose, readers of this collection will extend to a broad constituency; it will include scholars who use the terms *rhetoric* and *rhetorical* substantively. Among these are literary critics, historians, sociologists, anthropologists, and philosophers as well as rhetorical theorists and critics. To this group may be added scholars like Stephen Shapin or Bruno Latour, whose recent work is rhetorical criticism in all but name.[1] This broader constituency may judge for itself whether the issues raised by Gaonkar, and challenged, amplified, and modified by his respondents, speak directly to their concerns. In our view, they do. They may judge also whether, having read this volume, they can continue to work in their usual way. In our view, they cannot.

A COMPARISON WITH WINGSPREAD

This is a collaboration among thirteen scholars that spans three generations and crosses three disciplinary formations: Speech Communication, English, and Science Studies. The germ was planted in a seminar on the rhetoric of science at an annual conference of the Speech Communication Association, blossomed into a special issue of *Southern Communication Journal*, and has borne fruit in this volume, enhanced by new contributions and revisions/expansions of prior contributions.

Such collaborations inevitably produce rigorous dialogue, as this volume illustrates. But this volume is also an illustration of an encouraging *topos*. For all the differences among the contributors concerning answers, there is general agreement concerning issues worth addressing. Rhetoric is the art of producing public oratory, and was systemized in the ancient world. Can this *productive* tradition be transformed without significant distortion into the enterprise that is before us, one that is essentially *critical* and *theoretical*? If it can, what is its legitimate scope and reason for being? Must rhetoric observe its traditional limits—a restriction to strategic, agent-centered discourse in the public realm? Or is rhetoric to extend its analysis to all discourse and, beyond discourse, to nondiscursive means of persuasion—e.g., civil disobedience in the public realm, the authority of the crucial experiment in science? And what is the goal of rhetorical analysis? Is it empirical—the investigation of practice for its own sake? Or is it normative—the government of practice? In other words, is rhetoric a tool essential to democracy, and are its critics its caretakers? Has rhetoric now become the new Master Trope, an immense body of theory that draws virtually all the humanities into its irresistible gravitational orbit?

These issues do not originate either with Gaonkar or his respondents, as a little bit of history will confirm. We can understand the context for these issues by seeing how their trajectory extends through the postwar period to the present day. To illustrate this trajectory, we would like to reflect on the relationship between the essays in this volume and the concerns of papers in *The Prospect of Rhetoric* (Bitzer and Black, 1971), a volume often called "Wingspread" after the conference it chronicles. This volume was the outgrowth of two interdisciplinary conferences held in 1970, convened by the Speech Communication Association to "outline and amplify a theory of rhetoric suitable to twentieth-century concepts and needs" (v). In the context of social ferment, and (sometimes violent) new forms of rhetorical expression, scholars at the time were concerned about the expanding conceptual character of rhetoric and redirecting rhetorical scholarship. Their voices eerily anticipate the current dialog, dwelling as they do on analogous *topoi*: the scope and definition of rhetoric, attempts to theorize it, and its relationship to the polity.

Karl Wallace (1971) attempts to reclaim for rhetoric its traditional status as a tool essential to democracy. In light of poststructuralist critiques of power relations implicit in discursive structures, his faith in democratic process and in the normative role of rhetorical practice seems almost poignant:

> Doubtless it has occurred to some readers that the nature of public discourse is virtually the same as the nature of what used to be called liberal education. . . . Some [educators], in thoughtless moments, speak of mere rhetoric or mere speech or mere language, as if communication could occur without a material and substantive basis. Or they think that rhetoric is limited to forms and styles of writing and speech and that the content and ideas of discourse belong entirely to scientific fields of study and are derived primarily from them. . . . I suggest that rhetoricians in the next decades can make their greatest contribution to the general welfare of the free and open society by acting in part as educators essential to the development of the public self of the individual. (9)

The problematic scope and definition of rhetoric was apparent even in 1970. In his response to earlier papers, Wayne Booth (1971), prescient as always, is aware of the reflexive problem implicit in the globalization of rhetoric:

> A piece of rhetoric about rhetoric to a group of rhetoricians . . . ? Impossible, clearly. . . . I could of course begin on the offensive, scrutinizing each piece, especially the introductions, for weakness of *ethos*, or locating the fallacies in every argument, exposing the . . . But it is easy to see where *that* would lead. It would be like opening a conference of psychoanalysts with a paper psychoanalyzing each of the other analysts. Every statement would soon dissolve into the *true* reasons (hidden,

"rhetorical") why it was made: "Oh, I know why you said *that*. Your eccentric definition of the nature and function of rhetoric leads inevitably to . . . ." "Ah, yes, but *I* know why *you* say *that. Your* picture of us as audience requires . . ." (93)

Booth goes on to reflect about the work done on rhetoric in other fields (psychology, sociology, anthropology, linguistics, and philosophy), and while calling for more case studies and interventions, notes, "There is simply no point in debating about how wide a field the term rhetoric covers or should cover, as if there were a hope of fixing the word in a right usage" (113). This view conforms to one of the conclusions of Wingspread: "*Our recognition of the scope of rhetorical theory and practice should be greatly widened*" (238, emphasis in original).

But is the search for definition as quixotic as Booth implies? In a trenchantly honest essay, Barnet Baskerville (1971) challenges several of the contributors:

Each day it becomes more difficult to talk even with one another (to say nothing of the generality of mankind, or specialists in other areas) about "rhetoric." Different groups use the same terms to designate different concepts; new terms are coined for old concepts; familiar terms we thought had been clarified to everyone's satisfaction turn up in unfamiliar contexts. . . . In light of such confusion, it seems remarkable that the writers of these position papers devote so little attention to problems of definition. (157)

Baskerville goes on to argue that the general definition adopted by many of the participants (rhetoric being roughly equal to persuasive discourse) may forestall the conference's objective, given the mounting evidence of nondiscursive persuasion:

We may be forced to the position that such persuasive (sometimes coercive) devices, though important subjects for study, though relevant to the rhetoricians, are not his central concern and cannot be embraced by the suitable conception of rhetoric we have been asked to outline and amplify. . . . It may successfully be argued that such a position makes it impossible to adjust rhetoric "to twentieth-century concepts, learning and needs," [and] that it would place rhetorical theorists outside the mainstream of present day communicative processes. (158)

Few of the particpants are troubled by the contrast between current rhetorical criticism and its legitimation in a tradition whose raison d'être is the production of oratory. Edward P. J. Corbett (1971) is particularly serene in his confidence:

> But as I study the so-called "new rhetoric," I am simply amazed at how much that is proposed as new is just Aristotle in new trappings or new terminology. The limitations of Aristotle's rhetoric are due not to any fundamental myopia on his part but to his restricted purview . . . [he] did indeed concentrate on a single mode of discourse, persuasion, but that concentration was the result of choice not blindness. (169)

And Corbett later notes, without finding it problematic, that:

> It may seem paradoxical to propose that rhetoric, which Aristotle said had no proper subject-matter, has become a substantive art.

Although, by and large, rhetoricians have ignored Wallace's call for political relevance, they have taken to heart Baskerville's suggestion that the scope and definition of rhetoric be expanded, have heeded Booth's call for case studies, and have shared Corbett's easy assumptions about the compatibility of their critical practice with the classical tradition. In other words, they have conformed to the Wingspread admonition that "*it is imperative that rhetorical studies be broadened to explore communicative procedures and practices not traditionally covered*" (238, emphasis in original).

In this, Wingspread recognized that, as of 1971, rhetoric's globalization was not generally recognized. It is hard to doubt that the globalization of rhetoric is now complete. How quickly it has happened—how easily rhetoric has become a universal hermeneutic! In his essay, Gaonkar teaches us to reflect on the consequences of our disciplinary haste.

THE NATURE OF GAONKAR'S CRITIQUE OF RHETORICAL HERMENEUTICS

Gaonkar is a rhetorical theorist and critic himself, and accordingly he does not reject their possibility, or discard these practices themselves. Instead he turns his rhetorical eye on them: How do critics argue them? What are their characteristic tropes? How does

rhetorical theory represent itself as an academic discipline—or intellectual movement? Centrally, he unfolds the global ambitions of
rhetorical theory as a *general hermeneutic,* a master key to all texts
(similar in scope and success to Casaubon's *Key to All Mythologies*
in *Middlemarch*). For this purpose, the literature on rhetoric of science is a perfect site, since it is the "hard" case: If rhetoric can prove
itself of explanatory value in the inner sanctums of physics and
chemistry, its claims to wide scope become genuinely cogent. Gross
(1990) typifies the sweep of such views:

> suppose we alter the judgment of tradition; suppose, instead, we
> define dialectic and logic in terms of rhetoric. From this per-
> spective, dialectic and logic are rhetorics designed for special
> purposes: dialectic, to generate the first principles of the special
> sciences; logic, to derive from these principles true statements
> about the causal structure of the world. When logic and dialec-
> tic are defined this way, rhetoric cannot be dismissed as defec-
> tive. On the contrary, it becomes the more general term that
> includes logic and dialectic as rhetorics for special purposes.
> (206)

Gross has, indeed, become infamous for a remark about reducing
science to "rhetoric without remainder," which seemed, even for
some sympathizers to rhetoric, to raise the stakes to an uncomfortable level (McGuire and Melia, 1989, 1991 vs. Gross, 1992).

Against this rhetorical tide (in both senses), Gaonkar mounts a
skeptical response, which may be summarized in four claims:

1. Rhetoric's essential character, as defined by both Aristotelian and
   Ciceronian tradition, consists in generating and giving speeches,
   not interpreting them—and certainly not interpreting texts in
   general.
2. The productive orientation of rhetorical theory, as traditionally
   conceived, requires a strategic model of persuasive speech, one
   in which the agency of the author controls the communication
   transaction. Such a view is plausible only in ancient fora or their
   contemporary analogues (and not even there, if we take seriously
   critiques of agency by Foucault, Barthes, and Derrida).
3. As a consequence of its traditional focus on production, rather
   than interpretation, rhetorical theory is "thin." The amount of
   specification necessary for a handbook like the *Rhetoric* is less
   than that needed for a critical theory. Because rhetoric's central
   terms—e.g., *topos* , *pisteis, enthymeme*—elude precise definition,

there are few constraints on them. Consequently, they are open to unbounded use. With so few constraints on interpretation, there can never be enough evidence for legitimate interpretive consensus. The thinness of rhetorical theory, then, enables its *globalization*, its extension to every instance of text, artifact, or communication.

4. Globalization, in turn, is tied to a disciplinary anxiety: If rhetoric is in need of revival, that's because its identity has been erased (by philosophy, science, the Enlightenment, or whomever) and there is therefore the danger that marginality could be permanent, that is, "the tradition" might be lost. But there is no need to worry: globalization is predicated on a circular strategy of recovering rhetoric as a universal phenomenon by prefiguring it as something *suppressed* or hidden. On this account, there are many "rhetorical" theorists (e.g., Thomas Kuhn, Stephen Toulmin) who only use the word occasionally and have no grounding in "the tradition"—but we can see their work is *actually* rhetorical anyway, provided we can (re-)describe it properly.

Gaonkar has addressed these themes before, especially the last. In "Rhetoric and Its Double" (1990), he considered whether a discipline which takes other fields of study as its content ("the rhetoric of . . .") has not thereby doomed itself to marginality—since its substance consists in having no substance. This line of argumentation has its roots in Edwin Black's remarkable little book *Rhetorical Criticism: A Study in Method* (1967). Much of Gaonkar's critique extends what is implied (though not taken up) in Black. In particular, three theses stand out. First, Black describes in detail the turn from the productive tradition to the critical interpretation of speeches, in the form of "neo-Aristotelianism," a loose collection of critical approaches ostensibly based in Aristotle, but actually inspired by James Wichelns's (1925) seminal article.[2] Second, Black examines the strategic focus of neo-Aristotelian criticism. For these critics, the point of speaking is to persuade the audience, and a good speech is one that achieves its goal. Therefore the critical evaluation of a speech must turn on whether or not the rhetor achieved her goal with the immediate audience. This line of reasoning requires that discourse be read as strategic. Third, Black shows that neo-Aristotelianism is both false to Aristotle and inadequate to the requirements of a critical method. Aristotle restricts the range of rhetoric to those situations (forensic, deliberative, and epideictic) where the audience is attempting to make a reasoned judgment; the contemporary (and very broad) notion of "persuasion" per se does not seem to be present in the *Rhetoric*. A critical method for contemporary rhetoric, therefore, would require a vocabulary which goes beyond the Aristotelian *pisteis* (proofs) and "types of speeches" to address contemporary persuasion's varied manifestations.

But Gaonkar goes well beyond Black in several important respects. First, Gaonkar deepens Black's analysis of the production-to-criticism turn by making explicit the problem of "thinness." While Black's critique was predicated on his desire for a method, Gaonkar attempts to show that this productive vocabulary cannot be the basis for a method because it provides critics with insufficient constraints on interpretive practices, practices for which it was not originally designed. Second, Gaonkar points out that the strategic assumptions built into the Aristotelian vocabulary are at odds with the critique of agency made by so many "friends" of rhetoric, especially Continental ones. But why then, Gaonkar asks, would this vocabulary prove so popular, so durable? Perhaps because it responds to a genuine rhetorical exigence: Reviving a discipline is no simple matter. As a consequence of the strategy of globalization, rhetoric, once Cicero's "civil science," now appears to be ubiquitous in modern life, as ubiquitous as community, knowledge, or interpretation.

AN EXAMPLE OF CRITICAL PRACTICE

Gaonkar's critique is not based on programmatic statements (like Gross, above), but on the practice of critics.[3] An example of the kind of rhetorical criticism that leads Gaonkar to his skepticism about hermeneutic globalization is the following commentary on Watson and Crick's famous paper, "A Structure for Deoxyribose Nucleic Acid":

> Watson and Crick devote by far the largest portion of their paper to describing their model of the DNA molecule, a static construction made credible by means of the precision of its fit, the sense it makes of previously isolated chemical facts, especially the fact that the ratios of the base pairs consistently approximate unity. But the achievement of this task accomplishes only the lesser of their two persuasive goals. Watson and Crick promised that DNA was not just another moderately complex molecule, however correctly described, but was also "of considerable biological interest." Given the ironic pregnancy of this assertion, it seems odd that the two researchers should spend so little time in its support. Seemingly, we have

only the one sentence: "It has not escaped our notice that the specific base pairing we have postulated immediately suggests a possible copying mechanism for the genetic material."

The answer to this puzzle lies in the rhetorical function of the adverb "immediately," really an instruction to the reader to re-view the description and depiction of the DNA molecule, to see the dynamic possibilities of an entity hitherto viewed as static. We are asked to perceive a just-described static structure in a new way, to undergo a Gestalt shift. In one sense, "immediately" is a rhetorical exaggeration, a hyperbole; in another sense, it is not. We may not instantly see the dynamic possibilities of the molecule; but once we do, our perception must be immediate. The molecule then fits beautifully into its new, more interesting context, that of Mendelian genetics. It is the fit of the now-dynamic molecule into this second context that fully satisfies the promise of the paper's opening sentence. (Gross, 1990:64)

This passage of rhetorical criticism illustrates all the characteristics Gaonkar criticizes. Gross insists that he can discover something interesting about science through an examination of the rhetorical features of its texts. Yet his analysis is so unconstrained by the tradition he professes to represent that his two terms of art—*irony* and *hyperbole*—can be deleted without ill effect, as can the two instances of the adjective "rhetorical." In addition, Gross's criticism glories in its readerly versatility; his is, in effect, a virtuoso performance. Because of this, however, his claims for the text are not legitimately contestable: they are themselves rhetorical performances. (Would a cadenza improvised by Pinchas Zuckerman be contestable?) In addition, Gross views the text exclusively as a strategic performance of its authors. But is this really the case, or is the strategic effect a consequence, not of authorial intent, but of critical reading? The gap between these opposing claims is where Gaonkar probes most deeply, running his finger, as it were, again and again over the space between a vocabulary suited to a productionist reading and the reconstructive readings of critics. And he seems to find it empty.

This passage also exhibits characteristics in rhetorical criticism criticized by Steve Fuller and Andrew King (both in this volume): a neglect of real audiences and an avoidance of the political and social implications of cognitive activity. On Fuller's account, Gross's claim equivocates between the empirical and the normative. Is it a claim about the way texts are *actually* constructed and received? Or is it a normative claim about the way texts *ought* to be constructed and received? Not the former: it contradicts Crick's recollections in *What Mad Pursuit* (1988:66–67) and posits a reader more sensitive to textual nuance than any actual reader could be. Not the latter, because no norms are suggested. On King's account, Gross unreasonably isolates his text from the social and cultural contexts that gave rise to it. This isolation helps free from social and political criticism not only the original discovery but its contingent consequences: recombinant DNA technology, the rise of molecular biology as *the* hegemonic discipline within bioscience, and the Human Genome Project. On this construal, by avoiding these linkages, rhetoric of science tacitly supports the *status quo ante*.[4]

Examples of the critical practices criticized by Gaonkar are legion, across a range of disciplines. For readings analogous in virtuoistic intent to that of Gross, see, for example, Evelyn Fox Keller on Bacon, Stanley Fish on Freud, Stephen Greenblatt on Shakespeare, Steven Shapin on Boyle, or Clifford Geertz on Balinese cock-fighting. Examples of the elision of political relevance are also legion, also across a range of disciplines: such elision is the effect, if not the motive for deconstruction in literary criticism, the effect if not the motive of positivism in the social sciences. The spectre of political irrelevance thus haunts the theories of thinkers as different as Thomas Kuhn and Bruno Latour.

REPLIES TO GAONKAR

Examples of these tendencies could be adduced from many kinds of criticism, across a range of disciplines. So, despite a focus on the rhetoric of science literature, we take Gaonkar to be raising foundational issues for rhetorical theory and criticism. Their sharp and compelling quality insures a rich variety of responses. Each respondent takes up different threads of Gaonkar's argument, contesting, modifying, or extending his ideas.[5]

Production and Criticism

Gaonkar argues that the rhetorical tradition is essentially one of practice. When theory *is* in evidence, it is firmly subordinated to practice and teaching. Topical theory and stasis theory are typical. The *topoi* (topics) provide orators in deliberative and forensic contests with a fund of arguments; stasis theory provides them with a way of determining the points at issue. Gaonkar asks whether it is really possible for a theory so firmly grounded in practice for over two millennia to be translated into a theory of interpretation. The strengths of a productive theory—its "rule of thumb" qualities— seem like weaknesses in a theory of interpretation. (Aristotle is one of the few classical writers on rhetoric to take a theoretical stance, which is perhaps why his brief definition of rhetoric has been so influential in the revival of rhetoric.)

In response to this charge, Michael Leff counters that Gaonkar's view is too extreme, treating as opposites two positions that the tradition places in fruitful dialectical tension: rhetoric as production and rhetoric as interpretation. By isolating the interpretive turn, Gaonkar is able ingeniously to "[establish] a causal rather than an accidental relationship between [that] turn and the globalization of rhetoric" (90). In Gaonkar's view, interpretation requires a metadiscourse that would, in its hermeneutic perfection, efface the object of study: The rhetorical text itself is now subsumed and invisible as a consequence of complete theoretical redescription. But to speak thus, Leff contends, is to hold too rigid a notion of the gap between production and interpretation. Leff attempts to show that there is a (hidden) interpretative element to classical theories, as exemplified by the doctrine of *imitatio*; the extension of a practice is an interpretation of it. This interpretive function is intrinsic to any hermeneutic. In fact, says Leff, Black's *Rhetorical Criticism* itself illustrates how "the act of interpretation becomes part of a tradition rather than a detached observation of its history" (94). Indeed, Gaonkar's own practice in "The Idea of Rhetoric in the Rhetoric of Science" is analogous to Black's: "he describes an interactive and generative network of influence that shapes, though it does not determine, the positions of those who participate in it" (93). Leff seems to best Gaonkar at his reflexive game: In identifying a rhetoric of rhetoric, Leff claims, Gaonkar must at least make his account consistent with his (Gaonkar's) own rhetorical practice in reading the texts he critiques.

In his response, John Angus Campbell agrees with Leff, objecting that "in driving a wedge between performance and interpretation [Gaonkar] disables a rhetorical interpretation before it gets off the ground" (119). What Gaonkar misses, Campbell feels, is a point Leff has also continually made, "that criticism is *itself* a performance" (119). To recognize this is to "remove the absolute barrier between performance and understanding" (119) and to espouse the position that Hans Georg Gadamer states so well:

> Where, indeed, but to rhetoric should the theoretical examination of interpretation turn? . . . Convincing and persuading

without being able to prove—these are obviously as much the aim and measure of understanding and interpretation as they are the aim and measure of the art of oration and persuasion. (quoted in Campbell 120)

Carolyn Miller responds by extending Leff's claim that Gaonkar overdraws the binary opposition between production and interpretation. She points out that none of the distinctive pairs of classical theory—performance/interpretation, practice/theory, *rhetorica utens/rhetorica docens*—can be described in terms of complete opposition: "Rhetorica utens, or 'rhetoric in practice,' for example, occurred as performance and led to performance imperatives for the *orator perfectus*, but performance includes an audience, and rhetorica utens can thus be understood equally from the point of view of the auditor—as a matter of reception, a matter of interpretation" (158). She also find an inconsistency in Gaonkar's claim that the vocabulary of criticism is Aristotelian and the claim that it is primarily "fashioned for directing performance": "since Aristotle's vocabulary is not primarily productionist, our use of the classical vocabulary for interpretive criticism would seem to be less of a distortion than he implies" (158).

But Miller's main contribution to the debate consists in her careful analysis of *translation, dialectic, dialogue,* and *conversation* as metaphors for interpretation. Dialogue is the metaphor she prefers "because dialogue requires relationship between interlocutors, and such relations inevitably involve power" (166):

> Gaonkar . . . idealizes translation not only by implying that it should be an unproblematic process of lexical matching . . . but also by presupposing that it constitutes a helpful model for describing what is involved in the globalization of rhetoric. Rather than being a secondhand translated lexicon for interpretation, globalized rhetorical hermeneutics is doubly hermeneutic: it is a conceptual vocabulary for interpretation which has itself been created by the process of interpretation. (166)

Strategy

Gaonkar has a second quarrel with rhetorical theory as a global hermeneutic: He finds the strategic, agent-centered orientation of classical rhetorical theory inconsistent with postmodern views of the subject and its agency. After deconstruction, one might ask, how could anyone still make sense of intentional persuasion, in any psychologically real sense? He is supported in this by James Jasinski and Steve Fuller. Jasinski holds that appeals to intention based in textual analysis are not strengthened by invoking a notion of rhetorical context, since in practice historical reconstructions of rhetorical context have been little more than extensions of the textual strategies they were supposed to be evidence for. Fuller thinks that intentions are, in a sense, irrelevant: what matters is how people read the text, how they interpret it. He doubts, seeing no evidence, that the normal audiences for scientific discourse read "intentionally," and so can't see why it matters to critics.

Leff, Miller, Campbell, and Keith also deal with this issue. Leff counters that Gaonkar's notion of agency is unreasonably rigid. To Gaonkar, agency cannot circulate freely. But Leff prefers a theory in which "agency becomes a matter of circulation of influence, something that remains fluid as one positioned subject engages the work of another, altering the work while being altered by it" (94). Carolyn Miller questions the historical basis for Gaonkar's claim about the univocality of classical agency: she wonders "whether it is possible for the classical vocabulary to promote *any* strong ideology. . . . the classical tradition is far from univocal. . . . It comes to us in fragments; some authors are internally inconsistent; several 'strands' within it have been discerned (perhaps the best known version is George Kennedy's analysis of the tradition into technical, sophistic, and philosophical strands)" (159).

John Angus Campbell attempts a radical defense of intentionalist reading; he feels that the idea of agency is irreducibly present in any rhetorical theory that makes ethical, political, or psychological sense. Moreover, to see the agent/rhetor as *either* "the point of origin" of rhetorical discourse *or* its "point of articulation" hampers the critic with a choice that is both false and hermeneutically naive. William Keith attempts to rescue the strategic character of rhetorical reading without privileging them with a psychological reality (i.e., without saying "Here is what the author/speaker was really trying to do"). As with Daniel Dennett's "intentional stance" toward machines, we don't have to make dubious claims about *psychological* reconstruction in order to give readings that *rhetorically* reconstruct a sense of strategy and *kairos*. Perhaps subjects and agents have been eclipsed, says Keith, as *foundational* explanatory elements in cultural and political theory, but Gaonkar takes these views too seriously: They don't mean that strategy can't reappear in a nonfoundational role.

Thinness and Contestability

Gaonkar's third argument against seeing rhetoric as a global hermeneutic focuses on the epistemic properties of rhetorical precepts. Do they provide the critic with a respectable set of constraints? Do these constraints produce interpretations that are legitimately contestable? Let us take the first question first. Gaonkar argues that, to the extent that there is theory, it consists not of a systematic array of insights but of a set of rules of thumb which cannot be deepened systematically. Once you have penetrated the first layer of explanation, you do *not* find another set of theories to explain the terms, claims, and relationships of that first layer. As contrasts, Gaonkar cites Marxism and Freudianism. While the top layer of Marxist theory invokes "class," underneath can be found a host of theories to flesh out "class" both conceptually and historically. Is there really a "theory" of the enthymeme in the same way?[6] Gaonkar's metaphor for this problem is "thinness": the theories of rhetoric are thin theories. This property is exactly right, he feels, for a productive art, exactly right for pedagogical purposes. But, when translated from production to interpretation, it has the unfortunate consequence that claims derived from theory lack appropriate constraints. Because virtually "anything goes," the application of such theories to texts leads to conclusions that are not falsifiable, not even legitimately contestable.

Alan Gross and John Campbell counter that the "thinness" of the theory does *not* entail the absence of constraints. Gross claims the tradition constrains rhetorical criticism even in the absence of rhetorical terminology: In *Narratio Primo*, for example, the first work on Copernican astronomy, "style persuades." We can see for ourselves that the

> increase in Rheticus' conviction is also mirrored in the gradual elevation of Copernicus's symbolic status: from heir to Ptolemy, to king, to general, to philosopher, to mythical hero: like Atlas, shouldering the world, or like Orpheus, rescuing the muse of astronomy from the underworld. . . . It adds nothing to the intellectual content of these statements to present them in the technical terminology of rhetoric, the classical vocabulary of . . . *taxis* and *climax*. (142–143)

His argument does not entail the uselessness of the technical terminology of rhetorical analysis. On the contrary, as in the case of anatomy, a technical terminology both embodies and enables systematic understanding: "it adds nothing to intellectual content to call a *kneecap* a *patella*. But no one would argue that therefore the technical terminology of anatomy is useless" (153, n.1). Equally important, as in the case of the Watson and Crick passage cited above, a technical terminology evokes a tradition of analysis: even the adjective, "rhetorical," allegedly vacuous, serves this purpose.

Campbell 's argument is complementary. While Gross claims that the tradition constrains rhetorical criticism even in the absence of explicit rhetorical terminology, Campbell claims that the text itself and its tradition of interpretation forms a complementary constraint. In effect, these become a set of Burkean "recalcitrances," against which (and with which) the critic must work. Campbell's example is Eugene Garver's readings of Machiavelli and Aristotle:

> Garver is a deep and insightful reader, but his readings, while involving choice and perspective setting, are not voluntaristic. . . . In the hands of a Garver . . . rhetorical criticism (like hermeneutics) becomes a form of radical questioning and as such can combine a high view of textual fidelity with an expansive view of critical freedom. (118)[7]

James Jasinski, by contrast, thinks the situation is not quite so dark as Gaonkar paints it. He notes that the public address tradition, which would generally include Campbell, Leff, and Gross, attempts to ground itself—stabilize a set of contestable claims—through a kind of historicism, which masquerades as a critical appeal to context. Moving through a variety of critics (most of whom, admittedly, have not dealt with science), Jasinski shows how, on the basis of recent work by historians, a thin and flexible notion of historical context can provide the nonstrategic ground for criticism.

William Keith and David Kaufer take the issue in a different direction: They redefine rhetoric as a design art, analogous to engineering and architecture. Like engineering and architecture, Keith argues, rhetoric fulfills its purpose by accommodating itself to its exigencies: the computer keyboard seems well designed to the extent that it seems "naturally" to accommodate the data-entering fingers of the operator. The rationality of all these fields is *both* practical and deep. To recover the craft inherent in rhetorical artifacts, therefore, we need the idea of *reverse engineering*:

> Confronted with an artifact . . . an engineer might have the job of making something "like it" or that "works like it." She

> would thus have to understand how it works, and how it was
> made, and attempt to duplicate the process. (How *do* they get
> the lead into the pencil?) (236)

While reverse engineering cannot establish, a priori, how the lead
actually got into the pencil, it can specify the constraints on the
process tightly enough to enable one to say that one's solution
approaches the actual solution. Reverse engineering presupposes
only one kind of rationality is manifested in an artifact's design,
when there might be many plausible reconstructions; rhetoric conceived of as reverse engineering has analogous limitations. It cannot
reconstruct the actual historical/psychological process that engen-
dered the verbal artifacts it analyzes—usually abbreviated as the
rhetor's *intent*—and it cannot pretend that those artifacts are *essentially* rhetorical, that rhetorical interpretation is the privileged
method of analysis. But Keith does not see these limitations as
important—since they don't limit *practical* uses of criticism.

Kaufer turns Keith's programmatic account into a theory. His
chief methodological tool, which is borrowed from cognitive science, he calls "complexity theory": "the study of the minimal complexity needed to describe a system, either as it exists in the abstract
or for some specific application or purpose. . . . In a rhetorical theory,
complexity analysis seeks to develop an explanatory framework that
accounts for a significant portion of the observed results of a rhetorical artifact with minimal conceptual complexity" (248–249). Kaufer
wants a weak theory, one that models not the psychological reality
that was the source of the rhetorical artifact but the constraints that
any plausible model of psychological reality must accommodate.

To illustrate his theory at work, Kaufer uses the Lincoln-Douglas debates. He interprets these by tracking their *interpretations-by-
design*. These are interpretations of what the speaker could have
meant, those that can be *"rescinded through alternative rendering of
the speaker's productive choice"* (256). During the Freeport debate,
for example, Lincoln begged his audience for time to put on his spectacles, saying, "I am no longer a younger man." We can interpret
this comment culturally as a statement about what counts as being
older, scientifically as a statement about what counts as a loss of
optical accommodation, and sociolinguistically as what counts as
an apology (as distinct from an excuse). But rhetorically we can only
deal with the speaker's interpretation-by-design: Lincoln was appealing to his common humanity, and, through *litotes*, to a common
nostalgia for lost youth. At the same time, he was referring indirectly to his status as a man of experience, making the most of the

four-year age gap between Douglas and himself. Within the constraints of interpretation-by-design, Kaufer builds his model of an "architecture of rhetorical design," an impressive first pass at a successful marriage between the rhetorical tradition and cognitive psychology.

Gaonkar also argues that the "thinness" of rhetorical theory issues in interpretations that are not falsifiable, or, in his weaker formulation, not legitimately contestable. The charge is serious: it means that the results cannot be classified as knowledge. Kaufer and Gross face the problem directly. Kaufer thinks that "rhetorical accounts should be falsified and improved upon"; he is certain, moreover, that his is such an account (250). Gross also takes the bull by the horns. He demonstrates that his interpretations have been legitimately contested and, what is more, his claims have been legitimately generalized by others in later work building on his. He feels that this legitimacy derives from the generalizability of case studies, by means of methods already in use in comparative political science and in sociology. He therefore concludes that "Gaonkar's criticism should be taken less as dismissal than as admonition. In future . . . the case study method must be more systematically employed as a starting-point for generalization and theorizing" (152).

Effectiveness and the Polis

Steve Fuller and Andrew King differ from other respondents in that they seek to extend and deepen Gaonkar's critique, albeit in ways he might not agree with. Working outside the tradition, Fuller plays the naif in the fairy tale of the emperor's new clothes. He notices the obvious point that the adults in the story uniformly neglect: Rhetorical critics go about their business by performing virtuoso feats of reading whose special quality is their distinctive results, and these critics claim to see something in a work—"The Gettysburg Address," *The Origin of Species*—that everyone else has missed. Then they claim that this unique reading has explained the rhetorical effect of "The Gettysburg Address" or *The Origin of Species*. Fuller points to the obvious problem with this picture: Since nobody actually reads (listens) that way, how can what the critic unearths explain the effects on readers or listeners? To Fuller, when Aristotle said, famously, that rhetoric concerned only discovering the means of persuasion, he did not solve but only formulated the problem. How can you know they are means of persuasion *unless* you encompass actual effects? But the documentation and analysis of effects is an empirical, not a normative task.

Fuller illustrates this point from the work of John Angus Campbell, who, through his adherence to a classical, strategic model, fails in Fuller's view to capture the real effects of Darwin's rhetoric. To Fuller:

> it would be better to think of *Origin* as having been thrown into the middle of many ongoing debates, subject to the vicissitudes of several parties trying to get whatever mileage they can out of what the book says. In that case, the rhetorically interesting feature of *Origin* is its ability to restructure the debates in which it so variously figured. (286)

As might be expected, Campbell takes exception to these animadversions. He feels that it would be a serious mistake to avoid "the strategic qualities of a scientific text. . . . Our question is a historical and philosophical one about the fact and function of rhetorical invention, not merely an empirical question about success" (130). But Campbell insists that his work also grapples with the empirical question of rhetorical success in a manner appropriate to a rhetorical critic:

> Darwin's specifically rhetorical achievement—whether one examines it in the strategies manifest in his writing or in the actual public response to his work—is to turn convention against itself and thereby change the terms of public debate. This is a spectacular achievement and it is a specifically rhetorical one, on any definition of rhetoric. (132)

King plays a different game. He criticizes the rhetorical tradition as an insider with the aim of locating the failure of classical rhetorical theory not in the theory but in the absence of political community on which the theory depended: "classical rhetoric . . . has lost (temporarily) the center of gravity (community) and the locus of a social role (citizen) that gave it vitality and relevance" (297). This relocation may seem at first a substitution of one myth with another: the ideal polis for the ideal orator. But by shifting the problem of theory and criticism from the rhetorical skill of the speaker to the political health of the audience, King's relocation does serious intellectual work. With this relocation in place, he is able to dismiss Fuller (and his intellectual predecessor, Comte) as antidemocrats substituting their own wills for the absence of community: "while Comte's unacknowledged rhetoricians practice the engineering of consent, Fuller's [Social Studies of Science] specialists (despite his pretense of broadening the debate by including subalterns and silenced people) will act as guardians by framing the technical issues in ordinary language" (305). The attack on Fuller, then, as on Comte, stems from King's belief that "postmodernism . . . is only another name for broken community and the consequent fragmenting of traditional civic discourse" (309). Thus, King feels that Gaonkar may have got his story backwards: if the current disarray of rhetorical criticism cannot be solved by despotism, however benevolent, it cannot be solved either by having critics ally with the forces of disintegration.[8]

Globalization, Suppression, and Anxiety

For Gaonkar, globalization and suppression are intimately tied together. Keith accords this issue a central place in his response: efforts of the rhetor are effective to the degree that they seem effortless: "the invisibility of rhetoric is exactly accounted for by rhetoric's focus on strategy, which accounts for the disciplinary problem of repression/recognition" (233). To Keith, this invisibility is at the center of the interpretive problem. If rhetoric intrinsically tends to deny itself then it will always be difficult to decide exactly "where" it is. The logic of globalization and suppression—

"Rhetoric is everywhere."
"Why isn't that obvious?"
"It is suppressed."
"Then how do you know it's everywhere?"
"It's everywhere suppressed."

—does not develop, as Gaonkar seems to suggest, primarily from disciplinary difficulties attendant on developing a modern theory of rhetoric, but is intrinsic to the character of rhetoric itself. It represents a problem that will not go away or be solved, and so a field of rhetoric will have to come to grips with the possibility that it will not become "just like" psychology or physics. The worry that rhetoric is, or has been, suppressed reflects a real disciplinary anxiety: the worry that one's discipline might be marginalized or become, like the profession of the Roman haruspex or the modern astrologer, no longer intellectually intelligible.

For some, this anxiety gets the better of them. Those questioning the methods for the revival of rhetoric become heretics: D. McCloskey responds to the problems of globalization, suppression, and anxiety by dismissing them entirely. In the great revival of

rhetoric, McCloskey sees Gaonkar as a leader of the forces of dark-
ness, those voices of barbarism and backwardness characteristic of
the Enlightenment's worst face. For McCloskey, Gaonkar's case is
half bluster, half non sequitur—and all hogwash. McCloskey finds
Gaonkar's worry about the translation of practice to theory
unfounded: "On these grounds no applied subject could be continuous with a theoretical subject: medicine would be discontinuous
with anatomy and biology" (104–105). In addition, he finds that
Gaonkar's argument that rhetorical claims can't be falsified is nothing more than a throwback to the outmoded philosophy of Karl Popper. McCloskey cannot imagine why there would be any limitations
to an Aristotelian approach, and he is not impressed by the argument that if everything is rhetoric, we cannot be discriminating critics; the fact that "everything is atoms" doesn't hamper physicists.
Finally, he thinks that Gaonkar's argument that the position of relativists is incoherent is itself incoherent. In a word, McCloskey has
no problems with the globalization of rhetoric, *period*: "If the
rhetoric of science from Fleck to Gross had to be put in a sentence it
would be, The substance of science *is* its rhetoric" (111).

Conclusion

As the century turns and a new generation of scholars comes to
the fore, it will be a matter of some interest to see whether the four
questions we posed at the begining of this introduction continue to
be addressed. On the basis of the debates in this volume, we would
be willing to give odds that, however much the answers change, the
questions will remain the same.

Notes

1. See Latour (1987) and Shapin and Shaffer (1986), as well as Shapin
(1994).

2. In "Object and Method in Rhetorical Criticism" (1991), Gaonkar
discusses the development of neo-Aristotelianism, and how it may have
arisen from erroneous readings of Wichelns.

3. His privileging of practice over theory will turn out to be significant.
Although his *position* does not entail that rhetoric does not respond to well-
articulated theory, this inference seems like a legitimate extension of his
analysis.

4. Incidentally, Gaonkar's practice of rhetorical criticism conforms to his theoretical views. See Gaonkar and McCarthy (1994).

5. Some of these authors have replied before, in another forum; see *The Southern Communication Journal*, vol. 58, no. 4, 1993. Of these, Lawrence Prelli was unable to participate in the current volume.

6. Of course, there *is* such a theory for metaphor—but it's questionable whether it's a rhetorical theory, leading back to issues of suppression and globalization.

7. This view does not exclude the textual violence of readings such as Burke's: "The textual violence of Burke wears a grin. . . . His readings are not merely willful, for in opening up possibilities within received *texts* he invites us to complicate fruitfully our understanding of *contexts*. In reminding us of alternative interpretive possibilities Burke does not destabilize or reduce our decisions to groundless acts of will but informed acts of deliberation" (116).

8. As we understand King's challenge, it concerns neither criticism nor theory directly, but the polity itself, not speech acts, but social action. If this is the case, it will not be an argument against him that Keith (this volume) and Gross, in recent papers, have insisted that the theories they espouse make possible a criticism that can create a fruitful commerce between the cognitive and the political. Nor will it be an argument against King that Gross and Miller have written papers severely critical of one status quo or another. King is not talking about talking.

REFERENCES

Baskerville, B. (1971). Responses, queries and a few caveats. In L. Bitzer and E. Black (Eds.), *The prospect of rhetoric: Report of the National Development Project*, 151–165. Englewood Cliffs, NJ: Prentice Hall.

Bitzer, L., and Black, E. (Eds.). (1971). *The prospect of rhetoric: Report of the National Development Project*. Englewood Cliffs, NJ: Prentice Hall.

Black, E. (1967). *Rhetorical criticism, A study in method*. Madison: University of Wisconsin Press.

Booth, W. (1971). The scope of rhetoric today: A polemical excursion. In L. Bitzer and E. Black (Eds.), *The prospect of rhetoric: Report of the National Development Project*, 93–114. Englewood Cliffs, NJ: Prentice Hall.

Corbett, E. P. J. (1971). Rhetoric in search of a past, present, and future. In L. Bitzer and E. Black (Eds.), *The prospect of rhetoric: Report of the National Development Project*, 166–178. Englewood Cliffs, NJ: Prentice Hall.

Crick, F. (1988). *What mad pursuit: A personal view of scientific discovery*. New York: Basic Books.

Gaonkar, D. P. (1990). Rhetoric and its double. In H. Simons (Ed.), *The rhetorical turn*. Chicago: University of Chicago Press.

———. (1991). Object and method in rhetorical criticism. *Western Speech Communication Journal, 54*, 290–316.

Gaonkar, D. P., and McCarthy, T. (1994). Panopticism and publicity: Bentham's quest for transparency. *Public Culture, 6*, 547–575.

Gross, A. G. (1990). The tale of DNA. In A. G. Gross, *The rhetoric of science*. Cambridge: Harvard University Press.

———. (1991). Rhetoric of science without constraints. *Rhetorica, 9*, 283–299.

Latour, B. (1987). *Science in action*. Cambridge: Harvard University Press.

McGuire, J. E., & Melia, T. (1989). Some cautionary strictures on the writing of the rhetoric of science, *Rhetorica, 7*, 87–99.

———. (1991). The rhetoric of the radical rhetoric of science. *Rhetorica, 9*, 301–316.

Shapin, S. (1994). *The social history of truth*. Chicago: University of Chicago Press.

Shapin, S., and Shaffer, S. (1986). *Leviathan and the air-pump*. Princeton: Princeton University Press.

Wallace, K. (1971). The fundamentals of rhetoric. In L. Bitzer and E. Black (Eds.), *The prospect of rhetoric: Report of the National Development Project*, 3–20. Englewood Cliffs, NJ: Prentice Hall.

Wichelns, H. A (1925). The literary criticism of oratory. In *Studies in rhetoric and public speaking in honor of James Albert Winans*, 181–216. New York: Century.

PART I

Provocations

CHAPTER 1

THE IDEA OF RHETORIC IN THE RHETORIC OF SCIENCE*

Dilip Parameshwar Gaonkar

INTRODUCTION: RHETORIC AS A METADISCOURSE

A striking but insufficiently examined feature of the current revival of interest in rhetoric is its positioning primarily as a hermeneutic metadiscourse rather than as a substantive discourse practice. Today we frequently invoke rhetoric as a metadiscourse to describe and to interpret discursive practices of various sorts, including those that are subsumed under "science." When one invokes a metadiscourse to account for a discursive practice, what one hopes to achieve is minimally a "redescription" of the latter. Under ideal conditions, an agile reader might wish to dissolve a discursive practice into the interpretive medium of a preferred metadiscourse (be it Marxism, psychoanalysis, structural linguistics, or rhetoric). A perfect interpretation is one in which the object of interpretation loses all of its recalcitrance and becomes transparent. Such is the dream of interpretation, and we have been seduced by that dream. Rhetoric has entered the orbit of general hermeneutics (Eden, 1987, 1990; Hernadi, 1989; Hyde and Smith, 1979). Even our culture appears to promote this hermeneutic impulse in rhetoric. It is a habit of our time to invoke rhetoric, time and again, to make sense of a wide variety of discursive practices that beset and perplex us, and of discursive artifacts that annoy and entertain us, and of discursive formations that inscribe and subjugate us. Rhetoric is a way of reading the endless discursive debris that surrounds us.[1] What does it tell us about a culture that it finds interpretive solace in rhetoric rather than in religion or in economics or in science?

RHETORIC AS HERMENEUTICS:
GLOBALIZATION, REPRESSION, AND DISCIPLINARY ANXIETY

Contemporary rhetoric differs from its classical counterpart in two important ways. First, we have extended the range of rhetoric to include discourse types such as scientific texts that the ancients would have regarded as falling outside its purview. To be sure, there were two opposed conceptions of the range of rhetoric in antiquity. While Aristotle promoted a "restrained" view of rhetoric as confined to the civic realm, the sophists viewed rhetoric as ranging over the whole of human affairs. But despite the sophists' attempt to promote an enlarged vision of rhetoric, it remained as a cultural practice bound to the civic realm and later, with the erosion of the public sphere in the classical world, rhetoric migrated to the realm of art and aesthetics. Here, once again, rhetoric failed to establish its hegemony as the generative grammar of artistic prose. Gorgias may have imagined a rhetoric that would become the privileged site for a festival of language where, to borrow an image from Geoffrey Hartman, "the words [would] stand out as words . . . rather than being, at once, assimilable meanings" (Hartman, 1981). But such a festival never did take place. Rhetoric after Quintilian, now domiciled within the pedagogical institutions and driven by changing cultural needs as mediated by those institutions, found itself progressively reduced in scope from an idealized medium of "general culture" to a regimen for training of bureaucrats for the state and the church, and then to a technical study of stylistics, and finally to a brittle taxonomy of tropes and figures. According to an account popular among certain European writers of "structuralist" persuasion—Barthes, Gennette, Ricoeur, and Todorov—taxonomically ossified rhetoric finally died in the early nineteenth century with the emergence of the Romantic aesthetics that privileged genius and spontaneity as opposed to the classificatory order and stylistic conformity characteristic of rhetorical instruction (Todorov, 1977). Whether we accept or reject this engaging historical narrative about rhetoric as an "incredibly shrinking discipline," one thing is certain: rhetoric today, whether "revived" or "reborn," presents an exactly opposite spectacle of an "incredibly engulfing discipline." Rhetoric is everywhere. Never before in the history of rhetoric, not even during its glory days of the Italian Renaissance, did its proponents claim for rhetoric so universal a scope as some postmodern neosophists do today (Leff, 1987). The rhetoric of science is simply one manifestation of this contemporary impulse to universalize rhetoric.

How does one universalize rhetoric? This brings me to the second key difference between contemporary and classical views of rhetoric. We have reversed the priority the ancients accorded to rhetoric as a practical/productive activity over rhetoric as a critical/interpretive activity. As academics, we are more interested in rhetoric as interpretive theory than as cultural practice.

The ancients were not entirely unaware of these two aspects of rhetoric. They distinguished between *rhetorica utens* and *rhetorica docens*. The former refers to rhetoric as practice in a sense not dissimilar from its contemporary usage. But the latter refers to rhetoric as a pedagogically motivated network of critical terms, practical devices, prudential rules, and semitheoretical formulations regarding a set of interrelated topics: practical reasoning, figurative language, compositional structures and strategies, psychology of audience, and sociology of opinion. Rhetorica docens has little in common with our contemporary sense of rhetoric as an interpretive theory. Rather it is cast in the spirit of handbooks. Although the boundary between rhetorica utens and rhetorica docens is rather unstable, it is not very difficult to establish that the ancients privileged the former over the latter. This is evident in the *orator perfectus* tradition (inaugurated by Isocrates, developed by Cicero, and canonized by Quintilian) that dominated rhetorical instruction in the West up till this century. Unlike Plato and Aristotle, the ancient proponents of the orator perfectus tradition were not concerned with the troubled epistemic status of rhetoric: Is rhetoric an art or a mere routine as Plato insisted? Isocrates, for instance, viewed rhetoric as a civic force rather than as a mode of understanding. His interest in theory extends only to an extent it has some immediate bearing on practice, that is, oratory in the service of the *polis*. Similarly for Cicero, the governing ideal of rhetoric is not to achieve self-grounding as an art but to strive for a union of wisdom and eloquence in ministering (guiding and sustaining) the republic. Thus, "theorizing" among the ancients was dominated by a pedagogical interest in performance rather than by a "hermeneutic" interest in understanding.

The fact that the ancients had a sharply different estimate of theory than we do frequently escapes our attention because our understanding of rhetoric—both its history and its current possibilities—is mediated almost exclusively by Aristotle rather than by Cicero and Quintilian. Aristotle's text, perhaps uniquely in the entire Greco-Roman rhetorical canon, permits us to entertain a distinction between theory and practice, with the former in some sense regulating and rationalizing the latter. Aristotle's *Rhetoric* may be briefly identified by its functional stress on the concept of "persuasion" and by the tripartite structure with which it disciplines the unwieldy discourse of persuasion. Within this scheme, rhetoric is preeminently a means to an end.[2] It enables its practitioners to act upon an audience so as to instill in them desirable attitudes and beliefs and when appropriate to incite them to action. With so clear a vision about both the function and structure of persuasive discourse, Aristotle was able to theorize about the "rationality" of the rhetorical enterprise, systematize its resources, and prepare it for the status of an "art" (techne), while in other texts, even in Cicero's philosophically inspired De Oratore, it is practice that constantly interrogates the utility of the "art." Cicero is decisive in his insistence that "inborn talent" and "practice" are infinitely more important than the knowledge of "art" in the preparation of an orator. This Ciceronian claim was to become a pedagogical commonplace (and hence a governing principle) in the institutionalization of rhetoric that followed the collapse of the Roman Republic.

It is now an accepted bit of scholarly lore that in the classical world and in the subsequent history of rhetoric, the orator perfectus tradition has been far more influential than the Aristotelian tradition. But in this century Aristotle has virtually dominated rhetorical studies.[3] The two major texts in contemporary rhetorical studies— Perelman and Olbrechts-Tyteca's The New Rhetoric and Burke's A Rhetoric of Motives—attest to this domination.[4] It is well beyond the scope of this essay to analyze how and why rhetorical studies in this century, especially within the disciplinary matrix of speech communication, became Aristotelianized (Leff, 1992). However, the links between the interpretive turn and the Aristotelianization are fairly deep. In fact, the interpretive turn initially appeared in the guise of neo-Aristotelianism. And as we shall see in the next section, the interpretive turn in contemporary rhetorical studies, even as it seeks to break free from a "restrained" vision of Aristotle, remains fatally bound to an Aristotelian vocabulary.

The Cultural Identity of Rhetoric

In this section I will spell out the implications of what it means to privilege theory over practice in contemporary rhetorical studies. I must begin by removing two possible misunderstandings. First, in my view, neither Aristotle nor his contemporary followers view rhetoric as anything but a practical activity. But a contemporary Aristotelian (if not Aristotle himself) is prone to view rhetorical practice from an interpretive axis rather than from a performative/pedagogical axis. Second, our propensity to adopt an interpretive

stance does not imply that we are any less implicated than fifth-
and fourth-century B.C.E. Athenians in rhetoric as a cultural and
material practice. If we allow ourselves a simple equation between
rhetoric and persuasion, we will find a staggering amount of rhetoric
in our daily life. The twentieth century is marked by a proliferation
of practical activities and discursive artifacts that one can characterize unproblematically as persuasive. In McGee's words, we experience "the brute reality of persuasion as a daily social phenomenon"
(McGee, 1982). The extraordinarily rhetorical character of our daily
discursive practices is self-evident so long as we allow ourselves a
simple equation between rhetoric and persuasion. But therein lies
the rub. The equation between rhetoric and persuasion does not
enjoy the sort of cultural currency that would give rhetoric a distinct
identity. Aside from a common and continuing usage of rhetoric to
mean "mere rhetoric," we do not have a more refined and culturally
accessible notion of rhetoric based on its relation to persuasion. Our
sense of rhetoric has become so attenuated that even the ancient
connection between rhetoric and oratory has lost some of its taken-
for-granted character. In the absence of a clear cultural sense of what
is a rhetorical practice or a rhetorical artifact and in the absence of a
developed cultural appreciation of rhetoric as a mode of understanding certain expressive and communicative social fields, a putative rhetorical analyst is required to discharge a double burden: she
must simultaneously make the practice/artifact under scrutiny intelligible (either imminently or contextually or by some combination of
the two) and also specify how the intelligibility of her reading is
grounded in a theory of rhetoric. This, I believe, is evident in our critical practices.

However, what is not so evident are the two radical consequences which are implicit in our critical practices: *First, what is
rhetorical in any given case is invariably an effect of one's reading
rather than a quality intrinsic to the object being read. Second, if
what is rhetorical is an effect of one's reading, then a master reader
can produce such an effect in relation to virtually any object. Hence,
the range of rhetoric is potentially universal.* Thus, it turns out that
the interpretive turn in rhetoric is inextricably linked to an impulse
to universalize rhetoric. They are two aspects of the same tendency
in contemporary rhetorical studies.

It is interesting to note that some critics, especially Michael
Leff, have openly resisted this tendency. While remaining within
the interpretive orbit, Leff attempts to blunt the impulse to universalize rhetoric. His strategy is as follows: Leff claims that the double
burden that a putative rhetorical analyst must discharge is not neces-

sitated by our impoverished sense of rhetoric but is intrinsic to
rhetoric as an embedded art and the radical particularity of its manifestations. For Leff, the peculiar nature of rhetorical art can be
understood only in and through its local discursive manifestations.
As a global process (conceived either as figuration or argument),
rhetoric is susceptible to theoretical abstraction and formalization.
But to do so beyond a certain point is impractical because rhetoric so
conceived becomes purely taxonomic, and hence trivial. In Leff's
words, "rhetoric is a universal activity that finds its habitation only
in the particular" (1987:7). Whatever one might make of Leff's
maneuver and the accompanying program of "textual criticism," it
does point to a fundamental and unresolved tension within the interpretive paradigm constituted under the authority of Aristotle. This
tension can be formulated in the form of a question: *Is it possible to
translate effectively an Aristotelian vocabulary initially generated
in the course of "theorizing" about certain types of practical (praxis)
and productive (poesis) activities delimited to the realm of appearances (that is, "public sphere" as the Greeks understood it) into a
vocabulary for interpretive understanding of cultural practices that
cover the whole of human affairs, including science?* This question
cannot be profitably addressed in an a priori fashion. It must be
addressed in the historical context of our disciplinary practices.

The Interpretive Turn and Rhetorical Criticism

The interpretive turn coincided with the constitution of
"rhetorical criticism" as a subfield of study in our discipline. The
original program for rhetorical criticism as enunciated by the members of the Cornell school, especially in Wichelns's inaugural essay,
was based on a certain reading of Aristotle that sought to translate
his theory of praxis into a method of interpretation. But this translation did not occur in a vacuum. Wichelns' attempt to formulate a
method was deeply informed by what he took to be the privileged
object of critical study, namely, oratory. It is Wichelns's view of oratory—its fragility and temporality, its connection to power, its location in the public sphere, its preoccupation with leadership—that
led him to posit a "historical critical method." "Oratory," according
to Wichelns, "is intimately associated with statecraft; it is bound up
with the things of the moment; its occasion, its terms, its background, can often be understood only by a careful student of history." Thus Wichelns, like Aristotle, kept rhetoric confined within
the public sphere although his view of orator as a culture hero—
who must periodically tame that "Leviathan, the public mind," lest

he "threaten civilization"—has a distinctly Ciceronian flavor.[5]

The resulting critical paradigm known as neo-Aristotelianism sought to integrate a critical vocabulary derived from Aristotle with a program of historical research. The practical results were dismal in two respects: First, the transformation of Wichelns's broadly conceived critical injunctions into a rigidly codified methodology produced a spate of mechanical and unimaginative critical studies. Second, the critical enterprise was overwhelmed by historical research, with some critics, such as Nichols, openly admitting that a study of oratory was only ancillary to a study of history.[6] Neo-Aristotelianism eventually collapsed under the weight of its own massive failure. But the privilege of writing its obituary belonged to Edwin Black who, in his influential book *Rhetorical Criticism*, offered a brilliant diagnosis of how its critical failure stemmed from a flawed conceptual apparatus. While Black's critique of neo-Aristotelianism has been fully absorbed into the disciplinary consciousness, his detailed discussion of Aristotle's *Rhetoric* and its relevance for conducting rhetorical criticism has been largely ignored. It is not possible here to examine the details and merits of Black's interpretation of Aristotle's conception of rhetoric "as a faculty that realizes its end in the act of judgment (*krisis*)," a judgment arrived in accordance with a normative procedure (Black, 1978:108). But the conclusions that Black draws on the basis of his reading of Aristotle command our attention. Black flatly states that the Aristotelian vision of rhetoric is far too narrow, far too normative, and far too rationalistic to be of use in modern times, especially in the appraisal of rhetorical discourse, because it excludes certain types of discourses and certain types of audiences and the formation of certain mental states (beliefs and convictions) from the purview of rhetoric. He traces the failure of neo-Aristotelianism back to Aristotle himself. In questioning the usefulness of Aristotelian principles and vocabulary, is not Black also implicitly questioning the utility of the whole of the classical tradition and its network of rules and terms in the critical appraisal of rhetorical discourses? For some reason, this bold provocation failed to elicit a response within the critical community.

The collapse of neo-Aristotelianism was followed by a period marked by both the globalization of rhetoric (greatly facilitated by the works of Kenneth Burke) and the pluralization of critical methods. Two types of critics and critical studies came into prominence. What distinguished the two types was their respective attitudes towards theory. One group of critics scrambled to replace the discredited neo-Aristotelianism with a variety of competing theories: phenomenological, structuralist, dramatistic, etc., all of them gen-

erally committed to the view of rhetoric as "symbolic inducement."
But critical studies inspired by those theoretical perspectives were as
a whole no more insightful than an average neo-Aristotelian study.
Even studies inspired by Burke's dramatistic theory of motives failed
to leave a decisive imprint. And soon the talk of conceptual innovation gave way to a certain form of antitheoreticism. In the second
group, it became fashionable to view the critic as a sort of bricoleur,
who exemplified Burke's dictum that a critic should "use all that is
there to use" in making the critical object intelligible. Black himself
endorsed this view of critical enterprise when he came out in favor of
emic criticism against etic criticism (Black, 1980). The progressive
globalization of rhetoric also reinforced the atheoretical stance. Now
that rhetoric was seen as something so immensely rich and complex and coextensive with humanity itself, it was assumed that only
a flexible system of theoretical perspectives and critical procedures
employed on an ad hoc basis could do justice to it. What this pluralist critical stance actually concealed is the persistence and the recuperation of classical rhetoric. (The situation in rhetorical theory is
quite different; from Bryant through Bitzer to Farrell, the dominant
influence of Aristotle in rhetorical theory is explicit.) A critic might
eschew theory as constricting and cumbersome, but can hardly do
without a critical vocabulary. A language of criticism, however diffuse, is always already in place in the conduct of criticism. It would
not take a great deal of ingenuity on my part to show that an
allegedly atheoretical critical study is suffused with a critical vocabulary that is not simply derived from everyday language (Swanson,
1977a, 1977b). The question is not whether but which vocabulary is
in play. And it is my contention that, by and large, our critical studies are sustained by the vocabulary of classical rhetoric, a vocabulary
primarily fashioned for directing performance rather than facilitating
understanding. The question remains unanswered as to whether this
vocabulary of performance can be adequately translated into a vocabulary of interpretation. As I indicated earlier, this question cannot be
answered in an a priori fashion. It calls for reflexive critical engagement.[7]

A putative translator will have to keep three things in mind:
First, one must realize that the translation involves not simply a
technical vocabulary but an ideology: a view of speaker as the seat of
origin rather than a point of articulation, a view of strategy as identifiable under an intentional description, a view of discourse as constitutive of character and community, a view of audience positioned
simultaneously as "spectator" and "participant," and finally, a view
of "ends" that binds speaker, strategy, discourse, and audience in a

web of purposive actions. How should our translator deal with this particular ideology of human agency? Should it be discarded or be allowed to be reinscribed in the new interpretive vocabulary? The choice one makes will depend on one's sense of the historical conjuncture—the postmodern condition—in which the translation is being attempted. (In the final section of this paper, I will offer an extended critique of the "humanist paradigm" and its view of agency.)

Second, the refashioned interpretive vocabulary must be adequate to accommodate a wide range of objects that are now subsumed under universal rhetoric. There is no way to deglobalize rhetoric from within the interpretive paradigm.

Third, the "thinness" of the current productionist vocabulary would have to be "deepened" and made more specific. By "thinness," I am referring to the abstract quality of the traditional vocabulary as illustrated, for instance, in the tripartite scheme of proofs (*ethos*, *pathos*, and *logos*) that enables one to find its presence in virtually any discourse practice. In disciplinary politics, the more refined and specific a language of criticism becomes (be it deconstruction, psychoanalysis, or reception theory), the greater attention it gets and by the same token the more vulnerable it is to falsification. In its current form, rhetoric as a language of criticism is so thin and abstract that it is virtually invulnerable to falsification, and for that very reason, it commands little sustained attention.[8] I am prepared to concede that a "thin" rhetorical lexicon may have certain advantages when it functions heuristically as an aid to performance, but it is inadequate for a critical reading of what gets "said" (or "done") in performance. Here I am already presupposing a certain view of interpretive process, i.e., that it is not a simple reversal of the process of production (Jaffe, 1980). I cannot here rehearse Gadamer's well-known arguments against romantic hermeneutic view that one could move from expression (*Ausdruck*) to experience (*Erlebnis*) by an operation called *Verstehen*. (The basic assumption is that understanding involves a process of psychological reconstruction.) Besides, even if we were to abide by the assumptions of romantic hermeneutics, the classical vocabulary of production (structuration of discourse practice) does not give us sufficient resources to apprehend how a speaker imagines and fills out a project conceived in the face of an exigency. We don't have to invoke a skeptical reading of Wittgenstein to remind ourselves that "rules" and "practices" are not linked in a manner that one can unproblematically "read off" the latter from the former. Cicero reminds us of this fact in a more gentle tone quite frequently. Between precept and performance, there is talent and practice, the regimen of the body. Rhetoric is like dancing, says Quintillian.

Keeping these challenges in sight, can we translate the current rhetorical lexicon? Once again, there is no point in soliciting a speculative answer. The translation is already underway. The practical critics are already struggling with the problem. It is only in their critical labor and struggles that one can glimpse the translative process. The critics' blindness to the translative process that is underway in their work does not necessarily devalue the insight that they are transforming rhetoric in the course of illuminating some text or practice. We place (somewhat frantically these days) things under the sign of rhetoric more to make rhetoric intelligible than the things subsumed under it. The emergence of the "rhetoric of science" as a new and increasingly prominent subfield of study in our discipline presents us with an extraordinarily fertile site to study the unfolding translative process, a veritable cultural semiosis through which rhetoric struggles to reconstitute itself as a nomadic metadiscourse.

The Politics of Repression and Recognition

One might wonder why our allegedly rhetorical culture lacks resources for spontaneously recognizing what is and what is not "rhetoric." This question has exercised the minds of some of our scholars. We have three explanatory hypotheses: linguistic (the lacunae thesis), sociological (the differentiation thesis), and historical (the repression thesis). Since the third hypothesis is central to any discussion on the rhetoric of science, I will briefly identify the first two and elaborate on the third.

Donald C. Bryant once suggested that our difficulty in discerning clear and distinct instances of rhetoric may be due to a simple lack of an appropriate term (Bryant, 1983). While in the realm of poetry we have a set of three differentiating terms for artist (poet), art (poetics), and output (poetry), we have in rhetoric equivalent terms for only artist (rhetor) and art (rhetoric) and none for output. Consequently, while we can easily identify Homer's epic as well as Shakespeare's sonnets as instances of poetry, we cannot with equal ease identify Lincoln's speech and Paine's pamphlet as instances of "rhetory" because there is no such word. But this linguistic lacunae merely makes us aware of the problem of recognition without explaining it. What makes one recognize an epic or a lyric or a sonnet as an instance of poetry is not simply that we have an appropriate word. Rather, the recognition is made possible by a cultural tradition within which it takes place. Obviously, rhetoric lacks a tradition

that would enable an average but literate person to unproblematically identify at least the paradigm cases of rhetoric as rhetoric. This
raises a question: why do we lack such an identity-bestowing tradition? (An answer to this question will be furnished by the third
hypothesis.) *Good Q*

The sociological differentiation thesis pertains to the character
of modern/postmodern society. On account of the functional complexity and structural differentiation of modern society, activities·
and artifacts that were once allegedly legible as instances of rhetoric
no longer signal those marks or carry those traces by means of which
one can recognize their ancestry. Manifestly persuasive activities
such as political oratory, litigation, advertising, and public relations
have evolved in the modern age according to their own inner logic,
developed their own distinctive institutions, and formulated their
own professional norms. In carrying out their practical activities,
the participants in those spheres of life do not feel the need for the
comprehensive theory of persuasion that rhetoric professes to
deliver. Hence, those agents and institutions no longer invoke
rhetoric either for self-understanding or for social legitimation. For
them, rhetoric represents a nostalgia for a lost myth of origin and
unity. This perfectly plausible explanation is tacitly acknowledged in
the institutional arrangements of the modern university. We make
no attempt to subsume the study of advertising, public relations,
litigation, and empirical research in persuasive processes (within
our own discipline) under the rubric of rhetoric.

While Bryant's "linguistic" explanation never got off the
ground (and rightly so) and while the "sociological" explanation is
tacitly acknowledged, it is the "historical" explanation that dominates our self-understanding as a discipline. The historical explanation comes in the form of a dialectic between repression and recognition. There are many versions of the repression thesis, but the
basic ingredients are the same. It is generally cast in the form of a
narrative that begins with a certain reading of the quarrel between
philosophy (the Platonic Socrates) and rhetoric (the older Sophists)
for cultural hegemony in ancient Greece. It recounts the birth of
rhetoric in litigation and its rise to political prominence during the
Periclean enlightenment, its clash with philosophy and its cultural
marginalization by the victorious philosophical reason, its subsequent confinement within the educational curriculum after the collapse of democratic politics in the classical world, and finally after
centuries of attenuation (except for one or two brief revivals) its
rapid disintegration and dispersal in the modern world under the
double onslaught of subject-centered reason and romantic aesthetics

(Bender and Wellbery, 1990). Despite the glaring historical inaccuracies in this narrative, repeatedly corrected by professional historians like Conley, Kennedy, and Vickers, the moral of the tale survives intact, i.e., the current dispersed character of rhetoric and the attendant lack of cultural recognition are not intrinsic to rhetoric but the result of a historical deformation (Conley, 1990; Kennedy, 1980). While rhetoric as cultural practice continues to exist because its materiality cannot be erased, the requisite vocabulary to recognize it as such has been suppressed and maligned. This gives us a decisive motivational clue as to why contemporary rhetoric so insistently positions itself as an interpretive metadiscourse. The repression of rhetoric is only partial; it survives and goes about its business under a series of pseudonyms and misrecognitions. Such a shadowy existence will continue so long as the vocabulary of recognition and legitimation remains fragmented.[9] Thus rhetoric, in order to disclose its presence in discourse practices, must reconstitute itself into a second-order discourse, an interpretive metadiscourse. Hence the hermeneutic turn in rhetoric is inextricably caught up in a politics of recognition.

It is precisely within the conceptual framework of a historical dialectic between repression and recognition that a new formation called "the rhetoric of science" is located. In the following section, I will try to show how this new and increasingly prominent formation in rhetorical studies best exemplifies the interweaving of the three components I have identified so far: the interpretive turn, the globalization of rhetoric, and the politics of recognition.

My choice of this particular formation to illustrate some of the general problems in rhetorical criticism may seem a bit ironic, but it has certain strategic advantages. First, science is generally viewed as that discursive space in which rhetorical considerations are least relevant or welcome. The very idea of the rhetoric of science suggests that we are now turning our attention to the furthest outpost in rhetoric's quest for universal hegemony. Thus, we might here observe the perils and possibilities of globalization under conditions of determined resistance. Second, it is also here that the dialectic between repression and recognition gets played out with the greatest clarity. If science is that space where rhetoric was traditionally viewed as utterly irrelevant, it could only mean (for the champion of rhetoric) that here the suppression of rhetoric was carried out in the most thoroughgoing manner. Hence, an unpacking of the dialectic between repression and recognition would have visible consequences for self-understanding of both science and rhetoric. As for science, it would have to refashion its epistemological anxieties in a manner that does not involve a simple refusal to recognize the consequences of its textuality. On the other hand, a successful recuperation of rhetoric in science would shift the presumption, once and for all, in favor of the proponents of universal rhetoric. If science is not free of rhetoric, nothing is. Third, the repressed rhetoricity of science could be brought to light only through an interpretive redescription of science. Science, like religion or finance, does not offer itself as a rhetoric. It must be reread against considerable resistance from those who are committed to other readings or descriptions of science. And the fate of universal rhetoric will turn largely on the efficacy of those rereadings.

THE RHETORIC OF SCIENCE AS A DISCURSIVE FORMATION

The "rhetoric of science" (referred to hereafter as RS), as I understand it, refers to the work of those who study science from a rhetorical perspective. This body of literature is scattered over several disciplines: speech communication, English (the disciplinary host to composition programs), sociology, and history and philosophy of science.

My essay concentrates on work produced within the discipline of speech communication, with a few references to works by scholars in composition programs. This rather narrow focus calls for an explanation. I am, as the title of this essay indicates, primarily interested in analyzing what happens to our understanding of rhetoric when it is placed in a contested interpretive relation to a cultural/material/discursive formation such as "science." It is not that I am uninterested in the enterprise undertaken by some of my colleagues of illuminating "science" by recourse to rhetoric, but my current reading strategy (whatever its strengths and weaknesses) places me once removed from the discourse of science per se. I thus begin by thematizing the ways in which *rhetoric* is deployed and positioned in RS literature.

What is the purpose of such a reading? A brief answer to this query is this: In less than two decades rhetoric—a discipline that has been routinely pronounced dead at regular intervals (as if to make sure it was really dead) since the middle of the last century—has suddenly risen in prominence in scholarly discourse. A striking and commonly noted feature of this renewed interdisciplinary interest in rhetoric is the sheer promiscuity with which the term *rhetoric* is deployed. Such a promiscuous usage makes a traditionalist like Brian Vickers uncomfortable. In his recent book, *In Defense of*

Rhetoric, Vickers finds himself in an unenviable position of having to defend rhetoric not only against its old enemies (Plato and the usual suspects) but also against its new friends (de Man and the faceless horde of postmodernists). Vickers believes that rhetoric, despite its historical mutability, has a recognizable traditional core and that core must be kept in view in our contemporary uses and extensions of rhetoric. While Vickers is not exactly an essentialist, he regards the manner in which, say, Burke or de Man deploy the rhetorical lexicon, especially the lexicon of tropes, as having little in common with its traditional usage. Further, he avers that such a radical departure from tradition is fatal to any genuine and lasting recuperation of rhetoric. Thus, Vickers's response to today's promiscuous uses and invocations of rhetoric is normative. He wants to bridle (mis)uses of rhetoric through some sort of mediation of tradition (Vickers, 1988). This view has a considerable appeal among speech communication scholars such as Farrell and Leff. Unlike Vickers, Farrell and Leff are genuinely receptive to the current interdisciplinary excitement about rhetoric, but they do insist on recovering and rereading traditional texts as a point of necessary resistance to the postmodern habit of treating rhetoric as if it were a free-floating signifier. The strategy of vertical integration while admitting a modicum of horizontal dispersal is fairly common. This strategy, however reasonable, is also motivated by a deeply felt anxiety that promiscuous invocation of rhetoric and exaggerated claims on its behalf will only succeed in trivializing rhetoric.[10]

My own response to and readings of promiscuous uses and invocations of rhetoric is rather different. I am inclined to descriptively map the ways in which the term *rhetoric* is deployed and try to ascertain what sort of hermeneutic burden it is made to carry. Instead of regarding promiscuity as an indication of a failure of scholarly scruples, or of a disregard for tradition, or of a lack of commitment to rhetoric (all of which it may very well be), I am inclined to view it as the very object of cultural analysis. When the use of a term such as *rhetoric* becomes culturally so fervid, it hardly makes sense to bemoan its illicit deployment. I begin instead with two assumptions: First, the practice of invoking rhetoric is a culturally significant phenomenon and that practice is symptomatically related to the crisis in the human sciences marked by the demise of "foundationalism" in philosophy and of "high modernism" in art and literature. Second, the seemingly careless and ubiquitous uses and invocations of rhetoric deflect our attention from its strategic deployment. Sheer multiplicity of usage that stretches from the inane to the idiosyncratic makes an overwhelmed reader abandon the hope of

THE IDEA OF RHETORIC

ever finding what motivates and steers rhetoric. It is precisely in
this state—fatigue combined with a traditional distaste for rhetoric—
that one is prone to overlook its strategic deployment in criticism
and interpretation.

This being my proposed reading strategy, I believe it is appropriate to start with that body of literature on science generated primarily by scholars in speech communication and in composition
programs that consciously and explicitly employs a rhetorical perspective. However, it will not be possible to keep my analysis
securely confined within the boundaries of that literature because RS
as an intellectual enterprise stands in an embattled relationship to
two established traditions of scholarship: rhetorical studies and "science studies." To a certain measure, my own analysis of RS mimics
that embattled situation. In the first part of the essay, I examined
how RS is positioned vis-a-vis certain trends and concerns within
rhetorical studies, especially in rhetorical criticism. I approached
RS (without really entering into it) from the standpoint of the rhetorical studies as a whole, and further, I projected certain broader disciplinary anxieties, especially those pertaining to recognition, interpretation, and globalization, onto this newly emergent subfield. But
those anxieties function differently within RS because its proponents are exposed to yet another and arguably more immediate set of
anxieties that stem from the position of RS as a "latecomer" in the
game of "science studies" dominated by historians, philosophers,
and sociologists. The two sets of anxieties in their complex interplay
rise to the surface no sooner than one begins to specify the boundaries of RS. The RS literature is not extensive, but it is scattered
and largely unreflexive. There are no programmatic statements, nor
detailed critical reviews of existing literature in print.[11] Therefore, I
will begin by identifying what I regard as the salient features of the
RS literature in terms of its programmatic goals, primary audience,
analytic and critical methods, and preferred objects of study.

The general aim of the RS project is to show that the discursive
practices of science, both internal and external, contain an unavoidable rhetorical component. *Internal* here refers to those discursive
practices that are internal to a specific scientific language community; *external* refers to the discursive practices of that scientific language community in respect to its dealing with other scientific (or
nonscientific) communities and society in general. Although the
slippage between the two is recognized, the distinction is carefully
maintained. If we arrange the existing RS literature along an exter-
nal/internal continuum, we will find the following thematic types of
rhetorical studies of science: how and with what effect science is

The range of RS

made accessible to the general public through popularization; how and with what effect science intervenes in deliberation and decision-making of public policy; how and why science differentiates and dissociates itself from what it regards as non-science or pseudoscience; how and why and with what effect "findings" in one discipline are analogically translated into "premises" of another discipline (generally from a "natural" science to a "social" science as from biology to sociobiology, or from a "harder" science to a "hard" science as from genetic biology to paleontology); and finally, how scientific controversies involving theory choice or paradigm shift unfold and get resolved in terms of norms, resources, and practices that are internal to a given scientific community. This list of types of studies is not exhaustive, but it does illustrate how capacious is the range of RS. Further, a quick survey along such a continuum reveals that in the recent years rhetorical analysis of science has moved decisively towards the internal pole. This is predictable. The proponents of RS have long recognized that an attempt to read science rhetorically encounters greater resistance as one moves from the external to the internal. Further, they also believe that their collective endeavor can become fully legitimate in the eyes of the "science studies" establishment only when they have shown how rhetorical considerations are relevant and unavoidable in understanding discourse practices that are inscribed and framed strictly by the internal constraints and dynamics of a specific scientific community. That is to say: science is rhetorical all the way down, or in Gross's vision, which offers a rhetorical reading of science "without remainder" (Gross, 1990:33). In this regard, RS hopes to secure for the "rhetorical in science" the same sort of recognition that SSK (the sociology of scientific knowledge) has sought to secure for the "social in science."

However, the differences between RS and SSK are striking and instructive. Although both started roughly at the same time in the 1970s, SSK has developed into a complex empirical research program that displays considerable internal variation in theory and methodology, while RS remains little more than an uncoordinated research initiative carried out by a handful of committed individuals. While SSK has problematized right from the start the internal/external distinction to open up conceptual space for innovative empirical research, RS tenaciously clings to that distinction, even as it increasingly slides towards the internal pole, because studies conducted around the external pole, when viewed as critical explorations in public discourse, are easily assimilable within rhetorical studies as currently constituted. Further, while SSK and its allies (SSK–like approaches: laboratory studies, discourse analysis, ethnomethodological approaches, reflexivity, actor network theory) have reached a level of disciplinary consolidation that they have put into question the very category of the "social" in science studies, RS has yet to turn its reflexive gaze back on to the idea of the "rhetorical." Even in the study of scientific controversies, a topic eminently suited for rhetorical analysis, the work of Harry Collins exceeds anything RS has to offer both in terms of conceptualization and empirical work. These are disconcerting facts about RS. One could go on in this fashion comparing RS unfavorably with SSK and generate sufficient ammunition to dismiss the current state of scholarship in RS as inconsequential. But such dismissals miss the point. The fact is that RS, like so many other research projects based on a revived interest in rhetoric, has stalled after a promising beginning. There are two possible explanations as to why the RS project has stalled: first, it has misread science; second, it has misappropriated (not in the normative sense) rhetoric. While I am not qualified to pursue the first explanation, I am interested in entertaining the second for the light it might shed on the predicament facing not only RS but every other proposed contemporary extension of rhetoric into the zone of interdisciplinarity.

The RS literature is made up of two types of studies: general essays and case studies. Typically, a general essay explains what RS as a scholarly project signifies by specifying the conditions of its possibility, by providing a rationale, by identifying research programs and trajectories, and most important, by describing how it is positioned in relation to the received traditions in science studies. A case study typically takes some structured episode (say, a controversy) or some specifiable dimension (say, writing) of scientific practice and analyzes it from a rhetorical perspective. The two types of studies are closely related. The general essays invariably conclude by calling for more case studies insofar as only the latter can disclose through interpretive redescription the presence of rhetoric in science. And yet the case studies themselves display a palpable anxiety about redescribing a given scientific practice or artifact as an instance of rhetoric on a purely ad hoc basis lest such redescribing turn into a Sisyphean task. Hence, one can always find that hesitant gesture towards generalization, so very characteristic of case studies, about the inward connection between science and rhetoric derived from a certain version of philosophical anthropology (the tedious stuff about *homo symbolens*) that makes rhetoric simultaneously unavoidable and erasable.

What is important here is the form of the common framing (prefigurative) strategy we find in most general essays showing how science and rhetoric are linked. An analysis of this framing strategy gives valuable clues as to how the idea of rhetoric is deployed in RS. Moreover, the three larger disciplinary concerns pertaining to interpretation, globalization, and recognition discussed earlier become salient here. This strategy takes the form of a narrative that goes something like this: Under certain descriptions of science, and so long as those descriptions were dominant (leaving aside the question among whom), it was difficult to conceive of how science could have anything to do with rhetoric. These descriptions (variously identified as objectivism, foundationalism, and logical empiricism) were allegedly dominant in science studies till the beginning 1960s and under those descriptions a research project such as RS was unthinkable. Then came Kuhn, and everything changed. A new set of descriptions of science (variously identified as postempiricist, Weltanschauungen, and constructivist) became available and made it possible to articulate a connection between rhetoric and science. Thus, RS in its very inception becomes immediately implicated in a politics of recognition. The image is clearly one of visibility: under one description rhetoric is invisible and under another it is "dimly" visible. The interpretive problem arises from the fact that *even under the new description the visibility of rhetoric is not self-evident.* One still has to *recuperate* it through further redescription, and such redescription is seen as the distinctive task of RS.[12]

In RS literature one finds three basic recuperative strategies: *communitarian, epistemological,* and *inventional.* The first strategy focuses on the communal character of science and foregrounds the notion of rhetoric as "situated and addressed." The second strategy focuses on the revised epistemic status of science in the postpositivist framework and foregrounds the notion of rhetoric as "reason-giving" activity and more narrowly as "argument." The third strategy, analyzed later in this essay, focuses on the discursive dimension of knowledge production in science and foregrounds the notion of rhetoric as an inventional system for constructing socially intelligible knowledge claims.

An example of the communitarian strategy may be found in Philip C. Wander's "The Rhetoric of Science" (1976), one of the earliest general essays on the rhetoric of science. According to Wander, given the aura of infallibility surrounding science and "its place in the deliberation of public policy," rhetorical critics have an obligation to review its influence and interventions in civic life. After a swift anecdotal review of how the technical language of science is increasingly invoked to intimidate the laity and to elevate the expert by disenfranchising the citizen's voice, Wander reiterates that "science or use of science in public deliberation begs rhetorical investigation" (229). Interestingly, Wander does not seem to have a distinctive theory of science. While he does occasionally invoke a communitarian view of science, Wander does not attempt to link rhetoric and science systematically by recourse to that particular view of science. Wander's claim that the scientific "research report" is a persuasive document addressed to a historically specific audience is based on a mundane view of how scientists (like any other mortals) communicate rather than fashioned out of a special theory of scientific knowledge production.

In Overington's (1977) essay, published a year later, one can notice a major shift in the way the link between rhetoric and science is articulated. Overington wants to extend "rhetorical analysis and criticism to the process of knowledge production in science" (143). To justify such an extension, he begins by giving an account of "science as a community," drawing on the works of Polayni, Ziman, and Kuhn. He discusses topics such as the training of young scientists and how they are admitted to an "invisible college," the "practical art"–like character of scientific investigation, processes of consensus formation, the role of journal articles, the use of exemplars, etc., to highlight the communitarian character of science. Once that description of science is in place, for Overington, the link between rhetoric and science becomes obvious. One has to simply translate that description of science into a corresponding rhetorical terminology. The key move in this translation is to substitute "audience" for "community," and, lo and behold, the scientists become licensed speakers, research situations turn into rhetorical situations, and research reports becomes persuasive arguments. Thus, Overington mechanically reads off a rhetorical view of science from a communitarian view of science. When Overington, armed with this reading strategy, attempts to analyze the scientific discourse of sociology as a case study, the results are predictably dismal. What we get is a catalogue of rhetorical techniques and a typology of arguments (derived from Perelman) that are routinely present in sociological discourse. The only lesson one can extract out of Overington's essay is this: scientific knowledge production is a communitarian audience-bound activity, and hence amenable to a rhetorical analysis. This is simply neo-Aristotelianism in a communitarian garb. One does not find in Overington's essay an attempt to fashion a rhetorical approach that takes into consideration the distinctive features of scientific practice.

The epistemic strategy provides an interesting development of the communitarian approach. The idea that science is distinctive,

especially in its privileged epistemic status, is precisely the target of
Weimer's (1977) polemical essay, perhaps the most influential philosophical brief for RS in the 1970s. Weimer's rhetorical reconstruction
of science begins with a critique of what he calls "justificationism,"
which has allegedly dominated Western epistemology since the
Greeks became fascinated with Euclidean systems and equated scientific knowledge with mathematical derivation. Within the justifi-
cationist framework, according to Weimer: "knowledge has been
identified with proof and certainty: *genuine* or *'valid' knowledge
became proven assertion.* Knowledge, proof, and truth became defi-
nitionally fused concepts: knowledge *is* truth which *is* proven (assertion)" (2). With the subsequent emergence of logic as a formal system
of valid proof procedures, it became imperative to state any knowledge claims, including those of science, in appropriate logical form.
And in due course, "[s]cience became the epitome of logic and vice
versa." Within such a framework rhetoric was not only subordinated to logic, it was also completely removed from any connection
with scientific endeavor. Rhetoric dealt with *doxa*, logic and science with *episteme.* However, according to Weimer, the justifica-
tionist framework is now in complete disarray and the attempts by
"neojustificationists" to salvage it have also failed. So Weimer sets
out to reconceptualize logic, rhetoric, and scientific rationality
within an alternative framework called "nonjustificationism."

What is disappointing about this reconceptualization is that
here, as in Overington, once a new description of science is in place
it is assumed that the link between rhetoric and science is already
made evident. However, this maneuver is carried out differently in
the two essays. While Overington's rhetorical view of science is simply a mirror image of his communitarian view of science, Weimer
simultaneously generates out of his "nonjustificationist" framework
new descriptions of both science and rhetoric. But the two descriptions turn out to be virtually inseparable. In place of the justifica-
tionist equation of knowledge, proof, and truth, we now have a new
equation of knowledge, argument, and rhetoric. In a later essay,
Weimer actually states that the claim—"all knowledge is rhetorical"—is analytically implied in the "nonjustificationist" perspective (Weimer, 1984:65 n. 6). That is, to view science from a nonjustificationist framework is already to view it as a rhetoric. The fate of
rhetoric turns on the viability of a metatheoretical framework, a
precarious opening for rhetoric given the idiosyncratic character of
Weimer's framework.

From such a perspective, theoretical/explanatory discourse in
science turns out to be a set of warranted but contingent arguments

and its rationality rests in its openness to criticism. This discursive mode in which scientific rationality is articulated is precisely the link between rhetoric and science. But the link is mediated through an equation of rhetoric and nonjustificationism:

> In a nonjustificational framework that acknowledges the argumentative nature of theoretical explanation and understanding, *logic and dialectic are facets of rhetoric and have no independent existence apart from the rhetorical transaction.* Rhetoric has as its domain all aspects of the argumentative mode of discourse including logic, dialectic, and the methodology of science. (84)

Thus, rhetoric goes global and science becomes *sub specie rhetoricae.*

The disenchantment with epistemically driven RS is evident in two essays published by Melia (1984) and Bokeno (1987). In a brief but perceptive review essay, Melia examines the fluctuations in the philosophical understanding of science and how those fluctuations appear to alternately open and close the space for RS. In a compact narrative, Melia explains how, starting from Hume's destabilization of "cause" to Kuhn's now-familiar thesis about paradigm shifts, there has been a series of assaults on the privileged epistemic status of science and how each new assault has produced a recuperative countermove by philosophers. For example, Kant's a priori categories of mind sought to "provide an alternative source for the fundamental intuitions of science" as an antidote to Hume's skepticism; Popper's "falsificationism" sought to "tackle the problem of induction and to some degree refurbish the empirical foundation of science" after the four key developments in the twentieth century—"Gauss' non-Euclidean geometry, Maxwell's field theory, Planck's quantum theory, and Einstein's relativity theory—had shaken the foundation of the Great Newtonian synthesis" (304). From Melia's narrative, it is clear that at least for now the assaults have significantly breached the fortifications and the epistemic case for RS rests precisely in sustaining and widening that opening. After reviewing the erosion of certainty in science, Melia concludes: "[I]f the proper concern of rhetoric is with the merely probable, plausible, or contingent, then it seems plain that a great deal of ground has been surrendered to what might with justice be called the 'rhetorical point of view'" (304). In addition, Melia makes two basic points. First (and this is implicit in Melia's narrative), while certain crises in science and the philosophy of science have opened a space for RS, rhetoric appears to have had no discernible role in precipitating those crises. RS as an epistemic construct is largely an effect of a crisis in the philosophy of science. Second, after favorably reviewing three books by Kline, Munevar, and Weimer respectively, Melia notes that they have "established the possibility, in the most fundamental sense, for a rhetoric of science. Along with Kuhn, Feyerabend, Hanson, Polanyi, Bohm, et. al., they breach the once impenetrable wall of hard science. Inside these walls lies terra incognita for rhetoric. And no amount of debate about the work of philosophers of science, whatever its merit, will secure scientific territory for rhetoric" (311). Thus, Melia expresses serious reservations about following the philosophers along the epistemic trail and concludes by calling for case studies in RS.

R. Michael Bokeno (1987) mounts a forceful critique of the epistemic strategy in RS. He begins by showing how that strategy is grounded in the so-called Weltanschauungen philosophy of science (referred hereafter as WPS) as articulated in the works of Kuhn, Hanson, and Feyerabend. Bokeno's critique consists in showing how WPS involves a radical form of "conceptual relativism" such that "it cannot supply an acceptable account of the nature of scientific knowledge and the progress of science" (297). WPS questions the basic assumption that "science deals with a common world," and thus makes it impossible to formulate criteria "for comparing the empirical adequacy of rival theories or competing knowledge claims" (297).

Having stated his general critique of WPS, Bokeno turns to RS. Here his critique may be divided into two parts; I will here pursue Bokeno's second line of critique, which can be examined independently. Here Bokeno describes how RS, like WPS, by emphasizing "theory" related issues generates a series of loose connections between facts, meanings, theories, symbolic constructs, conceptual schemes, cognitive processes, persuasive languages, etc., that makes rhetoric virtually indistinguishable from science:

> The claim that science is a rhetorical process, then, apparently ensues from the idea that *any* process conducted via some conceptual scheme or framework is rhetorical, because language, meanings, and interpretations are inherent in that framework. Indeed, in the current rhetorical understanding of science, "rhetoric" seems to be conceptually inseparable from most if not all scientific process, including observation, description, theoretical understanding, and theory change. (301)

Further, such "global identification of rhetoric with the inherently suasive nature of language and influence provided by conceptual contexts" (301) does not shed any light on the actual scientific practice.

Bokeno's critique is often sharp and compelling. Even if one were to reject his neorealist critique of WPS, there is considerable merit to the way he unpacks the global pretensions of RS. What is disturbing about Bokeno's essay is not his diagnosis but his remedy. Bokeno makes three recommendations on how to use the term *rhetoric.* First make the term *rhetoric* conceptually precise: "If one prerequisite for a rhetorical view of science is more important than others, it is a communal, unambiguous, and consistent use of the term 'rhetoric' either in theoretical or operational definition (309)." Second restrain the scope of rhetoric: "If rhetorical study is to contribute to a new understanding of science, then a conception of rhetoric which is smaller than a conception of human conceptual activity is a minimum theoretical requirement" (306). Third he has a specific suggestion on how to make rhetoric precise and to narrow its range, return to the classical model: "[A] more traditional conception of rhetoric—intentional persuasion involving canons of logical, ethical, and emotional proof—may remain the most useful theoretical and methodological tool we have: perhaps rusty from disuse, but nevertheless sturdy and proven worthy" (309).

In my view, Bokeno's first recommendation is unrealistic, the second unjustified, and the third retrograde. The normative recommendation to make rhetoric conceptually precise flies in the face of the history of the term. Rhetoric is preeminently a cultural construct and what it means varies according to time and place. However frustrated a traditionalist might feel about the promiscuous deployment of *rhetoric* as an interpretive term, a program to bridle its uses is unlikely to succeed. At one point, Bokeno suggests that the need for conceptual precision is all the greater because rhetoric now has a high interdisciplinary profile. But it is precisely the arrival of rhetoric on the interdisciplinary scene that has made it radically promiscuous. The "use value" of the term *rhetoric* is quite astounding. I will have more to say about this vexing problem later when I discuss the phenomenon of "coarticulation," that is, how rhetoric is discursively linked to a variety of entities. For now it should suffice to note that Bokeno's recommendation opts for an easy way out. Instead of mapping what sort of hermeneutic burden rhetoric is made to carry in RS, Bokeno proposes to collectively legislate how the term ought to be used.

Bokeno's second recommendation about narrowing the scope of rhetoric seems reasonable, especially in light of his effective deconstruction of the global pretension of the epistemic strategy. But that deconstruction does not foreclose other strategies, such as the tex-

tual strategy to be discussed later, for realizing the hermeneutic aspirations gof RS which remain global. As I have indicated earlier, there
is no way to effectively deglobalize rhetoric so long as it remains
within the interpretive orbit.

Bokeno's third recommendation, about reviving the classical
model of intentional persuasion, strikes me as a retrograde move. I
do not see how such a model deeply implicated in the ideology of
human agency has the requisite interpretive resources to illuminate
contemporary science in all its material, cultural, and discursive
manifestations as RS aspires to do. Moreover, the idea of reviving the
classical model is a little confusing because it is already very much
active in the case studies, and in my view, adherence to that model
is more frequently a source of weakness than strength.

The Inventional Strategy
and the Humanist Paradigm

In the remaining part of this paper, I will try to show how
untenable Bokeno's recommendations are by examining the critical
practices of three key figures in RS—John Campbell, Alan Gross,
and Lawrence Prelli. I focus on Bokeno's recommendations because
they represent in a nutshell the traditionalist's admonitory critique
of RS. If one adds to Bokeno's threefold recommendations Melia's
sensible call to avoid philosophical debates about science and to get
on with case studies, it would seem that the basic ingredients for a
"conservative" research program in RS are now in place. I call such
a program "conservative" because it not only conforms to the pieties
of the "humanist paradigm" that dominates rhetorical studies but
also defers negotiating the anxieties (identified earlier) occluded by
those pieties.

The humanist paradigm is based on a reading of classical texts,
especially those of Aristotle and Cicero, and its governing feature is
the positioning of the rhetor as the generating center of discourse and
its "constitutive" power. The rhetor is seen (ideally) as the conscious and deliberating agent who "chooses" and in choosing discloses the capacity for "prudence" and who "invents" discourse that
displays an *ingenium* and who all along observes the norms of time-
liness (*kairos*), appropriateness (*to prepon*), and *decorum* that testify to a mastery of *sensus communis*. Within such a paradigm,
while one does recognize the situational constraints, including the
specificity of the audience addressed, they are, in the last instance, so
many items in the rhetor's design. The agency of rhetoric is always

reducible to the conscious and strategic thinking of the rhetor. The dialectic between text and context, a topic of considerable interest today, is already prefigured in the rhetor's desires and designs. Such is the model of intentional persuasion, still dominant but under trial.

It is rather ironic that the unfeasibility of this research ideology is attested by the work of Campbell, Gross, and Prelli because each of them in different ways struggles to respond positively to Bokeno's recommendations; and, as I shall show, their success as critics appears to be inversely related to their actual adherence to those recommendations.

If anyone exemplifies the case studies approach in RS, it is surely Campbell. Campbell has been working on and around the same text—Darwin's *The Origin of Species*—for nearly twenty-five years. His essays on the *Origin* provide a rare opportunity to study the shifts and turns in critical practice in relation to a relatively stable object. While Campbell has generally refrained from theorizing about the presuppositions of RS, both Gross and Prelli operate out of a clearly delineated theoretical and methodological framework in their recently published book-length studies. Each book contains a general statement that establishes a link between rhetoric and science and a series of case studies that explore that linkage. *In my judgment, the case studies by Campbell, Gross, and Prelli, though fascinating on their own, neither endorse a revival of the classical model, nor authorize deglobalization, nor make a case (even a practical case) for conceptual precision. On the contrary, they put into question the humanist ideology that gives rise to such recommendations that are largely divorced from the actual practice of criticism.* My reading of case studies by Campbell, Gross, and Prelli and the tensions I detect between the case studies and the theoretical formulations that underwrite them are quite different from the way the authors themselves see their work. I read the case studies, especially those of Campbell and Gross, *against* the avowed interpretive strategies of the authors.

In the pages to follow, I will examine several of Campbell's essays to show how he appears to have exhausted the possibilities of an agent-centered model of "intentional persuasion" and is now moving towards a discourse-centered model of "intertextuality." And yet Campbell refuses to let go of an image of Darwin as the rhetorical superstar who is always in command of the situation. In my reading of Gross's work I will try to show how his proposed approach—an updated neo-Aristotelianism—has little bearing on what he does as a practical critic. Gross succeeds as a critic largely by ignoring the approach he recommends. Prelli is a hard case because he does precisely what he says he is going to do and does it with a remarkable thoroughness. Prelli fashions a method of "topical invention" for analyzing scientific discourse and applies it to a series of case studies in a manner that admirably fulfills every one of Bokeno's recommendations—conceptual precision, deglobalization, and the revival of classical model. But Prelli's critical exegesis, forced to conform to a preconceived method, gets caught in a relentless taxonomic redescription that yields results that are mechanical and unexciting.

Campbell and the Model of Intentional Persuasion

John Angus Campbell is preeminently a critic (Campbell, 1970, 1974a, 1974b, 1975, 1987, 1989a, 1989b, 1990a, 1990b, 1990c). Unlike Gross and Prelli, he is not given to theorizing a particular version of RS. Having completed his dissertation in the late 1960s under the supervision of that nemesis of neo-Aristotelianism, Edwin Black, Campbell keeps a suitable distance from that discredited method for discerning effects of ephemeral texts. At the same time, Campbell's early work is free of that desperate search for an alternative critical framework characteristic of the 1970s. Campbell anchors himself securely in a critical object—Darwin's *Origin*—and begins to study its constitutive emergence and intervention in a specific historical/cultural/textual milieu. At one level, Campbell's approach is similar to that of intellectual history as he carefully traces the interaction of ideas and the influence of prior texts on later texts. Campbell's affinity with intellectual history is most evident in the attentiveness with which he examines how ideas and texts are mediated by the cultural grammar into which they are injected. What distinguishes Campbell's approach from a typical exercise in intellectual history is his consistent use of rhetoric as the interpretive instrument.

Two features of Campbell's critical practice stand out. First, Campbell's analysis is relatively free of rhetorical terminology. Except in his most recent essays published in 1989 and 1990, Campbell rarely uses it. This does not mean one would not find references to the ubiquitous three modes of proof. Rather, while discussing Darwin's textual self-fashioning or his positioning of audience or his preferred modes of practical reasoning (as in the famous breeder analogy), Campbell generally avoids invoking technical terms to mark the articulation of proofs. Second, Campbell's analysis is unequivocally committed to an agent-centered model of intentional persuasion. The discursive objects (practices and texts) that Campbell elects to analyze are invariably read from Darwin's point of view. These two features appear to be related. In Campbell's recent essays, as the grip of the agent-centered model begins to loosen and the focus shifts towards the intertextual dynamics technical vocabulary becomes increasingly prominent.

Campbell's earlier reticence about using rhetorical terminology is not atypical. Since the collapse of neo-Aristotelianism, rhetorical critics have deployed technical terms rather gingerly. Only recently it has become fashionable to linguistically thematize discourse processes, such as the fielding of arguments (*inventio*), narrative strategies (*dispositio*), and figuration (*elocutio*) in writing criticism and this fashion coincides with a renewed interest in textual criticism. But even textual critics who favor using rhetorical terminology tend to disavow its technical status. There is an ambivalence, a reluctance to endow rhetorical terminology with distinctive interpretive resources unavailable in ordinary language, a tenacious refusal to go beyond the "show and tell" approach that relies on the common intuitions about what Burke calls the "psychology of form." A rhetorical term is treated as if it were an abbreviation for a discourse process that can be described, albeit inefficiently, in everyday language. Thus, the interpretive power of rhetorical terminology, if it has any, is constantly eroded by presenting it exclusively in descriptive terms. Deprived of an interpretive function, rhetorical terminology tends towards a taxonomic pole, and becomes a translation machine.

Even though Campbell seldom uses rhetorical terminology, his essays on Darwin are unmistakably rhetorical. The indelible mark that makes Campbell's reading rhetorical is his absolute and sustained commitment to an agent-centered model of intentional persuasion. Here, once again, I believe Campbell's critical practice is not atypical. Campbell's work shows (perhaps on account of the relative stability of his object of study) more dramatically than any other critic's work that within the humanist paradigm rhetorical practice is in the last instance reducible to the contents of the rhetor's consciousness. One can do away with the entire rhetorical lexicon and still write criticism that bears a rhetorical signature so long as one reads a given discourse practice (or text) as a manifestation of the rhetor's strategic consciousness. This means that humanist rhetoric is more deeply implicated in the modernist project of subject-centered reason than is generally acknowledged. Strategic thinking is very much an affair of the consciousness: it marginalizes structures that govern human agency: language, the unconscious, and capital.

Campbell's work illustrates how influential and seductive this model is and how it holds the critical imagination captive. Campbell, indisputably one of the best critics in the field, invariably reads the text as a manifestation of the author's conscious design. In his recent essays, as he begins to map the evolution of Darwin's evolutionary insight and its rhetorical transformations, Campbell is led explore to the intertextual dynamics out of which the *Origin* emerged; here Campbell notices how textual unconscious and practical rationality merge in a manner that defies authorial design, and yet he refuses to yield the image of Darwin as the master rhetorician who unfailingly imposed his discursive will.

In Campbell's frame, Darwin stands over the *Origin* like a colossus. An account of the extraordinary circumstances under which the *Origin* was composed is merely a prelude to the great rhetorical saga. As Campbell tells it:

> In the June of 1858 Darwin was in the second year of writing *Natural Selection*, a book on transmutation he had been planning since 1837. On the sixth of that month Darwin was startled to receive from the young naturalist Alfred Russell Wallace the sketch of a theory virtually identical to his own. In the wake of the Wallace letter, Darwin put aside his mammoth text, then two-thirds complete, and in nine months produced the work on which his fame rests. (1987:70)

Thus, Darwin's *Origin* was composed under duress "at a time and in a form not of his choosing " (1989b:217).

Not only was the *Origin* composed under duress, it was fated to appear before an audience schooled in scientific and religious opinions inhospitable to the theory it promulgated. Aside from its revolutionary scientific import, Darwin's theory was culturally subversive. It called for a fundamental shift in the way Victorian England viewed the relationship between man, nature, and God. And yet within a decade Darwin had prevailed (1986:351). Campbell sets himself the task, in essay after essay, to give an account of the astonishing rapidity with which evolutionism became scientifically accepted and culturally assimilated.

Campbell immediately discards one possible explanation; viz., Darwin's theory prevailed because it was demonstrably true and its evidential base was unassailable. On the contrary, says Campbell, Darwin, who called the *Origin* "one long argument," was acutely conscious of gaps in his evidence and sought neutralize those gaps by practical reasoning that was closer to rhetoric than logic. "The Ori-

gin relies upon analogy in particular and imagery in general to develop an argument whose conclusions are not certain but, at best, probable" (1975:376–377). Aside from the use of analogy and imagery, Campbell discusses in some detail other textual features (always read as Darwin's conscious strategies) of the *Origin* that mitigate or deflect the problem of evidential weakness. In this context, Campbell discusses how Darwin constructs his authority to draw inferences from not-altogether-conclusive data and how he navigates the readers through the evidential stream as fellow investigators by shifting his pronouns from "I" to "We."

Campbell's preferred explanation focuses on Darwin's rhetorical labors, both textual and extratextual, that facilitated the rapid acceptance of evolutionism both by the scientific community and the educated public. Campbell portrays Darwin as engaged in three different types of rhetorical activities and roles. First, Campbell examines Darwin's textual performance in the *Origin* in terms of how he negotiated, subverted, and triumphed over the cultural grammar of his time. Second, Campbell portrays Darwin as a man perfectly capable of living with a certain discrepancy between his private beliefs and his public statements. Third, Campbell describes the campaign of activities Darwin mounted before and after the publication of the *Origin* to manage the reception and interpretation of his theory. Campbell's analysis of Darwin's rhetorical activities under each of these three categories is perceptive, detailed, and forcefully argued. It is also a model of "historical critical" method that survived both the collapse of neo-Aristotelianism and the pluralist hiatus that followed (Gaonkar, 1990). What is central to this method, as exemplified in Campbell's Darwin essays, is the reading strategy that connects certain textual features to their context of constraints and resources through the agency of the author/speaker. Campbell's work shows both the strength and limits of this model of intentional mediation between text and context.

On Campbell's account, the cultural grammar into which the *Origin* was interjected consisted of a complex interplay between science and religion. "To understand," writes Campbell, "the means by which Darwin's victory was won we must examine Darwin's rhetorical inheritance, that tangled legacy of incompatible assumptions— of scientific assumptions based partially on religion and of religious assumptions bolstered partially by science" (1970:2–3). Further, according to Campbell:

> The superordinate scientific field in Darwin's time, embodying the stereotypic and general paradigm of scientific rationality

per se, was "natural theology," and its rules were contained in what was called "Baconian science." Specific fields had their own rules, but they participated in the larger enterprise of "natural theology" and in the general grammar of Baconian science, which related fields to one another and science to the higher order of truths of natural theology. (1986:352)

Campbell's interpretive strategy is to connect these elements of cultural grammar to certain features of the text by ascribing to Darwin a distinct type of agency: conscious, strategic, and intentional. "My specific thesis," Campbell writes, "is that the key to Darwin's success—his truly extraordinary feat of making the core of his revolution so widely and rapidly intelligible, despite a variety of popular and technical disputes—was his skill in exploiting the Baconian categories to show the intelligibility of a worldview everyone thought the rules of the cultural grammar had excluded" (1986:352). In defending this thesis, Campbell repeatedly identifies and analyzes four textual features.

First, Darwin's flyleaf contained citations from two (and sometimes three) prominent works in the tradition of English natural theology. According to Campbell, Darwin deliberately chose these citations to encourage the readers to view his theory as compatible with the conventional religious view of nature as a product of divine design.

Second, Darwin's account of natural selection as analogous to the domestic breeder and the personification of nature it entailed was a conscious rhetorical choice. "To a public," writes Campbell, "steeped in a theological tradition which taught men to view the adaptations of the natural world as the artifact of a conscious designer, Darwin presented natural selection under the metaphor of a conscious, choice making intelligence" (1970:13). To make his theory "socially intelligible," Darwin was prepared to resort to those discursive conventions his audience understood, even if that meant putting his key insight in a form that was (from today's perspective) "scientifically unclear and even wildly inaccurate" (1975:381).

Third, Campbell dwells on the remarkable similarity between the linguistic practices of Darwin and William Paley, the epitome of natural theology. For instance, Paley's description of the human windpipe and the gullet (while arguing that so complex an organism could not have been created by blind chance but only by divine contrivance) is stylistically similar to Darwin's description of the "beautiful co-adaptations . . . in the woodpecker and the mistletoe" characteristic of "every part of the organic world" (1970:8–9). Campbell discusses at length how Darwin sought to inscribe the conventional terms of natural theology like "contrivance" with new evolutionary meanings by what Kenneth Burke calls "casuistic stretching," the process of "introduc(ing) new principles while theoretically remaining faithful to old principles" (1986:361). In short, Darwin uses the very language of natural theology to undermine it.

Fourth, the opening paragraph of the *Origin* gives an account of how Darwin, after years of careful observation and accumulation of facts, came to formulate his theory. The paragraph depicts Darwin as a passive observer, not given to theoretical speculation, who is "struck" by "certain facts" and who follows those facts to gradually arrive at his evolutionary insight. It is as if Darwin were following, step by step, the inductive procedure laid out by the Baconian science. According to Campbell: "Virtually every statement in this paragraph is socially correct and technically false" (1986:361). On the basis of evidence culled out of Darwin's letters and notebooks, Campbell has little difficulty showing that Darwin was theoretically inclined and "he delighted in far-ranging speculations and saw himself as creating ideas" (1987:73, originally in Gruber, n.d.). In an 1857 letter to Wallace, Darwin says: "I am a firm believer that without speculation there is no good and original observation" (1986:359). Campbell's explains the discrepancy between Darwin's private and public statements as follows: "The discrepancy, I believe, is explained by the view that Darwin was using a methodological convention important to his colleagues, though irrelevant to his science, to give a traditional warrant to a controversial thesis and hence make it persuasive" (1987:74–75). Campbell goes on to give an explicitly intentional description: "[T]he testimony of Darwin's notebooks argues strongly that Darwin thought long and hard, not only about nature, but about persuasion, and that he went to great lengths. . . . The fact is, however, that frontal assault was not Darwin's style, and thus a certain disingenuousness was necessary for Darwin to be persuasive" (1987:75–76). Noting Darwin's natural tendency to exuberantly speculate and theorize, Campbell says, "one is little short of awed by the massive restraint and carefully premeditated adaptation of his public argument" (1987:77).

Another striking instance of discrepancy pertains to Darwin promotion of the American botanist Asa Gray's pamphlet, "Natural Selection not Inconsistent with Natural Theology." In a letter of 1860, Darwin clearly rejects Gray's argument. However, as Campbell notes:

> Darwin's inability to accept the truth of Gray's argument did not prevent him from recognizing its usefulness. It was Darwin

who purchased Gray's untitled articles from *The Atlantic
Monthly*, it was on Darwin's initiative that Gray's articles
came to be printed in pamphlet form, and it was Darwin who
suggested the theme for their title, paid for their printings, and
had them distributed free of charge to various scientific and
religious leaders whom he felt might favorably incline towards
his views. (1975:384)[13]

The strategic deployment of Gray's pamphlet is but one
instance of Darwin's public relations campaign on behalf of his theory. In an essay on what he calls Darwin's "Third Party" strategy,
Campbell sets out to disabuse the traditional "view of Darwin as a
rhetorical indigent, dependent on the charity of the persuasively
gifted," such as T. H. Huxley, to conduct the public defense of his
theory (1989a:55). Campbell gives a vivid account of how Darwin,
both before and after the publication of the *Origin*, deployed his
friends and colleagues—Joseph Dalton Hooker, Charles Lyell, Asa
Gray, T. H. Huxley ("Darwin's bulldog"), W.F. Bates, Fritz Muller, G.
J. Romanes, Thomas Davidson, and John Scott—literally as "advance
men" to manage the reception and interpretation of his book. For
instance, Campbell describes in detail Darwin's near "obsession"
to secure Lyell's public endorsement for his theory. When at last he
did secure that endorsement, how "slyly" Darwin misread/misrep-
resented that endorsement to his own advantage.
    In discussing Darwin's rhetorical activities, especially his tex-
tual performance in mastering the prevailing cultural grammar,
Campbell repeatedly pays tribute to Darwin's "singular ability" to
"synthesize" and to "subvert" the situational resources and constraints. These tributes are an integral part of Campbell's explanation: the rapid acceptance of evolutionary ideas was made possible by
the agency of Darwin's rhetoric. The language of explanation is
unabashedly intentional. In discussing specific textual features, key
phrases like "the struggle for existence" are shown to be results of
Darwin's "strategic and intentional choice" (1987:81). If rhetoric is
an art of the "sayable," then Campbell's Darwin was "a past master
at saying the socially correct thing" (1986:360). There are moments
when Campbell strays from a strictly intentional reading (as when he
is discussing the similarity between the linguistic practices of Paley
and Darwin), but they are rare. And sometimes when he is confronted with textual data (i.e., the word *struck* and its variants occur
sixty-five times in the first edition of the *Origin*) that cannot be easily assimilated to a conscious design, Campbell speaks of a buried
intention: "While the frequency with which an author uses a term

may be beneath the threshold of his or her consciousness, its repetition provides an indication of an author's underlying intention" (1986:361). On the whole, Campbell's analysis assumes that Darwin knew exactly what he was doing and that his textual practices were intentional and premeditated. The intentionalist reading is further accentuated by the agonistic vocabulary used to characterize Darwin's achievement: "battle," "win," "triumph," "herculean," etc. By reading the rhetoricity of the *Origin* almost exclusively in terms of Darwin's conscious and strategic design, Campbell foregrounds a "functionalist" view of rhetoric. His early essays illustrate in a paradigmatic fashion Bryant's (1953) definition of rhetoric as a practical art of "adjusting ideas to people and people to ideas."

The question is not whether Campbell, while examining the textual performance in the *Origin*, is justified in ascribing agency to Darwin, but rather how one should characterize that agency. Is it necessary, as Campbell does, to persistently position Darwin as a conscious and deliberating agent to make sense of the performative dialectic between the *Origin* and its alleged context? Does an attempt to read the *Origin* under a strictly intentional description flatten out its textuality and defer consideration of the intertextual matrix out of which it emerged? I will address these questions not by an independent reading of the *Origin*, but rather by examining a shift in Campbell's reading practices in two recent essays (1990a and 1990c).

The shift is evident on three counts: First, there is a general weakening of the intentional model of persuasion. Instead of reading the *Origin* as an organic and self-standing strategic performance, Campbell begins to read it "intertextually," especially in relation to Darwin's "transmutation notebooks." Second, while mapping the textual movements, Campbell repeatedly invokes the rhetorical lexicon. Third, Campbell increasingly refers to rhetoric as "constitutive" rather than as "functional."

According to Campbell, the general idea of evolution—the present world of plants and animals are the modified descendants of earlier plants and animals—was not something original to Darwin. His own grandfather Erasmus was one among the six earlier thinkers who had propounded different versions of evolutionary theory. What made Darwin's version distinctive was his explanation of the mechanism which drives evolution, namely, natural selection (1990a:209).[14] According to Campbell: "The basic insight that gave Darwin the core of what became the theory of natural selection first occurred to him in late October 1838, a little over two years after he had returned from his celebrated round-the-world voyage on the

HMS *Beagle* (from 1831 to 1836)" (1990c:3). In the fourth chapter of
the *Origin*, the chapter Darwin once called "the keystone of my
arch," he spelled out the concept he had been working on for twenty
years in a language that continues to puzzle the modern reader.

In the two essays, Campbell meticulously tracks across those
twenty years (and more) the complicated itinerary of Darwin's
insight and its rhetorical transformations. Among other things,
Campbell describes how that insight was articulated in relation to
the available biogeological data, some of which Darwin himself had
collected during the *Beagle* voyage. Campbell shows how Darwin
read and misread the data as his insight evolved. Further, Campbell
describes how that insight was articulated in a series of "preselec-
tionist" and "early selectionist" theories Darwin entertained and
discarded before he finally settled on the version in the fourth chapter. Here Campbell's narrative attempts to show how the "path" (or
the "way") to the final version led through a series of contradictory
empirical findings, speculative theories, and textual encounters and
how *Darwin's conceptual itinerary was always already inscribed by
rhetorical habits and considerations*. While the earlier formulations
were either conceptually flawed or contradicted by the available
data or rhetorically implausible, only in the final version was Darwin
able to find "the semantic space midway between mechanism and
miracle" that would ideally balance the competing claims of conceptual innovation and social intelligibility. Campbell's narrative
takes the reader through a dense intertextual space that traverses
not only Darwin's evolutionary works before the *Origin* but also
his encounter with key texts of other thinkers, especially Lyell's
Principles of Geology.

There is a palpable difference between these two essays and
Campbell's earlier work and the difference pertains to the "difficulty" of reading. In the earlier essays, the dialectic between text
and context gets neatly mediated through the Darwin's intentional
design. However complex the cultural grammar into which the *Origin* was interjected, so long as Darwin is positioned as the conscious
and deliberating seat of discourse Campbell's reading remains clear
and crisp. But in the recent essays Darwin is positioned differently.
He is portrayed as someone struggling to articulate a theory whose
conceptual structure contradicted his own scientific beliefs and
rhetorical intuitions. This alters the equation between Darwin,
Campbell, and the reader. When Darwin struggles Campbell struggles, and so does the reader. With Darwin struggling, Campbell is no
longer content to read in terms of a conscious design the interplay of
practical reasoning and figuration in the *Origin* and how that inter-

play prefigures the cultural grammar of its time. At last, the *Origin* emerges from the shadow of Darwin's colossal presence and is seen to have a life and logic of its own that lures the reader into an intertextual space of notebooks, letters, and abandoned works. It is precisely at this point one finds Campbell increasingly drawing on the rhetorical lexicon—stasis, hypotyposis, anaphora, personification, presence, double hierarchy, parallel case, etc.—to map the vagaries of the text. Such an intertextual reading, the details of which defy paraphrase or quick illustration, is a messy affair compared to an intentionalist reading.

Campbell tries to tidy up his reading by occasionally going back to the intentionalist model. At various points, Darwin is portrayed as thinking hard about the problem of persuasion and tributes are paid to his rhetorical genius. These sanitizing moves tend to functionally split the insight from its articulation (that is, the context of discovery from the context of justification), even though Campbell no longer entertains such a distinction. For he writes:

> We must be careful, however, not to press too far the distinction between the form of Darwin's language and the substance of his thought. The inventional dimension of Darwin's thought goes much deeper than Darwin's conscious use of misleading diction. As we examine the genesis and early development of Darwin's ideas, we find form and content, what Darwin wanted to say, the social and linguistic resources available to him for saying it, and the audience he wished to say it to are constitutive of his logic. (1990c:15)

As Campbell begins to read Darwin's language and rhetoric as "constitutive" rather than as "strategic," two interpretations of the *Origin*—intentional and intertextual—continue to vie for allegiance. Campbell prefers to view the two interpretations as complementary:

> Darwin's logic, starting with his reading of Lyell on the *Beagle* and continuing through the *Origin*, was always situated in the midst of a living, ongoing, practical task, and this made it at once inadvertent and intentional, opportunistic yet rational. Darwin's reason was inadvertent—or dialectically ironic—in that both before and after the conversion to evolution, and before and after his coining of "natural selection," he frequently thought he was proving one thing when his arguments ended by convincing him of something else. Darwin's logic was inten-

tional, in that from the first, and continuously throughout the various stages of his career, he was ambitious for scientific success and readily seized every opportunity that the voyage, the heuristic resources of Lyell, and the turns of his own thought and experience opened to better make sense of nature. (1990c:22)

But Campbell's readers may not abide by his preference. As for me, after reading Campbell's recent essays, the balance has irretrievably shifted in favor of an intertextual reading. It is difficult imagine how an intentionalist reading could do justice to the *Origin* as a text.

Gross and the Neo-Aristotelian RS

Unlike Campbell's exclusive devotion to Darwin, Gross's rhetorical readings in science cover a wide range. His book—*The Rhetoric of Science* (1990)—contains a collection of case studies, most of them previously published. The introductory essay attempts to place the case studies within a general framework Gross identifies as an updated neo-Aristotelian approach. Gross's neo-Aristotelianism is different from its previous incarnation in "public address" studies in two ways. First, Gross is committed to globalizing rhetoric. He wants to "entertain a possibility Aristotle could never countenance: the possibility that claims of science are solely the products of persuasion" (3). Lest he be judged brash, Gross emphasizes the provisional character of his analytic strategy: "Whether, after rhetorical analysis is completed, there will be left in scientific texts any constraints not the result of prior persuasion, any 'natural' constraints, remains for the moment an open question" (3). In the meantime, Gross wants to proceed with rhetorical analysis "unabated." While Gross transgresses the Aristotelian boundaries that confine rhetoric to the public sphere (and to the manufacture of politico-juridical discourse), he insists on taking Aristotle's *Rhetoric* as his master text. He accomplishes this maneuver by decontextualizing Aristotle's definition of rhetoric as the art of finding "in each case the existing means of persuasion." For Gross, this definition, which he regards as essentially sophistic in spirit, authorizes a global view of rhetoric. Further, Gross believes that once science is shown to be susceptible to rhetorical analysis, the Aristotelian limits will simply wither away.

Second, Gross is committed to "starring the text." Most of his case studies take as their primary object of analysis discrete scientific texts such as Rheticus's *Narratio Prima*, Darwin's *Red Notebook*,

Newton's *Opticks*, Watson and Crick's *The Double Helix*, etc. Even when Gross is negotiating larger themes—analogy in science, taxonomic language, style in biological prose, the arrangement of scientific papers, the peer review process, etc.—it is textual materials that invariably command his attention. For instance, in analyzing "Style in Biological Prose," analysis centers on microfeatures of the texts, minutely examing what would seem to be the mundane mechanics of the editorial process. By privileging the text, Gross significantly departs from the historicist orientation of earlier neo-Aristotelianism that sought to dissolve the text within its context of constraints and resources.

For Gross, RS takes "as its field of analysis the claims to knowledge that science makes" (3). Gross establishes the general link between rhetoric and science by specifying scientific knowledge as follows:

> Scientific knowledge consists of the current answers to three questions, answers that are the product of professional conversation: What range of brute facts is worth investigating? How is this range to be investigated? What do the results of these investigations mean? Whatever they are, the "brute facts" themselves mean nothing; only statements have meaning, and of the truth of statements we must be persuaded. These processes, by which problems are chosen and results interpreted, are essentially rhetorical: only through persuasion are importance and meaning established. (4)

With this general rationale for RS, Gross turns to the practical task of applying a neo-Aristotelian rhetoric to scientific texts. The key interpretive move involves a substituting "invention" for "discovery":

> To discover is to find out what is already there. But discovery is not a description of what scientists do. . . . Discovery is a honorific, not a descriptive term; it is used in a manner at odds with the history of science—a history for most part, of mistaken theories—and at odds with its current practice, a record, by and large, of error and misdirection. The term invention on the other hand, captures the historically contingent and radically uncertain character of all scientific claims, even the most successful. If scientific theories are discoveries, their unfailing obsolescence is difficult to explain; if these theories are rhetorical inventions, no explanation of their radical vulnerability is necessary. (7)

This substitutive move presupposes a broadly constructivist view of scientific knowledge and representation. It also indicates Gross's theoretical affinity with SSK and SSK–like approaches. However, Gross does not specify how the constructivist thesis links up with (or updates) neo-Aristotelian critical approach he recommends.[15] What follows is a general account of how rhetorical categories—stasis, logos, ethos, pathos, arrangement, style—are applicable to scientific discourse and when applied yield valuable insights. In the introductory essay, Gross gives a series of short examples. For instance, he explains the difference between Aristotle's and Newton's view of motion in terms of different staseis that motivated their inquiries. In another illustration, Newton is shown to deploy the same common topics in his *Opticks* that one finds in everyday discourse. As for ethos and pathos, Gross describes how "all scientific papers . . . are embedded in a network of authority relationships" and how "the disciplined exclusion of emotional appeal from scientific prose is itself a rhetorical trope" (13–15). Further, Gross questions the view that in scientific reasoning "metaphor and analogy have only a heuristic function, that they wither to insignificance as theories progress" by recalling the centrality of the "breeder analogy" in Darwin's *Origin*.

But what do these examples signify? While Gross has little difficulty showing that one could profitably apply rhetorical categories in analyzing scientific discourse, one is left with a nagging suspicion that those categories are so capacious that it would be impossible not to find them in any discourse that is "situated," and "addressed." A rhetorical reading merits attention only insofar as it proffers a distinct and "contestable" (if not "falsifiable") reading of a given scientific text.

This is precisely what Gross attempts to do in his extended case studies. Take, for instance, his essay on "Copernicus and Revolutionary Model Building." The essay centers on a reading of Rheticus's *Narratio Prima* (1540), the first work on Copernicanism, published three years before Copernicus's own *De Revolutionibus*. On Gross's account, *Narratio Prima* revolves around a specific exigence: How to account for one's allegiance to the Copernican system when it was less than compelling by its own avowed standards of argument and evidence. "Until Brahe, Kepler, and Newton, the heliocentric view fell short of its own highest goal: 'to explain completely,' as Copernicus says in the *Commentariolus*, 'the structure and motions of the Universe'" (105). According to Gross, in the intervening years the allegiance to the Copernican system was not, as Feyerabend suggests, a matter of "blind faith" sustained *"by irrational means* such as propaganda, emotion, *ad hoc* hypotheses, and appeal to prejudices of all kinds" (97). Nor does Gross accept Bernard Cohen's view that Copernicus' masterpiece "had no fundamental impact on astronomy until 1609," and the idea that its publication (1543) immediately revolutionized astronomy is no more than "a fanciful invention of eighteenth-century historians of astronomy " (107). While Gross concedes that the Copernican system was not immediately accepted, he finds Koestler's characterization of *De Revolutionibus* as "the book nobody read" untenable. According to Gross:

> This scarcely seems fair to a work that Rheticus devoured, Brahe knew well, Kepler studied assiduously, and Maestlin annotated over a period of fifty years. These men formed a network of influence. Maestlin was Kepler's teacher, and Brahe his mentor. . . . To trace this network of influence is to chronicle a progress that takes us from the birth of modern heliocentricity to the threshold of its first significant intellectual flowering: Kepler's three laws of planetary motion. (107–108)

If Gross's reading simply identified this line of textual influence hitherto overlooked by students of the Copernican revolution, it would be an impressive contribution to historical understanding. But Gross makes no such claim. On the contrary, he draws on the previous historical scholarship of Moesgaard and Westman to identify that network of texts. What is distinctive about Gross's reading is his characterization of that network as consisting of a rhetorical chain of "rational conversions," of which *Narratio Prima* is the opening move.

Gross begins by noting that *Narratio Prima* is structured like a story and thus diverges from a typical Renaissance astronomical treatise composed in an Euclidean form. On Gross's account, *Narratio Prima* contains both a scientific case as well as a rhetorical case for heliocentricity. The scientific case is rather straightforward. It portrays the methods and arguments of Copernicanism as essentially conforming to the prevailing conventions of astronomy that privileged Euclidean forms of reasoning, observational accuracy, and a general conformity with Aristotelian physics. However, the scientific case was incomplete by standards enunciated by Copernicus himself. To compensate for that gap, Rheticus places the scientific argument within a rhetorical form. Gross's basic insight is that *Narratio Prima* enacts a drama of rational conversion: It portrays Copernicus as a "great traditional astronomer, steeped in Ptolemy," whose zeal for the accuracy of observations was second to none, who while "walking in the footsteps of Ptolemy," was nevertheless driven reluctantly "in obedience to command given by the observations" to question geocentricity. Further, he is portrayed as one who is neither rash nor smitten by "a lust for novelty" and fame: "Even after he himself was entirely convinced of heliocentricity, we learn, Copernicus was reluctant to publish his results lest other be upset. Only the repeated urging of the Bishop of Kulm that there was no place for secrecy in science finally persuaded the great astronomer to publish" his views" (103). For Gross, this is a consummate drama of rational conversion. Copernicanism may not have been a gapless system but the process by which Copernicus, pursuing truth in a manner Aristotle would have approved, arrives at heliocentricity appears to be rhetorically gapless. As Gross perceptively notes, *Narratio Prima* enacts a double conversion: "In recounting Copernicus' conversion to heliocentricism, Rheticus is also recounting his own" (103). Gross finds traces of a similar drama in the works of Maestlin and Kepler and goes on to argue that Rheticus provided the later Copernicans with a model of rational conversion that bridged the gap between reason and will (109).

What is striking about Gross's engaging reading of *Narratio Prima* is that it is devoid of rhetorical categories, Aristotelian or otherwise. Reading pivots on the idea of "rational conversion." There is but a single reference to a technical formulation—"argument field"—and it alludes to Stephen Toulmin's work on nonformal reasoning (Toulmin, 1958). Since many of Gross's other case studies are also free of rhetorical terminology, one is left with same question that surfaced after an initial reading of Campbell: what makes these case studies instances of rhetorical analysis?

In Gross's case, it is difficult to tease out the lineaments of a rhetorical signature for two reasons: First, Gross is eclectic in the choice of his case studies. There is no stable object (as in Campbell) against which his critical practice can be examined to elicit a common strategy. Second, Gross is relatively promiscuous in drawing interpretive constructs from various sources—speech act theory, Habermas's "ideal speech situation," Victor Turner on "social drama," Propp on narrative, etc. Each case study draws on a different set of conceptual material and Gross makes no attempt to incorporate that material within the neo-Aristotelian approach he recommends. It would not be an exaggeration to say that not even a single essay in Gross's book can be regarded as a critical illustration of a neo-Aristotelian approach. Gross's neo-Aristotelianism is a phantom; it does not exist. And his critical practice is unhampered by its absence.

If neo-Aristotelianism gives no clue as what makes Gross's readings unmistakably rhetorical, one has to consider other possibilities. In my judgment, the rhetoricity of Gross's readings is rooted in two basic strategies. First, on the negative plane Gross tries to show how in a given case the textual representation of a scientific knowledge claim derives its authority neither from an unassailable empirical base nor from a gapless inferential sequence. Second, on a positive plane Gross tries to show how, in fact, a given text constructs (or fails to construct) its authority to enunciate scientific knowledge claims. This is precisely Gross's reading strategy in relation to *Narratio Prima*. One can detect a similar strategy operating, though less explicitly, in several other case studies. Since we cannot examine each case study individually, I will make some general observations about Gross's critical practice.

First, Gross's case studies show that there is considerable variation as to how different scientific texts, from Newton's *Opticks* to Watson and Crick's *The Double Helix*, construct their authority. While unpacking that authority in its various textual forms and disguises, Gross eclectically draws interpretive constructs from a variety of sources. What is common to Gross's case studies is his constructivist stance (which signals his affinity with SSK) rather than application of a specific interpretive language such as neo-Aristotelianism. Second, Gross's readings gain in complexity and credibility whenever he focuses primarily on unpacking the textual representation of scientific knowledge claims. Inversely, the readings tend to be "thin" whenever the rhetoricity of a scientific knowledge claim is made to rest on the latter's deficiency in terms of logical form or empirical validation. Third, if there is weakness to Gross's essays it is not because he does not use the rhetorical vocabulary, but he does not adequately "star" the text. For instance, in the "Copernicus" essay Gross does not follow up his careful reading of *Narratio Prima* with an equally attentive reading of how rational conversion was replayed in the later texts in the rhetorical chain.

Prelli and the Model of Topical Invention

In his book, *A Rhetoric of Science* (1989), Lawrence J. Prelli proposes to apply the classical method of "topical invention" to the study of scientific discourse. Prelli's book has two relatively symmetrical parts. In the first, Prelli presents a general theory of rhetoric and a specific method for analyzing discourse; and in the second, he applies that theory and method to scientific discourse.

In the first part, drawing on concepts and insights from both classical and contemporary rhetorical theory, Prelli characterizes rhetoric in five distinct ways: rhetoric is the suasory use of symbols (Burke); rhetoric is situated discourse (Bitzer); rhetoric is addressed discourse (Burke); rhetoric is reasonable discourse (Perelman, Wallace, Fisher, etc.); and rhetoric is invented discourse (Aristotle and Cicero) (Bitzer, 1968; Burke, 1969; Fisher, 1978; Perelman and Olbrechts-Tyteca, 1969; Wallace, 1963). For Prelli, these five characterizations are interrelated in a harmonious fashion. However, I shall argue that this is not the case.

The first Burkean characterization of rhetoric as "the suasory use of symbols" furnishes the global framework within which the remaining four characterizations are given specific articulation. The three middle characterizations of rhetoric as "situated," "addressed," and "reasonable" are unproblematic insofar as they represent the taken-for-granted background assumptions in contemporary rhetorical studies. Prelli, quite rightly, does not discuss them in detail because his views here are in consonance with dominant disciplinary practices as he reiterates the agent-centered intentional model. Moreover, the middle three characterizations have a distinctly Aristotelian flavor of "rhetoric restrained."

Prelli devotes most of the first part of his book (three out of four chapters) to elaborating the fifth and the final characterization of rhetoric—as "invented discourse." For Prelli, rhetoric is a practical art of the "sayable." It provides a heuristic for constructing persuasive discourse: what one can say about x (with x generally conceived as field-variant) in a given "situation" that would be regarded as "reasonable" by the audience "addressed." To articulate such a heuristic, Prelli draws on the work of classical rhetoricians, especially Aristotle and Cicero. Prelli devotes most of the second part of the book, as in the first, to showing how scientific discourse may be best understood as "invented discourse." Once again, he devotes three chapters—one each to ends, issues (*stasis*), and lines of arguments (*topoi*)—to explain how the three steps of topical invention are applicable to scientific discourse. In each chapter, that claim to applicability is illustrated by a series of case studies on subjects as diverse as gravity waves, parapsychology, teaching apes to talk, and the memory transfer in planarian worms, the last being the most detailed. Finally, in chapter 10, Prelli deploys the method of topical invention in its entirety for analyzing two extended case studies—the struggle over the scientific status of "creationism" and the announcement of the "double helix" (a double-helical structure for DNA) by Watson and Crick in their historic *Nature* article.

In Prelli's version, the topical method is made up of three sequentially related components: ends, issues, and arguments. In the production of discourse, one first identifies "appropriate rhetorical purposes"; second, one applies "a doctrine of *stasis* to discover the legitimate points of dispute relevant to the rhetorical purposes"; and third, one applies "a topical method of generating arguments appropriate for resolving the disputes discovered by the application of *stasis*" (Peters, 1992:58).

Prelli's exposition of the method in the second part of the book turns into an endlessly complex affair as he offers a threefold characterization of rhetorical ends, a four-by-four stasis schema for analyzing issues, and a list of twenty-two possible and recurrent lines of arguments (topoi). The stasis theory is pivotal as it provides the coordinating structure for specifying ends, identifying issues, and generating arguments. According to Prelli, there are four general kinds of "stoppage"—*evidential, interpretive, evaluative,* and *methodological*—found in scientific discourse. He calls them "superior stases," that is, "arguable points concerning the four grand functions of doing science: adducing evidence, interpreting constructs and information, evaluating the scientific significance of matters discussed, and applying scientific methods" (146). Even when the scientists agree on the relevant superior stases in a given case, the questions arise "about how the problem should be formulated or about which specific issue needs to be resolved to solve the problem" (147). These are questions about "the availability, the meanings, and the usefulness of evidence, constructs, judgments, and procedures" (146). These questions admit only a limited set of responses that are mediated by what Prelli calls "subordinate stases": *conjectural, definitional, qualitative,* and *translative.* Thus, having set up a sixteen-fold stasis matrix for framing issues, Prelli proceeds to identify twenty-two topoi for generating arguments that can engage the points of disagreements in a manner acceptable to scientific communities. According to Prelli, these topoi, subsumed under four functional groups—*problem-solution, exemplary, evaluative,* and *scientific ethos*—are characteristic of all scientific discourse irrespective of specialty: "they are structures of acceptable reasoning used over and over in scientific discussions. . . . These themes constitute a stable, ever-present collection of discussable options that are, as it were, culturally 'authorized' by all scientific communities. Knowing what these options are is helpful to any scientist deciding what to say and how to say it to his or her colleagues" (216).

While this intricate analytic machinery might seem baffling to a neophyte, its governing assumptions are easy to identify: All rhetorical discourse aims to "persuade"; to persuade successfully one must have ends that are deemed "reasonable" by the "situated audience" addressed; what qualifies as reasonable is what coheres with the relevant "conventional norms" embraced by such an audience. Once the rhetor's "ends" are coordinated with the "field-variant norms" of the audience, it becomes possible to figure out what is "sayable." The stasis-based method of topical invention, by further coordinating the issues with possible lines of arguments, provides a heuristic for figuring the "sayable."

Let me begin by enumerating the comparative merits of Prelli's project. First, Prelli is conceptually precise as he carefully specifies what he means by rhetorical analysis. Further, he has articulated a system of topical invention which is specifically tailored for scientific discourse. Second, his case studies are carefully researched and documented. Third, Prelli's three middle characterizations of rhetoric both contain and expand the communitarian and the epistemological strategies discussed earlier. While rhetoric as "addressed" and "situated" gives a more precise reading of the communitarian strategy, rhetoric as "reasonable" gives a more concrete reading of the epistemological strategy. Moreover, Prelli rearticulates the two strategies in a distinctly rhetorical vocabulary and grounds them in the rhetorical tradition. These are some of the basic strengths of Prelli's approach.

Now to the difficulties. I will begin with an immanent critique; that is, I will evaluate Prelli's method in terms of his own claims and expectations as to what it does and can do. According to Prelli, the topical method enables one to do three things: to *describe* the dynamics of scientific discourse in a systematic and intelligible fashion; to *evaluate* the efficacy and appropriateness of a given discourse choice by the scientist; and to *instruct* scientists to communicate productively, especially when they are embroiled in controversies, by exposing them to the practical logic of the topical system.

It is clear that the discourse of science is amenable to topical analysis. In his major case studies, Prelli shows how it is possible to redescribe the dynamics of a scientific text in terms of a topical system. Take, for instance, Prelli's reading of James V. McConnell's 1967 paper—"The Biochemistry of Memory"—a key text in the planarian memory transfer controversy.[16] Prelli's "stasis analysis" of this twelve-page paper is quite straightforward. He dissects McConnell's arguments, step by step, in terms of how he identifies and addresses (or fails to identify and address) the central points of dispute. The sixteen-fold stasis machinery is put to work in excruciating detail. Prelli quotes extended passages from the paper (almost a third of it verbatim!) and comments on them in the "show and tell" fashion. Here the question is no longer whether a scientific paper such as McConnell's *can* be redescribed in the language of stasis analysis, but whether it is *useful* to do so. To answer this question, one must attend to two features of Prelli's reading: abstract generality (i.e., thinness) and systematicity. Earlier, I argued that rhetoric as a language of criticism is so thin that its applicability to any discourse is virtually guaranteed in advance. The same is true of stasis analysis. Further, in Prelli's case, the "thinness" of the interpretive vocabulary also gives the impression of circularity to the extent one finds his reading simply translates a scientific paper from one idiom to another. This sort of circularity would be tolerable if the translation brought to light hitherto occluded features of the text. But Prelli's translations tend to be highly abstract and arcane without enhancing explanatory power. To take a typical example, after analyzing a long passage of McConnell's prose, Prelli writes:

> McConnell was claiming that some skeptics rejected his data because they were too biased theoretically to accept his assessments of what the data meant. In the language of *stasis* analysis, McConnell was asserting that it was not logical to take *conjectural* stands against the reliability of evidence because one does not accept *definitional* efforts to assess evidential meaning. (165)

A translation of this sort is unlikely to convince an attentive reader of its usefulness.

While evaluating McConnell's response to his critics, Prelli introduces the notion of "stasis management." It refers to the ways in which the rhetor identifies, frames, sequences and addresses the interconnected points of dispute that block agreement. It also refers to the ways in which the rhetor might avoid, marginalize, and if possible reconfigure certain disputed points that are deemed unfavorable given the situational exigencies. All such discursive manuevers, Prelli believes, can be mapped with the aid of his sixteen-fold stasis grid. After a careful descriptive mapping of McConnell's argumentative moves, Prelli identifies the key points of "blockage" (mostly pertaining to the superior stasis of evidence in its definitional and conjectural aspects) McConnell could not address to the satisfaction of his critics and explains why that was so. To a degree, Prelli also speculates on what McConnell might have done to be more effective and concludes his analysis by specifying what the disputants need to do to resolve their differences. On the whole,

McConnell gets high marks for his stasis management. While Prelli's evaluative comments are eminently sane and quite insightful, one suspects that Prelli could have generated that commentary without deploying the elaborate machinery of stasis analysis. To be sure, Prelli believes that the stasis theory, both as a conceptual system and as a technical vocabulary, is the generative center of his readings and insights. Yet one finds Prelli continuously translating back and forth between a free critical reading using ordinary language and a stasis analysis. One cannot easily determine which of the two parallel readings is generative of the other, or at least, which one exceeds the other in explanatory force.

What is more, the veneer of stasis vocabulary conceals the ideological presuppositions of Prelli's critical practice. More than anything else, Prelli is interested in the pragmatics of scientific communication. For him, the stasis analysis is valuable only insofar as it aids the scientists (and their critics) in clearing up "stoppages" and "blockages" that impede communication. What Prelli aspires to do is to inject a stasis-driven "topical consciousness" into the discursive self-understanding of science. He believes that a familiarity with the method of topical invention would greatly facilitate scientific communication and thereby contribute to the advancement of learning. In fact, Prelli accounts for McConnell's success as partly due to his instinctive grasp of the topical method. Prelli also believes that had McConnell and his critics known the topical method they would have been more successful in negotiating their differences. The basic assumption here is that the scientist (as any other human being) is capable of discursive "self-monitoring" and that such a capacity, when exercised under the guidance of topical method, can facilitate communication. This is very much an Enlightenment notion: Not only is "self-monitoring" regarded as a virtue, but also as consequential in facilitating mutual understanding. This ideology of communication is blind to what Habermas would call the "systemic distortions" of institutionalized forms of social practice such as "science." Although Prelli constantly refers to "situations," "audiences," and "conventions" as constraining the discursive activity of the scientist, those references do not bring into focus the sheer materiality of science as an institutional practice. It is precisely when one begins to pay attention those institutional aspects (made familiar by the SSK research tradition), that one grows skeptical about Prelli's view of the scientists as self-monitoring rational actors who seek to advance knowledge through mutual understanding. Even if one were to concede à la Rorty that modern science as a "discursive community" is conducive to garnering a high degree of self-reflexivity and mutual understanding, it remains to be shown how a tuition in the topical method would significantly strengthen that communal disposition.

Now I want to shift my critique to another level and examine three more general features of Prelli's work: the promiscuous use of the term *rhetoric*, the attempt to ground the possibility of rhetoric in a certain version of "symbolic" anthropology, and an "overreading" of Kuhn's book *The Structure of Scientific Revolution*. These three features are most explicit in the pivotal sixth chapter, where Prelli attempts forge a systematic conceptual link between rhetoric and science (but cf. chapter 2). While these features are found in a somewhat amplified form in Prelli's work, they are characteristic of RS as a whole.

Prelli, who gives such a systematic method for analyzing scientific discourse, is also one of the most promiscuous users of the word *rhetoric*. Not content to give a topical analysis in a vocabulary that is already dense, Prelli saturates his reading with the word *rhetoric* and its two variants *rhetorical* and *rhetor*. They seem almost talismanic; it is as if Prelli wishes make his analysis rhetorical simply by repeating those words again and again. The most obvious case is when he refers to the scientist sometimes simply as the "scientist," sometimes as the "rhetor," and sometimes as the "scientific rhetor." There is no discernible logic as to why he uses one characterization rather than another. In one sentence he will identify an agent, say McConnell, as the "scientist," and in the very next sentence he will refer to him as the "scientific rhetor." In fact, one could delete these three words more than 80 percent of the time without doing violence to Prelli's meaning. Here is an example of Prelli's practice: "[T]he reasonableness of a rhetor's rhetoric about science can be diminished or enhanced through attacks or encomiums concerning a rhetor's 'scientific' qualities of thought or conduct" (142–143). In a sentence of this sort, the specificity of *rhetoric* is so attenuated that it becomes no more than a pleonastic qualifier.

This pleonastic usage is linked to Prelli's attempt to ground rhetoric in Burke's theory of symbolic action. "Following Burke," writes Prelli, "I take rhetoric to be the suasory use of language as a symbolic means of inducing cooperative acts and attitudes in symbolizing beings" (13–14). Prelli goes on to rehearse the now familiar thesis as to how, for the *animal symbolicus*, "reality is nothing other than that which is mediated through . . . symbol systems," how it "cannot think without symbols," and how "it names its experience, and through this symbolic act it creates, to a great extent, what it takes to be its world," and so on (15). The stage is thus set for the globalization of rhetoric as "symbolic inducement": "Rhetorical acts present allegations about what is; they symbolically advance contentions about how we should name, pattern, or define experiences and thereby make those experiences meaningful" (14). A rough equivalence among *rhetoric, language, thought,* and *reality* emerges, and at that point *rhetoric* loses its specificity. Prelli, again following Burke, attempts to recuperate a modicum of specificity by linking rhetoric with the concept of selection (its agent-centered variant, choice)—but to no avail. Observe how Prelli connects rhetoric with the ubiquitous human practice of selecting:

> Rhetoric explains the selective functions involved when we make, apply, judge symbols. A symbolic actor can only exercise his or her capacity by selecting symbols through which to mediate experience and render it meaningful. Furthermore, selection is necessarily persuasive in its consequences. In choosing one term over others, one directs attention toward particular meanings and relationships and excludes or minimizes those supplied by other terms. . . . Seldom if ever is there only one way to "see" a phenomenon. . . . All users of language are preachers insofar as their choices of words bring into view values, meanings, and purposes they desire. By not choosing other verbal options, they exclude alternative values, meanings, purposes. (16)

Here the problem is the same that one finds in Weimer. Symbol using, symbol selecting, and rhetoric are analytically inseparable. If choosing among symbols is always rhetorical and if we are always choosing among symbols, rhetoric is unavoidable, but alas, also unspecifiable.[17]

There are two sides to Prelli's project: On the one hand, he has fashioned a very specific "topical method" that draws its inspiration from Cicero. Whatever my reservations about its practical usefulness in resolving scientific controversies, it can be deployed with considerable precision and systematicity in a descriptive analysis of scientific discourse. It is still possible for Prelli to refine (by simplifying) his method and selectively apply it to discursive formations that are responsive to such a method. On the other hand, Prelli's attempts to theoretically ground the RS project in Burke's philosophical anthropology leads to a globalization of rhetoric. While this move brings "science" within the range of rhetoric, it also deprives rhetoric of any specificity. This has an adverse effect on the method of topical invention, which was not meant to sustain the mission of a globalized rhetoric. Thus, Prelli's first and fifth characterizations of rhetoric do not harmonize. Burke and Cicero do not make good bedfellows, at least not in the folds of Prelli's treatise.

Finally, I turn to Prelli's reading of Kuhn's *Structure*. It occupies a central place in Prelli's attempt to conceptually link rhetoric and science. Prelli begins by assuming that Kuhn's account of "science" is relatively accurate, and then tries to show how that account is "implicitly" rhetorical. (But see Fuller 1992 for the claim that Kuhn is a "positivist by other means.") This particular move is quite common among the proponents of RS. What is distinctive about Prelli's rereading of *Structure* is his elaborate and slow-moving translation of Kuhn's text into the language of rhetoric. Unlike Overington and Weimer, Prelli does not magically derive the possibility of RS from a certain description of science. Nor does he simply cite, as so many proponents of RS are content to do, the famous passages in which Kuhn stresses the importance of "persuasion" and compares paradigm shifts in science to religious conversions. Instead, Prelli unpacks *Structure*, step by step, as if he were probing into the "rhetorical unconscious" of the text. But the yield is not startling. Prelli simply translates Kuhn's key concept of "paradigm" as "selective symbolic orientation." Thus, Kuhn turns out have a view of scientific discourse that could be construed as a form of "symbolic inducement," although his view of persuasion, Prelli declares, is "conceptually underdeveloped" (87). Prelli's rereading of Kuhn is instructive, and characteristic of RS as a whole. It shows that Kuhn's work implicitly gives a rhetorical account of science, but, alas, does not go far enough, and so a bona fide rhetorician must come in to do his/her appointed duty.

CONCLUSION

Why is Prelli so laboriously trying to redescribe and extend Kuhn's insights into the language of rhetoric? This question alerts us to two distinctive and problematic features of the so-called rhetorical turn in contemporary thought: the distinction between "explicit" and "implicit" rhetorical analysis, and the phenomenon of coarticulation, where rhetoric cannot be articulated without a correlative concept, in this case science.

Explicit/Implicit Rhetorical Analysis

Explicit analysis is the one in which the analyst consciously employs rhetoric as an interpretive metadiscourse; this is what the proponents of RS themselves do. Implicit analysis occurs when the analyst neither understands nor describes what she is doing as a form of rhetorical analysis, but it would be recognized as such by someone familiar with rhetoric. An analysis of a given scientific practice/discourse may be viewed as implicitly rhetorical, if that analysis marks certain features—argumentation, figurative language, generic constraints, modes of constructing authority, and addressivity—and if the force and intelligibility of that analysis is firmly rooted in reading and foregrounding those markings. The difficulty with the idea of implicit analysis is that the perpetrators don't realize (or acknowledge) what they are doing is rhetoric. They need someone else, usually a proponent of RS, to redescribe what they are doing as rhetoric. The power of anointing certain analyses as "implicitly rhetorical" through vigorous rereading rests exclusively with the proponents of RS, a power of dubious value given the status asymmetry between the two groups.[18]

The proponents of RS, whenever they canonize a text as "implicitly rhetorical," as they have done insistently with Kuhn's *The Structure of Scientific Revolutions*, claim that they are drawing out rhetorical implications that never get adequately thematized in the text itself. The occlusion of rhetoric in the text is partly explained as an effect of the author's lack of familiarity with the rhetorical tradition and vocabulary. Further, it is implied that an understanding of rhetoric would have contributed significantly to the economy and effectiveness of the text in carrying out its mission. But it is not uncommon to find those who are celebrated as masters of "implicit rhetorical analysis" react indifferently, if not with hostility, to such interpretations of their work. To the best of my knowledge, none of those masters (and the list is formidable: Kuhn, Feyerabend, Gadamer, Habermas; Toulmin is the possible exception) so far has either conceded that what they have been doing all along is a form of rhetorical reading, or gone on to incorporate rhetorical vocabulary in their subsequent work. Nevertheless, the proponents of RS continue to find more and more evidence of implicit rhetorical analysis. To a certain extent, the site for discovering examples of implicit rhetorical analysis has shifted from HPS to SSK. Instead of Kuhn and Feyerabend, these days Steven Shapin, Bruno Latour, and Steve Woolgar are treated as doing implicit rhetorical analysis.

The persistent tracking of "implicit rhetoric" is understandable at one level. It is a way of making conceptual alliances, a perfectly natural thing for a latecomer to do. Moreover, it enriches the conceptual resources of RS. But it has also another serious consequence which is not sufficiently recognized. In short, the dialectic between implicit and explicit rhetoric makes the very idea of rhetoric undecidable. One can always redescribe any text, both in terms of what it says and what it does, in terms of its unconscious deployment of rhetorical categories. Thus, it turns out that Kuhn's book is not, in itself, an exemplary instance of implicit rhetorical analysis, *but its alleged rhetorical complicity is an effect of someone else's reading.* Any critical text can be shown to possess a level of reflexivity that makes it rhetorical. The lesson is invariably that there is no exit from rhetoric.

Coarticulation

The phenomenon of "coarticulation" refers to the fact that one rarely speaks of rhetoric in isolation, but always in relation to something: a person, practice, event, text, or formation. The most common linguistic form of coarticulation is "the rhetoric of X," as in the case of RS. In the last two decades instances of coarticulations in this form have been multiplying at a dizzying rate. Here is a selected list drawn from a restricted field of titles and subtitles of scholarly books, book chapters, and journal articles arranged in the alphabetic order: assent, antitheory, doubtful authority, economics, ethnographic holism, history, human sciences, image, inquiry, interpretation, irony, motives, modernism, mourning, passivity, pedagogy, philosophy, revolution, secularism, social history, social sciences, temporality, textuality, and so on.

A traditionalist reacts to such a proliferation of "the rhetoric of X" with predictable horror and laments how rhetoric is being trivialized. But there is something disingenuous about this lamentation. A traditionalist, when it is convenient, is as liable to use "the rhetoric of X" as promiscuously as any brazen postmodernist. At issue here is what class of items may be reasonably substituted for X. As a rule, a traditionalist (relying on the authority of Aristotle) expresses reservations about substituting "natural" as opposed to "cultural" entities. And even among cultural entities, a traditionalist is likely grow progressively skeptical as a substituted item becomes further and further removed from some palpable link to human agency or from a readable discursive mediation.

Thus, the ideologically motivated, normative lamentations of traditionalists altogether miss a serious issue. They remain entangled in the age-old divide between nature and culture. Rhetoric is more or less irrelevant in discourse on nature, even if nature turns out to be scripted like a book, and thus the traditionalists find the very idea of RS implausible (at least when it comes to talking about the constitution of scientific knowledge itself). This is mostly an a priori assumption based on the authority of Aristotle and what they take to be the dictates of common sense.

What the traditionalists fail to notice (being preoccupied with the paradigmatic pole of substitutability rather than with the syntagmatic pole of contiguity) is that the proliferating coarticulations *simultaneously* create the effect of both globalization (everywhere) and situatedness (here and now). Whether one arrives at the idea that rhetoric is everywhere inductively (based on the ubiquitous presence of the term) or deductively (as a derivation from a philosophical anthropology) makes little difference. The sheer usage and repetition emanating out of a hermeneutic stance is what creates the effect of globalization. Moreover, *globalization severely undermines rhetoric's self-representation as a situated practical art*. This dialectic between globalization and situatedness has been perceptively marked out by one politically attuned observer, Bruce Robbins (1990):

> There is already something paradoxical about taking rhetoric, defined by its local, conjunctural situatedness, and thus universalizing to cover "everything." But more innocuous expressions of the form "the rhetoric of x" also produce a multitude of indirect effects, options, agendas, principles, and values whose diversity is deviously or sophistically camouflaged by the all-embracing label "rhetoric." It is this deviousness in the ways "rhetoric" is currently functioning in our discourse, a deviousness which informs but also restricts various politicizing projects of interdisciplinarity, that I call "the rhetoric of rhetoric."

Before we can decide whether the all-embracing label "rhetoric" camouflages the "diversity" of entities in which it is presumably embedded, we have to figure out just what is going on. These coarticulations create the illusion of unidirectionality: rhetoric as an apparatus operating on or embedded in something, but always the same regardless of the embedding entity. This is one sense of the promiscuous, both universal and empty, and is what the traditionalist objects to. The other way of reading its promiscuous ubiquity is as what Althusser calls "overdetermination." It bears so much interpretive or strategic weight that it is literally flattened in its appearance. It is a dead metaphor, Derrida's "white mythology." Only a disciplined reading and probing can unpack the layers and layers of sedimented semantic structure, a venture whose value becomes more dubious as the sediments accumulate.

Placebo

Let me see if I can clarify the situation by using an analogy of ancient lineage. Since the time of Gorgias, rhetoric has been compared to a psychoactive drug. In the contemporary usage, it is not clear whether rhetoric is actually a drug, some sort of a (in current pharmacological jargon) "delivery system" for a drug, or a substitute for a drug. As a delivery system, rhetoric has at least two distinct forms: a nondescript mixer (such as water) that dilutes the potency of an alcoholic beverage, or a sweetener (such as sugar syrup) which camouflages the bitterness of a medicine. The difference is critical. In the case of a mixer no one confuses relative tastes of whisky or gin, even though both are mixed with water. Rhetoric in this sense is an ubiquitous but dull accompaniment, not something worth studying. At least one can learn fairly quickly the right proportion of water/rhetoric to mix. But in the case of the sweetener, there is room for ethical mischief and ideological distortion, since the underlying flavors are obscured. But the third alternative is the most critical. *When there is no drug, no substance, rhetoric itself functions as a drug.* More precisely, rhetoric becomes a placebo in the absence of a drug. Rhetoric, seemingly the supplement, becomes *substantial*.

What is centrally at stake in the RS literature (and perhaps in rhetorical criticism in general, *mutatis mutandis*) is this: In the construction of scientific knowledge/practice/culture, does rhetoric ever function as the placebo? That is, does it ever threaten to become part of the substance of science? No one doubts that rhetoric functions as the mixer, sometimes as the sweetener, but can one argue that science is a simulacrum (in Baudrillard's sense), a rhetorical construction without reference? Without some mediating reality, reference becomes a sort of placebo, a fiction created by rhetoric. There are thus different forms in which rhetoric's supplementarity functions: mixer (pedagogy), sweetener (critique), placebo (theory: power/persuasion or tropology). The question is not really whether rhetoric is one or the other, but how it functions in interpretive discourse.[19]

NOTES

*The core of this paper was initially written for a seminar on "The Rhetoric of Science: New directions for the Nineties" organized by Alan Gross and John Lyne at the 1991 SCA Annual Convention and published in *Southern Communication Journal* (Summer 1993). I am indebted to Gross and Bill Keith (a participant in that seminar) for encouraging me to expand the paper, innocent as they were of what "amplification" means to me. My debt to Bill Keith for arranging and editing the special issue around my essay is massive. He has been a model editor: patient, encouraging, and always available to discuss substantive issues. I am still grateful to Campbell, Fuller, Gross, Leff, and Prelli for taking time to read different and fragmented versions of the paper while preparing their responses. In writing this paper I have had numerous productive discussions with three of my colleagues—Daniel O'Keefe, Andrew Pickering, and Joseph Wenzel. I am particularly indebted to O'Keefe for his help in "normalizing" my alien English. Finally, this paper is offered as a token of affection to Trevor Melia—teacher, colleague, and friend—who has been promoting the idea of rhetoric of science for more than two decades at the University of Pittsburgh.

1. Literary critic Steven Mailloux (1989) has catchy phrase for this reading practice—"rhetorical hermeneutics." But, alas, in our postmodern times a clever turn of phrase invariably turns into a method. Unlike Nietzsche, we won't let aphoristic wisdom run its course.

2. For a "constitutive" as opposed to a "functionalist" reading of Aristotle, see Beiner (1983).

3. Until very recently the orator perfectus tradition has been virtually ignored. But recently, a number of scholars have turned their critical attention to that cluster of themes and concepts—eloquence, prudence, decorum, sensus communis, ingenium, dicta acuta and dicta arguta, the ideal orator, to prepon, kairos, judgment, etc.—that constitutes the vita activa tradition. For a representative text, see Mooney (1985).

4. See Perelman and Olbrechts-Tyteca (1969) and Burke (1969). While Burke's own acknowledged debt to Aristotle is well known, there is little justification to view Burke's rhetoric as basically Aristotelian.

5. Wichelns (1925). We must distinguish between the two components of the Aristotelian legacy: a view of rhetoric as a practical/productive activity and containing rhetoric within the public sphere. The significance of the former can be understood only by an understanding of Aristotle's elaborate classification of arts and sciences. However, it is clear that the Aristotelian vocabulary in Rhetoric is that of a practical productive art. As for the latter component, by locating rhetoric in the realm of the contingent and the probable Aristotle did not strictly contain it within the public sphere. But in the course of his own practical theorizing, Aristotle drew his material almost exclusively from that sphere. This choice was further solidified by Cicero's decision to confine rhetoric to questions dealing with hypothesis rather than thesis. Thus, restraining and containing rhetoric within a certain sphere is a fundamentally practical decision, but that practical decision has had theoretical effects in generating a certain kind of vocabulary.

6. At one point Marie Hochmuth Nichols (1963) asks: "What are historians doing that may well be supplemented by the work of rhetoricians?"

7. I am not suggesting that the current critical vocabulary is drawn exclusively from classical rhetoric. There have been some significant conceptual innovations and additions: Bitzer's "exigency," Black's "second persona," McGee's "ideograph," Leff's "time and timing," Perelman's "presence," and Burke's battery of terms headed by "identification." These are basically interpretive concepts that coexist uneasily with the background "productionist" vocabulary of Aristotle.

8. I am not suggesting that our current critical vocabulary produces interpretations of texts and practices which are not open to contestation/falsification. Frequently, what appears to be contestable about an allegedly rhetorical reading of a text is not the reading itself, but what the critic takes to be its effects: claims about the "context," the author's "design," the ideological "content," etc. Questions as to how a rhetorical reading *produces* its interpretive effects are generally elided.

9. Under such conditions, the "immediacy" of rhetoric is not a phenomenological given. For an opposite reading, see McGee (1982) and Natanson (1965).

10. When a group of speech communication scholars audaciously proposed that "all knowledge is rhetorical," Farrell shot back with his own codicil: "All knowledge is rhetorical in direct proportion to how trivial is one's initial conception of rhetoric" (1990:82).

11. One can find useful "literature reviews" in each of the two recent Ph. D. dissertations completed at the University of Illinois at Urbana-Champaign: Taylor (1990) and Peters (1992).

12. Thus, RS minimally aspires to redescribe science as a form of rhetoric. While not claiming that science is "mere rhetoric," RS insists on exploding the positivist myth that science is entirely free of rhetoric. In a more positive vein, RS seek to show how rhetoric is an integral part of scientific practice.

13. According to Campbell (1987:71), the general readers of the *Origin* (who were advised to consult the pamphlet beginning with the fourth edition) had no way of knowing that Darwin himself did not believe in Gray's arguments until 1867 when he publicly rejected them in his *Variation in Plants and Animals Under Domestication*. No mention of this refutation was made in the two subsequent editions of the *Origin* in 1869 and 1872.

14. The core of Darwin's theory of natural selection is stated in formal language by Stephen Jay Gould (1977) as follows: "1. Organisms vary, and these variations are inherited (at least in part) by their offspring. 2. Organisms produce more offspring than can possibly survive. 3. On the average, offspring that vary most strongly in directions favored by the environment

will survive and propagate. Favorable variation will therefore accumulate in populations by natural selection" (11; cited in Campbell, 1990c:4). Note Campbell's remarks about the difference between the formal language of Gould as opposed to Darwin's original ordinary language formulation.

15. Therefore, it is not necessary here to examine and critique Gross's constructivism in evaluating his critical performance. For detailed discussion on this topic, see Gross's exchange with McGuire and Melia: McGuire and Melia (1989), Gross's reply in Gross (1991), and their rejoinder in McGuire and Melia (1991).

16. McConnell claimed that memory is a chemical phenomenon that can be physically transmitted. To prove that hypothesis, McConnell and his colleagues conducted a series of controversial experiments on cannibalistic planarian worms. In one rather gruesome experiment, they classically conditioned a group of planarians to contract in the presence of light by administering electric shocks. Then, as McConnell describes it in his 1966 paper: "(We) cut them in half, and fed them to hungry cannibals. We also chopped up untrained planarians and fed them to another group of cannibals. Then a day or so later, all of the cannibals were trained. We found that the cannibals that had eaten the trained worms were, from the first trials, significantly more responsive to the conditioned stimulus (light) than were the cannibals that had eaten control animals." For McConnell, this meant that memory of the performance task had been transmitted physically from the trained planarians to the untrained ones through cannibalization. These experimental results were questioned and fiercely attacked by fellow researchers. McConnell (1967) answers his critics.

17. Prelli also attempts to delimit the concept of rhetoric by linking it with another Burkean concept—symbolic "orientation." But here again, the linkage fails to make rhetoric any more specifiable.

18. The relation between these two groups is itself an endlessly fascinating topic. The explicit rhetoricians of science usually belong to the low-status disciplines (speech communication and composition), while the implicit rhetoricians belong to the high-status disciplines (history, philosophy, and sociology). Thus far the referencing has been exclusively one-sided. Even here the marginality of rhetoric is made manifest institutionally.

19. One might read this essay either as an interrogation of some of the governing assumptions of contemporary rhetorical studies as exemplified in the "rhetoric of science," or as an interpretive survey of that subfield. Those who elect to read the essay as a survey should note two key omissions. First, I have not examined the work of Charles Bazerman (1987) who, working out the disciplinary matrix of English Composition, has extensively examined the "writtenness" of scientific knowledge. Second, I have not examined the growing body of case studies in RS. Among the case studies, particularly notable is the collaborative work of Henry Howe (a biologist) and John Lyne (a rhetorician) on the rhetoric of sociobiology.

References

Bazerman, C. (1987). *Shaping written knowledge*. Madison: University of Wisconsin Press.

Beiner, R. (1983). *Political judgment*. Chicago: Chicago University Press.

Bender, J., and Wellbery, D. E. (1990). Rhetoricality: On the modernist return of rhetoric. In J. Bender and D. E. Wellbery (Eds.), *The ends of rhetoric*, 3–42. Stanford: Stanford University Press.

Bitzer, L. F. (1968). The rhetorical situation. *Philosophy and Rhetoric, 1*, 1–14.

Black, E. (1978). *Rhetorical criticism: A study in method*. Madison: University of Wisconsin Press. Orig. pub. 1965.

———. (1980). A note on theory and practice in rhetorical criticism. *Western Journal of Speech Communication, 44*, 331–336

Bokeno, R. M. (1987). The rhetorical understanding of science: An explication and critical commentary. *Southern Speech Communication Journal, 52*, 285–311.

Bryant, D. C. (1953). Rhetoric: Its function and its scope: Rediviva. In D. C. Bryant, *Rhetorical dimensions of criticism*, 3–23. Baton Rouge: Louisiana University Press.

Burke, K. (1969). *A rhetoric of motives*. Berkeley: University of California Press. Orig. pub. 1950.

Campbell, J. A. (1970). Darwin and *The origin of species*: The rhetorical ancestry of an idea. *Speech Monographs, 37*, 1–14.

———. (1974a). Charles Darwin and the crisis of ecology. *Quarterly Journal of Speech, 60*, 442–449.

———. (1974b). Science, religion, and emotional response: A consideration of Darwin's affective decline. *Victorian Studies, 18*, 159–174 .

———. (1975). The polemical Mr. Darwin. *Quarterly Journal of Speech, 61*, 375–390.

———. (1986). Scientific revolution and the grammar of culture: The case of Darwin's *Origin*. *Quarterly Journal of Speech, 72*, 351–376.

———. (1987). Charles Darwin: Rhetorician of science. In J. S. Nelson, A. Megill, and D. N. McCloskey (Eds.), *The rhetoric of the human sciences*, 69–86. Madison: University of Wisconsin Press.

———. (1989a) The invisible rhetorician: Charles Darwin's third party strategy. *Rhetorica*, 7, 55–85.

———. (1989b). Of orchids, insects and natural theology: The evolution of Darwin's strategy after *The Origin*. In B. E. Gronbeck (Ed.), *Spheres of argument: Proceedings of the sixth SCA/AFA conference on argumentation*, 216–224. Annandale, VA: SCA.

———. (1990a). Darwin, Thales and the milkmaid. In R. Trapp and J. Schuetz (Eds.), *Perspectives on argumentation*, 207–220. Prospect Heights, IL: Waveland.

———. (1990b). Scientific discovery and rhetorical invention: Darwin's path to natural selection. In H. W. Simons (Ed.), *The rhetorical turn*, 58–89. Chicago: Chicago University Press.

———. (1990c). On the way to the *Origin*: Darwin's evolutionary insight and its rhetorical transformation. *The Van Zelst lecture in communication*. Northwestern University School of Speech, Evanston, IL.

Campbell, P. N. (1975). The personae of scientific discourse. *Quarterly Journal of Speech*, 61, 391–405.

Conley, T. M. (1990). *Rhetoric in the European tradition*. New York: Longman.

de Man, P. (1979). *Allegories of reading: Figural language in Rousseau, Nietzsche, Rilke and Proust*. New Haven: Yale University Press.

Eden, K. (1987). Hermeneutics and the ancient rhetorical tradition. *Rhetorica*, 5, 59–86

———. (1990). The rhetorical tradition and Augustinian hermeneutics in *De doctrina christiana*. *Rhetorica*, 7, 45–64.

Farrell, T. B. (1990). From the Parthenon to the bassinet: Death and rebirth along the epistemic trail. *Quarterly Journal of Speech*, 9, 82

Fisher, W. R. (1978). Toward a logic of good reasons. *Quarterly Journal of Speech*, 64, 376–384.

Fuller, S. (1992). Being there with Thomas Kuhn: A parable for modern times. *History and Theory*, 31, 241–275.

Gaonkar, D. P. (1990). Object and method in rhetorical criticism: From Wichelns to Leff and McGee. *Western Journal of Speech Communication*, 54, 290–316.

Gould, S. J. (1977). *Ever since Darwin*. New York: W. W. Norton.

Gross, A. G. (1990). *The rhetoric of science*. Cambridge: Harvard University Press.

————. (1991). Rhetoric of science without constraints. *Rhetorica, 9,* 283–299.

Hartman, G. (1981). *Saving the text: Literature, Derrida, philosophy*. Baltimore: Johns Hopkins University Press.

Hernadi, P. (Ed.). (1989). *The rhetoric of interpretation and the interpretation of rhetoric*. Durham: Duke University Press.

Hyde, M. J., and Smith, C. R. (1979). Hermeneutics and rhetoric: A seen but unobserved relationship. *Quarterly Journal of Speech, 65,* 347–363.

Jaffe, S. (1980). Freud as rhetorician: *Elocutio* and the dream-work. *Rhetorik: Ein internationales Jahrbuch*, Band 1. Stuttgart: Frommann-Holzboog, 42–69.

Kennedy, G. A. (1980). *Classical rhetoric and its christian and secular tradition from ancient to modern times*. Chapel Hill: The University of North Carolina Press.

Leff, M. C. (1987). Modern sophistic and the unity of rhetoric. In J. S. Nelson, A. Megill, and D. N. McCloskey (Eds.), *The rhetoric of the human sciences*, 19–37. Madison, WI: University of Wisconsin Press.

Leff, M. C. (1993). The uses of Aristotle's *Rhetoric* in contemporary American scholarship. *Argumentation, 7,* 291–296.

Mailloux, S. (1989). *Rhetorical power*. Ithaca: Cornell University Press.

McConnell, J. V. (1967). The biochemistry of memory. In W.C. Corning and S.C. Ratner (Eds.), *The chemistry of learning: Invertebrate research*, 310–322. New York: Putnam.

McGee, M. C. (1982). A materialist's conception of rhetoric. In R. McKerrow (Ed.), *Explorations in rhetoric: Studies in honor of Douglas Ehninger*, 23–48. Glenville, IL: Scott Foresman.

McGuire, J. E., and Melia, T. (1989). Some cautionary strictures on the writing of the rhetoric of science. *Rhetorica, 7,* 87–99.

————. (1991). The rhetoric of the radical rhetoric of science. *Rhetorica, 9,* 301–316.

Melia, T. (1984). And lo the footprint . . . : Selected literature in rhetoric and science. *Quarterly Journal of Speech, 70,* 303–313.

Mooney, M. (1985). *Vico in the tradition of rhetoric*. Princeton: Princeton University Press.

Natanson, M. (1965). The claims of immediacy. In M. Natanson and H. W. Johnstone (Eds.), *Philosophy, rhetoric, and argumentation*, 10–19. University Park: Pennsylvania State University Press.

Nichols, M. H. (1963). *Rhetoric and criticism*. Baton Rouge: Louisiana University Press.

Overington, M. A. (1977). The scientific community as audience: Towards a rhetorical analysis of science. *Philosophy and Rhetoric, 10*, 143–164.

Perelman, C., and Olbrechts-Tyteca, L. (1969). *The new rhetoric: A treatise on argumentation*. J. Wilkinson and P. Weaver (Trans.). Notre Dame: University of Notre Dame Press.

Peters, T. N. (1992). *A rhetorical project for understanding scientific change*. Ph.D. diss., University of Illinois.

Prelli, L. J. (1989). *A rhetoric of science: Inventing scientific discourse*. Columbia: University of South Carolina Press.

Robbins, B. (1990). Interdisciplinarity in public: A rhetoric of rhetoric. *Social Text, 25/26*, 103–118.

Swanson, D. L. (1977a). A reflective view of the epistemology of critical inquiry. *Communication Monographs, 44*, 207–219.

————. (1977b). The requirements of critical justifications. *Communication Monographs, 44*, 306–320.

Taylor, C. (1990). *The rhetorical construction of science: Demarcation as rhetorical practice*. Ph.D. diss., University of Illinois.

Todorov, T. (1977). *Theories of symbol*. C. Porter (Trans.). Ithaca: Cornell University Press.

Toulmin, S. E. (1958). *The uses of argument*. Cambridge: Cambridge University Press.

Vickers, B. (1988). *In defense of rhetoric*. Oxford: Clarendon.

Wallace, K. (1963). The substance of rhetoric: Good reasons. *Quarterly Journal of Speech, 58*, 239–249.

Wander, P.C. (1976). The rhetoric of science. *Western Journal of Speech Communication, 40*, 226–235.

Weimer, W. B. (1977). Science as a rhetorical transaction: Toward a nonjustificational conception of rhetoric. *Philosophy and Rhetoric, 10*, 1–29.

———— . (1983). Why all knowledge is rhetorical. *Journal of the American Forensic Association, 20,* 63–71.

Wichelns, H. A. (1925). The literary criticism of oratory. In A. M. Drummond (Ed.), *Studies in rhetoric and public speaking in honor of James Albert Winans.* New York: Century.

PART II

Dissensions

Chapter 2

The Idea of Rhetoric As Interpetive Practice: A Humanist's Response to Gaonkar

Michael Leff

> I admire your character too much, Marcus Cato, to con-
> demn your intention; some details I might perhaps alter
> and slightly change. "You do not make many mistakes,"
> says that well-known old guardian to a very brave man,
> "but you do make mistakes. I can correct you." But I can-
> not correct you. I would most truthfully say that you make
> no mistakes at all, and you seem the kind of man who
> deserves, not so much correction in anything as a slight
> restraint. . . . If some good fortune, Cato, had taken you
> with your natural ability to such teachers, you would not
> indeed have been better or braver or more temperate or
> more just, for that would have been impossible, but you
> would have been a little more given to kindness.
>
> —Cicero (1937:60–64)

The first thing to say about Gaonkar's essay is that it is exceed-
ingly ambitious. Attempting an intricate synthesis within a synthesis, Gaonkar folds his interpretation of the scattered literature on
the rhetoric of science within a still broader redescription of the current disciplinary scene in rhetorical criticism. Under the pressure
of this two-fold responsibility, the essay grows increasingly complex as it proceeds; thick descriptions of particular texts are inter-
larded with theoretical commentary, and the texture of the whole
becomes so dense and variegated that it resists any effort at brief
summary and response. Nevertheless, the conceptual architecture of

the essay seems reasonably clear and straightforward. Building upon a set of interrelated binary concepts, Gaonkar defines the interpretive function of contemporary rhetoric through a systematic contrast with the productive/performative function of classical rhetoric. The entire essay, as I read it, pivots on this distinction, and I want to direct my response to this fundamental point.

It is possible to quarrel with Gaonkar on extrinsic, historical grounds, but this strategy would stress matters of detail and deflect attention from the larger issues that he brings so sharply into focus. Consequently, I prefer to play Cicero to Gaonkar's Cato, and instead of searching for mistakes, I intend to assume the role of an immanent critic. My question is whether Gaonkar realizes his own ambitions, and to answer it, I must try to understand the logic of his position and test its internal coherence. Ultimately, this effort focuses on Gaonkar's central tenet: that the "ideology of human agency" associated with classical rhetoric radically separates the older, humanistic paradigm from the contemporary, interpretive turn in rhetorical studies. I must begin, however, by tracing the steps that lead to this conclusion.

Gaonkar's argument rests upon three key terms: *globalization*, *interpretation*, and *recognition*. Each term is paired with an opposite: A globalized conception of rhetoric stands opposed to a restrained conception (specifically, rhetoric restrained to civic or public fora); an interpretive rhetorical stance is opposed to a practical or performative stance; and recognition of the rhetorical function in discourse is opposed to its repression. The last of these pairs (recognition/repression), though important to Gaonkar's analysis of the rhetoric of science literature, seems derivative from the other two and less fundamental to his general characterization of the disciplinary scene. Consequently, I will concentrate on only the first two concepts— globalization and interpretation.

Using the binary opposition he builds into these concepts, Gaonkar distinguishes between "classical" and "contemporary" rhetoric. Classical rhetoric is restrained and oriented toward practice and performance; it looks forward to the doing or making of something in the civic arena. Contemporary rhetoric is global and interpretive; it retrospectively seeks to understand something done or made in any discursive arena. Then, through a rather ingenious move, Gaonkar establishes a causal rather than accidental relationship between the interpretive turn and the globalization of rhetoric. If rhetorical criticism is an interpretive act, then, on Gaonkar's account, it must invoke a metadiscourse (a conceptual "vocabulary") in order to comprehend particular discourses. But a metadiscourse is what it is because it stands above and is not restrained by any class of objects. Hence, rhetoric becomes whatever an interpreter can filter through the vocabulary of the metadiscourse, and the range of this activity is unlimited. The rhetorical "in any given case is invariably an effect of one's reading," and since it is possible to produce this effect on "virtually any object," "there is no way to deglobalize rhetoric from within the interpretive paradigm."

Gaonkar's next move is to demonstrate that the humanistic or classical paradigm is incompatible with the interpretive paradigm. Following a well-known distinction, Gaonkar divides humanistic rhetoric into two species: *rhetorica utens* and *rhetorica docens*. The first species, represented by Cicero and his conception of the *orator perfectus*, stresses practice per se, and because practice is always bound to particular circumstances, it deemphasizes any kind of theoretical vocabulary. The second species, represented by Aristotle, is theoretical, but the theory is directed toward a specific kind of practice, and hence its "productionist" vocabulary is inappropriate for an interpretive metadiscourse.[1] Any effort to make a direct, unreflexive application of this vocabulary to the task of interpretation must lead to confusion. Unfortunately, however, our disciplinary history began with this misappropriation of Aristotle, and long after the repression of Aristotle's authority, it still haunts and disables our critical practice.

If a direct, unreflexive appropriation of the "productionist vocabulary" is inappropriate, it still remains possible to "translate" this vocabulary and alter it so that it can serve interpretive purposes. Gaonkar, however, discounts this strategy, primarily because "the humanist paradigm" conveys not just a technical lexicon, but also an "ideology of human agency." He summarizes this "ideology" as a

> view of the speaker as the seat of origin rather than a point of articulation, a view of strategy as identifiable under an intentional description, a view of discourse as constitutive of character and community, a view of audience situated simultaneously as "spectator" and "participant," and finally, a view of "ends" that binds speaker, strategy, discourse, and audience in a web of purposive actions.

Since it runs counter to the interpretive function of a critical metadiscouse, Gaonkar maintains that this view of agency ought to be discarded, and he promises an extended critique of the "humanist paradigm." But I am not certain that he fulfills this promise. The issue is deferred until a much later section of the essay, where Gaonkar describes and assesses John Campbell's studies of Darwin.

The commentary here, although quite detailed about Campbell's work, is not very explicitly linked to the specific and strong theoretical claims that Gaonkar makes earlier in the paper, and as I will explain later, his conclusion indicates a personal preference rather than a systematic indictment of the humanistic stance. Moreover, even if we set this problem to the side and concentrate on the argument presented in the introductory section, Gaonkar's position still seems insecure. His theoretical ordering of terms does not actually discard a subject-centered conception of agency so much as it relocates it at a different level of discursive activity, and his theory is not fully consistent with his own interpretive practice as a reader of disciplinary history.

Interpretation is a slippery term that can be applied to rhetorical criticism in a number of different senses. As he formulates his theoretical position, however, Gaonkar narrows his focus to a single option: Interpretation is an activity of a reader designed to subsume particular discourses within the lexicon of a metadiscourse. Thus, in the opening paragraph of the essay, Gaonkar explains that:

> When one invokes a metadiscourse to account for a discursive practice, what one hopes to achieve minimally is a "redescription" of the latter. Under ideal circumstances, an agile reader might wish to dissolve a discursive practice into the interpretive medium of a preferred metadiscourse. . . . A perfect interpretation is one in which the object of interpretation loses all of its recalcitrance and becomes transparent. (25)

A striking feature of this account is the extremely active role played by the interpreter and the passivity of the interpretive "object." The reader "redescribes" the discursive practice, "dissolves" it, makes it "transparent." This point is reinforced, in a passage I have cited earlier, when Gaonkar asserts that the "rhetorical" is "an effect of one's reading rather than a quality intrinsic to the object being read," and as a result, "a master reader" can encompass an unlimited range of objects. Again the reader is active; the text is inert. From this perspective, of course, the rhetor ceases to function as a significant agent, but the ideology of agency still remains. Instead of the orator perfectus, we have the master reader, the *lector perfectus*. Agency is removed from the forum, the law-court, and the pulpit, only to be relocated in the places where metadiscourse dwells—the study, the lecture hall, and the library.

This equivocal view of agency reflects the rigidity of the binary method Gaonkar uses to construct his own critical metadiscourse.

Within the fearful symmetry of this method, one can change the locus of agency but cannot move agency across the line of demarcation between theory and practice. If classical rhetoric, by definition, has a practical/productive end, its conception of agency cannot serve the theoretical demands of the interpretive critic. Likewise, however, if the goal of interpretive criticism is to wield a metadiscourse, the critic must resist or dissolve agency as it appears in particular discursive practices. Critics, then, must lock their perspective either within the subjectivity of the rhetor or within the subjectivity of their own theoretical interests. There is no space where the two positions can meet and interact, and so, in both conditions, agency centers on an isolated subject. The only way to break out of this dilemma is to adopt an interpretive stance that allows a more fluid relationship between the agency of the critic and the agency represented in the texts studied by the critic.

When Gaonkar turns away from the theoretical aspects of his essay, he sketches an interpretive position that might solve the dilemma constructed by his own theory. In fact, the greater part of the essay consists of a reading of disciplinary history, and in assuming his role as interpreter, Gaonkar grounds his perspective within the internal workings of the literature. Implicitly rejecting the tendency to view the discipline from the top down through borrowed lens, he argues that the key issues "cannot be profitably addressed in a priori fashion" but must be approached "in the historical context of disciplinary practice." This task, he adds, calls for "reflexive critical engagement" and requires an understanding of the struggles and labors of practicing critics. In applying this perspective, Gaonkar reads the disciplinary literature by concentrating on particular texts and authors, but these particulars emerge neither as isolated bits nor as the product of wholly extrinsic forces. Instead, he describes an interactive and generative network of influence that shapes, though it does not determine, the positions of those who participate in it.

This network functions through rather informal and unobtrusive channels. Its influence, as Gaonkar demonstrates, often is not recognized consciously, and its operation has more to do with ingrained habits and taken-for-granted orientations than with openly examined doctrine. In other words, this intertextual network constitutes a tradition, and like all traditions, it cannot be understood or mastered by stepping outside the medium that sustains it. Thus, both the practicing critic and the disciplinary metacritic engage in interpretive practices as they work in and through a network of mutual influence. Viewed in this light, agency becomes a complex matter that cuts across the bias of the theory/practice distinction.

In order to illustrate and extend this point, I want to consider a single text, Edwin Black's *Rhetorical Criticism*—a work that Gaonkar (like almost everyone else) identifies as a landmark in the disciplinary literature. From the intertextual perspective, we recognize that, in one sense, the book is a product of the tradition, a reflection of earlier work in its history. At the same time, however, Black is not merely reflecting what came before him; he reinterprets the tradition, attempts to revise it and to leave his mark on its future development. The influence of the book, however, is unstable and something that Black cannot control since readers filter the book through their own interests and interpret it according to their own vision of the tradition. Yet, unless readers simply dissolve the book into a disembodied metadiscourse, they are not impervious to the agency of Black's text. As they study the book, their own vision of the tradition is likely to change and hence also the conception of their place within it.

Within this process of turn-taking, the act of interpretation becomes part of a tradition rather than a detached observation of its history, and agency becomes a matter of the circulation of influence, something that remains fluid as one positioned subject engages the work of another, altering the work while being altered by it. Moreover, at this point of intersection, the tension between production and interpretation softens. As Gadamer observes, when readers encounter texts distanced from their own position, "the grasping of meaning takes on something of the character of an independent productive act, one that resembles more the art of the orator than the process of mere listening." And for this reason, instead of dividing the productive vocabulary of humanistic rhetoric from the work of interpretation, Gadamer believes that "the theoretical tools of the art of interpretation (hermeneutics) have been to a large extent borrowed from rhetoric" (1977:24).

At times, Gaonkar verges toward explicit recognition of this fluid, interactive conception of interpretation, and the essay contains sustained passages that illustrate its application. Yet these tendencies are deflected (or perhaps repressed) by his commitment to a theoretical metadiscourse and the binary oppositions that maintain it. This inclination to divide and purify surfaces most clearly when Gaonkar assesses Campbell's studies of Darwin.

Through a perceptive reading of Campbell's work, Gaonkar notes a significant shift in critical orientation: In the earlier essays, Campbell views Darwin as a calculating strategist who shrewdly and consciously adapted his textual practices to the demands of the context. In the later essays, however, Campbell offers a richer, more complex reading of *The Origin of Species*, one that invokes a more precise rhetorical vocabulary, probes more deeply into the intertextual background, and acknowledges less than fully conscious elements in Darwin's rhetoric. Campbell himself seems well aware of the change and regards his more recent insights as a consistent expansion of his earlier work. He expresses this point elegantly: "Darwin's logic, starting with his reading of Lyell on the *Beagle* and continuing through the *Origin*, was always situated in the midst of a living, ongoing, practical task, and this made it at once inadvertent and intentional, opportunistic and yet rational." But Gaonkar, inhibited by his metatheoretical lexicon, finds it difficult to accept this effort to balance intertextual and intentional dimensions of criticism. Preferring to divide early Campbell from later Campbell, Gaonkar comments: "Campbell's readers may not abide by his preference. As for me, after reading Campbell's recent essays, the balance has irretrievably shifted in favor of an intertextual reading." Thus, a careful and patient reading of Campbell's work does not open new space for Gaonkar but ends in a judgment that protects his binary categories.

More generally, the same binary rigidity enters into Gaonkar's original and most fundamental premise—his categorical distinction between the productive/performative nature of classical rhetoric and the interpretive nature of contemporary rhetoric. This distinction is not unfounded and, up to point, is a plausible and useful way of interpreting the difference between broad and complex developments in the history of rhetoric. Classical rhetoric and the criticism associated with it surely place emphasis on reading as a resource for future production rather than as an exercise in assigning meaning, and the technical apparatus of traditional rhetoric is intended mainly as a guide to production and performance. Contemporary criticism, however, centers upon meaning and adopts an understanding of texts as its primary burden. (On this distinction, see Tompkins, 1980:202–206.) The two orientations are different, and Gaonkar is right to warn against a conflation between the instruments of the one and the purposes of the other.

Nevertheless, although this distinction between periods and focal interests indicates an important difference of tendency, it is misleading when considered as a categorical, global, and essential opposition. Production and interpretation are not discrete activities. They occur in association with one another, and unless they are purified through an artificial theoretical lens, a focal interest in one does not preclude a lively interest in the other. In fact, one of the major insights of recent literary theory is a recognition that interpretive theory itself is always grounded in a rhetorical context and always involves rhetorical production (e.g., Fish, 1989; Mailloux, 1989). Likewise, viewed from a certain perspective, we might conclude that the productive emphasis in classical rhetoric also incorporates hermeneutic activity. Unfortunately, the possibility of this interaction has been occluded from view in the discipline of rhetorical criticism. Modern rhetorical critics have concentrated on the technical lore of classical rhetoric as a free-standing system, and as a result, they have left little space for considering how that lore might participate in a larger and more flexible program of language studies. And Gaonkar, because he begins with a strong and unqualified binary opposition between production and interpretation, assumes that the problem in applying classical rhetoric to interpretive work stems from the *essence* of classical rhetoric. He does not consider that the problem may reflect the way that modern scholars *interpret* the tradition.

The appropriation of classical rhetoric by modern critics was not the result of an unmediated encounter with the classical sources. It occurred within an academic milieu that favored—almost demanded—foundationalist conceptions of theory and method.[2] In turning the tradition to their purposes, modern critics left the impress of their prejudices and needs on it, selecting and interpreting its elements to conform with an interest in abstract theory and objective methodology. Not surprisingly, then, they isolated the preceptive lore as almost the sole item of attention and treated the precepts as theoretical principles capable of being applied directly and rather mechanically to textual criticism. Other aspects of the classical program—e.g., its extensive program of reading, its compositional exercises, and its rather antitheoretical stress on pragmatic judgment— were largely ignored. The result was a critical approach that had little interpretive energy, but the fault here, I believe, was less a consequence of the original model than of the naive modernism that used and defined the model for its own narrow purposes. Moreover, subsequent attempts to reform rhetorical criticism typically have displaced the older tradition without considering how it could be reinterpreted. The result has been to reify a certain (foundationalist) conception of the history of rhetoric, and Gaonkar's binary method, despite its theoretical elegance, repeats this same pattern of looking backward and forward without ever a glance to the side.

Yet, the current hermeneutical turn ought to encourage a reinterpretation of the relationship between traditional rhetoric and contemporary rhetorical criticism. In saying this, I am not referring to the already well developed efforts at producing revisionist histories of rhetoric, though such histories often have relevance to the project I have in mind. What I am advocating is a hermeneutic understanding in Gadamer's sense of the term—a fusion of horizons between the traditional texts and our current interests. In this project, effort is directed not at placing classical rhetoric within an extrinsic category scheme, but at understanding the elements, objectives, and functions of older rhetorics on their own terms insofar as we can understand them in our own terms. As opposed to foundationalist approaches to history, this perspective would not encourage us to locate fixed essences that characterize different "systems of rhetoric" or rhetorics of different periods. Instead, we would assume that the tradition is itself complex, that its elements exist in a complex relationship with one another, and that our understanding of this relationship changes as a function of our own interests and preoccupations. From this perspective, the relationship between production and interpretation in the traditional "productionist" rhetorics takes on a more fluid aspect than it does in Gaonkar's binary history.

To illustrate this point, I want to consider the classical notion of *imitatio*. In classical rhetoric, the doctrine of imitatio marked the most obvious intersection between the reading of texts and the production of persuasive discourse. Although this doctrine held a prominent and persistent place in traditional rhetoric, modern scholars have only begun to give it serious attention, and it is sometimes badly misunderstood because of the aversion to "imitation" that we have inherited from the Romantic movement. Imitatio was not the mere repetition or mechanistic reproduction of something found in an existing text. It was instead a complex process that allowed historical texts to serve as resources for invention. Classical literary criticism, drawn into the orbit of rhetorical functionalism, largely served as a vehicle for developing productive skills through imitatio, and this orientation militated against reading a literary text as modern critics do—as a privileged unit of meaning. Nevertheless, within the larger program of rhetorical education, imitatio allowed interpretation to play a vital role in the formation of rhetorical judgment.

The function of rhetorical education, at least in its more liberal variants, was to impart the practical judgment and linguistic resources an orator needed to encompass particular situations. The oratorical faculty depended upon the ability to make the appropriate response to the circumstances at hand; hence propriety (*prepon* or *decorum*) in rhetoric, like prudence in ethics, could not be reduced to technical or theoretical rules. Rules were general, but rhetorical cases were particular and could not be resolved by theoretical knowledge per se. For this reason, the preceptive lore of rhetoric did not constitute a "theory" or "method" in the modern sense of these terms. The precepts could only indicate possibilities for use, and the body of precepts served as an armamentarium of strategies whose potential was realized only as put to use in practice. Consequently, as Quintilian put the point, anyone whose knowledge of rhetoric was restricted to theoretical principles possessed no more than a "dumb science" (*mutam scientiam*; see *Institutio oratoria*, 5.10.119). The goal of the rhetorical program was not to generate theory but to assist in developing a faculty for judging when to use a strategy and how to embody it appropriately in a concrete case.

Because of the inherent limitations of theoretical instruction, imitatio performed an especially important function in rhetorical education: It could show by example what the rules could not tell. This kind of instruction implied a two-step process. In the first step, the reader would learn to identify rhetorical strategies and forms as actually embodied in a text and to judge their significance relative to the text as a whole and its purposes. In the second step, such strategies and forms would be reembodied in a composition addressed to a new situation. Throughout both phases, invention and interpretation interacted with one another. Significant features of the historical text not only had to be recognized in isolation but applied to an understanding of how they functioned as part of a whole—an understanding realized only if the reader engaged in something like an act of invention; and then when the reader became a writer, interpretive judgment had to be used to determine whether, when, and how these strategies could be appropriated for new uses. This interaction between interpretation and production established an organic link between the historical text and the new composition. The old text left its impression on the rhetor's product, but the rhetor's productive act also left its interpretive impression on the original. Rita Copeland, in her perceptive analysis of imitatio, summarized this complex development when she commented that

> the relationship between model and copy, like the relationship of lineage, is predicated on the act of invention: the model, or ancestor, discovers and posits the ground for future invention. Such an evolutionary pattern is enabled or sustained by the very interpretive community it creates. Hence to justify the imitative enterprise, the copy produces, not conspicuous likeness of the original, but rather what is understood and revalued in the original. (1991:27)

As Copeland describes it, imitatio requires a dynamic balance between interpretation and production. Thus, while the end of the process is a productive act of invention, this act is so intimately connected to interpretation that production and interpretation virtually coalesce.[3] There is, then, an important interpretive dimension built into classical rhetoric; or at any rate, a contemporary reader concerned about interpretation can locate this dimension in the older texts and consider its application to current interests. Gaonkar's binary distinction between classical and contemporary rhetoric, between a rhetoric of production and rhetoric of interpretation, would preclude reading the older texts in this way; and by essentializing differences of tendency, his position ironically places the history of rhetoric outside the range of his supposedly global interpretive turn.

Gaonkar's binary terminology works effectively as an instrument of abstract critique, but the theoretical purity it demands renders it far less effective as an instrument for addressing "the historical context of disciplinary practice" or for "reflexive critical engagement." These tasks require what Gaonkar's own reading of disciplinary history often reveals—a vocabulary and an attitude flexible enough to adjust to the rough ground of practice. As Cicero might have said to his theoretically inclined friend Cato, a less rigid set of categories might not only lead to more charitable interpretation but might also yield a more self-reflexive and humane conception of the relationship between theory and practice.

This same principle of charity, however, should apply to my judgment of Gaonkar's effort. The problems in his essay reflect the complexity of the task he has sent for himself, and he has made a notable contribution to our disciplinary self-understanding. His patient and careful encounter with the literature has forced some largely unrecognized issues to conscious attention. Most notably, he has opened debate about the relationship between interpretation and agency in rhetorical criticism, and if his intention was to alert us to the complexity and urgency of this issue, then he has fully realized his ambition.

NOTES

1. Gaonkar's alignment of terms can be represented schematically as follows:

Range	Functions	Periods	Goal(s)
Global	Interpretation	Contemporary	Interpretive metadiscourse
Restrained	Production/ performance	Classical	1. Practice (Cicero's *orator perfectus*)
			2. Theory (Aristotle's theory of practice)

2. For a general account of the impact of foundationalist assumptions on rhetorical criticism, see Nothstine, Blair, and Copeland (1994:15–70). For a detailed account of how these assumptions influenced the reception of Aristotle's *Rhetoric*, see Atwill (1993).

3. Copeland, in fact, argues that Gadamer's model of hermeneutics " is already contained in a Roman rhetorical theory" (20). This theory engages the reader in "a dialectical relationship with the text, as intepretation is fused with application."

REFERENCES

Atwill, J. M. (1993). Instituting the art of rhetoric: Theory, practice and productive knowledge in interpretations. In T. Poulakos (Ed.), *Rethinking the history of Rhetoric: Multidisciplinary essays on the rhetorical tradition*, 91–118. Boulder, CO: Westview.

Cicero, M. T. (1937). *Pro murena*. L. E. Lord (Trans.). Loeb edition. Cambridge: Harvard University Press.

Copeland, R. (1991). *Rhetoric, hermeneutics, and translation in the middle ages: Academic traditions and vernacular texts*. Cambridge: Cambridge University Press.

Fish, S. (1989). *Doing what comes naturally: Change, rhetoric, and the practice of theory in literary and legal studies*. Durham: Duke University Press.

Gadamer, H. G. (1977). *Philosophical hermeneutics*. D. E. Linge (Trans.). Berkeley: University of California Press.

Mailloux, S. (1989). *Rhetorical power*. Ithaca: Cornell University Press.

Nothstine, W. L., Blair, C., and Copeland, G. (1994). *Critical questions: Invention, creativity and the criticism of discourse and the media*. New York: St. Martin's.

Tompkins, J. (1980). The reader in history: The changing shape of literary response. In J. Tompkins, *Reader response criticism: From formalism to post-structuralism*. Baltimore: Johns Hopkins University Press.

CHAPTER 3

BIG RHETORIC, LITTLE RHETORIC: GAONKAR ON THE RHETORIC OF SCIENCE

Deirdre McCloskey

Dilip Gaonkar notes that the rhetoric of science is an argument a fortiori: "If science is not free of rhetoric, nothing is." Yes. The rhetorical studies of biology, economics, and mathematics over the past twenty years have used just this tactic, reading even scientific texts rhetorically. Gaonkar does not like it, not one bit. He wants to keep Science distinct from the rest of the culture. He wants rhetoric to stay in its cage. He is a Little Rhetoric guy.

The arguments he marshals to support his distaste for Big Rhetoric are unconvincing, though conveyed in a lively and authoritative style. They are not—as would appear from the surface rhetoric—based on the evidence of the works being criticized. By the length of his respectful summaries, in fact, Gaonkar admits that the writers he surveys do good work. A posteriori, therefore, the rhetoric of science is possible and good, even in Gaonkar's opinion. He depends for making his case against the rhetoric of science on the a priori: a rule of method says that the definition of rhetoric must be narrow, therefore rhetoric could not possibly apply to science, and so anyone who says otherwise must be an anything-goes, touchie-feelie relativist. But these arguments are specious. They are supported mainly by bluster.

In a long paper, Gaonkar manages to cover a surprisingly small number of works. For all the self-conscious elaboration, he treats a small selection of pieces by some of the people in speech communication and English/Rhetoric departments who have written on the rhetoric of science. Gaonkar admits when he gets down to business that he "concentrates on work produced within the discipline of speech communication" (37). He narrows it further, to exclude for example John Lyne's or Henry Krips's work. His claim that "the rhetoric-of-science literature is not extensive" (39) is made true therefore by construction, by overlooking much of the work (as an embarrassing footnote admits). And in wider focus Gaonkar excludes the literature on the sociology and history of science, much of it rhetorical in character. This he does by labeling it "implicitly" rhetorical, and therefore not *echt* rhetoric. He gives no argument for ignoring the implicitly as against the explicitly rhetorical. This device for excluding most of the rhetoric of science would apply also to the literature by scientists themselves reflecting on their rhetorical practices, such as Fleck (1935), Polya (1954), Polanyi (1962), Chandrasekhar (1987), Gould (1993), and to all else beyond a tiny group of incoherently selected texts. Little wonder that he finds the field "not extensive."

The new sociologists and historians and rhetoricians of science call themselves "the children of Thomas Kuhn." Science studies have thrived since Kuhn spoke out in 1962, and the change can be summarized in one word: rhetoric. Gaonkar, by contrast, is the son of Edwin Black. He adopts Black's pre-Kuhnian view of how to treat the religion of Science in our culture. Gaonkar admires some of the children of Kuhn, especially the "Social Studies of Knowledge" undertaken by British sociologists such as Harry Collins, Trevor Pinch, Michael Mulkay, Barry Barnes, Malcolm Ashmore, Steve Woolgar—rhetoric of science by another name. But characteristically Gaonkar turns the success in Britain into an attack on his own department: "In the study of scientific controversies, a topic eminently suited for rhetorical analysis, the work of Harry Collins at the University of Bath exceeds anything the rhetoric of science has to offer both in terms of conceptualization and empirical work" (41).

I agree with the favorable assessment of Collins (Gaonkar does not seem to be aware of Michael Mulkay's work, which is still more rhetorical). We had a conference at the Project on Rhetoric of Inquiry some years ago that brought the British sociologists and the American rhetoricians of science together. We concluded that the two groups were doing essentially the same thing. Collins and I worked fitfully on a long paper drawing the analogy between Social Studies of Knowledge and the Rhetoric of Inquiry. Kuhn himself participated enthusiastically in the 1984 conference that initiated the rhetoric of inquiry. These people are rhetoricians, if sometimes ignorant of their own tradition.

Listen to how the SSK people talk. Collins:

> Scientists do not act dishonourably when they engage in the debates . . . ; there is nothing else for them to do if a debate is ever to be settled and if new knowledge is ever to emerge from the dispute. (1985:143)

And Mulkay:

> My chapters . . . investigate and describe certain recurrent forms of scientific discourse which occur in connection with technical debate. . . . They examine the relationship between participants' and analysts' discourse; between participants' and analysts' interpretative practices. . . . They explore the difference between monologue and dialogue. (1985:7)

More rhetorical one could not get. So hurrah for British sociology of science, and welcome to a late development in the 2500-year-old tradition of rhetoric.

What I do not agree with is Gaonkar's self-deprecating bluster against Speech Communication and its accomplishments in the rhetoric of science. Gaonkar uses social studies of knowledge against the rhetoric of science, making the best the enemy of the good. At seminars or conferences on rhetoric, someone from Speech Comm can be relied on to stand up and make the case against rhetoric. I have never understood this impulse. You would think the self-deprecator would be embarrassed to be caught making the bush-league point that speech, you know, is sometimes insincere. These are hard times for Speech Comm, and perhaps it is in such terms that one can understand the impulse to self-deprecation. Antirhetorical coastie deans full of zeal for science (as understood ca. 1965) view the Department of Speech Communication with suspicion—I need hardly remind the present readers that it is a midwestern field; or that in universities from Columbus to Seattle it is under administrative attack. You will find chemists trained at Cal Tech and turned administrators running around asking, "But what is speech communication?" and not staying for the answer. In the face of such an onslaught on her dignity, reinforced by the low place of persuasion in Western culture since Francis Bacon, rhetoric borrows prestige from her more respectable sisters. She dons philosophical white gloves and a pretty scientific pillbox hat, in the intellectual and sartorial style of 1965, and commences sneering at the lowly place from which she came.

It's a pity, an opportunity lost. Because of intersecting idiocies in American departments of philosophy and political science, the department of speech communication has been left in charge of the rhetorical tradition. Rhetoric is the guardian of democracy, the nurse of reason, the teacher of sense. Yet rhetoric itself (thus advertising and politics) and any department studying it (thus composition and journalism, too) has low status. The further a field is from democratic persuasion, the higher its academic prestige, in Plato's style: "You attempt to refute me," Socrates says in the *Gorgias*, "in a rhetorical fashion, as they understand refuting in the law courts. . . . But this sort of refutation is quite useless for getting at the truth" (471e). Or in the *Phaedrus*: "He who is to be a competent rhetorician need have nothing at all to do . . . with truth. . . . For in the courts . . . nobody cares for truth about these matters" (272d). The Platonic disdain for how we actually persuade each other is the central absurdity of our culture. To be left in charge of remedying the absurdity, as speech communication is, bringing us back to a proper understanding of word and action, is a great honor—though it must be admitted that in practice the honor works out like the Duke's in *Huckleberry Finn*, who, after being tarred and feathered and run out of town on a rail, allowed that if it weren't for the honor of the thing, he'd just as soon have skipped it.

Gaonkar implausibly claims that the rhetoric of science has "stalled after a promising beginning" (41). The claim of "stalling" is implausible on its face because in Gaonkar's narrow definition so few works in the field have been attempted. A car does not stall if it is never started. That Gaonkar claims to discern a "low status of rhetoric of science in comparison to philosophy, history, and sociology of science" shows where he lives. The "low status" has nothing to do with the quality of work and a lot to do with ancient Platonism and modern attacks on departments of communication. It's all most unedifying, this diffidence about his field of study.

Gaonkar's technique is to put the rhetoric of science in a double bind. If rhetoric of science does something empirical (for example, examining closely the rhetoric of scientific papers), it is in Gaonkar's eyes "routine and predictable" ("routine" is his favorite word of condemnation). If it does not do something very extensive (for example, produce fifty papers a year on its subject), it is "stalled."

Gaonkar's rhetoric of proof throughout is merely assertive; he hasn't any arguments worthy of the name. He depends on bluster, a "merely rhetorical" move: if you make assertions at length, portentously, with ample throat-clearing, you can depend on fooling some of the people some of the time. Gaonkar says that classical rhetoric is disabled from inspiring modern rhetoric because classical rhetoric was about performance and modern rhetoric about understanding. How's that? On these grounds no applied subject could be continuous with a theoretical subject: medicine would be discontinuous with anatomy and biology. The rhetoric of science has "stalled," says Gaonkar, justifying his lugubrious inquest into why, though the program is in its infancy. On these grounds any small field would be declared "stalled" and then closed down—shades of the coastie deans. Gaonkar's tropes of argument remind me of a spoof on medical diagnosis published a few years ago that identified "short stature syndrome," affecting an alarmingly high share of the population—to wit, children.

Gaonkar wants to assert against all the writings in science studies since Kuhn that science is not rhetorical. Galileo, Boyle and the air pump, DNA, and so forth "allegedly testify to the unavoidably rhetorical character of scientific enterprise." For the assertion Gaonkar has no argument, merely sneering modifiers. Thus in full his bluster against the pioneering paper by Overington:

> The key move in this translation is to substitute "audience" for [research] "community," and lo and behold, the scientists become licensed speakers. . . . Overington mechanically reads off a rhetorical view of science from a communitarian view of science. . . . The results are predictably dismal. What we get is a catalogue of rhetorical techniques and a typology of arguments . . . that are routinely present in sociological discourse. (43)

Gaonkar does not justify the diction "lo and behold," "mechanically," "dismal," "routinely." When he turns to substance he is confused. He complains for example that Overington does not "fashion a rhetorical approach that takes into consideration the distinctive features of scientific practice" (43). The complaint is bizarre, considering that it was Overington's purpose and the purpose of other science studies since Kuhn to show that scientific practice is precisely not "distinctive." The children of Thomas Kuhn repeat what the Father said, that "we have only begun to discover the benefits of seeing science and art as one" (Kuhn, 1977:343).

Gaonkar is indignant when the conventional dichotomies of art/science, persuasion/proof, rhetoric/knowledge are undermined. About Weimer he is reduced to sputtering "Thus, rhetoric goes global and science becomes *sub specie rhetoricae*." Gaonkar can think of no argument why rhetoric should not go global or why science should not be viewed sub specie rhetoricae, except, goodness, how frightful, to "go global." In short, Gaonkar on Overington, Weimer, and the rest is an *ignoratio elenchi*, bluster borrowing the surface rhetoric of argument without in fact giving any.

Gaonkar announces and reannounces (I count four times) the "collapse of neo-Aristotelianism." Again, no argument; mere bluster. Apparently he regards Edwin Black as the last word on the subject. But saying so doesn't make it so. The Stagirite, the World's First Graduate Student, has legs, as has been shown recently in ethical theory. For myself I see no reason in Gaonkar's bluster to revise John Stuart Mill's opinion of the *Rhetoric* (he read it in Greek as a boy), "which, as the first expressly scientific treatise on any moral or psychological subject which I had read, and containing many of the best observations of the ancients on human nature and life, my father made me study with particular care, and throw the matter of it into synoptic tables." Some collapse.

Gaonkar's main target is the "globalization of rhetoric" (30 and throughout). He is unhappy with a wide definition of the word, and wants to show by exercise of pure reason that a narrow definition is better. His distaste for Big Rhetoric borders on revulsion: he uses the word "promiscuous" throughout to refer to it. Gaonkar is a grim Puritan father thundering against "promiscuous uses and invocations of rhetoric" (38, and throughout).

For some reason his discussion of Trevor Melia is a respectful summary (45ff). No sneering or indignation. Similarly, he devotes five pages to a summary of Campbell's work on Darwin before raising a critical peep. As I've already said, the length of the summaries, and the many ingenuities and insights exhibited in the works, argues contrary to his surface theme for a brilliantly successful program of "globalization." Even when he summarizes Alan Gross, with whom he is less patient, or Lawrence Prelli, with whom he is still less so, the reader gets the impression of richness and intelligence in the texts criticized (as on 67–73), an impression which contradicts the merely a priori objections offered by Gaonkar himself.

The best question to ask in a seminar is "So what?" Most science and scholarship goes wrong by being irrelevant. In essence Dilip Gaonkar raises a bored yawn to the rhetoric of science: So what? But the weapon can be turned back on its wielder. All right, British departments of sociology in the 1970s and 1980s were open to the entry of people trained in science. The American departments of speech communication were then less ready, because of the Dilipian diffidence about rhetoric among its only defenders; because of the humanistic and therefore science-shy bent of rhetoricians; and, most fatally, because of a continuing interest in the politics that political science had abandoned in favor of misuses of statistical significance (a misuse invading now communication studies, too). Yes, such traditions for a while made rhetorical studies of science less exciting to young people, though now no longer. But: so what? Gaonkar wants the delay to mean that there is a "predicament facing not only the rhetoric of science but every other proposed contemporary extension of rhetoric into the zone of interdisciplinarity" (41). The argument has nothing to do with the conclusion. It does not show what Gaonkar wishes it showed, that Little Rhetoric rules.

Gaonkar has three philosophical warrants for Little Rhetoric, which look cogent to people who have not thought them through. The first is what may be called the "*si omnia, nulla*" argument: if everything, nothing. If rhetoric is "everything," says Gaonkar, then it is nothing. "Si omnia, nulla" is a popular figure of argument in such discussions (the email conversation on the H-Rhetor list had a lively debate in the fall of 1994 on precisely the Big/Little Rhetoric definition, and turned on si omnia, nulla). Popular though it is, probably for its air of snappy profundity, it is in fact a silly non sequitur. If something is "everything," it does not follow that it is nothing. Atoms are "everything." That does not make atoms nothing. That air is everywhere does not make air nothing (consult Boyle and his pump). That language is made of words does not make the words nothing. If most speech has a persuasive perlocutionary force, "mere" rhetoric, what exactly is the problem? So what?

For example, Gaonkar takes Alan Gross to task for using "categories . . . so capacious that it would be impossible not to find them in any discourse that is 'situated' and 'addressed'" (62). What of it? So what else is new? I realize that many people believe a rule of scientific method that words cannot be universally applicable. But the belief is false, even preposterous. Gaonkar asserts that "a rhetorical reading merits attention only insofar as it proffers a distinct and 'contestable' (if not 'falsifiable') reading of a given scientific text" (62). The assertion is imperious nonsense from the philosopher's easy chair, a notably worn chair at that, thirty years old. Gaonkar writes later, "I argued that rhetoric as a language of criticism is so thin [i.e., general] that its applicability to any discourse is virtually guaranteed in advance" (69). He did not in fact "argue" anything of the kind. But suppose he had, and had established "thinness" in this sense. Still the impatient seminar participant will want to ask: So bloody what?

Gaonkar finds "reasonable" R. Michael Bokeno's formulation of si omnia, nulla: "If rhetorical study is to contribute . . . then a conception of rhetoric which is smaller than the conception of human conceptual activity is a minimum theoretical requirement" (quoted 47). Who says? What rule of method requires so? Michael Billig (1987) has written a long and brilliantly persuasive book showing the opposite, that one can be said to be "arguing" (with oneself) when one is thinking. Gaonkar complains about Prelli: "the specificity of rhetoric is so attenuated that it becomes no more than a pleonastic qualifier" (71), and "there is no exit from rhetoric" (75). Well, what of it? Suppose there were not? "This is one sense of the promiscuous, both universal and empty, and is what the traditionalist objects to" (76). "While [Prelli's] move brings 'science' within the range of rhetoric, it also deprives rhetoric of any specificity" (73). Huh? Why? We are not told. Gaonkar never gets further than his alleged rule, unargued, that rhetoric must be defined narrowly. He does not show in what way the "specificity" is compromised, or whether it matters.

Gaonkar's second warrant for Little Rhetoric is, as I have observed, pre-Kuhnian, an antique philosophy of science. He argues that modern rhetoric is "thin," by which he means overgeneral. Anything fits its categories. So what? Here's what: such a framework is "invulnerable to falsification, and for that very reason . . . commands little sustained attention" (33; the self-deprecating anxiety in the phrase "commands little sustained attention" is palpable).

In someone claiming sophistication about the rhetoric of science, the Popperian flavor here is startling. "A critical statement is, in some sense, verifiable"—so says Edwin Black on page 7 of his classic, *Rhetorical Criticism: A Study in Method* (1978, originally published in 1965) in the spirit of 1965. But Gaonkar should know that Karl Popper's book of 1934, translated into English only in 1959, is not the last word on the philosophy of science. Gaonkar betrays no familiarity with what has happened since 1934, from the pens of Kuhn, Hesse, Lakatos, Feyerabend, and others, among them Karl Popper. What has happened is that falsification has been shown to be no criterion of science at all, and science has been shown to be rhetoric all the way down. Thermodynamics, for example, is a manipulation of an unfalsifiable definition of energy. That does not make the theory in any way doubtful. As Kuhn put it, "in scientific practice . . . the scientist often seems rather to be struggling with facts, trying to force them into conformity with a theory he does not doubt" (1977:193). Imre Lakatos (1976) argued that even in mathematics the alleged falsifications are fended off by a "protective belt" of redefinition.

Gaonkar's third and final warrant for Little Rhetoric is the fear and loathing that knows no name, the conservative's unargued horror of postmodernism retailed in the *New York Times* and the *Wall Street Journal*. Gaonkar approves again of Bokeno's "sharp and compelling" strictures on the rhetoric of science, namely, that rhetoric of science is "radically relativist." This is sharp and compelling? The newspapers dredge up the malarkey about "relativism" every time they comment on the culture wars. The charge is not sharp and compelling. It is routine (as Gaonkar might put it) and inaccurate and illogical.

Bokeno claims that the rhetoricians of science cannot be persuasive unless they accept absolutism. He's marshaling the usual *tu quoque* argument. You, oh relativists, must believe in absolutism, because you claim [here is the mistake] absolute truth for relativism. I have given the tu quoque argument a chapter's worth of attention in a recent book (1994), and cannot bear to go through it again. Suffice here to quote Bruno Latour's reply to a critic who had used the tu quoque on him. Here's sharp and compelling:

> Those who accuse relativists of being self-contradictory can save their breath for better occasions. I explicitly put my own account in the same category as those accounts I have studied without asking for any privilege. This approach seems self-defeating only to those who believe that the fate of an interpretation is tied to the existence of a safe metalinguistic level [thus also Stanley Fish, Richard Rorty, and D. McCloskey]. . . . This belief is precisely what I deny. . . . This reflexive position is the only one that is not self-contradictory. (Latour, 1984:266)

The one point Gaonkar makes beyond his vacuous three that has some bite is his criticism of early John Campbell for putting too much emphasis on Darwin's conscious intent. Gaonkar is here reinventing the New Critical "intentional fallacy" (he gives no sign that he knows that this is what he is doing). That Keats intended "Ode on a Grecian Urn" to be skillfully done is irrelevant to the question of whether it is. (Incidentally, Gaonkar himself commits the intentional fallacy in rejecting the identification of the British sociologists of science as rhetoricians. He claims that only if they say they are rhetoricians—as unbeknownst to Gaonkar some in fact have—are they to be accounted as doing the rhetoric of science.)

One can understand what battles Campbell had to fight against the naive view that scientific writing is entirely without intent at all, automatic "writing up the results," whose only intent is to "tell the truth." Scientists say so. Saying so is a good move in a scientific debate, my "facts" against your "prejudice" (as in the debate over oxidative phosphorylation (Mulkay, 1985:43, 45, 48, 105, and throughout). Gaonkar notes that in recent essays Campbell has opted for a more intertextual approach. Instead of praising Campbell for learning something new about criticism, however, Gaonkar uses Campbell Mark II to sneer at Campbell Mark I, and then to raise a general sneer at Campbell and his works. It's again making the best the enemy of the good. He notes that Campbell "prefers to view the two interpretations [that is, Darwin as conscious rhetor and Darwin as unconscious user of the rhetorical materials in his culture] as complementary" (59). "Readers may not abide by his preference" (60), says Gaonkar with a sneer, not pausing to articulate why. In truth it's hard to see how else one could view speech except as Campbell Mark II does, as intent and socialization together. So for any text. Gaonkar himself, for example, has a conscious intent to belittle the rhetoric of science, but an unconscious attachment to the sneer.

Gaonkar has a bad case of what Stanley Fish (1989) calls "theory hope," the notion that ruminations from the philosopher's chair can do things like "justify a general hermeneutics." Gaonkar will not let the evidence alter his a priori view that Big Rhetoric is an impossibility. He says, "Obviously, rhetoric lacks a tradition that would enable an average but literate person to unproblematically identify at least the paradigm cases of rhetoric as rhetoric." He asked "why do we lack such an identity-bestowing tradition" in rhetoric as we have in poetry? The answer of course is that we did, for twenty-five hundred years in the West and for comparable periods in the Indian and Chinese traditions. The evidence shows, without lifting a philosophical finger, that there is nothing impossible about the average person being able to recognize rhetoric as rhetoric. People like Richard Lanham (1993) and me point this out daily.

Gaonkar wants to take a dim view. He takes, for example, a dim view of Prelli's optimistic picture of science as involving "audiences" and "conventions." The "sheer materiality of science as an institution," says Gaonkar, undercuts the notion of scientists as "self-monitoring rational actors" (70–71). Puzzlingly, he cites the social studies of knowledge in support of his materialist views. Collins, Mulkay, et al. (Ashmore, et al., 1989; Latour and Woolgar, 1979; Pinch, 1986; Shapin and Schaffer, 1985), showed on the contrary that science is a matter of arguments and conventions (and power and money, too, but that is more typical of Robert Merton than Thomas Kuhn). Gaonkar speaks respectfully throughout of rhetorical sociology, but he doesn't get it. "Does [rhetoric] ever threaten," he asks rhetorically, "to become part of the substance of science?" He is forgetting that *res* and *forma* are intimately connected. If the rhetoric of science from Fleck in the 1930s to Gross in the 1990s had to be put in a sentence it would be *The substance of science is its rhetoric.* Gaonkar speaks of "reference" and "reality" as though now a long generation of the children of Thomas Kuhn had not made such talk look stunningly naive.

Gaonkar's distaste for the fragment of the rhetoric of science he has studied is therefore not to be given much weight. His distaste is misplaced, and what is more relevant here, unargued. It surely is a rule of method that unargued opinion, however finely expressed, is not to be credited. I have formulated a little joke about it: after one turn of the ignition key the movement against the rhetoric of science, whose chief member is Dilip Gaonkar, has stalled.

REFERENCES

Ashmore, M., Mulkay, M. and Pinch, T. (1989). *Health and efficiency: A sociology of health economics.* Milton Keynes and Philadelphia: Open University Press.

Billig, M. (1987). *Arguing and thinking: A rhetorical approach to social psychology.* Cambridge: Cambridge University Press.

Black, E. (1978). *Rhetorical criticism: A study in method.* Madison: University of Wisconsin Press. Orig. pub. 1965.

Chandrasekhar, S. (1987). *Truth and beauty: Aesthetics and motivations in science.* Chicago: University of Chicago Press.

Collins, H. M. (1985). *Changing order: Replication and induction in scientific practice.* Sage: London and Beverly Hills.

Fish, S. E. (1989). *Doing what comes naturally: Change, rhetoric, and the practice of theory in literary and legal studies.* Durham, NC: Duke University Press.

Fleck, L. (1979). *Genesis and development of a scientific fact.* Chicago: University of Chicago Press. Orig. pub. 1935.

Gould, S. J. (1993). The composition and reception of "The spandrels of San Marco." In J. L. Selzer (Ed.), *Understanding scientific prose.* Madison: University of Wisconsin Press.

Krips, H. (1992). Ideology, rhetoric and Boyle's new experiments." Unpublished ms. for "Narrative Patterns In Scientific Disciplines," April 27-

30, 1992, Cohn Institute, Tel Aviv University; Edelstein Center, Hebrew University; and the Van Leer Jerusalem Institute.

Kuhn, T. (1962). *The structure of scientific revolutions*. Second ed. 1970. Chicago: University of Chicago Press.

———— . (1977). *The essential tension: Selected studies in scientific tradition and change*. Chicago: University of Chicago Press.

Lakatos, I. (1976). *Proofs and refutations: The logic of mathematical discovery*. J. Worrall and E. Zahar (Eds.). Cambridge: Cambridge University Press.

Lanham, R. A. (1993). *The electronic word: Democracy, technology, and the arts*. Chicago: University of Chicago Press.

Latour, B., and Woolgar, S. (1979). *Laboratory life: The social construction of scientific facts*. Beverly Hills: Sage.

Latour, B. (1988). *The pasteurization of France*. A. Sheridan and J. Law (Trans.). Cambridge and London: Harvard University Press.

McCloskey, D. N. (1994). *Knowledge and persuasion in economics*. Cambridge: Cambridge University Press.

Mulkay, M. (1985). *The word and the world*. London: Allen and Unwin.

Pinch, T. J. (1986). *Confronting nature*. Holland: Reidel.

Plato. (1914). *Phaedrus*. H. N. Fowler (Trans.). Cambridge: Harvard University Press.

———— . (1925). *Gorgias*. W. R. M. Lamb (Trans.). Cambridge: Harvard University Press.

Polanyi, M. (1962). *Personal knowledge: Towards a post-critical philosophy*. Chicago: University of Chicago Press.

Polya, G. (1954). *Induction and analogy in mathematics* (Vol. 1 of *Mathematics and plausible reasoning*). Princeton: Princeton University Press.

Shapin, S., and Schaffer, S. (1985). *Leviathan and the air-pump: Hobbes, Boyle and the experimental life*. Princeton: Princeton University Press.

CHAPTER 4

STRATEGIC READING: RHETORIC, INTENTION, AND INTERPRETATION

John Angus Campbell

INTRODUCTION

Gaonkar's richly nuanced paper provides a cornucopia of insights for the field of speech communication as well as for any critical scholarship in the rhetoric of science. In addition to his comments on our work in the rhetoric of science, Gaonkar has traced in detail the specific disciplinary history that has led scholars in our field to the particular problems, tensions, and ambitions that characterize our work. For scholars pursuing the rhetoric of science he has identified crucial fault lines that, if we negotiate them well, will strengthen our contribution to learning. Much as I differ with his general perspective, his comments on my work in particular are deeply gratifying. In many places he has understood me better than I understand myself! Gaonkar places my work in the tradition of my teacher Edwin Black, and analyzes insightfully and instructively how it was shaped by the critical pressures following the publication of *Rhetorical Criticism*. Gaonkar has read all my Darwin essays and his assessment is a profound act of collegial friendship. I also add my hearty appreciation for the critical observations of Steve Fuller, whose assessments of my readings as a critic are generous and whose critical comments similarly raise important questions about the explanatory ambitions of my work.

I would be a far less perceptive reader than Gaonkar or Fuller credit me, were I unaware that their praise for my rhetorical criticism springs from a general critique. Since Leff has given an anatomy of the binary logic that governs Gaonkar's essay, and since I agree with Leff's analysis and with most of the particular points that Gaonkar makes about my essays, I will focus most of my attention on issues where Gaonkar and I most seriously differ: on his view of hermeneutics, the "ideology" of agency, and his critique of the "thinness" of the rhetorical lexicon. As a response to Gaonkar's specific observations on my work, and to his indictment of me as a rhetorical humanist, I will—true to type—cast my response in the figure *tu quoque*: I shall argue that since his critique of me recapitulates my critique of Darwin, he has, despite himself, given a powerful endorsement to my methods. In the case of Fuller, I have no difficulty with the framing of his critique and I will address his points in due course.

ANTIHERMENEUTICS, TRANSLATION, IDEOLOGY, AND THICK LANGUAGE

In his opening sentence Gaonkar observes that the remarkable feature of rhetoric's current incarnation "is its positioning primarily as a hermeneutic metadiscourse rather than as a substantive discourse practice" (25). It is difficult to quarrel with the idea that hermeneutic practice requires a "metadiscourse." Precisely because a text, or a person, is distant or in some sense strange, one needs to find a way of "redescribing" the text or finding common ground with the person to mediate between the horizon of one's present and the horizon of the other. Discovering a language appropriate for making known or sharing meaning is, in the rhetorical sense, artistic—it must be *invented*. Gaonkar hermeneutically errs, however, when he calls the aim of a "redescription" as "dissolv[ing] a discursive practice into the interpretive medium of a preferred metadiscourse" (25). One might quibble with the "all" when Gaonkar says, "A perfect interpretation is one in which the object of interpretation loses *all* [my emphasis] of its recalcitrance and becomes transparent." But then he adds, "Such is the dream of interpretation and we have been seduced by that dream," and there is no quibble possible. Not one of the great representatives of the hermeneutic tradition—Gadamer, Heidegger, and Ricoeur among them—has been seduced by this dream, and the rest of us may look to their examples for encouragement as we pray for strength to resist the temptation to which Gaonkar himself may have succumbed.[1]

The problem with the view of hermeneutics that Gaonkar expresses is that his account of the dissolution of a discourse practice into a metadiscourse is not an "interpretation" but a form of academic one-upmanship or "trumping" that has little in common with the interpretive ideals of hermeneutics, including Heidegger's use of *aletheia*, Gadamer's "fusion of horizons," Ricoeur's notion of "narrative," or the idea of dialogue central to them all. In his essay "Hermeneutics as a Theoretical and Practical Task," Gadamer explicates hermeneutics by "invok[ing] the model of the practical philosophy that could also be called politics by Aristotle." He reminds the reader that it included rhetoric and aimed at giving each science its proper and secure place within an all encompassing and variegated whole.

> the claim to universality on the part of hermeneutics consists of integrating all the sciences, of perceiving the opportunities for knowledge on the part of every scientific method wherever they may be applicable to given objects, and of deploying them in all their possibilities. (1981:137)

Gadamer's observation is particularly important for our discussion, for he is specifically talking about science and clearly does not see hermeneutics as dissolving science into a metadiscourse.

Gaonkar, however, is not entirely mistaken. What he has described with exquisite precision is an *antihermeneutic*. Concerning the true object of his description he could not be more correct: It is a seductive dream. He is equally correct that Marxism, psychoanalysis, structural linguistics, and, alas, even the rhetorical analysis of science can supply examples of it.[2] The list could be extended. Sociobiology is almost entirely the kind of reductive trumping operation Gaonkar has described, as was positivism before it and the more radical versions of the sociology of science since (Howe and Lyne, 1992; Bock, 1980). The risk of academic conversations turning into a game of disciplinary one-upmanship is one of the most conspicuous and least pleasant aspects of contemporary university life. The rhetorical tradition, however, is a great storehouse of ways to slow down hostile epistemic takeovers, or avoid them entirely by urging arguers to advert to their practices and come to their senses.

Happily, the differences between Gaonkar and myself concern only matters of theory; in practice we are oddly aligned. In light of the (not altogether undeserved) drubbing he gives me later in his essay for making Darwin a rhetorical colossus bestriding history, his account of the critic's power to create rhetorical discourse through a mode of reading is ironic. If I rightly understand Leff's analysis, Gaonkar and I differ little on whether agency figures in criticism, but merely on where to find it! Since I endorse the agency of the critic just as strongly as Gaonkar shows I endorse the agency of historical actors, I am obliged to allow considerable latitude to

Gaonkar's claim for the critic's freedoms and powers. But I resist his formulation anyway.

I want to agree with Gaonkar that the critic indeed has a considerable latitude in the interpretation of a text. Kenneth Burke's "perspective by incongruity" is a perfect example of appropriate critical freedom even though it can be, in its comic way, an act of violence against a text (Burke, 1954, part 2). Where I differ from Gaonkar is on the reason for this freedom, and thus why apparent textual violence is sometimes permissible, and indeed necessary. I also want to point to constraints on reading.

The textual violence of Burke wears a grin; we know he's pulling our leg. Burke's aim is therapeutic; he approaches us in the spirit of Kierkegaard to deceive us out of our deceptions by seeming to side with them, and then upholding us, or falling with us, when we slip (as he rather thought we would) on our own rug (Kierkegaard, 1939; see also Webb, 1988). Burke's critical violence is disciplined by a political or moral aim; he offers alternative interpretations to lead us to more open and insightful critical practice and ultimately to a better life. His readings are not merely willful, for in opening up possibilities within received *texts* he invites us to complicate fruitfully our understandings of *contexts*. In reminding us of alternative interpretive possibilities, Burke does not destabilize our decisions or reduce them to groundless acts of will but instead treats them as informed acts of deliberation (Burke, 1969:xv–xxiii).

By the same token that critics have latitude because the object of their analyses and judgments is complex and must encompass a wide variety of contexts, they are also constrained. Free play is part of criticism because contexts are variegated, interconnected, and because a central feature of intelligence, the consideration of varied possibilities, is a prerequisite to deliberation and judgment. Because criticism ends in judgment, criticism (and rhetorical criticism preeminently) is practical reason and operates both under conditions of freedom and of constraint. The necessarily playful contributions of intelligence, in suggesting discursive possibilities, prepare the mind for judgment, for determining the sufficiency of evidence, and for deciding whether an interpretation is "correct" or how much weight it should be given. I agree with Gaonkar that there is a moment in rhetorical analysis when the freedom of the critic is almost unbounded. A competent critic, in the creative moment of play proper to invention, should be prepared to consider a wide variety of interpretive possibilities no matter how violent, silly, or far-fetched. I differ from Gaonkar because I advert to the step that immediately follows the moment of free play—the neces-

sity for the critic to decide which of her mere ideas makes sense
(Lonergan, 1978; Campbell, 1993). Because rhetorical criticism, like
all other forms of rhetorical practice, ends in judgment, *the freedom
of rhetorical critics and the situation of their subject are symmetrical.* Prudential judgment is required by rhetorical critics not primarily because they have decided to read a discourse a certain way,
but because judgment, and its attendant constraints, is as inherent to
critical practice as it is to performance. Critics try to make sense of
texts as rhetorical action even as rhetors constructed the text to
address the need for action in their particular situations. Again,
much as I appreciate Gaonkar's generous tributes to my readings of
Darwin, and after all appropriate credit is given to relevant features
of his intertextual context, the man himself, through his insight,
timing, and verbal skill, produced real effects. Some of these I have
brought to light, others I have explicated as possible readings given
my reconstruction of his context (in light, of course, of my interpretation of our own).

Gaonkar's view of rhetorical criticism as either voluntaristic or
gratuitous is closely tied to his view of rhetoric as either oratory or a
universal quasi logic lacking concreteness. In principle, and despite
Gaonkar's well-taken point that we have no locus for rhetoric as
concrete as classical oratory, the presence of rhetoric is not impossible to detect even when it does not appear in its most visible guise
as oratory. Rhetoric is subtle, but so is reality. Rhetoric is another
name for practical reason and practical reason is ubiquitous—without being, or having pretensions of being, a universal logic. Whenever
we are deliberating, whatever the forum, wherever there are no fixed
rules, or where there are very few, or those few conditioned by our
decisions, we are in a province as surely rhetorical as ever was classical oratory. Nor is there anything novel about this. Even in highly
technical fields, people reason practically all the time and always
have. The novelty of a rhetorical reading of nonoratorical texts is
merely the novelty of returning health after a long positivist illness.
Once one gets used to being well, the ubiquity of rhetoric is neither
surprising nor destabilizing. Examples of serious scholarly projects
that are nothing but sustained reflective and philosophical rhetorical
readings, even when oratory is only one or even a minor focus of
their investigations, are not hard to find. A good example is Eugene
Garver's project of a history of prudence.

Garver offers a view of rhetoric that is very large—indeed,
indeterminate in scope—yet which is clearly constrained. In the
introduction to his brilliant study of Machiavelli, Garver notes that
Machiavelli stands to the history of prudential reason as Descartes

stands to the history of algorithmic reason (Garver, 1987). This is not
to say that Descartes cannot be analyzed rhetorically, but it is to
say that in Machiavelli we find a project of reason alternative to
Cartesian reason, an alternative mode of reason resting partly on
character, partly on craft, and, though suasory throughout, clearly
recognizable as reason. Yet if one asks, "Well, what exactly is 'prudential reason?'" expecting a short answer such as "It is this and it is
always found right here," the question itself shows a certain failure
of understanding. Garver might well call his project a "history of
prudence," even though it is almost impossible to define "prudence"
per se, let alone specify exactly where one will find it. To talk about
and understand "prudence" one talks about, and works through,
cases. It does not matter what the "subject" is or what the genre is.
In Machiavelli's case, for example, the *Prince* makes for an odd manual, since the very capacity it would teach is the prerequisite for
reading it. Nor is it the case that the *Prince* is just about winning. In
one of the drollest parts of his book Garver notes that there is at
least one hard and fast rule in Machiavellian prudence: "Never hire
mercenaries" (37). When victory costs one freedom of action—the
ability to operate out of one's own resources—it is indistinguishable from defeat. There is a lesson here for rhetoricians who place the
"rigor" of the method above the art of the critic.

Similarly in Garver's new book on Aristotle's *Rhetoric*, aptly
subtitled *An Art of Character* (1994), Garver underscores the tension
in Aristotle's project between an art that could be taught for a fee and
an ethical practice appropriate to citizens. To imagine a "technical"
rhetoric is relatively easy: There are ways of systemizing persuasive
speech, and what one teaches for a fee is (by definition) a system.

But—imagine this technical art adapted to a context of authentic political engagement with one's fellows in the *polis*. Rhetoric at
this point becomes complicated, by its very nature. While the three
Aristotelian genres help identify rhetoric in its political context, in
the end they participate in the larger problematic of rhetoric: the
problematic of practical reason.

Garver is a deep and insightful reader, but his readings, while
involving choice and perspective setting, are not voluntaristic. If so
many features of the thought of Machiavelli or Aristotle become
clear in his readings, it is because he has submitted to these texts'
discipline, has found their grain and read along it. And this is the
invitation he gives his reader. As one reenacts his reading one has to
work, but one can do the work because one can recognize the projects of Aristotle or Machiavelli in one's own life, as well as in other
texts. Garver does not make texts practical or rhetorical merely by a

willful decision to read them that way; he makes clear through his reading why certain texts belong to a history of prudence by making clear what prudence means and what it is. In the hands of a Garver, a Nancy Struever, or Michael Leff, rhetorical criticism (like hermeneutics) becomes a form of radical questioning and as such can combine both a high view of textual fidelity with an expansive view of critical freedom.

How one combines critical freedom with textual discipline leads us to Gaonkar's claim that the idea of "translation" involved in rhetorical criticism is caught in a disjunction with performance. According to Gaonkar, a critical language grounded in the performative standards of classical rhetoric is unable to do the work required of translation because it cannot be converted back into an account of performance. Gaonkar's comments on translation are the most potentially damaging aspect of his critique; for in driving a wedge between performance and interpretation he disables a rhetorical interpretation before it gets off the ground. His critique pivots on how one understands hermeneutics, particularly a "romantic hermeneutics." Since it is Gaonkar's thesis that the classical vocabulary of my project (Gross adds that the same holds true for his) is informed throughout by a romantic hermeneutics, things do not look good for critics.

As Gaonkar correctly points out, the problem with romantic hermeneutics via Schleiermacher is that in clinging to a notion of the psychological subject it was fatally compromised by an insufficiently historical view of understanding. Romantic hermeneutics, as Gadamer argues, failed to appreciate the historicity common to all understanding. As Linge notes, even when we look at one of the greatest monuments of the scientific school of German historians, Mommsen, we inevitably see the man in his time, not just a history of the Papacy (Gadamer, 1976:xviii). Because of the historical complicity of all understanding, whether we will or no, there is no privileged vantage point from which to understand subjects better than they did themselves. Hence, Gaonkar's critique of me does not really prove he understood me better than I understood myself (though thanks to it I understand myself better). Gaonkar's critique inevitably reveals the separate horizon of his own struggle to understand my work as my apprehension of his essay reveals my complementary struggle to appropriate his evaluation.

Once we see, as Leff has cogently argued in various essays, that criticism is *itself* a performance, we remove the absolute barrier between performance and understanding that for Gaonkar disqualified the language of classical rhetoric from serving double duty as an instrument of analysis. Indeed not only, as Leff shows, does Gadamer insist on interpretation as a performance, but he endorses the language of classical rhetoric as uniquely well qualified for the job:

> Where, indeed, but to rhetoric should the theoretical examination of interpretation turn? Rhetoric from oldest tradition has been the only advocate of a claim to truth that defends the probable, the *eikos* (verisimilitude), and that which is convincing to the ordinary reason, against the claim of science to accept as true only what can be demonstrated and tested! Convincing and persuading without being able to prove—these are obviously as much the aim and measure of understanding and interpretation as they are the aim and measure of the art of oration and persuasion. (Gadamer, 1976:24)

Given then that an interpretive enterprise free of the romantic subject and committed to a robust use of the classical rhetorical lexicon is not only possible, but appropriate—indeed exemplary—how does that get me off the hook (and Alan Gross as well) for our alleged view of agency? Gaonkar's rejection of agency per se because the romantic version of it is untenable, is ultimately indefensible.

At one point he says, quite appropriately, "This question [the question of a vocabulary adequate for the translation of performance to critical understanding] cannot be profitably addressed in an a priori fashion. It must be addressed in the historical context of our disciplinary practices." Fair enough. But then in the course of his general, and otherwise helpful, survey of our disciplinary history he announces, "one must realize that the 'translation' involves not simply a technical vocabulary but an ideology." The "ideology" he then describes could double as a handlist of *topoi* that could characterize rhetorical analysis on virtually any description:

> a view of speaker as the seat of origin rather than a point of articulation, a view of strategy as identifiable under an intentional description, a view of discourse as constitutive of character and community, a view of audience positioned simultaneously as 'spectator' and 'participant,' and finally, a view of 'ends' that binds speaker, strategy, discourse, and audience in a web of purposive actions. (32–33)

A minimalist definition of *ideology* suggests that an ideology is a perspective imposed arbitrarily and, once exposed, opens up alternative interpretive possibilities. If "agency" as a mode of reading is arbitrary, let us see if we can rid ourselves of this "ideology," and its related arbitrary notions of strategy, discourse, community, and audience, and still make sense of discourse.

As a test case, let us try an anti-ideological reading of Gaonkar's essay.[3] Let us regard "Dilip Parameshwar Gaonkar," whose name appears at the beginning of this essay, as a "point of articulation" rather than the "agent" or "the seat of origin" of "The Idea of Rhetoric in the Rhetoric of Science." No reading of "his" essay recovers strategy, nor finds a persona, or an implied view of community constituted by the essay (even though it discusses *our* "disciplinary history!"). Though the essay names "John A. Campbell" and he intends to respond, I could not be "simultaneously a 'spectator and participant' " and there are no "ends" that bind Gaonkar, Gross, Keith, Prelli, Leff, Fuller, and myself and other readers and scholars "in a web of purposive actions," even though we have all corresponded with one another about this very volume and about the *Southern Communication Journal* issue which preceded it. I submit, granting full sway to Gadamer's critique of the romantic subject, and also to Gaonkar's critique of me for placing too much emphasis on agency, that Gaonkar has not identified something imposed arbitrarily that blocks an intelligible alternative. What Gaonkar has called an "ideology" is the necessary background assumption under which communication, including his own, is intelligible and perhaps possible. When Gaonkar takes exception to what I have said and offers a rebuttal, he will confirm my point. Any competent reader could identify in his statement a strategy, a persona, a community, and a view of audience that bound Gaonkar and all our colleagues and readers together by common ends. If further proof were needed, it does not take much imagination to figure out what would happen if someone else published all or part of Gaonkar's essay under her own name. The person would be thrown out of the profession. And the reason would relate to every one of the items Gaonkar identifies as part of the "ideology" of agency. To say that the invocation of "agency" is an "ideology" and we can set it aside in favor of an alternative that dispenses with it is not merely false. It is nonsense.

Talk about agency, responsibility, intentions, and community is more secure than anything that could question them, precisely because they are practices in which we are all complicit—and a good thing too. Deny agency and the very idea of practical, political, or ethical reason becomes a non sequitur. Deny community, with all its complex ties to discourse conventions, and what sense is there in someone trying to plan a political campaign, or crafting a new course proposal (say "The Ideology of Agency 101") that will get through departmental review, let alone pass muster with the college curriculum committee? If Gaonkar's denial of agency is extreme and possibly incoherent, I have to say that my own formulations of agency that he aptly critiques are not exactly philosophic bargains. I agree to take the stand and place my hand on a copy of *Of Grammatology*: "I solemnly swear I do not now, nor have I ever, believed in romantic hermeneutics"; though perhaps it was not unreasonable of Gaonkar to suppose that I did, given the way I formerly wrote.

A way to question agency and intentionality, without falling into the opposite absurdity of trying merely to dismiss them, is suggested by Gadamer's notion of play (1975:91–98). For Gadamer, the to and fro of play describes the human condition: life, language, and the possibilities of understanding that emerge within language. In the play of life there is no position for a neutral observer. The game was here before we arrived. To live is to participate. The Gadamerian field is Heraclitus's fire, or his river, and its governing "laws" are *kairos* and *to prepon*. Under this description, when an opening appears in the field of play it is not simply the case that so and so sees the opening, seizes or hits the ball, and fumbles, trips, misses, or scores. It is also the case that the players are played by the game. In a sense the opening on the field of play draws the ball and the players to itself. The opening may be an occasion for novelty when a player does something unexpected, or when an absorbed and self-forgetful researcher catches the answer that had eluded everyone else, or when a heckler sees her moment and blurts out just the right thing at precisely the right instant. Gadamer's play takes us beyond the autonomous subjects of Schleiermacher, common sense and copyright laws, and ethical, practical, and political deliberation, and shows us how even towering works of genius have been the wanton gift of a high-strung tensile flow of synergistic action and reaction, like the instant shifting of a school of fish or the precision turns in the flight of a darting flock of shorebirds.

Seen, not from some Kantian position above the game or a Hegelian one at the end of it, but from the perspective of the kairotic instant within it, there is a level, or moment, in the play of meaning that transcends agents, strategies, and what sense and practical reason constrain us to call their "intentions." To describe rhetorical action at this level one need merely shift, in the language of Burke's pentad, to "scene" in place of "agent," or make appropriate similar shifts in the various combinations of foci set out in Rosenfield's "Anatomy of Criticism." To see the action from the standpoint of the game playing the players and language speaking the speaker requires talent, for a narrative must have actors, even if the actors are technically "scenes." But though I have surely erred in my earlier essays in placing too much emphasis on Darwin as an agent, exactly as Gaonkar has pointed out, my principle, unlike his proposal to abolish agency as a category, is not dogmatic. When cases admit of a more instructive reading from a scenic standpoint, they should be read from that standpoint. Or, if critics have a particular talent for scenic readings, then let them exercise it. There are good and practical reasons, however, why "agent" is ordinarily a prominent feature in rhetorical criticism.

The viewpoint of the Gadamerian play of language is not and cannot be the perspective of the work-a-day rhetorical critic any more than, in the case of ordinary sport, can it be the perspective of the coach, the players, or the fans. For the players there is discipline, sacrifice, taking personal responsibility, teamwork, and training, including the watching of endless replays while the coach (whose very profession is the intentional fallacy) says, "Gaonkar, here is where you screwed up . . . do you see that opening, now look . . . what were you thinking? Don't give me that crap about not being the 'point of origin.' Next time—and this applies to you Campbell! wipe that smirk off your face—here is what I want you to do." Indeed, Gaonkar's comments about performance and dancing are exactly on the mark. If we put set aside his binary distinction between the speaker being "the point of origin" *rather than* the "point of articulation" we can recognize that from different perspectives the speaker can be described accurately one way or the other or as a tensional fusion of both. Each is real, exacting, analytically rigorous, and functionally distinct. From the standpoint of the kairotic moment, the speaker is subsumed in the larger dynamic of play and in Gaonkar's terms is quite properly "the point of articulation." From the standpoint of the slogging work-a-day perspective, the perspective of training, preparation, diet, coaching, teaching, teamwork, daily workouts, fire in the belly (what my karate instructor called "the *bushi-do* [warrior] spirit"), journalism, the fans cheering for the home team "Go Rhets!" and rhetorical criticism, the speaker is, again in Gaonkar's terms, "the point of origin." We will come out right at last if we refuse reductionism outright and insist on the functional distinctions necessary to understand the intelligibility of the elements in persuasive communication without concluding either that any element can be dispensed with or that the sum of them explains the whole.

But, whether it seems best in this case to emphasize "agent" or in that one "scene," in what language is the rhetorical play of meanings to be described? Gaonkar insists that this language cannot be the rhetorical lexicon, which he affirms strenuously and repeatedly is woefully abstract and inferior to other lexicons:

> By "thinness" I am referring to the abstract quality of the traditional vocabulary as illustrated, for instance, in the tripartite scheme of proofs (*ethos*, *pathos*, and *logos*) that enables one to find its presence in virtually any discourse practice. In disciplinary politics, the more refined and specific a language of criticism becomes (be it deconstruction, psychoanalysis, or reception theory) the greater attention it gets and by the same token the more vulnerable it is to falsification. In its current form, rhetoric as a language of criticism is so thin and abstract that it is virtually invulnerable to falsification, and for that very reason, it commands little sustained attention. (33)

These claims are extraordinary for their perfection in missing the point of rhetoric as the mode of practical reason. But Gaonkar's next sentence virtually unsays what the previous half of the paragraph sought to establish:

> I am prepared to concede that a "thin" rhetorical lexicon may have certain advantages when it functions heuristically as an aid to performance, but it is inadequate for a critical reading of what gets "said" (or "done") in performance. (33)

Since, as we have noted, and as Leff and Gadamer have both established at length, criticism is in fact a form of performance, Gaonkar's statement in this passage renders his earlier point moot. The earlier statements, however, are so extraordinary and fit so well with the antihermeneutic posture of his opening paragraph that they cannot be allowed to pass without remark. Let us consider Gaonkar's point about the thinness of classical rhetoric.

Two of Gaonkar's alternative models for a "dense" language—deconstruction and reception theory—are both 99.9 percent classical rhetoric. Deconstruction, whatever else it may be, owes its very life to Nietzsche (a distinguished student and master practitioner of rhetoric if ever there was one) and his rediscovery of the Sophists. Deconstruction is an integral part of a rhetorical movement we might refer to as the "postmodern sophistic." As a rhetoric undisciplined by community and relying on the pyrotechnic skills of individual virtuoso performers, deconstruction represents a problematic and dangerous (but ancient) strand of the rhetorical tradition. As for the rhetorical lexicon, how is Gaonkar's claim that "deconstruction" is "denser" than rhetoric even coherent when de Man, for one, takes most of his critical arsenal not only from rhetoric, but right out of the allegedly "thin" classical version of it? As for "reception theory" (I assume Gaonkar is referring to reader response theory), like deconstruction it too is a variant of classical rhetoric. Stanley Fish, certainly a reader to be conjured with, makes use of rhetoric not only in his more recent works but demonstrates the analytic power of both the classic and Ramist versions of rhetoric in *Surprised By Sin: The Reader In Paradise Lost*. I do not think anyone has ever claimed that Fish's vocabulary was too thin or abstract, and certainly the language of his criticism receives much critical notice in the academy.

When Gaonkar recommends the language of psychoanalysis, he has indeed identified a "thick" language that is different from the "thin" language of rhetoric. The language of psychoanalysis no doubt does adequate service when deployed by a practitioner who can thin it by careful listening. In the hands of one less gifted, who (to use one of Gaonkar's more happy expressions) does not know how to "dance," it has serious limitations. The "thickness" of psychoanalytic language allows the unskilled analyst to answer questions before they are asked, or indeed to impose them, as gays, women, and philosophic theists could readily attest. Ricoeur (1970) refers to the central concept of "identification" as "the thorn in the side of psychoanalysis" (131) precisely because of the way it throws into stark relief Freud's failure to grasp the negotiated and perspectival character of all knowing. All that saved Freud from fitting his patients within the constricting categories of his positivist science was his intelligence—which unfortunately could not always free itself from the thick, densely woven and viscous strands of his language.

Earlier in his paper, Gaonkar listed Marxism along with psychoanalysis as an example of a suitable "metadiscourse." Though he does not include it in this part of his essay, Marxist language also has the "thickness" Gaonkar prizes. The theoretic thickness of Marxist language is exactly the point at issue in Gadamer's complaint against Habermas. As Gadamer notes, Habermas's desire to preserve the Enlightenment ideal of a privileged analytic discourse beyond the play of history, language, and tradition is exactly why he resists the full historicization of understanding central to hermeneutics—and exemplified superbly from the earliest antiquity by rhetoric.

In sum, two of Gaonkar's candidates for a "thick" language— deconstruction and reader response—are in fact "thin" because they are nothing but rhetoric (in the best sense of nothing) and consequently rely, almost absolutely, on the skill of the critic or reader and not on the conceptually freightedness of a lexicon. Gaonkar's thick terms are downright heavy and thus (as Gadamer shows contra Habermas's Marxism and Ricoeur contra Freud's scientism) are clumsy instruments for capturing thought in kairotic flight.

Even more extraordinary than the contradictory concepts in Gaonkar's call for lexical "thickness" is his claim that the alternatives to the language of rhetoric that he cites are superior because they are "falsifiable." Surely he jests! Has anyone ever heard of a case where a claim by one deconstructionist was "falsified" by another? Since when is "falsificationism" even part of the deconstructionist lexicon? (These de-con artists read and go free to read again. And in broad daylight!) As for psychoanalysis, the very expression of skepticism about it is proof that one is guilty of repression! Marxism one has to respect for having stuck its neck out in making a falsifiable prediction. Marxism predicted that the advance of capitalism would lead to greater misery for the masses, worse crises, and ultimately its own demise due to its internal contradictions. And what has been the effect on Marxism's academic adherents of the worldwide resurgence of market economies and of capitalism showing no signs of creating a proletariat that would destroy it? In a *New York Review of Books* essay, Habermas responds to the question "What remains of socialism?" with the riposte "radical democracy." Habermas then recommends that "welfare state measures [must be used] to tame capitalism to some point where it becomes unrecognizable as such" (Michnik and Habermas, 1994:26). To which a conservative journal offers the following riposte:

> (1) The failure of socialism does not lead to the approval of capitalism. (2) State power should tame capitalism to the point where it is not recognizable as capitalism but is recognizable as socialism. (3) Socialism has not failed. Take our word for it, Habermas is a very famous philosopher. (Neuhaus, 1994:67–68)

Even in the face of Gaonkar's concession of a "thin" lexicon's desirability for the analysis of performance, and my argument (from the very author he uses to establish his claim) that criticism is indeed a performance, his characterization of rhetorical terms as "abstract" invites closer analysis. It is understandable, given Gaonkar's attraction to the lexicons of Marxism and psychoanalysis, why he would choose that term. Sciences and ideologies that want to appear scientific seek to develop terms or law-like generalizations that reduce (or seem to reduce) lower-level phenomena to higher-level descriptions of greater conceptual precision. Without "abstraction" and hence the "reduction" of lower-level phenomena to higher regularity, a science cannot fulfill its legitimate conceptual aims. Rhetorical terms, precisely because rhetoric shares almost nothing in common with the explanatory ideals of the natural sciences, are not "abstract" but indeterminate. It is the indeterminacy of rhetorical terms that allows rhetoric, especially in the tradition of the topics, to guide investigation without determining the outcome (Jost, 1989:17–20). One initiates an inquiry by discovering what is at issue; preliminary inquiry reveals subordinate issues which are examined in turn, until the appropriate questions, values, and facts relevant to responsible decision or informed interpretation are clarified.

It is through open inquiry guided by preliminary understandings of what seems to be the case that rhetoric, specifically in the form of topical reason, proceeds in a manner that is neither free play nor the thick and prematurely closed language of expertise. Free play and thick, viscous, expert language are alike false alternatives. Topical reason allows room for discovery and this makes it at once thin yet strong, open yet structured. At the end of the day, when the relevant facts and values, rules, persons, and circumstances are gathered, weighed, and arranged, then topical reason is at last thick, and only as thick as the circumstances of the case allow or require. As for "testing," the products of rhetorical reason are tested all the time as in courts of law or in debate. Unlike Marxism or psychoanalysis, the products of rhetorical reason are rebutted every day and in this sense (for that moment or case) "falsified." Again, rhetorical topics are thin only on their first appearance, when their mere heuristic relevance has been established. Once topics are filled with the content appropriate to them, they can rival the thickness of any technical language of expertise. As for the interest that the language of rhetoric is gaining in the academy, I would make bold to suggest Gaonkar expand his circle of acquaintances. From theology to law to literature to classics to philosophy, rhetoric is receiving sustained attention.[4] As for the history and philosophy of science, the classical version of rhetoric—the very version that Prelli represents preeminently—has recently received an unprecedented reception that shows no signs of abating (for example, Pera and Shea, 1991).

Which brings us to my project. Gaonkar is right. In my early essays I have given an exaggerated portrait of Darwin's agency. *Mea culpa!* But, as he also documents, I have changed my emphasis. Here I should make a strong methodological point. Rhetorical theory is— or ought to be—grounded in practice. The exacting and relentlessly changing demands of practice are what keeps it, or any part of it, from hardening into an ideology. As Leff (1980) has put it, in criticism a theory should be the theory of its case. In my case, aside from an occasional essay or two, such rhetorical theory as I have written is chiefly the theory of one case. The inevitability of something like the *topoi* that structure my on-going Darwin project are abundantly confirmed by the way Gaonkar temporarily suspends his binary logic to investigate it. Gaonkar opens his analysis of my work not by attempting to absorb it into a metadiscourse but by establishing a topical horizon in which its questionableness can be engaged. His remarks on what, in hermeneutic terms, would be the horizon of my own initial understanding facilitates his inquiry without (at this point) prejudicing its outcome. The historical John Angus Campbell, as foreign to me now as another person, could not possibly have known about himself the things that Gaonkar finds in his account of the critical situation in which I began my work. In his deft account of my early career, Gaonkar answers through his practice the very question that he finds impossible to resolve on the level of theory. His superb and informative account of my context does not prevent him from giving an equally and strikingly well articulated picture of me as an individual. While he is more artful than I was in my earlier essays in negotiating the relation between the recoverable strategies manifest in a work and the intentions of the writer, he just as clearly identifies the critical tactics that have informed my disciplinary practice. Gaonkar is a skilled rhetorical biographer of me precisely because in his critical practice he is able to keep author, text, situation, and intertextual context in heuristic play. His account is interesting as a story precisely because there is a "there" there; he tells us the story of an agent who does things with words, and then does new things with them as new circumstances arise, including the new circumstance of understanding his subject more fully.

The curious point in Gaonkar's assessment of my work is that exactly where his own topical analysis has reached its appropriate density or "thickness," when he successfully has brought into play through his patient and painstaking analysis my account of the full problematic of Darwin's enterprise, Gaonkar's logic itself becomes woefully thin. Having shown that I no longer view Darwin as a Super Rhetor, bestriding history like a strategic colossus (he really has caught me in some beauts!), he therefore concludes that Darwin must be folded into the anonymity of his intertextual ambience. The inadequacy of Gaonkar's logic could not be more evident. Tested by the contrapuntal tensions of merest rhetorical complexity, his logic snaps like a desiccated wishbone. But the remedy is simple. The interpreted fact of the matter is this: Were Gaonkar to reason on the basis of his practice, aside from his superior deftness in handling text, author, situation, and context, he and I would be found at most to differ in emphasis, nothing more. On the basis of the principles established through practice there can be few substantive disagreements between us.

Not only has Gaonkar accurately exposed the excesses of my earlier accounts of Darwin but he is equally correct in placing me in the tradition of civic humanism. I am not only a humanist (a successful divination of rhetorical motive on his part if ever there was one), but an evangelical humanist. In that spirit, I invite Gaonkar to come home and reformulate his theories in light of his practice. Struever well captured the deeper imperatives of humanist critical practice when she observed of one of its premier practitioners "there is an urgent conviction investing the Petrarchan texts that investigation is *lived*: theory must be considered as a practice and practice must be redesigned as 'free' " (1992:4). In marrying thought with life, humanism makes criticism urgent, civic, demanding, and worthwhile. In the wideness of its understanding of practice—a practice constrained by its subject, circumstances, and setting yet dependent more on the critic than on set method—the classical tradition provides a rich store of critical tools, not least of which is the example of able performers. My critique notwithstanding, I consider Gaonkar a superb performer gifted in the dance.

FULLER AND THE VERY IDEA OF A RHETORICAL STRATEGY

If Gaonkar takes my readings to task for excessive intentionality, on grounds that the author is but the "site of articulation" rather than "origination," Steve Fuller (this volume) objects to the whole idea of studying rhetorical strategy in the first place:

Do readers engage scientific texts as rhetorical episodes? (That is, as if the author were publicly addressing them with the purpose of moving them to act one way or another.) By simply taking for granted that readers engage texts rhetorically, the rhetorician of science appears to be naively passing off a normative theory of how scientific texts should be read as though it were already implicitly applied by some actual readers whose interpretive processes the rhetorician then wants to capture. (283–284)

I find it of some interest that both my critics focus on different aspects of the same thing. Gaonkar opposes the notion of a strategist, Fuller the notion of a strategy.[5]

In answer to Fuller's first question, "Do readers engage scientific texts as rhetorical episodes?" I can only say that Darwin certainly thought they did. Otherwise what would have been the point of all that preparation? He knew most of the members of the British—and the American—scientific establishment of his time. He knew their modes of argument, turns of phrase, and characteristic objections, and he was abreast of the religious and general culture of his time. Within certain tolerances, for which we all have analogues within our own experience, he could anticipate the probable responses of many of his colleagues. But he did not know for sure how they would actually respond. Nor was Darwin's world entirely of one mind. Fuller's comment on Whewell as an exception to inductivism is of course pertinent; Darwin's references to how a false theory was unlikely to explain so many different classes of fact was his gesture to Whewell's alternative concept of the "consilience of inductions" (Whewell, 1847).

The first issue, for me, is not whether scientific texts can be engaged as rhetorical episodes, but what status are we to give the rhetorical engagement between author and reader—which is too patent a fact of literary experience to ignore—and how are we to address it in our understanding of scientific texts? The most obvious reason for attending to the strategic qualities of a scientific text is that these qualities provide an answer to a central issue the text poses. How did the author see her ideas interacting with the values and beliefs of the audience that would condition her text's reception? Our question is a historical and philosophic one about the fact and function of rhetorical invention, not a merely empirical question about success. Understanding how the author attempted to position her ideas in relation to other and competing ideas is part of what it means to understand the rhetorical dimensions of a culturally revolutionizing idea. If there is something distinctive about the contribution of a rhetorical analysis to the history and philosophy of science, it surely will be here.

I have to add that there is something odd in Fuller calling his query about whether scientific texts can be read as rhetorical episodes "Feyerabendian." Feyerabend is a truly masterful reader of exactly the kinds of strategies for which Fuller takes me to task for examining. Again and again *Against Method* focuses on what we can only call Galileo's *ingenium* in how he "publicly addressed [his audience] with the purpose of moving them to act [or at least to believe] one way or another."[6] *Against Method* is not primarily about the responses of actual readers; it is primarily about how the persuasive strategies of a particular author refigured the terms of the debate.

Having urged the appropriateness of attending to a text's strategies as a first issue, I do not mean to dismiss the appropriateness of Fuller's question. I believe Aristotle's comparison of rhetoric to medicine provides an appropriate bridge between my emphasis on "invention" and Fuller's insistence on results. Neither in medicine nor in rhetoric, Aristotle insists, should results alone be the test of "art." As the aim of medicine is not health but to bring the patient as near to health as the case will allow, so in rhetoric the aim is not persuasion but to discover the possible means of persuasion (1355b). Analysis of the internal strategies of the text gives us our interpretive grasp on the inventional issue.

On the issue of results I would suggest the appropriateness of applying one of Darwin's central biological insights to rhetoric, the notion of *imperfect adaptation*. On one hand, adaptation in nature (even at its very best) can always be improved; on the other hand, it can only get so bad before the organism, or the species, will go extinct. The only general point about adaptation (whether biological or rhetorical) is that, while it always might be better, it only has to be good enough. Applying this principle to Darwin's own adaptation, we do not have to impose so rigorous a test as propositional persuasion. As Fuller suggests, and Peter Bowler documents in detail, only a handful of scientists in England or America accepted the theory of natural selection (Bowler, 1988; Campbell, 1989). When we begin to examine Darwin's supporters more closely, we immediately discover further wide differences of opinion on very fundamental issues (for example, between Darwin and Wallace on the strictness of selectionist criteria, or between Huxley and Gray on its theological implications).

And yet, by any serious *rhetorical* measure, even when Darwin "lost" he won. First, central to Darwin's persuasive aim, as he indicated in his letters, was to gain acceptance for the general belief in what he called "descent" or "descent with modification" (1911:163–164). Indeed, this was his original project long before he ever came up with the theory of "natural selection." That his advocacy of selection was governed by the more general rhetorical consideration of advancing "descent" can be seen in his readiness, in later editions of the *Origin* and in his *Descent of Man*, to compromise with his critics by admitting the relative efficacy of mechanisms other than natural selection. Indeed, in one of his later letters to the editor he became indignant at the idea that any one would accuse him of teaching that natural selection was the exclusive mechanism of evolution (1903:388–389)! Second, the same pattern can be seen in Darwin's public stand on design. On the one hand, the theory of natural selection challenges conventional religion; on the other, through his language Darwin seems to invite a compromise. (And in fact in his "deal" with Asa Gray, who offered to "baptize" natural selection, Darwin bought, paid for, and helped circulate a pamphlet containing an argument he emphatically rejected philosophically [Campbell, 1989:70–74].)

As I have suggested elsewhere, we need to judge the popular impact and reception of the *Origin* by how the inherent ambiguities in Darwin's position are the essence of his position. If ever a scientific author manifested the central intellectual quality Garver sees in Machiavelli's *Prince*, it is Darwin. Again, we are not talking about sheer (or at least not mere) deviousness, let alone superhuman mastery of history, but about a steady policy of "stable innovation." Darwin's specifically rhetorical achievement—whether one examines it in the strategies manifest in his writing or in the actual public response to his work—is to turn convention against itself and thereby change the terms of public debate. This is a spectacular achievement and it is a specifically rhetorical one, on any definition of rhetoric. It is for this reason that I have positioned my reading of Darwin as a "cultural grammar." In so doing, I have read the *Origin* primarily against the tradition of natural theology as epitomized by Paley and have underscored the way Darwin's text was written with an eye to the popular inductivism associated with the Scottish Common Sense school's canonization of Bacon. I am concerned also with actual affects (even effects) and, as a representative anecdote, my "sudden death" test of rhetorical utility is this: The first edition of the *Origin* of Species was 1859. The last edition of Paley's *Natural Theology* (first edition, 1802) was 1863.

In general, however, I prefer a more refined empiricism. In considering the impact of Darwin on his milieu, and in response to Fuller's concern that I may be going uncritically from textual strategy to audience affect, not only do we need to take seriously Darwin's notion of "imperfect" adaptation, we also need to take seriously his related notion of "differential adaptation." Darwin's strategies no more reproduce themselves directly in readers than in a Darwinian world are adaptations in nature the direct and immediate effects of the intentions of God. One Darwinian reader will become an atheist or an agnostic, another a devotee of Asa Gray's reconciliation with natural theology; one will reject natural selection, another will see it as one mechanism among others. Professional scientists (and science was beginning to be professionalized in the generation after the *Origin*) might pick up parts of the program of the *Origin* and not others. There are many possible ways of reading Darwin, and Darwin himself was genuinely amazed at the diversity of interpretations placed on his work by various readers (1911, 2:299). But diversity and unpredictability are not evidence against careful attention to its strategy. Darwin did decisively decenter the tradition of natural theology and altered fundamentally the terms of the conventional debate over "design," the foundation of morality, and much else besides. Attending to strategy against the backdrop of audience provides one way of understanding the operation of the strategy—how it was designed to engage salient features of its rhetorical situation. The focused study of audience effects is a separate issue and provides a different locus for criticism. The following overlapping analogies will conclude what I have to say about the imperfect adaptation and the differential relation of authorial or textual strategy to audience affect/effect.

A person (in this following example a reckless one) may loosen a boulder on a cliff knowing it will probably impact in a clump of trees further down the slope. But she cannot know what other particular things it will crash into on the way—though she does know there will be other things. Similarly with a text; it may be designed to have an impact, but once it is placed in circulation, one is no longer in control. The role of strategy was to produce the text, position it, and get it moving, and this involved knowledge, strength, timing, skill, and judgment. To put the same point in a different way, once while leafing through an old popular aviation magazine in a repair shop waiting room while my car was being fixed, I read an article by an airline pilot who told of his experience in flying the Goodyear blimp. The "lift off" and the trip were a piece of cake. Then he described how, when it came time to return to the airfield, he turned the controls and nothing happened. The regular blimp pilot instructed him to be more forceful, to which the author responded, as I remember his expression, by "executing a maneuver that would have knocked an airliner on its ear." Again, nothing happened. Then gradually the blimp began to come around.

Generally speaking, history does not turn on a dime either. And we would be mistaken to make too much of the idea of rhetors—let alone rhetorical critics—as scientists seated before a dense panel of technical gadgets which they mistake for the levers of destiny. And yet, at least in good weather, (or for those who know how to fly and to read the signs of the times) there are occasions when certain people (and seemingly out of thin air) execute spectacular deeds through words. In the case of Paine's *Common Sense*, a particular persuasive strategy may have an immediate effect—an effect palpably persuasive and potently political. Probably there is also a point to Fuller's concern that readers of scientific texts do not read them as rhetorical episodes—or, as I believe, the episodes function differently. Nor do I mean to dismiss Gaonkar's preference for seeing the author also as a site of production and not only as a site of origination. Most of what even a genius says will be conventional. Yet history does turn, intellectual innovations do happen, and the strategy of great texts, in conjunction with numerous ancillary conditions, has something, sometimes everything, to do with it. But in bad weather, in a high wind, and in a blimp (and with Gaonkar and Fuller), it would be pathetically heroic not to believe in deconstruction.

NOTES

1. The aims of Gadamer's project are admirably set forth in his book *Philosophical Hermeneutics* (1976). That the aim of Heidegger's philosophy is "to call his audience to authentic existence" is argued by Henry W. Johnstone, "Rhetoric and Communication in Philosophy" (1978:68). See also Paul Ricoeur (1965:xi–xxi), and also Ricoeur's own excellent chapter "Work and the Word" (197–219).

2. That Marxism is a seductive dream is a point only academics—and only Western ones at that—would need to have documented. But rhetoricians have no ground for refusing to honor local pieties. See Kolakowski (1978); for example, vol. 1, p. 80; or vol. 3: "Marxism has been the greatest fantasy of our century" (523). That Freudianism is no better is well documented in Sulloway (1982): "we may well ask whether psychoanalysis is perhaps unique among the sciences in having sought so strenuously to shroud its origins in myth" (502). On the rhetorical sins of structuralism see Vickers (1988) on Jakobson et al. (442–453). For rhetorical reductionism, see Alan Gross (1990:33).

3. This parody makes less gently a point that Leff makes in his response, viz., that Gaonkar's criticism of Campbell and Gross is as agent-centered as any of their work.

4. For theology and law together, see Ball (1985); McKeon (1982); Maranhao (1986); Ober (1989); Kimball (1986); Farrell (1994).

5. Scene at *Postmodern State Correctional Institution For Habitual Humanists:*

Inmate 1: What are you in for?

Inmate 2: First-degree metaphysics of presence. I claimed in print that somebody meant something when they said something, and my colleagues thought I meant it!

6. Feyerabend (1980), see esp. ch. 11. Feyerabend's synopsis says it all: "Galileo prevails because of his style and his clever techniques of persuasion, because he writes in Italian rather than in Latin, and because he appeals to people who are temperamentally opposed to the old ideas and the standards of learning connected with them" (13).

REFERENCES

Aristotle. (1982). *On rhetoric.* J. Freese (Trans.). Cambridge: Harvard University Press.

Ball, M. S. (1985). *Lying down together: Law, metaphor, and theology.* Madison: University of Wisconsin Press.

Bock, K. (1980). *Human nature and history: A response to sociobiology.* New York: Columbia University Press.

Bowler, P. (1988). *The non-Darwinian revolution: Reinterpreting a historical myth.* Baltimore: Johns Hopkins University Press.

Burke, K. (1954). *Permanence and change,* Los Angeles: Hermes.

———. (1969). *A grammar of motives.* Los Angeles: University of California Press.

Campbell, J. A. (1989). The invisible rhetorician: Charles Darwin's third party strategy. *Rhetorica, 7,* 55–85.

———. (1993). Insight and understanding: The "common sense" rhetoric of Bernard Lonergan. In T. J. Farrell and P. A. Soukup (Eds.), *Communication and Lonergan,* 3–22. New York: Sheed and Ward.

Darwin, F. (Ed.). (1903). *More letters of Charles Darwin.* Vol 1. London: John Murray.

———. (1911). *The life and letters of Charles Darwin.* New York and London: D. Appleton.

Farrell, T. B. (1993). *Norms of rhetorical culture.* New Haven: Yale University Press.

Feyerabend (1980). *Against method.* London: Verso.

Gadamer, H. G. (1975). *Truth and method.* New York: Seabury.

———. (1976). *Philosophical hermeneutics*. D. E. Linge (Trans. and Ed.). Berkeley: University of California Press.

———. (1981). *Reason in the age of science*. F. G. Lawrence (Trans.). Cambridge: MIT Press.

Garver, E. (1987). *Machiavelli and the history of prudence*. Madison: University of Wisconsin Press.

———. (1994). *Aristotle's* Rhetoric*: An art of character*. Chicago: University of Chicago Press.

Gross, A. (1990). *The Rhetoric of Science*. Cambridge: Harvard University Press.

Howe, H., and Lyne, J. (1992). Gene talk in sociobiology. *Social Epistemology*, 6, 1–54.

Johnstone, H. W. (1978). Rhetoric and communication in philosophy. *Validity and rhetoric in philosophic argument*. University Park: The Dialog Press of Man & World.

Jost, W. (1989). *Rhetorical thought in John Henry Newman*. Columbia: University of South Carolina Press.

Kebley, C. A. (1965). Introduction. In P. Ricoeur, *History and truth*, xi–xxi. Evanston: Northwestern University Press.

Kierkegaard, S. (1939). *The point of view for my work as an author*. W. Lowrie (Trans.). Oxford: Oxford University Press.

Kimball, B. A. (1986). *Orators and philosophers: A history of the idea of liberal education*. Columbia: Columbia University Press.

Kolakowski, L. (1978). *Main currents of Marxism*. 3 vols. New York: Oxford University Press.

Leff, M. C. (1980). Interpretation and the art of the critic. *Western Journal of Speech Communication*, 44, 347–349.

Lonergan, B. (1978). *Insight: A study of human understanding*. New York: Harper and Row.

Maranhao, T. (1986). *Therapeutic discourse and Socratic dialogue*. Madison: University of Wisconsin Press.

McKeon, Z. K. (1982). *Novels and arguments: Inventing rhetorical criticism*. Chicago: University of Chicago Press.

Michnik, A., and Habermas, J. (1994, 24 March). More humility, fewer illusions: A talk. *New York Review of Books*, Vol. XLI, 26.

Neuhaus, R. J. (1994, Nov.). While we are at it. *First Things*, 47, 67–68.

Ober, J. (1989). *Mass and elite in democratic Athens: Rhetoric, ideology, and the power of the people.* Princeton: Princeton University Press.

Pera, M., and Shea, W. R. (1991). *Persuading science: The art of scientific rhetoric.* Canton, MA: Science History Publications.

Ricoeur, P. (1965). Work and the word. In *History and truth,* 197–219. Evanston: Northwestern University Press.

———. (1970). *Freud and philosophy.* New Haven: Yale University Press.

Struever, N. S. (1992). *Theory as practice: Ethical inquiry in the Renaissance.* Chicago: University of Chicago Press.

Sulloway, F. (1982). *Freud, biologist of the mind.* New York: Harper and Row.

Vickers, B. (1988). *In defence of rhetoric.* Oxford: Clarendon.

Webb, E. (1988). *Philosophers of consciousness.* Seattle: University of Washington Press.

Whewell, W. (1847). *The philosophy of the inductive sciences, founded upon their history.* London: John W. Parker and Sons.

CHAPTER 5

WHAT IF WE'RE NOT PRODUCING KNOWLEDGE? CRITICAL REFLECTIONS ON THE RHETORICAL CRITICISM OF SCIENCE

Alan G. Gross

Surely Gaonkar's assault on my work, mounted with such panache, requires, if not a retreat, at least a strategic withdrawal to previously occupied positions. For if Gaonkar is right, it seems to me, what I and my fellow rhetoricians of science have been producing in the last decade is not an instance of classical rhetoric's strength but a demonstration of its intellectual bankruptcy, not knowledge but nonsense. This is largely because Gaonkar thinks that critics like myself are mistaken in considering classical rhetoric as an adequate epistemic or methodological resource. Classical rhetoric is not about the analysis of texts, he insists, but about their production. To rely on this fund of pedagogical lore for the analysis of scientific texts is a category mistake; it is like appointing the volleyball coach to a chair in physiology on the grounds of her intimate and thorough knowledge of the functions of the human body. And there is little question that Aristotle would have been appalled that a framework designed to perfect *technê* would be applied as an *epistemê*.

Arguably, a history of successful use belies this concern for historical niceties. But Gaonkar claims that this success is an illusion enabled by the "thinness" of an Aristotelian framework as an interpretive tool, an absence of appropriate constraints that licenses an intellectual promiscuity so thorough as permanently to guarantee its popularity. Classical rhetorical theory is easy—too easy, in Gaonkar's view. Its applicability to any text is an index not of its power but of its vacuity. Its tools of analysis—*stasis, enthymeme, topoi,* and so forth—are routinely described in a manner so vague as to provide virtually no respectable guardrails on critical activity. Classical rhetorical analysis functions not as a micrometer, but as a Cuisinart: its use does not illuminate the texts of science so much as it homogenizes them, producing in each case a similar shapeless mass in which the original ingredients are virtually unrecognizable.

There are two epistemic consequences to this misguided practice. Since the rhetorical analysis of science is unconstrained by legitimate intellectual limits, its products cannot be contested. But what cannot be contested ought not to be affirmed. It is not knowledge. The lack of legitimate constraints has a second unfortunate consequence: in rhetorical analysis, what is distinctive about science virtually disappears. To say that scientific communication is rhetorical, therefore, is to say nothing much, and nothing interesting. It is no wonder that philosophers, historians, and sociologists of science largely neglect work in that field.

In Gaonkar's view, I survive as a critic only to the extent that I avoid Aristotle, despite my insistence to the contrary. Against Gaonkar, I shall argue that classical presuppositions clearly drive my enterprise and are directly responsible for the class of insights to which I lay claim. Moreover, I shall contend that these presuppositions are far less limiting than Gaonkar contends. Although I agree with him that classical rhetoric cannot provide an intellectual framework sufficient for the analysis of scientific texts, I differ from him in claiming that this insufficiency does not arise from any alleged vacuity of rhetorical theory. Classical rhetoric ought not to be abandoned; instead, it should be enriched by the insights into language and its contexts of use that two millennia of reflection have bestowed upon us. It is because of this abundant harvest that the effective use of an Aristotelian framework requires that it be extended and supplemented.

Against Gaonkar, then, I argue that the understanding of the rhetorical aspects of scientific texts counts as knowledge. The claims of rhetoric of science can be—indeed, they have been—legitimately affirmed, fruitfully contested, and effectively incorporated into more comprehensive theoretical formulations. It follows that the price of the routine neglect of rhetorical analysis by philosophers, historians, and sociologists is their misunderstanding of their central texts: if they continue to ignore the work of rhetoricians, rhetoricians may suffer in prestige, as Gaonkar affirms. But the real cost of this neglect is not social, but epistemic and methodological.

ARISTOTLE OR BUST?

Gaonkar (1993) asks a question central for any rhetoric of science founded on classical theory:

> Is it possible to translate an Aristotelian vocabulary initially generated in the course of "theorizing" about certain practical (*praxis*) and productive (*poesis*) activities . . . into a vocabulary for interpretive understanding of cultural practices that [includes] science? (30)

This seems exactly right, even to the scare quotes around "theory." Even the theoretical status of the *Rhetoric* cannot be presupposed. And it is the *Rhetoric*, certainly, that is the master text for current rhetoricians of science, the text to struggle with, and to struggle against: "the interpretive turn in contemporary rhetorical studies, even as it seeks to break free from a 'restrained' vision of Aristotle," Gaonkar avers, "remains fatally bound to an Aristotelian vocabulary" (28).

According to Gaonkar, the literature of rhetoric of science, because it is "largely unreflexive" (39), remains deaf to this central paradox. This lack of theoretical self-consciousness, however, will not save the critic from criticism, because even "an allegedly atheoretical critical study is suffused with a critical vocabulary that is not simply derived from everyday language. The question is not whether but which vocabulary is in play" (32). And it is not a matter of language alone. An Aristotelian rhetoric of science is marked by ideological allegiances far deeper than any terminology:

> a view of the speaker as the seat of origin rather than a point of articulation, a view of strategy as identifiable under an intentional description, a view of discourse as constitutive of character and community, a view of audience positioned simultaneously as "spectator" and "participant," a view of "ends" that binds speaker, strategy, discourse, and audience in a web of purposive actions. (31–32)

This characterization of classical rhetoric as a set of terms and a network of presuppositions, each inadequate to its putative task, is crucial to Gaonkar's analysis of my work, an analysis designed to show that my "proposed approach—an updated neo-Aristotelianism—has little bearing on what [I do] as a critic" (50). The general view is that my use of classical theory is intermittent and perfunctory; that it is, in any case, irrelevant to my accomplishments as a critic. In Gaonkar's opinion this is just as well, since he does not "see how such a model, deeply implicated in the ideology of human agency, has the requisite interpretive resources to illuminate contemporary science in all its material, cultural, and discursive manifestations" (48).

The chapter from *The Rhetoric of Science* Gaonkar chooses as the focus of his criticism has for its subject the composition and reception of *Narratio Prima*, the first Copernican treatise, a work that predates *De Revolutionibus* by three years. He might have chosen instead the chapter on evolutionary taxonomy, or on Isaac Newton, or on Charles Darwin. In these cases, my recourse to classical theory is more explicit, and in the last, my analysis and that of John Angus Campbell overlap, a coincidence that might have provoked fruitful comparisons. But Gaonkar has chosen *Narratio Prima*, a choice that permits me to show that even in this chapter, a chapter free of classical terminology, the critical categories deployed and the ideology presupposed are pervasively Aristotelian. Having done this, I shall show just how my work and Campbell's jointly illustrate that a rhetoric centered on human agency is no bar to the understanding of science.

My study of *Narratio Prima* concerns the extended historical moment that constitutes the European reception of Copernicanism. This moment stretches from the publication of *Narratio Prima* in 1540 to the first decades of the eighteenth century, a time when astronomy finally possessed, in the physics of Newton and the calculus of Newton and Leibniz, the means to make full scientific and mathematical sense of heliocentricity. At the beginning of the period, scientists might be excused from believing in a system not clearly an improvement over its predecessor; by the end of the period, being an astronomer meant being a Copernican. As early, however, as the sixteenth century a small group of serious astronomers, of whom the most famous are Maestlin and Kepler, kept Copernicanism alive. How did they manage this adherence, in the absence of the grounding they themselves considered adequate? They managed, I suggest in this chapter, by supplementing science with reasons that would not bear close scientific scrutiny, and with a faith in their intuitions and in the intuitions of respected colleagues and teachers. This union of science, reason, and faith, a union I call "rational conversion," is, I contend, dramatized in *Narratio Prima*. *Narratio Prima* is a work that frames and undergirds the scientific arguments for Copernicanism with a narrative whose model is Paul's conversion in *Acts*.

What has this analysis to do with classical rhetoric? Nothing, in Gaonkar's view: "not even a single essay in Gross's book can be regarded as a critical illustration of [a] neo-Aristotelian approach. Gross's neo-Aristotelianism is a phantom; it does not exist" (65). Gaonkar's hyperbole is pardonable, a striving for effect. But his point is real, and telling, if true. It is not true. Gaonkar is correct in noting that my study of *Narratio Prima* is free of classical terminology. Despite this absence, however, the chapter embodies throughout an awareness of Aristotelian categories without which its analysis would be impossible, its claims without theoretical support. I could have said, "Here is *pathos,* there is *enargeia.*" But for an audience in speech communication, such *deixis* would be pedantry; for a general audience, a mere hindrance to understanding. It is no denigration of Aristotelian analysis that in this case exposition requires no technical terminology. Despite the absence of technical terms, my analysis of *Narratio Prima* is everywhere undergirded by the presuppositions of classical rhetoric and of the classical oration, presuppositions Gaonkar so insightfully summarizes: "a view of the speaker as the seat of origin rather than a point of articulation, a view of strategy as identifiable under an intentional description, a view of discourse as constitutive of character and community" (31–32). The author of *Narratio Prima* is clearly the seat of origin of a strategy designed to inculcate belief in heliocentricity; his audience is clearly one of scientists who are at the same time Christians, a double identification prerequisite to their participation in a discourse able to mediate between character and community.

To nail this point down, let us look at some specifics. I begin the section "The Rhetorical Case for Heliocentricity" by analyzing the structure of typical Renaissance astronomical treatises, all modelled on Ptolemy's *Almagest.* To this structure *Narratio Prima* is an exception. Its structure is essentially "story-like: the scientific case for Copericanism is embedded in a framework of conversion" (Gross, 1990b:100–101). Throughout this analysis of the *Narratio,* moreover, I remain sensitive to the persuasive function of a narrative structure whose central event is the simultaneous conversion of Copernicus and Rheticus. I take it that this narrative event redefines "astronomical truth" (104) by altering the ontological status of astronomical hypotheses. In the scientific tradition that Copernicus and Rheticus shared with Ptolemy, hypotheses are matters of mathematical convenience; at the end of the *Narratio* they "become what they are throughout *De Revolutionibus*: physical truths about the universe" (104). In the course of *Narratio Prima,* moreover, style persuades, as well as arrangement: "[the] increase in Rheticus' conviction is also mirrored in the gradual elevation of Copernicus' symbolic status: from heir to Ptolemy, to king, to general, to philosopher, to mythical hero: like Atlas, shouldering the world, or like Orpheus, rescuing the muse of astronomy from the underworld" (103). It adds nothing to the intellectual content of these statements to present them in the technical terminology of rhetoric, the classical vocabulary of *narratio, taxis,* and *climax.*[1]

But, apparently, Gaonkar has me whipsawed. Any victory I can claim is, at best, pyrrhic: to the degree that I convince readers that my approach is Aristotelian, I also convince them that my rhetorical criticism can add little to the understanding of science. Gaonkar makes this paradox clearest in his analysis of Campbell's contribution to the field, an analysis that focuses on Campbell's "absolute and sustained commitment to an agent-centered model of intentional persuasion" (277). He feels that this commitment seriously impedes the understanding of scientific texts. Their meaning cannot be captured unless an intertextual reading supplements (or, perhaps, actually replaces) its intentionalist counterpart. Gaonkar indicates a preference for intertextuality on the grounds that "it is difficult to imagine how an intentionalist reading could do justice to the *Origin* as a text" (282). Accordingly, Gaonkar approves of Campbell's gradual "conversion" from a strictly strategic view of rhetoric in which Darwin is a master rhetorician playing his audiences to a more intertextual view in which Darwin is one force in a field of forces.

Gaonkar feels that in his latest essays Campbell frees himself from an intentionalist reading and thereby, he implies, from a strictly classical approach:

> [Darwin] is portrayed as someone struggling to articulate a theory whose conceptual structure contradicted his own scientific beliefs and rhetorical intuitions. This alters the equation between Darwin, Campbell and the reader. When Darwin struggles Campbell struggles, and so does the reader. With Darwin struggling, Campbell is no longer content to read in terms of a conscious design the interplay of practical reasoning and figuration in the *Origin* and how that interplay prefigures the cultural grammar of its time. At last, the *Origin* emerges from the shadow of Darwin's colossal presence and is seen to have a life and logic of its own that lures the reader into an intertextual space of notebooks, letters, and abandoned works. (58–59)

Gaonkar's criticism of Campbell applies as well to my own work on Darwin. In my chapter on Darwin's notebooks I pay explicit attention to such classical matters as style, arrangement, and invention; at the same time, I am sensitive to the textual interactions that are a necessary part of any intellectual history of the *Origin*. I trace a single crucial observation, which Darwin made while eating a Christmas dinner of ostrich in 1833, from its first appearance in private to its first appearance in print twenty-two years later in the first edition of the *Origin*. Only by tracing the history of this observation, I contend, can we see its importance for Darwin, an importance not reflected in the final text. The importance of this observation and its eventual placement in the *Origin* are both, I conjecture, consequences of rhetorical transactions within Darwin's self, a self that is, like all selves, simultaneously individual and social, simultaneously, therefore, intentional as well as intertextual:

> The significant distinction in argument between the Notebooks and the *Origin* lies in the contrast between what convinced Darwin and what Darwin thought would persuade his first audience. . . . This explanation applies also to the most striking difference in argumentative strategy between the Notebooks and the *Origin*: the fact that the analogy between artificial and natural selection, which looms so large in the latter, is if such trifling importance in the former. (1990b:157)

To account for science rhetorically, however, an Aristotelian framework cannot simply be extended; it must be supplemented as well. An example of such supplementation is my recourse to Habermas in a chapter on peer review. I justify this recourse on the basis of the coincidence of aim between Habermas's ideal speech situation and peer review: "rational consensus, the explicit *telos* of the ideal speech situation, is the avowed *telos* of peer review. If Habermas's theory is plausible at all, the application of its machinery must be plausible in this instance" (129). In making use of Habermas, however, Gaonkar considers that I have transgressed against theoretical coherence: "Gross is relatively promiscuous in drawing interpretive constructs from various sources" (64), of which Habermas is one. This accusation of textual misconduct is difficult to fathom, given Gaonkar's reading of classical rhetoric (30ff). In Habermas's ideal speech situation, as in classical rhetoric, speakers are the origin of speech acts that are intentional in nature. In the aggregate, these acts constitute the speaker's character and her community; they bind speaker and audience in a system of common means and ends.[2]

The philosophical common ground Aristotle and Habermas share is not, however, shared by alternative views of peer review, views I reject as unrhetorical. I reject both functionalism and "strong program" explanations. I reject functionalism because it gives insufficient consideration to people: "its self-regulating systems can account for communicative action only by the reduction of such action to a systems function from which it differs in essence" (1990b:142). I reject explanations like Latour's in *Science in Action* because they are so unrhetorical as to refuse to distinguish as a matter of principle between human actors and their instruments. To Latour, considerations of power dissolve such distinctions. But "to equate communicative action with power," I maintain, "is to remain insensitive to real differences between rationality and irrationality, between communication oriented toward understanding and systematically distorted communication. Analyzed in terms of power only, peer review is, quite simply, unrecognizable" (141–142).

In my view these alternative explanations of peer review, and of science, however influential, are fundamentally mistaken because they are unrhetorical. They systematically neglect what rhetorical theory (and its twin, ethical theory) forces us to make central: human actors responsible for their actions, actions that in the aggregate constitute our social and political worlds. Efforts such as Latour's, which demote human actors to counters that "can be cumulated, aggregated, or shuffled like a pack of cards" (1987:223), are helpful in so far as they underline the limitations of individual wills and the degree to which those wills are constituted by cultural imperatives. But these efforts are misguided, even mischievous, to the extent that the zeal of their defenders eliminates the possibility of purposive action.

WHO'S AFRAID OF ARISTOTLE?

My defense has not yet touched on the contestability of the rhetorical analysis of science, its openness to falsification, and, therefore, its status as knowledge. This will be the subject of the next section of this rejoinder. Before beginning that task of defense, however, I would like to comment on another status relationship, that between rhetoric of science and its more established counterparts, the history, philosophy, and sociology of science. Gaonkar rightly points out that the intellectual traffic is stubbornly one-way, rhetoric of science consistently cast in the role of borrower. For him, this asymmetry underlines the dubious state of rhetorical analysis, the fact that "the current state of scholarship in RS [may be] inconsequential" (41). Gaonkar is especially exercised that rhetoricians of science rely for their legitimacy on finding common cause with such scholars as Kuhn and Feyerabend. He sees these alliances as entirely wrong-headed since "none of these masters . . . so far has either conceded that what they have been doing all along is a form of rhetorical reading, or gone on to incorporate rhetorical vocabulary in their subsequent work" (74).

The indifference of "the masters" to rhetorical analysis has never been as wholesale as Gaonkar implies. It is true that Kuhn shows no interest in rhetorical analysis, but the same cannot be said of Feyerabend. In *Against Method* (1975), Feyerabend asserts that allegiance to the Copernican system in Galileo's day amounted to a "blind faith" supported not by evidence and argument but *"by irrational means* such as propaganda, emotion, *ad hoc* hypotheses, and appeal to prejudices of all kinds" (153–154; his emphasis). In the index, "rhetoric" is a general entry for pages 1–309, indicating that this remark is not an aside but a reflection of a concern central to Feyerabend's argument (337).

The current attitude of historians and philosophers oscillates between increased need to take a rhetorical point of view into consideration and an occasional hostility to the possibility of rhetorical analysis. We can see the need to take rhetoric into consideration in the title of a collection by Marcello Pera and William R. Shea, a collection whose contributors are historians and philosophers of science: *Persuading Science: The Art of Scientific Rhetoric* (1991). We can see it also in the title of Peter Dear's collection, *The Literary Structure of Scientific Argument: Historical Studies* (1991). This orientation is no a mere matter of titles; we can see it also in the way problems are constructed. In *World Changes* (Horwich, 1993), a collection most of whose contributors are historians of science, J. L. Heilbron follows a quarrel between mathematicians in the Royal Society, a quarrel that "opened extensive rhetorical opportunities" (86); Jed Buchwald notes the importance of *staseis*, though he does not use the term: "Arguments," he says, "may revolve about physical issues (was ether a better physical foundation than light particles?) or about analytical complexity (were Fresnel integrals less acceptable as primary apparatus than equations for particle motion?)" (180–181); in his study of eighteenth-century science, M. Norton Wise has an instrument, a calorimeter, *"mediat[ing]* between the potentially divisive interests of Laplace and Lavoisier" (212; emphasis added).

Established scholars in allied disciplines have also reacted to rhetoric with hostility, both in print and behind the scenes. In *World Changes*, historian Noel Swerdlow identifies his text, an oration of Regiomontanus, as "a species of *epideictic*, that is, *demonstrative*, oratory which is devoted to the praise or blame (*laus vel vituperatio*) of someone or something" (141). Nevertheless, he dismisses the rhetorical analysis of this oration as intellectually trivial: "the general characteristics of Regiomontanus's oration as oratory can easily be understood by reference to standard treatises like the *Rhetorica ad Herrenium* and *De inventione*. But we shall leave such analysis to those who write about rhetoric (or is it now 'discourse'?)" (141).

This hostility has also been played out behind the scenes, by the gatekeepers of knowledge. The publication history of my study of the rhetoric of Copernicanism bears out the contention that the judgment that rhetorical analysis is of dubious value to the history of science may be as much a matter of intellectual politics as intellectual worth. Prior to its Harvard publication, the study was rejected by the *Journal of the History of Ideas* on the basis of a split review. The positive reviewer, a historian of astronomy from Princeton, recognized the value of my work to history; the negative reviewer dismissed my analysis because, by the standards of professional history, it was everywhere lacking in distinction. Although on the positive reviewer's intellectual side, the editor, unwilling to incur the wrath of the negative reviewer, who "owned the field," chose not to publish. By such means is the asymmetrical traffic between history and rhetoric of science maintained. For such reasons we may have to wait a decade or two to see the true influence of rhetoric of science on its older siblings.

THE EMPEROR'S NEW KNOWLEDGE?

Gaonkar has, apparently, undermined my effort to create rhetorical knowledge of science by showing that, since rhetorical analysis can demonstrate virtually anything, it can demonstrate absolutely nothing. "In its current form," he says, "rhetoric as a language of criticism is so thin and abstract that it is virtually invulnerable to falsification and, for that reason, it commands little sustained attention" (33). In an accompanying note, in apparent contradiction, he comments: "I am not suggesting that our current vocabulary produces interpretations of texts and practices which are not open to falsification" (79). Later, in reference to my work, he clarifies his intent: "a rhetorical reading merits attention," he states, "only insofar as it proffers a distinct and 'contestable' (if not 'falsifiable') reading of a given scientific text" (62).

To this indictment there is one seemingly devastating reply, an attack on falsifiability itself as a criterion of knowledge. *Falsifiabil-*

ity is Karl Popper's term; he saw its development as a response to a problem central to logical positivism, the problem of the confirmation of theories. Popper noted that, while no amount of positive evidence could confirm a theory, one piece of negative evidence could disconfirm it. Simple logic was the source of this insight. Suppose a hypothetical syllogism of which the antecedent is a theory, the consequent its evidence. For example, if inertia is real, this satellite will continue with fixed velocity toward Alpha Centauri. Suppose that the satellite behaves as predicted: can we say that inertia is real? We cannot. If we do, we will have committed the fallacy of affirming the consequent. But suppose that the satellite does not behave as predicted: can we deny the antecedent? Logic tells us that we can. Good scientific theories, Popper averred, were those that had, so far, resisted falsification.

Although elegant and attractive, falsifiability has been criticized because, it has been repeatedly pointed out, theories do not come individually packaged as hypothetical syllogisms. Any interesting scientific theory, classical mechanics, for instance, is a complex web, a vast interconnected network of propositions. A disconfirming instance in one part of the network can always be neutralized by adjustments elsewhere. As a result of his famous experiment with Edward Morley, Albert Michelson said that, because the stationary aether had no effect on their apparatus, it did not exist. But Henrik Lorentz said that, on the contrary, the aether only *seemed* to have no effect; actually, its pressure had shrunk the measuring rod. Lorentz's theory-conserving explanation is perfectly consistent with the facts. Experimental results, no matter how firm, cannot falsify theories, which can always be modified to accommodate them.

On the basis of this argument, most philosophers of science reject falsifiability as a criterion of scientific knowledge. I think this wholesale rejection is a mistake. True, falsifiability will not solve all of our epistemological problems; but it is not therefore empty. This is because, in the hard sciences at least, the constraints within the propositional networks of theories are often very considerable. Because of these, there is some valuable sense in which we can say that Newton's *experimentum crucis* falsified all theories that made white light simple; that Michelson-Morley's experimentum crucis falsified all theories of physics that relied on the luminiferous aether as their indispensable component; that Alain Aspect's experimentum crucis falsified all quantum theories that depended crucially on local hidden variables. However contestable such assertions may be in the history or philosophy of science, the conclusion for rhetorical theory and criticism seems inescapable: unless analogous constraints exist,[3] rhetorical theory and criticism cannot produce knowledge. In a real sense, rhetorical theorists and critics know nothing; worse, they *can* know nothing.

This claim may seem overly bleak. But it isn't a question of how comforting; it is a question of how true. In my view, the conclusion that rhetorical theorists and critics can know nothing presupposes the unreasonable premise that unless rhetorical critics and theorists can duplicate the constraints of contemporary physics, Popper's model of a falsifiable science, their efforts cannot produce knowledge. That this standard is overly Draconian even Gaonkar realizes when he agrees to another, the standard of contestability (62). (This is just as well, since the standard of falsifiability is overly Draconian even for contemporary physics.) Gaonkar does not define contestability. He might, however, agree that *claims to knowledge in the rhetoric of science depend on the degree of epistemic certainty with which they may be legitimately held, a degree dependent on the plausible analysis of exemplary cases whose typicality is presupposed.* On this construal, claims can be contested by two means: the critic can offer counterexamples or she can reanalyze existing examples.[4]

My views on the form of the experimental report, on Darwin, and on the rhetorical ontology of scientific objects and events have been contested by just these means, a contestability Gaonkar unreasonably disallows. According to Mike Markel, the form of the experimental report is not, as I say, the outcome of an outmoded philosophy of science, inductive in form and Baconian in origin. Its purpose is not to embody and, indirectly, to endorse Baconianism, but "to enable the reader to assess the quality of the scientist's logical reconstruction of the laboratory work" (1993:7). According to Markel, my claim entails that authors systematically "overstate the influence of their ideas" (15). To undermine this claim, Markel adduces what he takes to be typical instances of nuanced claims in the experimental papers he examines (15–16). The cogency of Markel's claim depends on the cogency of his counterexamples as refutations of my thesis.

In his interpretation of *Origin of Species*, Stuart Peterfreund does not contest my view of Darwin's most creative phase "as a rhetorical transaction within the self" (1990b:145; quoted in Peterfreund, 1994:250) In his opinion, however, the *Origin* is "about" colonialism and racism just as much as it is "about" science, a truth I fail to uncover. In pursuit of his thesis, he forges links between the *Origin* and the writings of Gilbert White, John Milton, and Samuel Taylor Coleridge, links that bind these writers and Darwin together in a web of colonialism and racism. The cogency of these links depends on the cogency of Peterfreund's reanalysis of the language of the *Origin* . For example, Peterfreund reinterprets the following as "racially charged" (244): "I crossed some white fantails, which breed very true, with some black barbs—and it so happens that blue varieties of barb are so rare that I never heard of an instance in England; and the mongrels were black, brown and mottled" (245). The plausibility of Peterfreund's claims depends on the plausibility of such rereadings.

In their essay "The Rhetoric of the Radical Rhetoric of Science" (1991), J. E. McGuire and Trevor Melia contest my call for a rhetoric of science without constraints, one that takes as a premise the possibility that the objects and events of science share a *rhetorical* ontology. They insist that I have science wrong. It is not mostly theory, as I assume, but mostly the discovery of facts. It is not mostly textual, as I suppose, but mostly practice. Their views are not neo-Kantian, as I assert, but a version of "minimal realism"; they see science as a set of empirical techniques for making sense out of the Burkean "recalcitrances" of the material world. Our disagreement concerns not the facts of science but their interpretation as evidence for or against an ontology that is specifically rhetorical. For example, I contend that "even within science, constants can change their character: after quantum electrodynamics, c, the *constant* speed of light, turns out to be an average, not a constant" (1991:289). McGuire and Melia agree and disagree: "The light constant, c, does change its character when we move from the context of the special theory of relativity to quantum electrodynamics [but] although the shift entails a different characterization of the parameter c, it is still a constant, and it continues to pick out *the same thing*, the speed of light" (313; emphasis added). The point of contention between us is the phrase *the same thing*. The reader must decide whether or not McGuire and Melia are begging the question. To decide one way or another is to prefer one exegesis of the texts of relativity over another.

Case studies in the rhetoric of science perform a second function that Gaonkar disallows: they permit the construction of robust generalizations and theories of wide scope. In Gaonkar's view rhetoric of science is a "stalled" project (41). This criticism stems from the purported epistemic and methodological limits of rhetorical case studies, their alleged incapacity to lead to robust generalizations and contestable theories of wide scope. It is one thing to claim that "rational conversion" is a bridge between early and late Copernicanism; it is another altogether to assert that "rational conversion" is a bridge that characterizes a whole scientific/literary genre, a bridge whose presence and structure we can predict in unexamined cases. In the former instance, we make a limited claim about a single text or suite of texts; in the latter, we make a robust generalization across cases and build a contestable theory of wide scope.

Can such generalizations and such theories be legitimately constructed from rhetorical cases? Given the labor-intensive nature that limits the production of cases and the complexity that makes case analysis so recalcitrant to quantification, can cases lead to robust generalizations and to contestable theories of wide scope? Alexander George (1979) has explored an analogous issue in his field of interest, comparative political science. In this field, relatively few cases are available for analysis because the discipline deals only with large units, typically nation states. But, George contends, nation-state comparisons focused on a particular problem, and structured to solve that problem, *can* lead to robust generalizations and contestable theories, generalizations and theories that benefit also from the analytical richness inherent in the case study method. Comparisons so well focused and so tightly structured imitate the constraints of experimental control. In a more recent effort, Charles Ragin and Howard Becker (1992) and their collaborators extend their methods from comparative political science to sociology (see also Ragin 1987). The structured, focused comparison of George, Ragin, and Becker offers rhetoricians of science methodological and epistemic hope, the hope of building generalizations and theories from an initially unpromising source, single case studies. In some recent work in rhetoric of science, case studies perform in just this way.[5] Kenneth Zagacki and William Keith (1992) use existing case materials to build a rhetorical theory of scientific revolutions; Richard Harvey Brown (1994) builds a single case of rational conversion in science into a rhetorical theory of genre.

In their rhetorical analysis of scientific revolutions, Zagacki and Keith use Bernard Cohen's four stage typology. At each of Cohen's revolutionary stages, these scholars claim, a "crucial exigenc[y] demands fitting rhetorical response" (59). In the first two stages, the *intellectual revolution* and the *revolution of commitment*, there is "the technical exigence of *uncertainty*"; in the third stage, the *revolution on paper*, there is "the problem of creating appropriate scientific *personnae* during revolutions, [and] the exigence of *preserving* revolutionary ideas"; finally, at the fourth stage, the *revolution in science*, there is "the problem of *transforming* revolutionary change into established practice" (59–60). Using as their *donné* Prelli's discussion of the topoi appropriate to science, Zagaki and Keith elaborate their theory, incorporating the work not only of Prelli but of Lyne and Howe and myself. Their purpose is "to integrate some of the diverse threads in the rhetoric of science literature and to extend systematically our understanding of that important domain" (60). By placing that literature in "a coherent theoretical framework" (74), as they note in their conclusion, they have transformed it into its theory, an accomplishment that Gaonkar disallows on theoretical grounds.

In his paper on the logics of discovery, Richard Harvey Brown extends my analysis of *Narratio Prima*: "I draw heavily on the work of Alan Gross . . . who showed how Rheticus's logic of discovery was a narrative of conversion. I conclude that logics of discovery are narratives of conversion generally, and not just for science" (4). In building his case, Brown first analyzes fictional narratives such as *Moby Dick*. According to Brown, these are stories of conversion designed to draw the reader into the mores of an alien culture, in the case of *Moby Dick* the culture of whaling. Brown then moves from such novels to ethnographic narratives. He establishes a commonality between these fictions and ethnographies: in both, the understanding of an alien culture is the goal; in both, the systems of belief of the narrator and reader are altered as a consequence of a double journey, an actual journey into an alien culture and a metaphorical journey into the self. At this point in his argument, Brown shifts from ethnography to philosophy. In *Discourse on Method*, he contends, Descartes is taking two journeys, a real European journey and metaphorical journey into the self. This double journey has a radical impact on Descartes's system of belief. In the last part of his argument, Brown turns from philosophy to science. In *Narratio Prima*, he contends, Rheticus's is also a double journey: an actual journey to Copernicus and, simultaneously, a metaphorical journey to Copernicanism. The avowed purpose of Brown's essay is "to define narratives of conversion as a literary/scientific genre" (26). To the extent that Brown succeeds in his assigned task, he shows that rhetorical analysis can yield not only generalizations but also theories.

CONCLUSION

Gaonkar's criticism should be taken less as dismissal than as admonition. In future work in the rhetoric of science, the mechanical rhetorical redescription of the texts of science must be avoided, and a continuing reflexivity concerning theory must be encouraged. Intertextuality must be forthrightly addressed, the case study method must be more systematically employed as a starting-point for generalization and theorizing, and more attempts must be made to bridge the interdisciplinary gap between rhetoric of science and its history, sociology, and philosophy.[6] Moreover, these tasks must be undertaken while continuing to struggle with the primary texts and actual practices of the sciences as the central objects of study. Only these sites of investigation offer sufficient resistance to vapid speculation; equally important, in the on-going contest for intellectual status between the rhetoric and the history and philosophy of science, only these sites provide appropriate resistance to those who dismiss our discipline as parasitic, slavishly dependent on the work of others.

NOTES

1. This is not a claim against the usefulness of this terminology to rhetorical critics and theorists. The technical terminology of anatomy may serve as an analogy. It adds nothing to intellectual content to call a *knee cap* a *patella*. But no one would argue from this that therefore the technical terminology of anatomy is useless; without such a system of terms for the parts of the body, how could medicine count as a science? The parallel with rhetorical terminology, however, is not immediately apparent; if after over two millenia, no such system of rhetoric terms exists serving a purpose parallel to the terms of anatomy, it does not seem far-fetched to argue that no such system is possible.

2. My later use of Victor Turner's concept of "social drama," to which Gaonkar also alludes, is *not* consistent with an agent-centered rhetoric. It must be justified by analogy, by turning cultures into agents. Whatever one may think of such a transformation, it moves unquestionably in the direction of a rhetorical formulation flexible enough to address issues of science and science policy.

3. My coeditor thought if might be worthwhile to spell out the constraints in the case of science. In Newton's case, as an example, we have the constraints of Euclidean geometry as realized in geometrical optics in the modelling of the action of light, and the constraints of Newton's experimental design—the sunlight, the configuration of prisms, etc.—as depicted in words and in diagrams. Presumably, these constraints were conditions sufficient for replication, though in the event, replication proved a matter of continuing contention.

4. Since arguments in rhetoric of science always commit the fallacy of affirming the consequent, and since they are based on cases perpetually subject to reanalysis, they are always contestable in principle, if not in fact. This hardly surprising conclusion holds also for contemporary physics.

5. Since there is no mention of these sociologists and political scientists in their work, I can only conclude that the grasp of these rhetoricians of science of this methodology is intuitive at this point.

6. For my attempts in that direction, see the references.

REFERENCES

Brown, R. H. (1994). Logics of discovery as narratives of conversion: Rhetorics of invention in ethnography, philosophy, and astronomy. *Philosophy and Rhetoric, 27,* 1–34.

Dear, P., (Ed.). (1991). *The literary structure of scientific argument: Historical studies.* Philadelphia: University of Pennsylvania Press.

Feyerabend, P. (1975). *Against method.* London: Verso.

George, A. (1979). Case studies and theory development: The method of structured focused comparison. In P. Lauren (Ed.), *Diplomatic history: New approaches in history, theory, and policy,* 43–68. New York: Free Press.

George, A., and McKeown, T. J. (1979). Case studies and theories of organizational decision-making. In R. F. Coulam and R. A. Smith (Eds.), *Advances in information processing in organizations: A research annual,* 21–58. Greenwich, CT: JAI Press.

Gross, A. G. Defining occupational disease: An archaeology of medical knowledge. In M. Huspek and G. Radford (Eds.), *Transgressing scientific discourses: Communication and the voice of the other.* Albany: State University of New York Press.

———. (1988). Philosophy versus science: The species debate and the practice of taxonomy. In A. Fine and M. Forbes (Eds.), *PSA 1988: Proceedings of the 1988 biennial meeting of the Philosophy of Science Association,* 223–230. East Lansing: Philosophy of Science Association.

———. (1990a). Reinventing certainty: The significance of Ian Hacking's realism. In A. Fine, M. Forbes, and L. Wessels (Eds.), *PSA 1990: Proceedings of the 1990 biennial meeting of the Philosophy of Science Association,* 421–431. East Lansing: Philosophy of Science Association.

———. (1990b).*The rhetoric of science.* Cambridge: Harvard University Press.

———. (1991). Rhetoric of science without constraints. *Rhetorica, 9,* 283–299.

———. (1993). The experiment as text: The limits of literary analysis. *Rhetoric Review, 11,* 290–300.

———. (1994a). Ending it all: Closure in science and its philosophy. *Argumentation, 8,* 9–20.

———. (1994b). Is a rhetoric of science policy possible? *Social Epistemology, 8,* 273–280.

———. (1994c). The roles of rhetoric in the public understanding of science. *Public Understanding of Science, 3,* 3–23.

———. (1995). Renewing Aristotelian theory: Cold fusion as a test case. *Quarterly Journal of Speech, 81,* 48–62.

Horwich, P. (Ed.). (1993). *World changes: Thomas Kuhn and the nature of science.* Cambridge: MIT Press.

Latour, B. (1987). *Science in action.* Cambridge: Harvard University Press.

Markel, M. (1993). Induction, social constructionism, and the form of the scientific paper. *Journal of Technical Writing and Communication, 23,* 7–22.

McGuire, J. E., and Melia, T. (1989). Some cautionary strictures on the writing of the rhetoric of science. *Rhetorica, 7,* 87–100.

———. (1991). The rhetoric of the radical rhetoric of science. *Rhetorica, 9,* 301–316.

Pera, M., and Shea, W. R. (Eds.). (1991). *Persuading science: The art of scientific rhetoric.* Canton, MA: Science History Publications.

Peterfreund, S. (1994). Colonization by means of analogy, metaphor, and allusion in Darwinian discourse. *Configurations, 2,* 237–256.

Popper, K. R. (1965). Science: Conjectures and refutations. In *Conjectures and refutations: The growth of scientific knowledge,* 33–66. New York: Harper and Row.

Ragin, C. C. (1987). *The comparative method: Moving beyond qualitative and quantitative strategies.* Berkeley: University of California Press

Ragin, C. C., and Baker, H. S. (1992). *What is a case? Exploring the foundations of social inquiry.* Cambridge: Cambridge University Press .

Zagacki, K., and Keith, W. (1992). Rhetoric, topoi, and scientific revolution. *Philosophy and Rhetoric, 25,* 59–78.

CHAPTER 6

CLASSICAL RHETORIC
WITHOUT NOSTALGIA:
A RESPONSE TO GAONKAR

Carolyn R. Miller

In his well-known essay on rhetorical situations, Lloyd Bitzer took a position on the rhetoric of science: he maintained that scientific discourse is not rhetorical because it doesn't require an audience in the same way that rhetorical discourse does; that is, it doesn't need an audience capable of mediating change (1968:8). More recently, and from the same geographical direction, Edwin Black delivered an opinion on this same issue: "we do not have and cannot have rhetorical critiques of a prodigious body of discourses produced by the physical and biological sciences," because "their formulary language unites form and substance into an indissoluble whole, leaving no room for even the most timorous rhetorical interpretation" (1992:10). In spite of these warnings from two of our most eminent rhetorical critics, many have gone ahead anyway and attempted to commit rhetorical critiques of scientific discourse. Some of the most perceptive of these have rushed in precisely where Bitzer and Black told us we couldn't tread. Studies by Greg Myers and John Campbell, for example, show the essential mediating role of scientific audiences; studies by Alan Gross of inductive form, by Charles Bazerman of the APA style manual, by Michael Halloran of the topical structure of Watson and Crick's paper, all show the diremption of form and substance in scientific texts (Bazerman, 1988; Campbell, 1987; Gross, 1990; Halloran, 1984; Myers, 1989).

Now we have Dilip Gaonkar's much longer and more detailed comments about the rhetoric of science "project" (this volume). He makes, in effect, both a narrow case against it and a broad case. The narrow case consists in his examination of specific critical projects; specifically, it consists in the failings he finds in them: Gross has

156

been inconsistent, Campbell has been ideological (and inconsistent), and Prelli has been unenlightening (276). But since other critics of other forms of rhetoric have undoubtedly been, at one point or another, inconsistent, ideological, and unenlightening, we cannot attribute these failings to the rhetoric of science project itself. Many of Gaonkar's observations about the work of these three authors are illuminating, as the authors themselves have acknowledged. Good critics learn from their own critics. But what Gaonkar has given us is negative evidence: the most that we could conclude from his narrow case is that rhetoric of science hasn't been done right yet, not that it can't—or shouldn't—be done.

The broader case is the theoretical one, in which Gaonkar argues directly that rhetoric of science really can't be done under any defensible "idea of rhetoric." The question he asks is whether

> it [is] possible to translate effectively an Aristotelian vocabulary initially generated in the course of "theorizing" about certain types of practical and productive activities delimited to the . . . "public sphere" as the Greeks understood it . . . into a vocabulary for interpretive understanding of cultural practices that cover the whole of human affairs, including science. (30)

He sees this "translation" as part of a wider movement in disciplinary politics, a movement he characterizes as the return of the repressed. His real interest, as he acknowledges, is in what happens to "the idea of rhetoric" not only as it is translated but more importantly as it makes itself a tool of disciplinary politics. His argument is complex, but I want to focus on two claims: first, that the translation can't succeed because the classical vocabulary was "fashioned for directing [the] performance" of a rhetor or a student and not for interpreting cultural practices; and second, that the translation can't succeed because the classical vocabulary necessarily carries with it an untenable ideology of human agency. Then I will examine the notion of "translation" as a metaphor for transhistorical appropriation and interpretation. This examination will show, I hope, that Gaonkar has begged a central question about the nature of the exchange between contemporary rhetorical theory and criticism and the classical tradition.

The distinction between performance and interpretation is important to Gaonkar's case because it illustrates the extent of translation that is called for: "we have," he says, "reversed the priority the ancients accorded to rhetoric as a practical/productive activity over rhetoric as a critical/interpretive activity. As academics, we are more

interested in rhetoric as interpretive theory than as a cultural practice" (27). He ties the performance/interpretation distinction closely
to the distinction between practice and theory as well as to the
ancient distinction between *rhetorica utens* and *rhetorica docens*.
But none of these pairs is identical or directly parallel to the others,
and none of them creates mutually exclusive terms. Rhetorica utens,
or "rhetoric in practice," for example, occurred as performance and
led to performance imperatives for the *orator perfectus*; but performance includes an audience, and rhetorica utens can thus be understood equally from the point of view of the auditor—as a matter of
reception, a matter for interpretation. On the other side, while
rhetorica docens for the ancients was centrally concerned with
enhancing performance, it relies on and sometimes develops theory, since performance can be improved not only by practice but
also by theory-based precept. Both performance and interpretation
draw from practice and incorporate theory, although in different
ways. Interpretive criticism should be a way of keeping the practice
in theory, of generating theory *from* practice.

Aristotle's work, as Gaonkar points out, may be unique in the
classical literature in permitting the distinction between practice
and theory (27). His work rests on a delicate, and sometimes teeter-
ing, balance between theorized description of practice and prescrip-
tion based on both theory and practice. Gaonkar acknowledges that
the *Rhetoric* is a "theory of praxis" (30). This may be why it has
survived and why it is available for—and seems to invite—the translation that Gaonkar finds troubling. However, given this view of
Aristotle's thought, it seems inconsistent to claim both that our
current vocabulary is primarily Aristotelian (28) and also that it is
primarily "fashioned for directing performance" (32). Since Aristotle's vocabulary is not primarily productionist, our use of the classical vocabulary for interpretive criticism would seem to be less of a
distortion than he implies. The more clearly productionist emphasis
in Isocratean–Ciceronianism is harder for us to discuss—and is less
discussed—precisely because it failed to develop a strong (easily
translatable?) conceptual vocabulary. Gaonkar does suggest in a footnote that some recent scholarship has resuscitated this alternate
tradition that emphasizes performance; he mentions specifically the
themes and concepts of eloquence, prudence, decorum, *sensus communis*, *ingenium*, *dicta acuta* and *dicta arguta*, the ideal orator, *to
prepon*, *kairos*, judgment, "etc." (78, n. 3). This alternate, non-Aris-
totelian vocabulary may prove to be a way to enrich, complicate,
and "thicken" the conceptual resources available to rhetorical studies today. The increasing use of these performance-oriented terms

may help transform interpretive criticism, although they are resistant to easy translation. However, the Aristotelian vocabulary has proven sufficiently difficult to translate that it seems unfair to call it "thin."[1]

The second line of Gaonkar's argument that I want to call into question is that the requisite translation can't succeed because the classical vocabulary of rhetoric necessarily carries with it an "ideology of human agency" (32). He contrasts the classical vocabulary with its "view of the speaker as the seat of origin," a view in which intentions and strategic thinking govern performance and serve as touchstones for interpretation, with the needs of the "postmodern condition," a view in which a speaker becomes a "point of articulation" (32) for "structures that govern human agency: language, unconscious, and capital" (52). I can see three reasons for resisting the conclusion he urges that the classical vocabulary must therefore be inadequate. The first is simply that these two views do not have to be seen as mutually exclusive: we can understand rhetorical action as a function that is both intended and governed (and both, imperfectly), a function for which neither the humanist ideology of agency nor the postmodern ideology of ventriloquism is sufficient explanation but for which both can offer insight. Second, since this argument presupposes a great historical discontinuity between classical humanism and postmodernism, we should look more closely at the period between them. This period, loosely called "modernity," is both the time of rhetoric's lowest ebb and the time of highest faith in human agency. Enlightenment confidence in the efficacy of human reason and rationalized strategy as well as Romanticist commitment to the author as subjective origin contribute more to the ideology of agency than pre-Enlightenment humanism. The ideology of agency is more a product of modernism than of classicism.

Third, we might question whether it is possible for the classical vocabulary to promote *any* strong ideology. As Leff suggests, the classical tradition is far from univocal on many matters (Leff, 1987). It comes to us in fragments; some authors are internally inconsistent; several "strands" within it have been discerned (perhaps the best known version is George Kennedy's analysis of the tradition into technical, sophistic, and philosophical strands [Kennedy, 1980]). Although Bender and Wellbery (1990) emphasize the coherence and doctrinal "codification" in the classical tradition, and its connection with property and social position, we might just as easily emphasize the disagreements, the fissures, the possibilities for rabble-rousing and subversion, the differential interests and ideologies of Aristotelian and Isocratean rhetoric, of descriptive and normative

conceptualizations. This is not to say that the tradition can be anything we like or that translation is unnecessary. But it is to say that
translation will be troublesome and may itself be the source of any
ideology we discern in the tradition.

Both of Gaonkar's specific arguments stem from his general
skepticism about the current interest in "globalizing" or "univer-
salizing" rhetoric, an interest he finds wrapped up with the politics
of recognition. He uses unusually vivid language to characterize this
hypertropic impulse, an impulse that not only expands the scope of
rhetoric but also makes it an interpretive "metadiscourse": rhetoric
(he says) is an "incredibly engulfing discipline" (26); it is "ubiquitous" (30, 38, 77) "hegemonic" (35), "promiscuous" (37, 38, 47, 75);
its use has become "culturally fervid" (38). This is a strong version of
an argument we have heard before, about whether rhetoric can be
transformed to meet new cultural, communicative, and disciplinary
conditions, or whether it should be understood pretty much in the
terms in which the classical tradition presents itself to us. Michael
Leff calls versions of these two views "liberated rhetoric" and
"restrained rhetoric" (1987:1), and D. McCloskey refers to "Big" and
"Little" Rhetoric (McCloskey, 1994). Brian Vickers, one advocate
of restrained rhetoric, has objected to the "widening" of rhetoric to
apply to "systems of belief and practice" in the human sciences
(1988:439 n. 9). Richard McKeon, in contrast, was convinced that
the history of rhetoric should be "the history of a continuing art
undergoing revolutionary change" (1987:22). Similarly, although he
has sympathies with a classically restrained version of rhetoric,
Black accepts the notion that rhetoric is fundamentally "mutable"
(1992:185–186).

There are several points to be made about this general issue.
One is that, in spite of what Gaonkar implies, the hypertrophy of
rhetoric may not be due only or primarily to disciplinary opportunism on the part of rhetoricians. Much of the interest in rhetoric
has come from elsewhere—from literary studies (which has grown
interested again in social effects and contexts), from sociology and
anthropology (which have found reasons to want to discuss discourse
as nontransparent), and from philosophy and a number of other disciplines that have engaged in reflexive self-examination. (It is, of
course, hard for rhetoricians educated under the repression narrative not to feel finally vindicated when this happens and to react
with what is perhaps unseemly enthusiasm. To the extent that they
are opportunists, however, they are failures at the game of disciplinary politics, judging by the still precarious status of rhetoricians
within the academy.) A second point, which Leff has made, is that

the argument about restrained versus liberated rhetoric is not new: it occurs throughout the history of rhetoric (Leff, 1987). Part of the fragmentation of the tradition noted earlier is a longstanding argument, indigenous to the rhetorical tradition, about whether rhetoric is a container or a thing contained, to use Leff's metonymy. The problem, then, is not only one of translation or cultural difference but also an essential ambiguity within rhetoric itself.

A final point is that there are really two forms of the argument about Big and Little Rhetoric: one in which rhetoric itself is a relatively continuous tradition and one in which sharp discontinuities figure. The discomfort that Vickers and others (like Bitzer and Black, to some extent) exhibit about the hypertrophy of rhetoric presupposes that there can be—*and is*—a relative continuity between the original rhetoric and rhetoric today. The objection they pose is that there is something quite definite meant by the rhetorical vocabulary and that for the sake of conceptual clarity and integrity we ought to—*and can*—keep meaning the same things by it, no translation needed.[2] Gaonkar's argument rejects such nostalgia: it emphasizes the historical discontinuities that both require translation of the classical vocabulary and at the same time make the success of such translation unlikely. To simplify his claim just a bit, because the classical vocabulary embeds within it assumptions that we cannot accept, or at least assumptions that undermine the uses to which the translation is to be put, we cannot mean anything useful or relevant by it—no translation possible. To use a slightly different metaphor, Gaonkar suggests that the classical world and the postmodern world are incommensurable. This argument from discontinuity is by now the more common form, relying on the historicist understanding that what is meant by a vocabulary in a given cultural context cannot be retained in a sharply different context. Black's discussion takes this form. Another and particularly dramatic version of this argument is that of Bender and Wellbery, who, in emphasizing the primary discontinuity of modernity, claim that

little rhetoric

> the new rhetoric is no longer that of the classical tradition; . . . its fundamental categories are markedly new. Rhetoric today is neither a unified doctrine nor a coherent set of discursive practices. Rather, it is a transdisciplinary field of practice and intellectual concern, . . . [sharing] with its classical predecessor little more than a name. (1990:25)

another version of Gaonkar's argument

Others who argue for Big or historically liberated rhetoric, in contrast, accept the notion of historical and cultural difference, but

Big
rhetoric

they also believe that some kind of "translation" is possible so that
rhetoric today retains a relationship to the rhetoric of the classical
tradition. Because the metaphor of translation plays such a central
and yet unexamined role in Gaonkar's argument, I want to devote
some time to exploring its uses and implications in this and similar
contexts. The concept of translation is used figuratively to describe
what is necessary for understanding across sharp differences, whether
historical, cultural, or cognitive; this problem has come to be of central interest in a number of disciplines, and the translation metaphor
has played a prominent role especially within history of science and
ethnography.[3] The general conclusion in these fields is that translation is not impossible but that it is never perfect.

The notion of translation, according to Talal Asad, has long
been one of the conceptual tools of British social anthropology; he
quotes a foundational 1954 essay establishing this point: "The problem of describing to others how members of a remote tribe think
then begins to appear largely as one of translation, of making the
coherence primitive thought has in the languages it really lives in, as
clear as possible in our own" (Asad, 1986:142). Clifford Geertz, one of
the most eloquent explicators of cultural ethnography, also uses the
concept of translation. Ethnography, he says, is "dedicated to getting
straight how the massive fact of cultural and historical particularity
comports with the equally massive fact of cross-cultural and cross-
historical accessibility—how the deeply different can be deeply
known without becoming any less different" (1983:48). He suggests
that the "translation" by which an anthropologist achieves and
transmits such understanding involves a "continuous dialectical
tacking between the most local of local detail and the most global of
global structure in such a way as to bring them into simultaneous
view" (69). He rejects the notion that such understanding comes
primarily from any unusual empathy with those who are deeply different; rather, he says, "it comes from the ability to construe their
modes of expression, what I would call their symbol systems" (70).
Elsewhere, he emphasizes that cultures, and the people who inhabit
them, are not impervious to each other, are not isolated "semantic
monads, nearly windowless" (1986:113). Geertz is convinced that
the very effort involved in cultural translation—generalized to our
dealings with all individuals and groups who differ from us—is essential to our growth as moral beings: it forces us to "imagine difference" (120). "Life," he says, "is translation, and we are all lost in it"
(1983:44).

The translation metaphor has also become important in science studies, made so primarily by Thomas Kuhn. He puts the prob-

lem of understanding difference in both historical and cognitive-linguistic terms, using the mathematical metaphor of commensurability as well as the linguistic one of translation. Kuhn began his work in the history of science by trying to understand Aristotle's physics. In the preface to his collection of essays, *The Essential Tension* (1977), he recounts his experience as a graduate student in physics asked to prepare a set of lectures on the origins of seventeenth-century mechanics. His research led him back to Aristotle's *Physics*, where he found little knowledge that could have served as a foundation for what Galileo and Newton meant by mechanics. Kuhn reports that he was puzzled by Aristotle's obtuseness about motion: "When dealing with subjects other than physics, Aristotle had been an acute and naturalistic observer. . . . How could his characteristic talents have failed him so when applied to motion? How could he have said about it so many apparently absurd things? And, above all, why had his views been taken so seriously for so long a time by so many of his successors?" (xi). Eventually and "all at once," Kuhn says, those questions were answered when he saw that what Aristotle meant by motion was quite different from what had been meant since the seventeenth century, and when he read the Aristotelian texts with that new understanding, the "perplexities suddenly vanished" (xi). In gaining "a new way to read a set of texts" (xii), Kuhn had discovered his first paradigm shift, his first understanding of "a global sort of change in the way men viewed nature and applied language to it" (xiii).

Different views of nature, Kuhn says, like natural languages, are "incommensurable," but this does not make them mutually untranslatable or incomparable. The comparison of different views can never be done from a neutral or mutually encompassing view point, just as a translation must always be from one particular language into another: "Proponents of different theories . . . speak different languages—languages expressing different cognitive commitments, suitable for different worlds. Their abilities to grasp each other's viewpoints are therefore inevitably limited by the imperfections of the processes of translation" (1977:xxii–xxiii). To his critics who complained that his statements on the incommensurability of worldviews seemed to preclude rational theory choice by isolating scientists within paradigms, Kuhn observes that we can and do in fact learn other languages (and other worldviews) but that even adept bilinguals can find translation difficult: "Translation . . . always involves compromises which alter communication" (1970:268). He suggests that those involved in the kinds of "communication breakdowns" that theory-choice presents can learn to

talk to each other "if they have sufficient will, patience, and tolerance of threatening ambiguity" (277). The process he describes
sounds much like Geertz's dialectical tacking.

Kuhn's more recent discussion of this issue, however, reduces
the notion of translation to lexical matching between languages (or
worldviews); in this view, translation can occur only between languages that are commensurable, in other words, that share large lexical structures. When this condition does not pertain, "where translation is not feasible, the very different processes of interpretation
and language acquisition are required" (1982:683). Interpretation and
language acquisition are the processes that ethnographers and historians engage in when they encounter alien cultures and theories.
Unlike the translator, who knows two languages, the interpreter (or
child learning a language) confronts "unintelligible" material (672).
Through a process of trial and error, inquiry and hypothesis, the
interpreter acquires, learns to think with and to speak, the alien language. Translation back into a native language may, or may not,
ensue (673). In suddenly understanding Aristotelian motion, Kuhn
did not have to translate it into Newtonian mechanics: rather, in
his account, he understood it on its own terms and was able to interpret it. What his account leaves mysterious is how this understanding occurs and how it may be facilitated or inhibited by the native
language or controlling worldview of the inquirer.

In his study of translation, *After Babel*, George Steiner (1992)
takes a much different position. He rejects the restricted philosophical sense of translation that Kuhn ultimately adopts, insisting that
interpretation is necessarily part of translation. He emphasizes that
all "human communication equals translation," with the same general processes involved in historical interpretation as in contempo-
raneous cross-language translation (49). He rejects as extremes both
the argument that no translation is really possible because any linguistic expression is a complete monad and the assumption that an
underlying universality of language guarantees the eventual perfection of translation. To penetrate the difference embodied in any linguistic expression, what is needed is a hermeneutic effort involving
knowledge, familiarity, and "re-creative intuition"; something will
be lost from the original, something may be gained in the new
expression; some translations work, and some fail (29).

In all three of these accounts, what emerges as essential to
translation, even replacing it as the central concept, is interpretation:
the metaphoric power of translation ultimately fails to explain the
real task in understanding difference. Geertz acknowledges that his
account of ethnographic work is more like interpretation than trans-

lation, seeing in the "dialectical tacking" motion between local and global the "familiar trajectory" of the hermeneutic circle (1983:69). Kuhn recognizes that interpretation (which he does not explain carefully) is much more important than translation to the historian of science and to scientists involved in paradigm debates. And Steiner assimilates technical accounts of translation to a wider and more general "hermeneutic motion." He characterizes this motion as having four moments: an initial investment of trust in the significance of the alien text, an aggressive appropriation or penetration, an incorporative embodiment or "bringing back" to the target language, and a restitution or contribution of meaning to the original language or text through exchange (312–319). These four moments give a structure to the hermeneutic circle that keeps it from being vicious, but it remains circular in that the translator can overcome difference only by relying on what is initially familiar. It is the dialectical tacking—between part and whole, new and familiar, trust and aggression, taking and giving—that generates incremental understanding.

The dialectical view of understanding-through-interpretation suggests another metaphor for our struggles with difference—dialogue, rather than translation. And indeed dialogue is a model frequently used by historians and historiographers. Stephen Greenblatt, for example, the Renaissance literary critic who is probably most responsible for the movement known as the "new historicism," says he "began with a desire to speak with the dead" or at least to "re-create a conversation with them" (1988:1). Dominick LaCapra, the intellectual historian, advocates a dialogic history, in contrast to objectivist or documentary history: the latter treats its sources as locations of factual reference that simply convey information; the former treats its sources as texts with "voices" that raise questions of "commitment, interpretation, and imagination" (1983:30). This dialogic process, he says, requires attention and patience, an openness and sensitivity to the "network of resistances" in the text, which may transform the very questions one had posed about the past.

Richard Rorty has described a similar distinction in the historiography of philosophy, using *conversation* as a central term. Historians typically attempt what he calls "historical reconstruction," which attempts to recapture the past on its own terms, understanding ideas and events as they would have been understood by those living at the time. Philosophers, in contrast, typically engage in rational reconstruction, which attempts to understand the past in terms of the present, to treat "dead philosophers . . . as contemporaries, as colleagues with whom [we] can exchange views."[4] He puts the distinction as a dilemma: "either we anachronistically impose enough of our problems and vocabulary on the dead to make them conversational partners, or we confine our interpretive activity to making their falsehoods look less silly by placing them in the context of the benighted times in which they were written" (1984:49). But it's only an apparent dilemma, he says, because both kinds of history are necessary.[5]

If we take the model of dialogue (or conversation) seriously, the task of historical work becomes even more complex, because dialogue requires relations between interlocutors, and such relations inevitably involve power. Rorty says, for example, that we "want to imagine conversations between ourselves . . . and the mighty dead" because such conversations assure us of our own superiority, due to the progress that our predecessors would have to acknowledge (51). LaCapra notes that "the act of interpretation has political dimensions" (63); the temptation to master and control the text can lead to forms of "subjectivist aggression" such as "creative misreading" or "active rewriting" (64). And Asad points out that even the cultural translations of ethnographers are "inevitably enmeshed in conditions of power—professional, national, international" (163). Such translations carry the authority of scientific, Western economies and presume the authority to "uncover the implicit meanings of subordinate societies" (163). It is naive, then, to understand either translation or dialogue as a neutral or equalizing model. The balance between appropriation and restitution cannot be taken for granted—and can never really be balanced.

Gaonkar is thus right to raise the question he does about the feasibility and fruitfulness of translating an ancient performative vocabulary into a critical lexicon for contemporary interpretive purposes. But he fails (inevitably) to alert us to the implications of his particular way of asking the question. He idealizes translation not only by implying that it should be an unproblematic process of lexical matching (the position Kuhn ultimately takes) but also by presupposing that it constitutes a helpful model for describing what is involved in the globalizing of rhetoric. Rather than being a second-hand translated lexicon for interpretation, globalized rhetorical hermeneutics is doubly hermeneutic: it is a conceptual vocabulary for interpretation which has itself been created by the process of interpretation. The rhetorical vocabulary has been appropriated and transformed from a tradition that is continually being appropriated and transformed. It thus presents an elusive target for critique.

In this rejoinder, I have not attempted any wholesale critique of Gaonkar's complex and provoking essay; I have only been able to tweak one thread in it. This thread, the thread of "translation," passes through much of his argument but does not by any means stitch together the entire fabric. Globalizers and rhetoricians of science alike would do well to ruminate on his admonitions about the relationship between their theories and practices. But we should also be aware that Gaonkar's critique may have overshot its mark. Just as it assumes that something other than interpretation, namely translation, is the method of globalizers, it implies that something other than interpretation, namely knowledge, is the aim of the rhetoric of science project. In claiming that it hasn't succeeded and implying that it can't, or shouldn't, succeed, Gaonkar both attributes too much to and expects too much from the rhetoric of science: falsifiable knowledge claims and an omnipotent hermeneutic metadiscourse. In this, he implicitly holds rhetoric of science to the disciplinary standards of science, and some of his respondents have been quick to concede this point more explicitly.[6]

But what *are* the appropriate disciplinary standards? What *would* success in rhetoric of science—or in any other interpretive enterprise—look like? Interpretation generates not knowledge but understanding. Understanding is not falsifiable or guaranteed by method, but rather is contestable and, let us say it, promiscuous, in that it draws upon whatever conceptual tools are available and seem promising. Interpretation aims not at replicable and predictive factual statements but at the construction (or transformation) of perspectives from which statements are made. It is not disabled by supposed contradiction, such as that between globalization and situatedness but finds in such conflicts productive ambiguity. Indeed, as Gaonkar recognizes, the efforts of much recent science criticism (by rhetorical and other means) have helped us to see science itself as an interpretive enterprise rather than a knowledge-producing one. Given the contributions that rhetorical studies have made to this understanding of science, has the rhetoric of science project "stalled," as he claims (41)? Perhaps the better question is whether it is producing as much understanding about rhetoric as it is about science.

NOTES

1. See, for example, Green's discussion of the various interpretations of "antistrophos" (Green, 1990), Leff's discussion of the confusion about "topos" (Leff, 1983), Grimaldi's commentary on Book I (Grimaldi, 1980), and Kennedy's annotations to the text in his recent translation (Aristotle, 1991).

2. McKeon ridiculed such rhetorical purists as interested only in "the monotonous enumeration of doctrines, or preferably sentences, repeated from Cicero or commentators on Cicero" (1987:120).

3. In parts 1 and 2 of *Beyond Objectivism and Relativism*, Richard Bernstein (1983) presents a very useful discussion of this issue, its treatment by different scholars, and its potential for providing a hermeneutical resolution to the Cartesian Anxiety.

4. Two recent studies of Progatoras position themselves in exactly this way, using Rorty's model. Schiappa's work is avowedly a historical reconstruction, and Donovan's is rational (Donovan, 1993; Schiappa, 1991).

5. Like most historians, historians of rhetoric have worried over how to access and interpret the past. Vitanza (1987) has suggested a taxonomy of approaches to history, including traditional, revisionist, and sub/versive historiography; a full exploration of these categories and their relation to the positions on translation and dialogue that I have summarized is beyond the scope of this essay, fortunately. Some of the revisionist work in rhetorical history is like the American emphasis in the literary new historicism—it is primarily interested in recovering from the past what had been omitted, suppressed, and forgotten, and in understanding more fully the relationships between whatever texts are of interest and their discursive and nondiscursive contexts (for example, most of the recent work on the Sophists). Other work is more like the British new historicism—it is interested in "the uses to which the *present* has put its versions of the past" (Montrose, 1986:7).

6. Kaufer, for example, seeks to make the art of rhetoric "fully systematized"—in effect, a platonized "science of design" (this volume). Gross seeks "robust, contestable generalizations" whose "aim is general knowledge" (this volume; 151). Gross has reacted very pointedly to Gaonkar's essay, not only in his response but elsewhere. He has, in effect, disavowed his earlier statement that "science is not the privileged route to certain knowledge but . . . another intellectual interprise . . . beside, but not above, philosophy, literary criticism, history, and rhetoric itself" (1990:3). He has replaced this with the conviction that rhetoric must compete with science by producing knowledge with generalizable social-scientific methods. His current position takes a curious form in a recent essay about the public understanding of science; in this essay he claims that "public understanding has genuine . . . epistemic status, different in kind, but not in significance from the epistemological status conferred by the methods of science"; but he also claims that in order to establish the epistemic status of such understanding, social-scientific case study methods are necessary to create "legitimate social and political knowledge" (1994:19). Academic understanding must, it seems, be authorized by scientific method; public understanding has an epistemic authority that is differently grounded and to which rhetorical critics apparently may have no recourse.

REFERENCES

Aristotle. (1991). *On rhetoric: A theory of civic discourse.* G. A. Kennedy (Trans.). New York: Oxford University Press.

Asad, T. (1986). The concept of cultural translation in British social anthropology. In J. Clifford and G. E. Marcus (Eds.), *Writing culture: The poetics and politics of ethnography,* 141–164. Berkeley: University of California Press.

Bazerman, C. (1988). *Shaping written knowledge: The genre and activity of the experimental article in science.* Madison: University of Wisconsin Press.

Bender, J., and Wellbery, D. E. (1990). Rhetoricality: On the modernist return of rhetoric. In J. Bender and D. E. Wellbery (Eds.), *The ends of rhetoric: History, theory, practice,* 3–39. Stanford: Stanford University Press.

Bernstein, R. J. (1983). *Beyond objectivism and relativism: Science, hermeneutics, and praxis.* Philadelphia: University of Pennsylvania Press.

Bitzer, L. F. (1968). The rhetorical situation. *Philosophy and Rhetoric, 1,* 1–14.

Black, E. (1992). *Rhetorical questions: Studies of public discourse.* Chicago: University of Chicago Press.

Campbell, J. A. (1987). Charles Darwin: Rhetorician of science. In J. Nelson, A. Megill, and D. McCloskey (Eds.), *The rhetoric of the human sciences: Language and argument in scholarship and public affairs,* 69–86. Madison: University of Wisconsin Press.

Donovan, B. R. (1993). The project of Protagoras. *Rhetoric Society Quarterly, 23,* 35–47.

Gaonkar, D. P. (1993). The idea of rhetoric in the rhetoric of science. *Southern Communication Journal, 58,* 258–295.

Geertz, C. (1983). *Local knowledge: Further essays in interpretive anthropology.* New York: Basic Books.

———. (1986). The uses of diversity. *Michigan Quarterly Review, 25,* 105–123.

Green, L. D. (1990). Aristotelian rhetoric, dialectic, and the traditions of antistrophos. *Rhetorica, 8*(1), 5–27.

Greenblatt, S. (1988). *Shakespearean negotiations.* Berkeley: University of California Press.

Grimaldi, W. M. A., S. J. (1980). *Aristotle, Rhetoric I: A commentary*. New York: Fordham University Press.

Gross, A. G. (1990). *The rhetoric of science*. Cambridge: Harvard University Press.

————. (1993). What if we're not producing knowledge? Critical reflections on the rhetorical criticism of science. *Southern Communication Journal, 58*(4), 301–305.

————. (1994). The roles of rhetoric in the public understanding of science. *Public Understanding of Science, 3*(1), 3–23.

Halloran, S. M. (1984). The birth of molecular biology: An essay in the rhetorical criticism of scientific discourse. *Rhetoric Review, 3*(1), 70–83.

Kennedy, G. A. (1980). *Classical rhetoric and its christian and secular tradition from ancient to modern times*. Chapel Hill: University of North Carolina Press.

Kuhn, T. S. (1970). Reflections on my critics. In I. Lakatos and A. Musgrave (Eds.), *Criticism and the growth of knowledge*, 231–78. Cambridge: Cambridge University Press.

————. (1977). *The essential tension: Selected studies in scientific tradition and change*. Chicago: University of Chicago Press.

————. (1982). *Commensurability, comparability, communicability*. Paper presented at the Biennial Meeting of the Philosophy of Science Association, East Lansing, MI.

LaCapra, D. (1983). Rethinking intellectual history and reading texts. In *Rethinking intellectual history: Texts, contexts, language*, 12–71. Ithaca: Cornell University Press.

Leff, M. C. (1983). The topics of argumentative invention in Latin rhetorical theory from Cicero to Boethius. *Rhetorica, 1*(1), 23–44.

————. (1987). The habitation of rhetoric. In Joseph W. Wenzel (Ed.), *Argument and critical practices*, 1–8. Annadale, VA: SCA Publications.

McCloskey, D. N. (1994). *Knowledge and persuasion in economics*. Cambridge: Cambridge University Press.

McKeon, R. (1987). *Rhetoric: Essays in invention and discovery*. Woodbridge, CT: Ox Bow Press.

Montrose, L. (1986). Renaissance literary studies and the subject of history. *English Literary Renaissance, 16*, 5–12.

Myers, G. (1989). *Writing biology: Texts in the social construction of scientific knowledge*. Madison: University of Wisconsin Press.

Rorty, R. (1984). The historiography of philosophy: Four genres. In R. Rorty, J. B. Schneewind, and Q. Skinner (Eds.), *Philosophy in history: Essays on the historiography of philosophy*, 49–75. Cambridge: Cambridge University Press.

Schiappa, E. (1991). *Protagoras and logos: A study in Greek philosophy and rhetoric*. Columbia: University of South Carolina Press.

Steiner, G. (1992). *After Babel: Aspects of language and translation*. 2nd ed. Oxford: Oxford University Press.

Vickers, B. (1988). *In defense of rhetoric*. Oxford: Clarendon Press.

Vitanza, V. J. (1987). "Notes" towards historiographies of rhetorics; or the rhetorics of the histories of rhetorics: Traditional, revisionary, and sub/versive. *Pre/Text, 8*(1–2), 63–125.

CHAPTER 7

RHETORIC'S LOT

Charles Arthur Willard

INTRODUCTION

When rustic rites become cosmopolitan fashions, the artifice is often more interesting than the original folkway. Self-flagellation, for instance, is an unworthiness ritual in dirt road villages but a refined art form in the social sciences. The sight of a lush research tradition prompts the pious to fall to their knees, bowing toward Vienna or a passing physicist, intoning "we're not worthy, we're not worthy." Organizational theorists are the cheeriest of these dour methodists. As there are roughly as many kinds of organizations as there are species in the phylum mollusk, a general theory of organization is roughly as informative as the label "mollusk." But the fact that no one can see the coherence of the field doesn't mean it isn't there, Karl Weick argues (1987:118). Working in the field requires a faith "that collective omniscience is significant and growing."

Anthropologists have a more original sin: Clifford Geertz is famous for underscoring the impressionistic, dialogical nature of anthropological observations, the uncertainty and elusiveness of the field's founding concept, and for the heresy of doubting the importance of culture in a cosmopolitan world. Nancy Scheper-Hughes (1995), in a respectful but disapproving review of Geertz's memoirs argues that, though "culture itself might not be so terribly important" (22), Geertz's avuncular disengagement in "a Victorian gentleman's pastime" is not at all amusing: "Among younger anthropologists today—especially those working in situations of political emergency, genocide, and war—are those who choose to engage as active witnesses, who record and react to grisly events" (23). If this makes anthropology seem like journalism, it also suggests that another "would-be science" has bitten the dust. Once hard, it is now soft; once factual, it is now interpretive; once universal, it is now a catalogue of local conditions.

And so, apparently, is sociology. Or at least no sociologist goes unbeaten in a symposium in *Social Epistemology* about Stephen and Jonathan Turner's *The Impossible Science*. The title of this book fairly captures its contents; and from the essays it provokes, one gathers that sociology lost its golden age of disciplinary coherence to the wiles of funding agencies, which saw disciplinarity as an impediment to solving social problems. The result was fragmentation, a proliferation of subspecialties, and a diaspora, a dispersion of sociological ideas to other disciplines. Sociology thus has no organizing identity. It is not one science but many, each "too small to sustain itself as a viable entity" (Bulmer, 1994:7). The sciences of sociology are getting funding and doing good work, so apparently they are "too small to sustain" themselves because they are local pictures that make no pretense of being whole pictures. Sociology is thus everywhere; it is marked profoundly by local characteristics, and no one expects the situation to change anytime soon.

Nor for many of the same reasons does Dilip Gaonkar expect rhetoric to become convincing and unifying. It is "thin" sui generis, by nature "parasitic," with "no subject matter of its own." Its universality is a diaspora, not a triumph, for it can be a rich interpretive framework only as welfare hermeneutics, a subculture of interfield dependency caught in a cycle of intellectual poverty.

There is perhaps solace in knowing that rhetoric is not alone in its "thinness," that it shares the plight of other *-ists* and *-ologies*. Persuasion is variously practiced, so rhetoric's identity should be no easier to negotiate any of the others. And there are grounds for optimism in the answers Gaonkar has provoked. The essays in this book exemplify, I submit, the best sort of skeptical moment, one from which the research tradition emerges the better for the experience.

Gaonkar and his fellow critics embody a premier disciplinary virtue, a public spiritedness, a sense of curatorship, a belief that the health of one's discipline matters. A discipline's beliefs should be, as T. S. Eliot says, "ideas severely looked-after," for a skepticism about grand claims is often warranted, and so is the hope to say clear and determinate things about as many things as possible.

With this collective virtue, however, comes a certain collective guilt. For in asking whether a field's practices are living up to its ideals, it matters very much how the question is posed. Great expectations make for extravagant disappointment, and impossibly high ideals virtually ensure that a "crisis" of something or other will be found (Willard, 1996). The horrors of "thinness" and "impoverishment," then, turn on the charm of such ideals as "thick" universality and "rich" theory. Bulmer (1994) thus wants "a convincing and unifying general theoretical sociology," one that encompasses all local instantiations so transparently that they cannot be construed otherwise, and so inclusively that each local instantiation will be connected with and reverberate to every strand of the mother theory.

This is real Quinian stuff, holism in the first degree, and though it is perhaps feasible in small conceptual ecologies, it is arguably a quixotic goal in larger ones. The genres have blurred, as Geertz says, for sound reasons. Humans and their practices vary, like mollusks and theirs, thanks to "splendid local adaptations," as Stephen Jay Gould says. To adapt to all this particularity, big fields have increasingly subdivided into specialties; and hybrid fields whose subject matters cross professional boundaries (cytology, immunopharmacology, public health) have proliferated to the point that they are almost too numerous to catalogue. Their sheer numbers suggest the futility of grand theory: The myriad structures, practices, and events of the world may never be coherently interpretable in a holistic and detailed way. And if this proliferation stems from adaptation to genuine differences, it suggests that social phenomena of any complexity can't be reduced exclusively to psychology, message attributes, or what-have-you. Explanations that emphasize any one thing at the expense of others are likely to be distortions. The diffusion of the old genres and their increasing specialization are thus a kind of progress, against which the concern for thickness and richness seems increasingly nostalgic.

In assessing the usefulness of skeptical moments, the trick is to know by how much a field's reach should exceed its grasp. Only in reaching does a field extend its grasp, so the hope to find coherent generalizations amid the clutter of specialist detail is indispensable. But as the case of theoretical thickness suggests, the deeper trick is to know the difference between wild-eyed ideals and conceivably achievable standards.

To assess Gaonkar's criticisms of rhetoric, then, I will begin with his standards, for each criticism he levels at rhetoric invokes explicitly or implicitly some ideal against which rhetoric seems to fall short. Later, in the second half of this essay, I will focus on *what* is being held up to judgment, for Gaonkar's vision of rhetoric is a surprisingly Aristotelian one; and the result, I will contend, is a rigged language game, a way of posing the problem of rhetoric's identity so that it can't be solved.

What Does Gaonkar Want?

"The politics of recognition" is, I imagine, a deliberately enigmatic phrase. It has the vagueness one associates with authors who have thought at length about things best left unsaid. What Gaonkar does say is that rhetoric "has never been able to determine its own fortune" (1990:360). Its prospects—feast or famine—have depended on outside events, and its identity has not, till lately, thrived. So rhetoric needs a clear and distinct identity.

Clear and Distinct for Whom?

The nature of this ideal, however, has a lack of clarity analogous to a brand recognition problem for which the advertiser doesn't specify the population to be sampled. The lack of clarity arises from the claim that "the equation between rhetoric and persuasion does not enjoy the sort of cultural currency that would give rhetoric a distinct identity" (29). "Cultural currency" means academic currency, one guesses, but other comments suggest a more populist vision: "Our allegedly rhetorical culture lacks resources for spontaneously recognizing what is or is not rhetoric." Rhetoric "lacks a tradition that would enable an average but literate person to unproblematically identify the paradigm cases of rhetoric as rhetoric" (34).

To the extent that these phrases evoke the "educated public," it is worth noticing that claims to the contrary have been made: "The residue of more than two millennia of association with instrumental considerations remains in common usage and lay perception, where 'rhetoric' is almost always synonymous with the study of persuasion" (Hauser and Whalen, 1995:1). This claim is as well-proved as Gaonkar's, which is to say there isn't a whiff of proof anywhere in its vicinity. But it is clearer, at least, about what would have to be measured to assess it: common usage and lay perception.

These competing assertions could be debated, I suppose, but is it worth the trouble? *Is* an idea impoverished if it lacks cultural currency? One never hears this sort of claim about the sciences, yet if the scientific literacy movement is to be believed, most scientific concepts lack cultural currency, including the most basic and least esoteric. Most college graduates can't answer rudimentary questions about science (Hazen and Trefil, 1991). We know that Einstein, from 1909 on, resisted the popularization of relativity because he thought that it referred to an order of reality unavailable to common sense; and it is a trade-book bromide that the world of quarks and leptons is profoundly counterintuitive to outsiders.

We might also debate whether chaos theory plays better in Peoria than the labor theory of value. But *is* an idea vindicated if it has cultural currency? Ignoring the 90,000,000 Americans who are barely literate, focusing solely on the politically engaged who can express opinions, or at least nod when pollsters ask them questions, one can mount a substantial case that comprehension by the laity is the litmus test of bad ideas: On the evidence of polls, creationism would be taught in the schools were the matter put to a plebescite. A study of *McLean v. Arkansas* (Taylor and Condit, 1988) puts the blame partly on the public ineptness of scientists, but chiefly on the *leveling* practices of journalists. *Leveling* refers not to the mob common denominator the federalists feared but to a side effect of the journalistic ethic of objectivity and fairness: By virtue of being given equal time, crackpots and experts are put on an epistemic par.

Journalism is perhaps the crux of the matter. Journalists are presumably "average but literate" people, and their fairness ethic is a public commitment to the idea that all voices should be heard. But here one is reminded less of Habermas than of H. L. Mencken, who doubted, emphatically, that most voices are worth hearing. Journalists fell on Mencken's food chain somewhere just above Baptists and the "simian gabble of the crossroads," but well below the "airy heights" at which literature professors practice philosophy without a license. They were an anti-intellectual intelligentsia, a rabble of failed sophomores, committed to a belief in "common sense" (meaning that when one doesn't understand an idea, the fault lies in the idea, not oneself), and champions of "general knowledge," a medium of thought within which all sights and sounds are reduced to a dull gray and low hum.

Darwinism, creationism—the matter is "controversial" on the journalistic plane. And on that plane rhetoric is not entirely invisible: American journalists consistently use the term as if it is the antonym of *reality*—as if its most invidious meanings (*bombast, verbosity, bravado*) are its only meanings. They do the same, by the way, to *argument*—using it largely to mean *quarrel* or *altercation*. Both conventions are apparently taken for granted (neither *rhetoric* nor *argument* are among the problematic terms arbitrated by the Associated Press *Stylebook*). But leaving aside the question of whether cold fusion or hermeneutics (or any idea that is not concrete, self-evident, and wrapped in authoritative assurances) would fare any better, the problem seems to be that a critical tradition with populist pretensions has not effectively competed for public attention.

Perhaps rhetorical criticism has been straitjacketed by its Aristotelianism, desperately seeking Pericles in the Age of Geraldo. But it has also been "thinned out" by infanticidal critiques. Movement studies, for instance, "went from hundreds of published studies in the 1970s to few or none in the late 1980s, ironically at a time when new social movements were springing to life." While metadiscussions of methodology may illuminate areas for development and needs for correction, "they can also produce a chilling effect on research so that new exploration atrophies and lines of discussion are closed, not by evidence gathered in the field but by speculative disapprovals from well rehearsed theoretical positions" (Goodnight, 1995).

In any case, if on no other grounds than that creationism *does* have cultural currency, I prefer to think that legitimacy *ad populum* is not the argument Gaonkar has in mind. The politics of recognition is more an academic matter. And it is on this trickier terrain that two very dubious ideals take center stage.

Falsifiability and Disciplinary Uniqueness

Is it rhetoric's dismal kismet to fade into hermeneutics whenever it becomes insightful or participates in the creation of special knowledge? Or is it odd in this day and age that we are asking this question, and given the blurring of the genres would the answer much matter? One could dismiss the question as another "point of articulation" in the "impulse to universalize [hermeneutics]," saying of hermeneutics what Gaonkar says of rhetoric: It is "culturally fervid," "hegemonic." It has extended the diremption of the author from *Grundelagen der Geometrie* to *TV Guide*, and the ambit of textuality to almost everything. But what is striking is the degree to which Gaonkar's prognosis replicates Aristotle's diagnosis. If one starkly contrasts performance and interpretation, instrumental action and architectonic thought, one will fully expect a "fade to substance" wherein rhetoric bleaches into a "genuine" form of knowledge.

Gaonkar is less inclined to be cavalier about the sources of the field's methods and the blurry fusion of rhetoric and hermeneutics. In academic politics, identity is everything, and blurry subject matters are easy prey. But this says more about academic politics than subject matters. Given the proliferation of hybrid fields, disciplinary uniqueness is a very dubious idea. It is, I submit, exclusively a creature of turf battles, budget wars, and academic pogroms. It has little to do with the daily work of academics, and as an intellectual matter has an unnatural fit with the world of ideas.

One clue to how other-worldly disciplinary politics can be comes early in Gaonkar's argument:

> In disciplinary politics, the more refined and specific the lan-
> guage of criticism becomes . . . the greater attention it gets and
> by the same token the more vulnerable it is to falsification. In
> its current form rhetoric as a language of criticism is so thin
> and abstract that it is virtually invulnerable to falsification, and
> for that very reason commands little sustained attention. (33)

There is a category mistake here. *Claims* might be falsifiable,
Gaonkar says as much in a footnote, but a "critical vocabulary," a set
of concepts and categories, is precisely the sort of thing Popper held
to be unfalsifiable. His aim, remember, was to denounce the "his-
toricisms" (Platonism, Marxism, etc.) as "mere" vocabularies. The
more Popperian expectation, one would think, is that critical vocabularies are best judged by whether they give rise to useful descriptions.

And *is* falsifiability the litmus test of academic attention and
respect? Conceivably, *falsifiability* means "fundability," the strategic planner's shorthand for reasons to under-fund the humanities.
That meaning would square with Popper's intentions. Had *he* admin-
istered the NSF, the likes of Platonists, Marxists, and Hegelians
would have been left to the tender mercies of state legislators. But
"language, unconscious, and capital," Gaonkar's taken-for-granted
realities, virtually ooze from the walls of humanities buildings; and
where concrete deterministic claims are falsifiable, as I will shortly
show, their more phlogiston-like manifestations are arguably as
unfalsifiable as ideas can be.

But the inexplicable appearance of Popper's least convincing
idea, with no defenses entered on its behalf, suggests that academic
politics occurs on another plane of discourse entirely, one in which
ordinary rules of reason and conduct are suspended or altered. For it
is only at an altitude elevated enough, or sunk low enough, that the
proliferation of hybrids is invisible and that disciplinary uniqueness
acquires respectability.

Universities are unique organizations: Durkheim's brain work-
ers do their work, pausing occasionally for a form of democracy reminiscent of the Kerensky government just before Lenin had everyone
shot; and the whole thing is encased in a Tayloresque bureaucracy
whose guiding telos has only tangential relevance to the first two
domains, and is often at odds with them. The result is a bizarre
mélange of intellectual brilliance, shameless demagoguery, and (in
the words of one dean) "administration by neat idea." This would be
amusing were it not also a zero-sum game. When FTEs are at stake,
one uses "all that is there to use." The expression is Burke's but the

sentiment is Hobbes's. One fights, and fights back, with whatever bludgeons are handy; and in roughly this spirit, we often find disciplinary uniqueness defended (or used) much as Uzis are defended (or used) as sporting weapons. Once stature puffs up and chastity bristles, palpably weak arguments acquire the glow of enduring truths. In at least the one case for which I claim the status of a combat veteran, disciplinary uniqueness was both entirely disingenuous—its advocates privately disavowed it—and could have been silenced had we been able to point to some respectable *bodies of work*. Such desiderata as whether *this* practice fits *that* theory would scarcely have mattered.

It seems oddly nonrhetorical to think about uniqueness as if it is something more than flim-flam, and thereby take on a burden of proof no one else would bother with. Anthropologists face the same problem: Anthropology is everywhere, and means so many things that some have argued that it means nothing. But instead of playing a loaded language game, Geertz has the good sense to see that the more unique anthropology makes itself, the more intellectually untenable it would be. The same can be said of rhetoric, which has spread to niches here and there—often in hybrid border fields. For this cosmopolitanism suggests not an idea so thin as to be meaningless, but an idea whose time has not only come but will keep on coming. To appreciate how and why this is so, I need to raise what will possibly be a discordant note among the essayists in this volume. One gathers from Gaonkar and others that pointing out that discourses *are* rhetorical is a mundane accomplishment, and that once done it stays done. I respectfully disagree.

The Cunning of Realism

Debunking claims to epistemic authority is, I submit, an indispensable skepticism in a democracy. It very much matters how knowledge claims are taken in the fuss and hustle of political life, whether they are trusted blindly, or shaped and formed by political agendas, or interrogated knowledgeably. Any number of things pass as self-evident truths, and all sorts of things pass as scientific facts, so the nuts and bolts of the appearances of factuality are arguably vital public knowledge. The architecture of knowledge claims is a complex issue, certainly, that in all likelihood will demand the theories and methods of many fields. But about discourses that deny or camouflage their own rhetorical character, one would think that people blessed with rhetorical sensibilities would have much to say, and much the world needs to hear.

The rhetoric of science certainly does. John Campbell's work, for instance, speaks directly to the standoff in Gaonkar between an "ideology of human agency" and "the postmodern condition." Ignoring the partiality of those labels (the false consciousness of the former being exposed by the manifest truth of the latter) and the question of whether wild-eyed determinisms are as false a consciousness as overly heroic claims about agency, notice that, as Gaonkar makes his case, an insinuation frosted with early-Foucauldian language passes as an argument. Not a *defense* of Foucault, mind you, or an exegesis of Foucault's later attempts to confront the problem of agency. It is simply a taken-for-granted reality: The agency model "marginalizes structures that govern human agency: language, unconscious, and capital" (52). Gaonkar doesn't make a case for believing in these "realities," so one can only speculate about how deterministic he means to be. He *sounds* like Mary Douglas (1986), for whom the "social control of cognition" seizes and eclipses the individual. Like a conquering pure intelligence in science fiction, and like Foucault's discourse formations, Douglas's institutions have motives of their own, and are thus analogous to rides in an amusement park: like them or not, once on them, one finishes the ride. Perhaps this is what Gaonkar means by "the sheer materiality of science" (70).

This catchphrase is widely used to insinuate a baseline reality without arguing the point. Thus West (1989:3–4), arguing that everything under the sun is inextricably linked to structures of domination and subordination, claims that a preoccupation of humanists "with the materiality of language—such as the ways in which styles of rationality and science or identities and subjectivities are socially constructed and historically constituted—has focused cultural investigations on the production, distribution, and circulations of forms of power, be they rhetorical, economic, or military powers." And that is the sum total of the argument: Humanists have this preoccupation, therefore it is valid.

Gaonkar explains the expression by referring to "SSK" (the sociology of scientific knowledge). But though SSK certainly explores institutional constraints and includes determinists in its ranks, the likes of Michael Mulkay and Harry Collins (to name just two) would resist the inference that their work undermines every view of agency. Both rest important chunks of the materiality of science, to use the expression differently, on what argument scholars would call "arguing from evidence." But arguing from evidence is not what Gaonkar is doing, so one can only speculate about how the implied reality behind his assertion might be redeemed. Language might be the determinist's strong suit, but I assume I needn't argue from scratch that proving linguistic determinism is a difficult undertaking—scarcely a completed one, and scarcely a nonempirical one: The proliferation of new argots is something of an obstacle; and so is the ability of Barbara O'Keefe's "rhetoricals" to strategically select conventions and modes of expression. The unconscious is a more religious matter: One either believes or doesn't; though certainly a powerful deterministic argument can be mounted against unreflective thought and its parallel susceptibility to peripheral route persuasion. And finally, in reading Frederick Jameson, for instance, one could substitute "phlogiston" for "capital" without harming the arguments. Like rhetoric, apparently, capital is everywhere. But where rhetoric is "thinned" by its dispersion, capital is presumably "thickened" into a holistic superintelligence that affects everything.

But though Gaonkar can be accused of merely witnessing for another literature, as things stand in this debate his claim is not only falsifiable but has been falsified. Put it this way: Did Darwin do what Campbell says he did? Campbell stands accused of marginalizing determinism's triumvirate, but the only evidence on the floor is Campbell's. And since the quality of Campbell's research is not at issue, and no one has claimed that Darwin *didn't* do what Campbell says he did, then in this debate, at least, the idea that Darwin was a "point of articulation" has been falsified. Revolution happens.

It would be nice to know how. Fuller (this volume) thus chides Campbell for lacking an old-style effects analysis. Fuller argues that new works burst upon a near infinity of scenes, ongoing projects, and disputes. The mystery is how the citation classics, some only half-read or disinterestedly browsed, worm their way into many discourses. Darwin's strategies are interesting, certainly, but it would be equally interesting to know how his ideas figured in multiple conversational turns. Therein might lie the evidentiary key to confirming Campbell's intuition that views of human agency and of the dispersion of discourse formations are compatible. This intuition is surely the heart of the matter, for if the Darwinian revolution wasn't exclusively intellectual or institutional, then *contra* Gaonkar, one can read Campbell not as shifting away from the intentionalist model but merely as starting with it. One asks what Darwin did, and then about his constraints, and then about what was happening around him, and then about how and why his ideas caught on in this circle and that. One might thereby produce the sort of portrait Fuller suggests, science as an exemplary mode of decision making.

I want to consider one more instance of the rhetoric of science having much to say. For if the concern is theoretical "thinness," it is in case studies that the critical vocabulary will encounter concrete particulars and thus "thicken." One body of work notably missing from Gaonkar's analysis (as he himself notes) is that of John Lyne, the Iowa rhetorician-cum-argumentation theorist (see Lyne, 1989, 1990a, 1990b, 1991). Lyne argues that "arguments for genetic interpretations of human behavior are largely unbounded by disciplinary constraints," and thus that both journalists and nonspecialist academics generally appeal to genetics-as-warrants for arguments in ways unjustified by scientific evidence (1989:232). In a series of studies written with biologist Henry Howe (Lyne and Howe, 1986, 1990), Lyne catches E. O. Wilson scampering from one field to another, escaping intellectual scrutiny. The negotiation of intellectual authority along the fault lines between established fields is arguably an important problem and one that most established fields are more or less equally incapable of solving alone. And the problems of "facts" that do not survive intact as they are translated for outside audiences and of external politics worming their ways into the internal affairs of technical fields are surely interesting ones per se, and arguably central to discussions of modern democracy.

Now it might be thought that to conclude this discussion of what Gaonkar wants, the final criticism would be that he doesn't argue in favor of a postmodern alternative to the language of production and performance. But such a criticism would suppose that there *is* some postmodern ideal up to which rhetoric might live, as opposed to merely a plight with which rhetoric must live. For reasons that will soon be clear, Gaonkar is more inclined to the latter view, and the reason, I will argue, is that there is nothing postmodern about his vision of rhetoric.

EVENTUALIZING THE STAGARITE

Gaonkar certainly knows that rhetoric neither begins nor ends with Aristotle, yet he presents the rhetoric of science with a dilemma that does: Because the American rhetorical tradition is dominated by Aristotle, science studies seem most rhetorical when they are most Aristotelian, yet most interesting when they are least Aristotelian. As the rhetoric of science is obviously interesting, it must be still another failed attempt to escape rhetoric's "mereness."

This "mereness" has the appearances of a postmodern impasse. But behind the Foucauldian veneer is a premodern pentimento. Aristotle's rhetoric is being put in its place by Aristotle's philosophy. For it is only within that system that rhetoric "cannot escape its mereness," "its status as a supplement" (Gaonkar, 1990:341).

Is the rhetoric of science being skewered by the sensibilities of an Aristotelian realist? Well, at the center of things is a vision not of what rhetoric is becoming or might become, or how it mingles with the social sciences, or what its various guises are like, but what it inescapably *is*. A thing's essence, in Aristotle, is what it is by its very nature. And in the telling analogy that appears toward the end of Gaonkar's essay (rhetoric as mixer, sweetener, and placebo), one can almost hear Hannibal Lecter's voice: "First questions, Clarice: What is its nature? What does it *do*?"

Rhetoric in its Purity-of-Essence

The analogy arises as Gaonkar considers the question of how much ground science must surrender to the plebeian art, or more precisely, the degree to which rhetoric may "threaten to become part of the substance of science." This is a telling question in itself, for it sets science—and therefore rationality—apart from language and discourse. Indeed, the analogy makes no sense unless reason is seen as *not* constituted within language and discourse, but rather in some sort of pure realm that can only be diluted or distorted by language. And that, I contend, is Aristotle talking, or even Plato, and it explains why Gaonkar cannot conceive of a satisfactory rhetoric. If the art is judged by a standard that requires the separation of reason and discourse, then it will always fall short.[1] And the fall, in this analogy, is precipitous:

> Since the time of Gorgias, rhetoric has been compared to a psychoactive drug. In the contemporary usage, it is not clear whether rhetoric is actually a drug, some sort of . . . "delivery system" for a drug, or a substitute for a drug. (77)

Already the deck is stacked. The only question is what sort of threat rhetoric poses for an entity to which it is alien; and though the analogy at first seems to be about current conventions, it quickly displays the infallible mark of the realist, a metaphor that is stone cold dead:

> As a delivery system rhetoric has at least two distinct forms: a nondescript mixer (such as water) that dilutes the potency of an alcoholic beverage, or a sweetener (such as sugar syrup) which camouflages the bitterness of a medicine. The difference is critical. In the case of a mixer, no one confuses the relative tastes

of whisky or gin, even though both are mixed with water. Rhetoric in this sense is a ubiquitous but dull accompaniment, not something worth studying. (77)

Would he say the same, one wonders, of water used to dilute toxic emissions, or air used to dilute insecticides as they are pumped into aircraft cabins, or of dilutants used in inoculations to weaken viruses? Such dilutions create realities that are for practical purposes more important than the materials one begins with. Café au lait begins with coffee that by itself is undrinkable, but joined 50-50 with milk it becomes ambrosia. And were I to say that Gaonkar is the sort of fellow who waters his whisky, he might take it as an insult. I would be accusing him not of a dull accomplishment but of a barbarianism that every self-respecting whisky drinker would denounce. Finally, let's say that Jonathan Edwards's "Sinners in the Hands of an Angry God" is grain alcohol—short of shouting "fire" in a crowded theater, the strongest imaginable fear appeal—and that the lyrics of "In the Sweet Bye-and-Bye," represent a considerable dilution. We know that extreme fear appeals are counterproductive and that even strong fear appeals fail without high ethos and an emphasis on solutions. Add to that knowledge the element of self-persuasion entailed in public singing, and there are reasons to think that the dilution is everything. But Gaonkar goes on:

> But in the case of the sweetener, there is room for ethical mischief and ideological distortion, since the underlying flavors are obscured. (77)

Notice the poisoned well: There is room only for mischief and distortion, not for improvement and insight. One can imagine examples of the former, certainly, but also of the latter. Every memoir about the Manhattan Project, for instance, attributes the scientists' cooperation to funding, patriotism, and curiosity. There was nothing especially ideological about the first two: The military was blatant, and many of the scientists themselves believed that the bomb might be necessary to win the war. The only ideology at work, arguably, was the trait we are inclined to respect the most. The Alamagordo scientists were curious about whether it could be done, and that, joined with patriotism, overshadowed doubts some had about whether it should be done. Then, after contemplating what they had wrought, some of them became disarmament advocates. For once the puzzle was solved and the overriding purpose of the program became less compelling, other considerations arose. Second thoughts set in; conscientious objections were raised; and even at the height of McCarthyism, there was room for ethical scruples.

Notice, too, the sweetened well, the nostalgic vision of science as a pristine Mertonian priesthood, squaring up eyeball to eyeball with reality itself. Something so pure can only be corrupted. This misty idealization is reminiscent, in letter and spirit, of *Wissensoziologie*. Mannheim and Durkheim depicted social life as so irrational, so determined by social structures, that it was imperative that science be *not* social. Their solution was to proclaim, arms waving, that scientists were exempt from the existential determination of thought.

There is a sizeable literature that denounces this idealization. It argues that the structure, incentives, and language of large-scale research "have more in common with business than with the academy" (Nisbet, 1969:311), that science is structured like agencies and corporations because it is interdependent with them (Kohn, 1986). Read generously, this literature suggests that the root metaphor for understanding the sciences is the *organization*—meaning governments, funding agencies, professional guilds, labs, etc. The processes said to animate organizations are communication flows and argument practices.

This debunking is as open to exaggeration as the misty idealization. Its arguments sometimes take the idealization as a standard, and then condemn virtually everything for not meeting the standard (Willard, 1996). But when too many studies are chasing too few dollars, researchers will adapt to their audiences. Thus, with apologies to Donald Bryant, the conduct of science is to an important degree the adjustment of studies to agencies and of agencies to studies. And if the former half of this equation is valid, if one studies X and not Y because one can get funding for X, then the next move in Gaonkar's argument is mistaken:

> But the third alternative is the most critical. *When there is no drug, no substance, rhetoric itself functions as a drug.* More precisely rhetoric functions as a placebo in the absence of a drug. Rhetoric, seemingly the supplement, becomes *substantial.* (77)

This argument misunderstands both drugs and placebos. There is a substantial literature proving that pharmacologically active drugs have placebo effects, and often only barely beat placebos in double-blind trials. From experimenter effects to patients' faith to planted expectations, medicine clearly has a nontrivial persuasive dimension. But Gaonkar goes on:

> In the construction of scientific knowledge/practice/culture, does rhetoric ever function as the placebo? That is, does it ever threaten to become part of the substance of science? No one doubts that rhetoric functions as the mixer, sometimes as the sweetener, but can one argue that science is a simulacrum (in Baudrillard's sense), a rhetorical construction without reference? (77)

If one studies X and not Y because of funding imperatives, or takes one's predecessors' research for granted based purely on the predecessors' ethos (as Bruno Latour describes), or parades Nobel laureates in Washington to save the supercollider, then the substance of science is already rhetorically framed, and to some extent incomprehensible apart from the political world within which it functions.

But notice the straw man at the end of the passage. If style is integral with substance, then science is "without reference" in the most extreme sense, that of Baudrillard. Rhetoricians of science have not defended so powerful a claim, so far as I know. The closest anyone has come is perhaps Werner Heisenberg's argument that measurement in quantum physics, though it isn't utterly without reference, is without reference in any ordinary sense. The act of measurement is a reality in and of itself, and to some extent the only available reality, so as one measures from different perspectives, one is moving from one reality to another. This reasoning, of course, has profound consequences in the social sciences, which have their own recalcitrant quanta to track. But rhetoricians of science, withal, needn't defend anything close to a science without reference: Reasoning-from-evidence suggest the existence of evidence; marshalling one's case suggests the ordering of materials; and audience-adaptation suggests among other things, surely, considering the available standards for what counts as evidence.

The subjects of measurement and reference do suggest, however, a way of speaking about the rhetorical dimensions of technical discourses. Measurements are in one sense simply measurements, just as a cigar, as Freud said, is sometimes just a cigar. But though SO_2 emissions are SO_2 emissions, the question of what constitutes health risks from certain emissions is a genuine hybrid, technical certainly, but centrally a matter of inference and argument. The technical side is easy; the rhetorical side is hard, for the question of what constitutes morally or politically acceptable risks expands the range and complexity of issues.

At any rate, in squabbling with Gaonkar I have perhaps proved that the rhetoric of science is being held hostage to a realism that can be fairly called "Aristotelian." I have suggested that the question of rhetoric's place in the scheme of things has been posed in a distinctly Aristotelian way, that Gaonkar, like Aristotle, gives *rhetoric* an identity by subordinating it to "genuine" forms of knowledge and by contrasting it to its antonym, *reality*. So it is appropriate to muse a moment about the sheer oddness of viewing the rhetoric of science through the lens of a philosopher for whom a rhetoric of science would have been inconceivable, a contradiction in terms, or a category mistake.

With Friends Like Aristotle, Rhetoric Scarcely Needs Plato

Aristotle's legacy is subtler than it seems. For though systematic philosophy has gone the way of the unicorn, the authority of Aristotle's system is still sometimes invoked to justify rhetoric's place among the disciplines. It is a hard place, and one can imagine that those who point to it hope that it isn't looked at too closely: a "Department of Supplementarity" would be the paradigm case of a service department. But it is a place nonetheless, and the sort of port to which one steers when survival or subsistence are at stake.

Let us imagine a conversation without politics looming in the background, and thus without the need for the ethos appeal. In that case, very few people I imagine would embrace Aristotle's rhetoric wholly, or give it the same place among the disciplines, or arrange the disciplines in anything like Aristotle's hierarchy, or espouse the whole of the Aristotelian system. There are too many things undreamt of in his philosophy: a nonteleological world, for instance, or one in which the truth doesn't have a natural tendency to triumph over its opposite, or in which women have the same number of teeth as men, or in which slavery is not the natural price of leisure-class philosophy. Conspicuously missing is anything like Mead's "inner parliament," wherein one balances one's aims against social expectations and institutions. True, Aristotle's rhetors wrestle with the available means of persuasion, his dialecticians weigh point and counterpoint in a process of argumentation and criticism. But Mead's parliament is at the center of things and applicable to everything. Aristotle's parliament, if we can call it that, applies only to practical affairs; it is excluded from the sciences, wherein one's syllogisms simply do their work. Aristotle's disciplines and their hierarchical positions have the feel of natural categories, in letter and spirit. Rhetoric fits into this scheme, as Gaonkar says, as a *supplement*, at most a kind of practical knowledge or practical art, as distinct from genuine knowledge as the container is distinct from its contents.

Mead's parliament is perhaps overrational, and perhaps over-estimates the powers of reflection while underestimating the invisibility of institutions. But it also suggests that the matter is not either/or. Just as light is both wave and particle, human agency is a composite of determinism and freedom—which suggests, in turn, that the heroic view of agency and the Marxists' existential determination of thought are local contingencies, not grand contrarieties. One can read into Aristotle, certainly, the idea that means and ends inform one another, and that means become ends in themselves; and more tenuously one can read Aristotle's instrumentalism as a very creative and adaptive art. But Aristotle's monism is something of an obstacle to reading a creative version of reflective thinking into his philosophy. Hogtied to an object-language, reflective thinking is a matter of seeking essences.

Pre-Mead, let's say, rhetoric was more a blunt instrument than it needed to be. Post-Mead, it is more adaptable, its nature changing as discourses change. Its subject matter is adaptation, the balancing of intentions and constraints, the creation of message strategies, and the negotiation of alternative situations and selves in order to enhance cooperation. Such goings-on can't be understood apart from their local instantiations, and no single local case will do.

Preeminently, it would be stretching things to read anything like the modern meaning of "interdisciplinarity" into Aristotle. His hierarchy of disciplines depended on a fixity of subject matters; their interrelationships were clear-cut subordinations of one field to another, so a rhetoric of ethics would have been as inconceivable in that system as a rhetoric of science. The creation of new discourses in which the hybrids are more than the sums of their parts (e.g., pragmatics, forensic medicine) is unimaginable in Aristotle. Yet the idea of interdisciplinarity is inconceivable without rhetoric, for no one who studies the creation of new discourses reduces mergers and hybrids to evolution or revolution *simpliciter*. The language in the interdisciplinarity literature, rather, is one of permutation, crossbreeding, adaptability, balancing, and strategic negotiation; and its most common image is of the ebb and flow of influence.

But there is, I submit a lacuna in Aristotle—a hole in his system right where an inner parliament should be. If one posits a fully determined physical world, and reduces human thought to physical processes, then it comes as something of a surprise if one also posits the possibility of human choice. It takes some doing to find action in causation, and Aristotle, one would think, would have made heavy weather of it. Yet the extant Aristotle is silent about why teleology waxes in the physical world but wanes in the human. One can imagine a lost, unifying treatise, but one can scarcely imagine what it would say. For *De Anima* presents a materialism and monism so consistent with the view of causation in the physical treatises that microfreedom amid macrodeterminism seems impossible. Perception is like a signet ring stamping itself on wax; mind is of one substance with the external world, so thought and language are not mirrors of nature so much as replications.

One would think, too, that handbooks on populist arts would refute popular philosophies that preached the futility of action. Unless Greek fatalism was merely the gothic fiction of its day, a horrifying but entirely theatrical possibility, one would expect a refutation of what might be called "teleology with bad motives." It had a mythic side: Olympus being to the Greeks roughly what the administration building now is to academics, humans were pawns of the whims and vendettas of the gods. And it had a "selfish gene" side: The vision of fate that powers the plot in *Oedipus Rex* mocks as an illusion the very idea of agency, and in tragedy, Aristotle says, plot is everything, character is secondary.

Yet there in the midst of it all are the social treatises, wherein interested actors pursue their quests for advantage, frame their intentions, weigh their alternatives, draw opposite conclusions, haggle and compromise, and presumably affect events. One can infer from this jostling, hustling world, despite the famous claim to the contrary, that rhetoric and dialectic together have a subject matter. They are about human agency, about action concerning matters that can be other than they are. The realm of practical affairs lies on the horizon of uncertainty, a place where truth needs help to triumph over its opposite. Among the arts, Aristotle says, only rhetoric and dialectic draw opposite conclusions; and the only reason to do that, presumably, is that human deliberation counts for something.

So the great mystery is why, if Aristotle's system is largely a historical curiosity, the lacuna is not. The missing explanation is still missing, for instance between middle and late Foucault, where an apparently inexplicable possibility of human agency arises from a thoroughgoing determinism (Willard, 1996), and in the stark choice that presents itself in Gaonkar's essays as the intentionalist "ideology" is set against a Foucauldian determinism. Perhaps since Aristotle's day, or at least since Kant's, the determinists have merely gone one way, and the free-agency crowd another, the twain meeting only for periodic flare-ups. But dependent on Aristotle's authority, and under-determined by the sort of data the rhetoric of science provides, the study of rhetoric may well have been doomed to cycle manically between exhilarating highs and depressive plunges.

A CONCLUSION, OF SORTS

The disciplinary status of classical rhetoric is scarcely one of the great questions that vex the world. Compared to matters of war and peace, or even faculty parking, the question of whether classical rhetoric is thick or thin, universalizable or local, seems *academic* in the worst sense of the word. After all, it is the *word* rhetoric that is chiefly at stake. Everyone, apparently, knows what persuasion is, and no one doubts that persuasion and influence are pervasive and important: Even in Gaonkar's terms, the sweetener is important and the placebo a threat.

But it is true that even in the company of the penitent, Gaonkar's essays stand out. They are marked by a mood, an Ecclesiastes-scale weariness that in tone and tenor suggests that "all is vanity." This mood is not incidental: It functions as data and warrant for many of the arguments. And though it can be dismissed as a vestigial Greek quirk, it is best dismissed for lack of evidence.

At one point Gaonkar says of Philip Wander's (1976) "The Rhetoric of Science" that Wander has no "special theory of scientific knowledge production" (43). That claim is odd in itself, as if all the varied sciences could be fitted into a single theory, and as if the sciences' interventions in civic life and their "aura of invincibility" are separable from a satisfactory account of their knowledge production. All this supposes that there is something special about science per se that sets it off from the mundane world of influence flows and persuasion. Whether this something special is Fuller's open forum of debate or Latour's mixture of instrumental confidence and hedged bets, the next step after Wander, so to speak, would be concrete studies of the concrete activities of scientists. And that, I submit, is what the rhetoric of science is doing.

NOTES

*The author thanks Daniel J. O'Keefe for helpful comments and criticisms.

1. I owe this argument to Daniel J. O'Keefe.

REFERENCES

Bulmer, M. (1994). The institutionalization of an academic discipline. *Social Epistemology, 8,* 3–8.

Douglas, M. (1986). *How institutions think.* Syracuse, NY: Syracuse University Press.

Goodnight, G. T. (1995, 9 May). Personal correspondence.

Hauser, G. A., and Whalen, S. (1995). New rhetoric and new social movements. Paper for the 8th Summer Conference on Argumentation, Alta, UT.

Hazen, R. M., and Trefil, J. (1991, 13 Jan.). Quick! What's a quark? *New York Times Magazine*, 24–26.

Kohn, A. (1986). *False prophets*. Oxford: Basil Blackwell.

Lyne, J. R. (1989). Arguing science. In Bruce E. Gronbeck (Ed.), *Spheres of argument: Proceedings of the sixth SCA/AFA conference on argumentation*. Annandale, VA: Speech Communication Association.

———. (1990a). The culture of inquiry. *Quarterly Journal of Speech, 76*, 192–224.

———. (1990b). Bio-rhetorics. In H. W. Simons (Ed.), *The rhetorical turn*. Chicago: University of Chicago Press.

———. (1991). Claiming the high ground. D. W. Parsons (Ed.), *Argument in controversy*. Annandale, VA: SCA Publications.

Lyne, J. R., and Howe, H. F. (1986). Punctuated equilibria. *Quarterly Journal of Speech, 72*, 132–147.

———. (1990). The rhetoric of expertise. *Quarterly Journal of Speech, 76*, 134–151.

Nisbet, R. (1990). *The quest for community*. New York, NY: ICS Press.

Scheper-Hughes, N. (1995, 7 Jan.). Review of *After the fact: Four decades, two countries, one anthropologist* by Clifford Geertz. New York Review of Books, 22.

Symposium on *The impossible science*. (1994). *Social Epistemology, 8*.

Taylor, C. A., and Condit, C. M. (1988). Objectivity and elites. *Critical Studies in Mass Communication 5*, 293–312.

Turner, S. (1994). The origins of 'mainstream sociology' and other issues in the history of sociology. *Social Epistemology, 8*, 41–67.

Weick, K. E. (1987). Theorizing about organizational communication. In Jablin, F. M., Putnam, L. L., Roberts, K. H., and Porter, L. W. (Eds.), *Handbook of Organizational Communication*. Beverly Hills: Sage.

West, C. (1989). *The American evasion of philosophy*. Madison, WI: University of Wisconsin Press.

Willard, C. A. (1996). *Liberalism and the problem of knowledge: A new rhetoric for modern democracy*. Chicago: University of Chicago Press.

PART III

Extensions

CHAPTER 8

INSTUMENTALISM, CONTEXTUALISM, AND INTERPRETATION IN RHETORICAL CRITICISM

James Jasinski

INTRODUCTION

At the end of his essay "The Idea of Rhetoric in the Rhetoric of Science," Dilip Gaonkar acknowledges that his text may be read in two different ways: "either as an interrogation of some of the governing assumptions of contemporary rhetorical studies as exemplified in the 'rhetoric of science' or as an interpretive survey of that subfield" (80, n. 19). My reading of the essay emphasizes Gaonkar's diagnosis of the "disciplinary anxieties" in rhetorical studies and his use of the "rhetoric of science" literature to "illustrate some of the general problems in rhetorical criticism" (36). As previous commentators have noted (e.g., Leff, 1993), Gaonkar's essay resists quick summarization. Rather than attempt such a task, I want to begin by pursuing one thread in its dense argumentative fabric in order to establish the contours of my project.

Gaonkar argues that cultural as well as disciplinary conditions require rhetorical critics to employ "recuperative strategies" (42) capable of revealing the repressed rhetoricity of a text. Recuperation is necessary in order to render the textual object "intelligible" as an instance of rhetorical practice and establish the "intelligibility" of rhetoric as an appropriate interpretive metadiscourse (29).[1] The recuperative strategies Gaonkar detects in the rhetoric of science literature, and by extension the larger practice of rhetorical criticism, reveal the "persistence" of key assumptions of classical rhetorical theory. Despite the demise of the neo-Aristotelian paradigm that dominated rhetorical criticism in the middle of this century, Gaonkar contends that "our critical studies are sustained by the

vocabulary of classical rhetoric" (32).[2] The dominant recuperative
strategy in current critical practice employs a "particular ideology of
human agency" (33) in order to support a "model of intentional persuasion" (48). This model situates "the text as a manifestation of the
author's conscious design" (51) and embodies a "functionalist" or
instrumental view of rhetorical practice (57).[3] The functionalist or
instrumental understanding of rhetorical practice, along with the
productionist vocabulary that helps sustain it, provides Gaonkar
with an explanation for the "thinness" of much current rhetorical
criticism.

In this essay I want to explore this "thinness thesis" and suggest one possible way that the problem of thin interpretive practice
in rhetorical criticism might be overcome. I want to pursue what is,
at least initially, a complementary critique of the instrumentalist/
intentionalist model of persuasion. Whereas Gaonkar's critique concentrates on the "ideology of agency" embedded in this model, I
want to examine the dominant understanding of context or "rhetorical situation" within the instrumentalist/intentionalist tradition.
This line of inquiry is, in fact, an extension of a point Gaonkar made
in an earlier essay. In his reflections on the rise of textual criticism in
rhetorical studies, Gaonkar (1989) suggests that "the very idea that
oratory as radically situated discourse robs it of a certain kind of
autonomy and influence" (273).[4] The instrumentalist orientation is,
it seems, flawed in terms of both its mode of contextualization and
its assumptions about human agency. But the contextualization of
discursive practice in rhetorical criticism needs to be unpacked historically in order to understand the limitations of the instrumentalist orientation and possible alternatives to it. Two general questions, both framed in the spirit of Gaonkar's strategy of
metacriticism, merit additional attention. First, how has context
been prefigured in critical practice? What tensions, if any, exist in the
discipline's "rhetoric of context?" What alternative modes of contextualization have been repressed and what possibilities for interpretive practice might follow from their recovery? Second, what
"hermeneutic burden" (38) has context carried in rhetorical criticism? How do alterations in a critic's mode of contextualization
alter this hermeneutic burden? What form of contextualization
might contribute to the hermeneutic project of "thickening" rhetorical criticism?

My analysis of context in the disciplinary tradition affirms
many of Gaonkar's critical observations concerning the instrumentalist model of criticism. While our diagnoses run along parallel
lines, our prognoses differ on two key issues. First, Gaonkar's claim

that the interpretive turn in criticism commits the rhetorical critic to a process of "redescription" does not, in my view, fully circumscribe the possibilities of interpretive practice. In the second section of the essay I sketch what might be considered a "reconstructive" version of interpretation as one alternative.[5] A key element of the interpretive burden faced by rhetorical critics is to reconstruct textual production through a reinvigorated engagement with context, specifically the performative conditions or performative traditions that enable and constrain discursive action. Second, Gaonkar's indirect endorsement of "more refined and specific" interpretive metalanguages (33) seems to suggest that the problem of thin criticism can be overcome through the incorporation of more sophisticated conceptual languages of interpretive theory into the practice of rhetorical criticism. In the final section of the essay I consider the question of whether the conceptual language of interpretive theory or the historical language of practice provides greater potential for thickening critical practice. While I argue that greater attention to the language of practice, to the performative traditions from which texts emerge, is necessary, I try to suggest that the theory-versus-practice question actually poses a false disjunction. Building on Gaonkar's reading of Campbell, I want to show that it is not a simple choice of either "more theory" or "more history." Greater attention to the historical language of practice invites, indeed demands, thicker interpretations and more elaborate conceptual reflection from the critic.

RECUPERATING RHETORIC; OR, WHAT DOES IT MEAN FOR RHETORIC TO BE A RADICALLY SITUATED PRACTICE?

Rhetorical critics generally agree that the key modern founding text is Wichelns's essay "The Literary Criticism of Oratory" (1925). Gaonkar's (1990) reading of this essay corrects the common misreading that "with Wichelns method masters the object." What Gaonkar observes is that " 'method' is determined by his prefiguration of the object domain of oratory." In unpacking this "structure of . . . prefiguration," Gaonkar notes its "antithetical form" and the "dispersed but coherent set of statements that characterize the object domain" of oratory (293–294). That Wichelns follows Hudson (1923) in exploiting the antithesis between literature and oratory is clear. But the asserted coherence of Wichelns's account of the object domain of oratory is problematic. Further attention to the essay's prefigurative structure reveals not just the founding dialectic between object and method but an internal dialectic with respect to context that has helped shape the discipline's critical practice.

The tensions inhabiting Wichelns's account of context can be seen on two levels. First, Wichelns vacillates between two modes of temporal emplotment. In one of the widely quoted passages from the essay, Wichelns contends that "the man, his work, his times, are the necessary common topics of criticism; no one of them can be wholly disregarded by any critic" (183). Wichelns's statement reworks material from an earlier of account of criticism that he quotes at the beginning of the paragraph: " 'There are,' says a critic of literary critics, 'three definite points, on one of which, or all of which, criticism must base itself. There is the date, and the author, and the work'" (183). Wichelns's paraphrase substitutes "times" for "date" and in so doing appears to broaden the temporal frame of critical activity. But the broader temporal scope inscribed in the substitution is not maintained in the course of the essay. For example, in one of the many passages evaluating the merits of extant oratorical criticism, Wichelns reintroduces "date" as a key critical focus (191). Toward the end of the essay, in Wichelns's account of the nature of rhetorical criticism, the broader temporal horizon is discarded as critical attention narrows to "a specific audience" (209) and the "occasion" (212). In the programmatic conclusion to section seven, Wichelns makes no mention of "the times" as a factor requiring critical reflection. Wichelns does admonish his reader to remember that "throughout such a study one must conceive of the public man as influencing the men of his own times by the power of his discourse" (213), but "times" now functions as a measure of "effect" and not a contextual frame.

The tension between "date" and "times" is muted through Wichelns' invocation of the opposition between literature and oratory. Temporal emplotment is crucial here as well, as Wichelns echoes the growing consensus that literature and literary critics focus on the timeless world of permanent values while oratory and rhetorical critics engage the timely world of immediate effects. As Gaonkar (1990) suggests, by removing any middle ground the antithetical or disjunctive form of Wichelns's exposition works to bind the rhetorical critic to the immediate occasion, to the "date," thereby bracketing the broader temporal horizon represented by the idea of "the times." The result of this reductive focus set in motion by Wichelns is, I will argue, a hypervalorization of the particular.[6] This mode of contextualization is central to the instrumental model of persuasion that both Gaonkar and I find problematic. There is, however, a second level of contextual tension in

Wichelns's text that complicates its rhetoric of context.

Gaonkar (1990:296–298) notes one of the key prefigurative moments in Wichelns's essay: "For poetry is free to fulfil its own law, but the writer of rhetorical discourse is, in a sense, perpetually in bondage to the occasion and the audience; and in that fact we find the line of cleavage between rhetoric and poetic" (212). The image of bondage in this passage echoes an earlier observation that "oratory . . . is bound up with things of the moment" (182). As the second passage makes clear, there is link between temporal emplotment ("of the moment") and the prefiguration of the object domain (advocates are "bound" to audience and occasion). The issue I want to address is the purported coherence of Wichelns's prefigurative structure. Does Wichelns figuratively destabilize or contest his apparently narrow and highly functionalist account of context? Two pages after the "bondage" passage, Wichelns writes: "A statesman's wisdom and eloquence are not to be read without some share of his own sense of the body politic, and of the body politic not merely as a construct of thought, but as a living human society. A speech, like a satire, like a comedy of manners, grows directly out of a social situation; it is a man's response to a condition in human affairs" (214). The organic imagery in this passage leads Wichelns from "date" and occasion back to a broader temporal frame: "On no plane of thought—philosophical, literary, political—is Burke to be understood without reference to the great events in America, India, France, which evoked his eloquence; nor is he to be understood without reference to the state of English society" (214).

Wichelns's mode of contextualization is, I contend, bifurcated. On the one hand, temporal emplotment and figurative imagery produce a narrow, truncated sense of context. Advocate and text are figuratively chained to the context which has been narrowed to audience and occasion or "date." In the process, rhetoric is instrumentalized, conceived as the advocate's individual and particularized struggle with the controlling "exigence" (Bitzer, 1968).[7] Rhetoric is also doubly confined; first, to the "public sphere" (Gaonkar, this volume, 31) and, second, within a highly circumscribed context. Extending the prefigurative structure, context functions as a prison cell that contains advocate and text. The advocate's bondage to the occasion is reinscribed in the critic's bondage to the advocate; the critic's task is to enter the context in order to locate "constraints" and then describe the advocate's strategic management of these factors. On the other hand, temporal emplotment and figurative imagery also construct a broader, organic sense of context. The advocate's actions are rendered as part of the organic development of the

larger public "body" and must be understood in that context. The
text is positioned as an outgrowth of context; context does not simply surround or contain the text but permeates or saturates the text
as the result of an organic process of emergence and development.[8]
The organic metaphor leads the critic deeper into the context in an
effort to comprehend the "birth" of the text. Critical energy is
directed toward describing the discursive traces of context in both
the form and substance of the text. Like Aristotle's *Rhetoric*,
Wichelns's essay has been appropriated and incorporated into the
dominant instrumental understanding of rhetoric. But the history of
its reception should not lead to the obliteration of its prefigured
internal contextual dialectic.

The reception and circulation of Wichelns's essay is part of the
often recited narrative of the emergence of the field of rhetorical
criticism. That reception process gave special emphasis to the situ-
ation-*bound* side of Wichelns's dialectic. The dominant pattern in
the rhetoric of context after Wichelns features a gesture toward a
broader, more organic sense of context overwhelmed by a particularized focus on audience and occasion. We find the gesture toward
an enlarged conceptualization of context in a number of programmatic essays. Baird and Thonssen (1947), for example, write: "The
speech cannot be isolated from its social milieu. A reconstruction of
the social background is therefore necessary. An adequate explanation of the complex economic, social, political, literary, religious,
and other movements must be made" (137). In practice, however, the
text is in fact isolated. Critical attention devolves from social and
historical context to occasion; when "social background" is included
in a critical study it functions as a passive container that frames the
text but plays virtually no substantive role in the critic's interpretive
response. Wrage's (1943) well-known study of Henry Clay's 1850
compromise address exemplifies the pattern. Wrage paints the historical scene in extremely broad strokes (sectional discord, Congressional gridlock over the Wilmot proviso) in order to establish
an exigence. Minute attention, however, is given to the particulars of
the speech occasion: the crowd gathering, the dress of the women,
the weather outside, Clay's physical appearance. Wrage effectively
isolates Clay from his "social milieu." Neither historical and social
background nor, for that matter, the meticulously reconstructed
occasion play a significant role in Wrage's engagement with Clay's
text.[9]

The same pattern of gesture and focus can be detected in the
critical reflections of Marie Hochmuth Nichols. In her "The Criticism of Rhetoric," Nichols (1955) employs organic imagery in an

effort to identify the object domain of rhetoric; the "speech," she writes, can be thought of as a "multi-celled organism" (9). One organic component, one "cell," of any rhetorical performance is "place," and Nichols notes that "place, of course, is not merely a physical condition. It is also a metaphysical condition, an ideological environment" (11).[10] But the physical or particular aspects of place dominate Nichols's critical imagination. In her well-known study of Lincoln's "First Inaugural," Nichols (1954) describes "place" in vivid detail: the weather, the size of the crowd, the security precautions, Lincoln's dress. Attention to the political climate (the process of secession in the South, discordant voices of reaction in the North) is evident as well. But this lengthy discussion is contained in the first part of the study and it, in turn, functions as the passive container of her explicit critical reflections in part two. Despite her programmatic directive, place is particularized and reduced to the material aspects of the occasion.

Nichols, even more than Wrage, helps disclose the hermeneutic burden of context within the instrumental tradition and how the fulfillment of this burden helps hypervalorize the particular. For Nichols, context apparently determines purpose and, in turn, guides the critic's engagement with the text.[11] Nichols notes that "occasion" alone is an insufficient determinant of purpose in the case of Lincoln's "First Inaugural." In order "to discern the purpose," she writes, "we must recall the experience of the nation between his election as President and the day of his inauguration" (57). At least initially, Nichols moves beyond the narrow confines of occasion in order to discern purpose and interpret the text. But notice, first, the narrow temporal frame she constructs. While she gestures toward a broader historical context (for example, she notes that Lincoln used Clay's 1850 compromise address, Andrew Jackson's proclamation against nullification, Webster's reply to Hayne, and the Constitution as inventional materials, inviting what Gaonkar [57] describes as an "intertextual" reading), this context, and its performative traditions, plays no role in her reading of Lincoln's text. Consider, secondly, Nichols's treatment of this broader sense of context. Nichols reduces the "experiences of the nation" to a little more than two expository paragraphs. Most of this discussion focuses on concerns over Lincoln's character. If this brief discussion in section two is combined with the overview of the political climate in section one and then compared to the discussion of "place" in the opening section, the dominance of the particular—over the historical—moment is abundantly clear. This hypervalorization of the particular severs the text and context from the flow of history. Lincoln's text is recuperated as rhetoric but it is prefigured as an isolated fragment, contained by a mode of contextualization that detaches the particularized context, and with it the text, from the historical field.[12]

After Nichols reconstructs Lincoln's purpose, she writes: "In evaluating the Inaugural, we must keep in mind its purpose, for the purpose of the speech controlled Lincoln's selection of materials, his arrangement, his style, and his manner" (59). As Gaonkar notes, in the instrumentalist/intentionalist model of persuasion, "the dialectic between text and context . . . is already prefigured in the rhetor's desires and designs" (49; cf. 58). In other words, context only enters the interpretive process through the agency of purpose; contextual elements not mediated by purpose are of no interest to the critic operating within the instrumentalist model. A more recent critical study of another speech by Lincoln illustrates how this injunction contributes to thin interpretation in rhetorical criticism. Leff and Mohrmann (1974) employ a revitalized classical perspective in analyzing Lincoln's 1860 speech at Cooper Union. Based on their assessment of "context," primarily the nascent 1860 presidential campaign, they write: "The central concern [of the speech] is ingratiation, and recognition of this purpose unifies the elements of analysis by giving them a more precise focus; awareness of the ultimate goal becomes shuttle to the threads of structure, argument, and style" (348). The weaving metaphor highlights a concern with textual action (text is derived from the Latin texere, "to weave") largely absent from the formative period of rhetorical criticism; purpose fulfills a substantial hermeneutic burden in Leff and Mohrmann's essay as it leads them to analyze closely various aspects of Lincoln's argument (e.g., ad hominem), style (e.g., prosopopoeia), and structure (repetition and parallel development). But the reliance on the mediating function of purpose exacts a cost. Leff and Mohrmann note how Lincoln "caps th[e] appeal" of the first section of the address in the following passage from the oration:

> Let all who believe that "our fathers who framed the government under which we live understood this question just as well, and even better, than we do now," speak as they spoke, and act as they acted upon it. This is all Republicans ask—all Republicans desire—in relation to slavery. As those fathers marked it, so let it be again marked, as an evil not to be extended, but to be tolerated only because of and so far as its actual presence among us makes that toleration and protection a necessity. (quoted in Leff and Mohrmann, 1974:352)

This passage from Lincoln is interesting because of what Leff and Mohrmann fail to say about it. Throughout the essay, Leff and Mohrmann exhibit a keen eye for stylistic nuance, but for some reason they fail to note Lincoln's use of chiasmus in this passage (the reversal "marked it . . . it be again marked"). The reason for the omission would seem to be the "shuttling" function of purpose; the chiasmus does not contribute to the purpose of ingratiation, hence it needs no interpretive explication. But the potentially destabilizing presence of chiasmus becomes visible through a different mode of contextualization. Ideologically, the nineteenth century is marked by an intense "filiopiety" (Forgie, 1979), a devotion to the "fathers." Lincoln's historiographic struggle with Douglass in the Cooper Union address (itself a continuation of the struggle begun during the senatorial campaign of 1858) is embedded in, even as it reinscribed, this ideological context. Lincoln is not only contesting Douglass's interpretation of the founding period, but struggling to fashion an appropriate relationship with the nation's founders (a struggle begun at least as early as his 1838 Lyceum address). In this context, the chiasmus embodies Lincoln's continued struggle with the burden of the founders; Lincoln wants to act—and calls on the nation to act—"as they acted," but the possibility of performative imitation or repetition is called into question by the figurative reversal. There is, then, an ironic element in the passage that merits interpretive reconstruction. The passage is, however, not simply ironic (content and form being at odds with each other) but also iconic. The iconicity of the passage can be grasped if we move beyond the limited context of the politics of ingratiation and situate the text clearly within the intense struggle over slavery (which Leff and Mohrmann do to a degree). As Leff and Mohrmann note, Lincoln sought to construct and inhabit a "middle ground" on the issue of slavery (347). If the chiasmus is read in the context of Lincoln's substantive position, his tertium quid, it assumes an iconic function by revealing the precariousness and instability of the middle course. The text tries to establish what Leff (in Leff and Sachs, 1990) refers to as "local stability," but the chiasmus testifies to the precariousness of the endeavor. The passage also contains an important argumentative move that eludes Leff and Mohrmann's attention. Lincoln justifies the Republican Party's position on the grounds that slavery's "actual presence among us makes that toleration and protection a necessity." Lincoln relies here on the argumentative "locus of the existent" (Perelman and Olbrechts-Tyteca, 1969) that bases judgment on the conformity of a policy proposition to the constraints of existing circumstances. Given that this argumentative form does not contribute to the purpose of ingratiation, Leff and Mohrmann have no reason to bring it the reader's attention. Yet the move is significant in the context of the performative tradition of prudential appeals in American public argument (see Jasinski, 1995). Appeals to the locus of the existent constitute a key element in the performative tradition of prudence and the presence of this argumentative form in Lincoln's text places Lincoln within this tradition. The text itself appears to invite an "intertextual" reading that explores Lincoln's participation in this performative tradition.

RECONSTRUCTING CONTEXT; OR, DOES RHETORIC EMERGE WITHIN DENSE PERFORMATIVE TRADITIONS WHOSE RECONSTRUCTION CAN HELP THICKEN CRITICAL PRACTICE?

It is a mistake to characterize, as Gaonkar does (1989:264; this volume: 61), neo-Aristotelian critical orthodoxy as predominantly "historicist." A more accurate characterization, as the previous section tried to suggest, is that it was radically particularist. We should not confuse particularist with historicist. Despite programmatic gestures and biographic and historiographic frames that suggest a historicist preoccupation, the situated recuperation of rhetoric in the first half of this century isolated context and text from history. Thankfully, the prison house of "occasion" has been dismantled. But as Leff (in Leff and Sachs, 1990) notes, the overthrow of the old orthodoxy brought with it a tendency to abandon the situatedness of rhetoric rather than, for example, an attempt to recover the neglected "organic" pole in Wichelns's original dialectic. Instead, rhetoric became associated with recurring formal structures (thereby contributing to the universalization of rhetoric described by Gaonkar). The rise of textualist studies in the last decade has helped shift debate from conceptual abstraction to concrete cases, but this move also contains the seeds of a new particularism (e.g., Hariman, 1989; Warnick, 1992). And while the relationships between form and content, intrinsic and extrinsic, and text and context were being considered in the metacritical literature, the spirit of particularism persisted in the numerous critical studies organized by the instrumentalist/intentionalist model of persuasion. In this section, I want to analyze some of the discipline's responses to this conceptual predicament. My principal concern is to explore how we might, in Gaonkar's (1989) terms, "deepen our sense of the dynamic relationship between public address and its ideological background" and "complicate and enrich our capacity to understand the interaction between texts and contexts" while still "attending to the integrity of the text as a field of action" (268; cf. LaCapra, 1983). Rethinking the relationship between context and text may help stimulate thicker interpretive practice.

One of the first sustained assaults on the dominant mode of contextualization in rhetorical criticism is in Black's highly influential book *Rhetorical Criticism* (1978). Black accepts the broader programmatic vision of the context and text relationship that we saw in Baird and Thonssen. "It is generally true," Black writes, "that the work of rhetoric is fragmentary outside its environment; it functions only in a particular world. . . . This fact gives the discovery of context an enhanced importance in rhetorical criticism as compared to the criticism of fine arts" (39). While Black adopts a form of particularism in this passage (the contrast in Black is between "particular occasion" [38] and "particular world" [39]), he goes on to critique the radical or hypervalorized particularism of the neo-Aristotelian tradition. He employs Nichols's essay on Lincoln to illustrate the "restricted view of context" (39) that dominates critical practice. This restricted view of context is manifest in the tendency of critics "to comprehend the rhetorical discourse as tactically designed to achieve certain results with a specific audience on a specific occasion" (39). The consequence of this mode of contextualization is that it shapes the critic's selection of data; Nichols only selects "data pertinent to the immediate audience of the First Inaugural and the specific occasion of its delivery" (41). The result is an extremely truncated reconstruction of Lincoln's purpose that guides Nichols's critical inquiry. The reconstructed purpose is reliable as far as it goes but the problem, Black suggests, is that it does not go very far; the critical insights produced by such a procedure are inherently limited.

Black develops his analysis of Nichols's essay by comparing it to the work of three other "critics": Edmund Wilson, Richard Hofstader, and Harry Jaffa (the attribution of the label "critic" to Hofstadter and Jaffa seems problematic). Their work is introduced in order to establish Black's interrelated claims that alternative reconstructions of purpose are possible, so Nichols's narrow account of purpose must then be attributable to her neo-Aristotelian presuppositions. But is this the only conclusion that can be reached from comparing these studies? Black's critique of Nichols via the work of Wilson et al. is based on a key, but only partially articulated, assumption. Black assumes that Nichols, Wilson, Hofstader, and Jaffa all subscribe to an instrumentalist understanding of discursive practice. These critic-historians apparently share a view of public rhetoric as primarily a means to a predetermined purpose or end (where the "ends" themselves are pursued through, but typically not constituted by, rhetorical practices) whose force is the result of fully conscious strategic decisions (so Black writes that Hofstader believed Lincoln "consciously molded his discourse" to a particular end and summarizes his discussion of the three critics with the claim that there are "some compelling reasons for suspecting that Lincoln's discourses were consciously designed to be strong and enduring forces" [39–40]). Based on this assumption of shared perspective, Black is able to argue that Nichols's neo-Aristotelian perspective explains her narrow sense of context and her limited account of purpose.

But is it fair to assume that the instrumentalist orientation constitutes a common ground for these critic-historians? For instrumentalist critics like Nichols, context appears to determine purpose. On closer examination, however, we see the equation to be reversed. Within the instrumentalist perspective, mode of contextualization follows purpose; the search for instrumental purpose governs the critic's mode of contextualization. Occasion emerges as the preferred mode of contextualization because it is normally capable of disclosing purpose. When confronted with a case where occasion is insufficient, as Nichols believed was the case with Lincoln's "First Inaugural," the critic gradually increases the scope of contextualization until purpose can be located. Once located, purpose organizes the critical study while context, and mode of contextualization, recedes into the background; with its single hermeneutic task completed, context functions in the instrumental tradition as inert frame or passive container.

Black reads Wilson et al. as operating within this critical tradition. Wilson et al. conceive Lincoln's purpose (his "paramount objective" [41]) more broadly than Nichols, so they contextualized his utterances in a way that exceeded audience and occasion. The search for purpose still seems to guide critical contextualization. But what instrumental purpose could warrant Wilson's going "beyond the limits of peculiarly American experience to cull ideas from the psychology of religion and the nature of tragedy" [42]? Black is silent on this point. The reason is, I suspect, because Wilson's mode of contextualization does not rely solely on or does not follow from an instrumental reconstruction of Lincoln's purpose. Wilson situates Lincoln within the broader existential contexts of religion and tragedy because he is not constrained by a thoroughly instrumental understanding of public rhetoric. Lincoln's discourse warrants this manner of contextualization because of what it does as a discursive "event," not because of what Lincoln consciously or intentionally tried to do through his discourse.[13] If we admit the possibility that the instrumentalist orientation is not shared by all these critic-historians, then Black's explanation of the limitations of Nichols's critical imagination is suspect, and space for an alternative account is thereby created. It may be the case that it is not Nichols's neo-Aristotelian methodology that limits her understanding of context; rather, the neo-Aristotelian methodology might be understood as valorizing a tendency inherent in an instrumental understanding of rhetoric. Understanding purpose as mediating agency will always constrain the critic's mode of contextualization since only those aspects of context that enter into the advocate's conscious design strategies are relevant; those aspects of context that cannot be linked directly to strategic choices are rendered irrelevant. Abandoning the narrow neo-Aristotelian categories of occasion and audience and expanding context, as Black proposes to do, without challenging the broader instrumentalist presuppositions that undergird the neo-Aristotelian critical strategy, which Black is generally unwilling to do (see, for example, his discussion of intention [15–17]), does not fundamentally alter the critic's mode of contextualization or substantially modify the hermeneutic burden of context.

Consider, for example, Black's reading of Chapman's "Coatesville Address." As he notes, the neo-Aristotelian critic is unable to appreciate the text, in part, because the critic cannot locate "its proper context" (83). In an even more radical way than Lincoln's "First Inaugural," occasion is an insufficient mode of contextualization. The context of the address, Black argues, is "the dialogue participated in by Jefferson, Tocqueville, Lincoln, Melville, Henry Adams, Samuel Clemens, Santayana, and Faulkner—a dialogue on the moral dimension of the American experience. . . . The context of the Coatesville Address is less a specific place than a culture. . . . It is a context whose place must be measured by a continent and whose time must be reckoned in centuries" (83–84). Consistent with the instrumentalist presupposition that mode of contextualization follows purpose, Black writes: "our warrant for taking the context of the Coatesville Address so broadly is suggested by Chapman himself" (84). Black reads the opening paragraphs of the address as a strategic decision made by Chapman to situate the address in the broad contours of American history. What interpretive burden does this reconstruction of context fulfill? The answer to this question is little, if any. After his reconstruction of the context, Black concludes: "So much for context. Next we must consider what the speech actually says" (84). But Black's analysis of the speech does not treat it as a moment in a dialogue; the reader gets no sense of how participating in "a dialogue on the moral dimension of the American experience" shapes Chapman's address. The other "voices" of the dialogue are strangely absent. Context may no longer be figured as something to which an advocate is bound, but it still functions as a passive container that exerts little influence on the shape and texture of the utterance (cf. Gaonkar, 1989:262–263).

What critical conclusions does Black reach about the speech itself? Black writes: "Chapman would have us perceive the event [the lynching] as a scene in a morality play. The play itself is the history of this country, seen as the death-through-sin and the potential rebirth-through-purification of a whole people" (87). The speech provides instruction on how a nation can negotiate the fundamental problem of "guilt" (88-9). Black reaches these conclusions, however, without any explicit invocation of purpose. Like Wilson's reading of Lincoln, Black recontextualizes Chapman's oration in terms of ritual drama based on what the text does, not what the author intentionally tried to do. Black's critical insights depend, I suggest, on an implicit destabilization of the instrumentalist paradigm.[14] Black remains committed to an understanding of rhetoric as fundamentally intentional and purposive but his own critical practice demonstrates a mode of contextualization that escapes the constraints of authorial purpose in order to articulate critical insights. Without this type of destabilizing moment, the critic remains a captive of an overly particularized sense of context. Within the instrumentalist orientation, appeals to context can only function as a formulary gesture (establishing the passive container that frames the text but fulfills no substantive interpretive purpose) and/or a way of uncovering authorial purpose. But since mode of contextualization follows the search for instrumental purpose, the critic, like the advocate, remains bound to a narrow, prefigured context. The potential interpretive insights that could be generated through a recuperation of Wichelns's "organic" sense of context are continually deferred by the instrumentalist paradigm.

Black's reflections on the category of context and the process of contextualization in rhetorical criticism have been continued in the more recent work of his colleague Stephen Lucas. Echoing Black, Lucas (1988) writes: "Because rhetorical discourse occurs only within a particular world, we need to comprehend the very identity of any given text as inextricably interwoven with its world" (248; cf. Lucas, 1981:6). Lucas identifies a number of specific elements as constitutive of world-as-context: intellectual, institutional, political, religious, and economic forces or factors can "condition both the development of the text and its internal operation" (248). One element of context merits "special consideration." Influenced by the "linguistic turn" in the work of intellectual historian J. G. A. Pocock, Lucas argues that rhetorical critics need to devote additional attention to "linguistic context." Quoting Pocock, Lucas (1988) writes: "every rhetorical text is situated within a particular linguistic context with its own vocabulary, conventions, idioms, and patois. One cannot hope to plumb what the text means or to chart its internal dynamics without recapturing 'the full wealth of association, implication and resonance, the many levels of meaning,' which a language possesses in a given society at a given time" (248–249; cf. Lucas, 1981:6). Lucas (1989) illustrates the critical value of the idea of "linguistic context" in his meticulous study of the American Declaration of Independence. In that essay, linguistic resources, situational controversy, and generic conventions are all employed to unpack and interpret the language of the text.

Lucas's metacritical observations on the category of context as well as his practical instantiations merit further reflection. To begin, consider Lucas's prefiguration of context in terms of Wichelns's dialectic. Lucas does not explicitly invoke Wichelns, nor is his prefigurative structure unambiguously organic in nature. What we do find in Lucas is the common gesture toward an expansive, potentially organic sense of context inscribed in what might best be called an "intertextual metaphor" (text as "inextricably *interwoven*" with context). Text is not simply bound to context nor does context merely surround or contain the text. Text and context are, in Burke's terms, "consubstantial"; they both are made from the same material or fabric. So, while Lucas's prefigurative strategy does not draw upon organic imagery, the entailments of each metaphor are similar. The organic and the intertextual metaphors both figure context as permeating or saturating the text. This relationship is most obvious in the case of linguistic context. The linguistic context of a text, the idioms, conventions, and figurative structures out of which it is fashioned, saturates the text or, in Lucas's terms, is "interwoven" with it. While McGee's critical perspective is, in the context of disciplinary politics, often seen as antithetical to Lucas's, his observation that "the apparently finished discourse is in fact a dense reconstruction of all the bits of other discourses from which it was made" (1990:279) is fully consistent with Lucas's intertextual metaphor. Lucas's reflections on the category of context, intentionally or not, function to recover the repressed element of Wichelns's dialectic. In so doing, the hermeneutic burden of context is enhanced as critics are directed to investigate how context is inscribed in the text.

That recovery is, however, only partial. I say partial because the interpretive insights that might be generated via Lucas's intertextual metaphor are negated by a lingering preoccupation with the particular. For example, Lucas (1981) writes: "rhetorical discourse invariably occurs within a particular world; and not only within a particular social, political, religious, economic, and intellectual world, but also within a special rhetorical world" (6); this same emphasis on the particular appears in the 1988 "Renaissance" essay, where it is reinforced through an appeal to Black's disciplinary authority. While the particular may not be hypervalorized in Black and Lucas (to a large extent "occasion" has been dropped from the critical vocabulary of the field), its continued emphasis promotes a problematic mode of contextualization as it reinforces the dominant instrumental paradigm. The problem with particularism is that it often becomes a quest for singularity.[15] Take Lucas's discussion of linguistic context: "every rhetorical text is situated within a particular linguistic context" (1988:248–249). To substantiate his account of linguistic context, Lucas invokes the authority of Pocock. The problem with this move is that Pocock's writings on the study of political language call into question Lucas's particularist thesis. According to Pocock (1987), texts do not exist in a particular, or singular, linguistic context but within "layers of language contexts" (25). Lucas's "particular linguistic context" is not a discrete, unified language-game with rules that a critic can employ to determine the contextual meaning of an utterance.[16] Following Pocock and other linguistically inclined intellectual historians and political theorists, language context is most appropriately understood as an ongoing process of creating and diffusing multiple idioms or modes of speaking. The critic's challenge is, I would argue, to appreciate the multiplicity of, and the inherent tensions in, the particular.

Lucas's assumption of a stable, seemingly self-evident context reinforces the dominant instrumental paradigm even as his intertextual metaphor (and some of his critical practices) helps to destabilize it. Lucas's version of particularism contributes to set of interlocked assumptions that constitute the instrumental tradition: a mode of contextualization that assumes situational stability, a sense of agency that assumes that intentions are unambiguous, fully present, and capable of directing textual production, and a sense of the text that assumes its coherence and its ability to represent authorial intention fully and without significant distortion. The limitations of this critical tradition can be seen more fully by comparing Lucas's detailed study of the Declaration of Independence with Fliegelman's (1993) recent examination of the Declaration and its "culture of performance." Lucas recuperates the Declaration via the norms of the instrumental tradition: it was a document whose "immediate object was to persuade" and it was "designed to meet the particular rhetorical situation faced by the American revolutionaries in July 1776" (1989:69). Fliegelman's recuperative strategy is, in comparison, decidedly textual. Whereas Lucas relies on intention and situational responsiveness to justify a rhetorical reading of the text, Fliegelman begins with the "diacritical accent" marks found in a part of Jefferson's rough draft of the final Declaration that were inadvertently included in a proof copy of Dunlap's official broadside printing of the Declaration (5–6). These textual marks lead Fliegelman into a consideration of eighteenth-century oratorical theory and, most importantly, the nature of oratorical performance. Lucas is by no means blind to the performative conditions, or traditions, that shape the Declaration. Consistent with his intertextual metaphor, Lucas locates the Declaration within the tradition of British constitutionalism. So, for example, Lucas notes that the appeal to necessity in the opening paragraph not only "carried strongly deterministic overtones" (75) but also "followed long-established rhetorical conventions" traceable to at least the start of the English Civil War in 1642 in Parliament's declaration on the "Necessity to take up Arms" (76). Fliegelman's treatment of performative conditions and traditions differs from Lucas's in its emphasis on tension. Lucas, of course, situates the Declaration in the context of the British-American conflict, but he does not probe the tensions within the performative context and relate those tensions to the action of the text. Fliegelman, on the other hand, reads the appeal to necessity within the context of the "conflicting obligations" (15) experienced by eighteenth-century public actors. One of those conflicts was between necessity and human agency. When Fliegelman turns to the "necessitarian context" invoked in the first paragraph, he discloses latent tensions within the action of the text. So, for example, he notes that "by demonizing George, the Declaration stigmatizes individual willfulness at the same time that it articulates an ideology of individual liberty" (144). Or, more fundamentally, he points to "the tension in the Declaration between the description of independence as the necessary consequence of George's actions and the document's own status as a performative utterance" (151). Fliegelman's account of the tensions within the text is a direct consequence of his reconstruction of the performative conditions, and the tensions in those conditions, that shaped the eighteenth-century public world. Fliegelman is able to capture the multiplicity in the particular. Lucas's version of particularism calls attention to important performative traditions but assumes an overarching stability that inhibits a rich engagement with the text/context relationship.

Lucas's work on the Declaration, much like Campbell's work on Darwin, reflects an emergent trend in rhetorical criticism. While Campbell and Lucas-remain committed to a form of instrumentalism, they also destabilize some of its dominant assumptions. What is most significant in Lucas and Campbell, if not developed as fully as it might, is the recovery of the neglected organic pole of Wichelns's contextual dialectic. In implicitly recovering this pole, Lucas and Campbell restore the historicity of the text by expanding the hermeneutic burden of context and, in particular, linguistic context. Context is more than a passive frame or repository of purpose. Textual interpretation cannot proceed if the text is isolated from the linguistic context or "cultural grammar" (Campbell, 1986) from which it emerges. The text must be read within, and against, this intertextual matrix. This mode of contextualization helps to account for the power and depth, the thickness, of Lucas's and Campbell's critical performances.

The continuing challenge is to extend and expand this line of critical inquiry. Part of that process involves, I contend, a decentering of the lingering instrumental orientation in their work. If purpose is decentered, removed as the governing principle of rhetorical analysis, what would constitute the "center" or hub of critical activity in rhetorical studies? The answer to this question depends, in part, on the objectives constituted within the field of rhetorical criticism. If the objective of critical analysis is a thick description of the text, then sustained attention to the text/context relationship becomes essential and can function as a hub for critical activity. Of particular importance is the relationship between text and linguistic context or performative traditions. This does not imply that other modes of contextualization are inappropriate. My claim parallels Pocock's (1987) when he writes: "We do not say that the language context is the only context which gives the speech act meaning and history . . . we say only that it is a promising context with which to begin" (20). Performative traditions are a promising context in that they constitute the conditions of discursive possibility or, in the neo-Aristotelian idiom, the "available means of persuasion." Rhetorical advocates are always situated within multiple performative traditions and these performative traditions function as the discursive resources for all rhetorical action. Critical analysis as thick description involves charting the organization of, and interaction among, performative traditions within the field of the text.

Space prevents a systemic exposition and detailed illustration of performative traditions as a mode of contextualization. In the remainder of this section, I want to address three questions. First, in more specific terms, what constitutes a performative tradition? Second, if performative traditions are essential to rhetorical activity, why are they, or why have they been, typically unnoticed? Third, what model or form of interpretive practice does the text/performative-tradition mode of contextualization suggest? My discussion of these three questions is by no means exhaustive or comprehensive.

Leff's (1993) account of a disciplinary tradition as "an interactive and generative network of influence that shapes, though it does not determine, the positions of those who participate in it" (299) captures the functional nature of all performative traditions. These traditions do not determine (on the issue on linguistic determinism, see Farr, 1988) discursive practice; rather, they shape, they enable certain practices (never completely determining) while constraining others (never completely excluding or prohibiting). The dialectic of enabling and constraining is a central facet of the functioning of performative traditions (on this dialectic, see Giddens, 1979; Foucault, 1982; Montrose, 1989). Performative traditions can have a relatively narrow scope (e.g., the tradition of conspiracy in American political discourse) or can be quite broad (e.g., civic republicanism as a performative tradition). They can be tightly bound to an institution (e.g., the common law) or diffused throughout a political culture. As Pocock (1987) and others emphasize, the process of linguistic diffusion is a crucial component of civic life. Languages and traditions that emerge within the confines of an institutional structure migrate into other spheres of life (e.g., social Darwinism) or they might be appropriated and used to challenge dominant institutions (e.g., Christianity as a performative tradition appropriated by Black Americans).

Performative traditions consist of specific elements that may be more or less fully developed or present in different traditions. First, a performative tradition is embodied in a linguistic idiom or language. The tradition of civic republicanism, for example, is embodied in its terms of value (virtue, disinterestedness, public good) and opprobrium (corruption, self-interest, factionalism). Second, a performative tradition is enacted through particular speaking voices. Civic republicanism is enacted by "citizens" while Puritanism is enacted by the "elect" and Christianity generally by "saints" and "sinners." Third, a performative tradition is marked by various figurative and argumentative patterns or structures. The accommodationist tradition of prudence is marked by its reliance on the locus of the existent

(Jasinski, 1995) while the scientific tradition of evolution, as Campbell illustrates, is marked by its underlying metaphoric structure. Finally, a performative tradition is perpetuated by a range of textual practices and organized into generic forms that are structured through generic conventions. The eighteenth-century tradition of civic republicanism is perpetuated through the practice of discursive anonymity (Warner, 1990) while the tradition of Puritanism is organized around the sermon and, in particular, the jeremiad (Bercovitch, 1978).

Thematizing the relationship between text and performative tradition(s) calls into question a romantic model of textual production and rhetorical invention. Texts do not emerge from the inspiration or genius of the author. Invention is a social process in that the words employed by any author are always already part of a performative tradition in which the author is situated and from which the author draws. Textual production or rhetorical invention is also not a process of following rules or precepts (cf. Gaonkar, this volume: 33). Traditions enable and constrain practice but do not dictate or proscribe. Attention to performative traditions leads to a conceptualization of invention as the discursive management of multiple traditions. To use Bakhtin's (1981) metaphor, rhetorical invention is the "orchestration" of performative traditions.

If, as my argument suggests, performative traditions are pervasive and provide the material for rhetorical invention, why has so little explicit attention been given to tradition in rhetorical studies? Bineham (1995) suggests an answer in his discussion of the transparency of tradition. Gaonkar's (1990) "transparency thesis" identifies part of the dilemma of contemporary rhetorical studies: rhetoric is difficult to recuperate as a general discursive process, and specific texts resist close critical analysis due to the transparency of rhetorical art. Unlike the aesthetic object, the rhetorical artifact does not call attention to itself as such. It appears artless; it is the result of inspiration, genius, common sense—anything, in short, but art. The turn to close reading over the last decade or so has done much to recover the artfulness of the seemingly innocent text. But the problem of transparency has a second level or dimension that requires attention. While the techniques of rhetorical art receive increased emphasis in close textual analysis, the materials of art still remain rather transparent. The problem, as Bineham notes, is that tradition, understood as the medium of human existence, "is encompassing but unnoticed; it is transparent" (5). Quoting Richard Palmer, Bineham writes: "Tradition is 'not over against us but something in which we stand and through which we exist; for the most part it is so transparent a medium that it is invisible to us—as invisible as water to a fish'" (8). It is relatively easy to notice when advocates are obviously positioning themselves within a specific performative tradition or when they try to take advantage of intertextual reverberations. Clinton's attempted appropriation of the Kennedy mystique or William Lloyd Garrison's invocation of the seemingly antithetical tradition and language of Fisher Ames are examples of this sort. But critics don't usually notice how Frederick Douglass's river metaphor extends and subverts a common nineteenth-century metaphoric structure (Jasinski, in press) or how Henry Clay enacts a prudential tradition that can be traced back to Edmund Burke and John Dickinson (Jasinski, 1995). Attention to the techniques of rhetorical art will not, I contend, elude the charge of abstract formalism. Leff's (1992) turn toward controversy is one way of confronting the problem of abstract formalism.[17] An alternative approach to thickening critical practice is one that "learn[s] from formalism without accepting its more extreme claims at face value" (LaCapra, 1983:15), and it would center on the orchestration of performative traditions—idioms, voices, argumentative and figurative patterns, textual practices and generic conventions—in textual action.

The interpretive practice implied by this mode of critical analysis is something other than Gaonkar's notion of "redescription." It can best be characterized as a rhetorical reconstruction of textual production. Different versions of reconstructive analysis can be found in contemporary social theory. Habermas offers a model of rational reconstruction that identifies the transcendental conditions of communicative understanding, while Foucault's work developed a sociological form of reconstruction for mapping discursive formations. Rhetorical reconstruction, as I envision it, is closer to Foucault's approach than Habermas's. The critical difference is that rhetorical reconstruction assumes the existence of what Bakhtin (1981) termed "linguistic heteroglossia": the "internal stratification present in every language at any given moment of its historical existence" (263). Bakhtin is preeminently a theorist of linguistic multiplicity. The language of a culture consists of multiple idioms, speech types, and voices. Inventional practices orchestrate linguistic multiplicity but, Bakhtin argues, individual authors never gain absolute control over linguistic heteroglossia. Individual authorial agency is decentered in the act of textual production as intentions are "refracted" through the spectrum of languages and voices that the author seeks to organize. As an interpretive practice, rhetorical reconstruction seeks to "chart" (to use Burke's metaphor) the play of languages and voices, what I've termed *performative traditions*,

within the field of textual action. Reconstructing the appropriation
and diffusion of, and the play among, performative traditions moves
rhetorical criticism beyond a formalist recounting of discursive techniques. It seeks to provide a thick description of the organic emergence of text from its performative context, recognizing the radical
multiplicity of the text's context.

A critical program of rhetorical reconstruction could degenerate
very easily into an intellectual study of influence. In my view,
rhetorical reconstruction, to be a viable critical approach, must do
more than note the intellectual influences on a Lincoln or a Clay. As
textualists in intellectual history have discovered, the task is to
locate influence in textual action. LaCapra (1983) puts it this way:
"The question then becomes how precisely the discursive practice,
deep structure, or ideology . . . is situated in the text other than in
terms of instantiation or simple reflection. . . . One must elucidate in
a more detailed way how the borrowed or the common [languages]
actually function in the texts in question" (42, 51, see also 56; cf.
Gaonkar, 1989:268, 275). Understanding how performative traditions "actually function" in the field of textual action is the
hermeneutic burden of rhetorical reconstruction.[18]

CONCLUSION: AGAINST METHODOLOGICALLY DRIVEN CRITICAL PEDAGOGY; OR, WHAT DOES IT MEAN TO STUDY TEXTS IN CONTEXT?

Gaonkar's insightful reading of Campbell leaves an important
question unasked. While he discloses a key shift in Campbell's strategy for reading Darwin's *Origins*, Gaonkar leaves unasked the question *Why?* Or, put a little differently: How do we account for the
shift in Campbell's critical practice? Why the change in interpretive perspective? It may be that Gaonkar's critique of the ideology of
agency embedded in the instrumentalist tradition makes this question unimportant, but I think raising the question can contribute
to ongoing disciplinary dialogue regarding the nature of critical pedagogy.

Two general answers to the question appear reasonable given
the nature of disciplinary practices discussed by Gaonkar. First, we
could explain Campbell's shift as the result of a theoretical or conceptual intervention. On this account, Campbell's reading strategy
changed as the result of his encounter with strands of interpretive
theory that run counter to the dominant context-purpose interpretive nexus prominent in the instrumentalist tradition. By incorpo-

rating these theoretical or methodological reconceptualizations into his critical project, Campbell fashioned, if only intuitively, a new "intertextual" interpretive framework that resituated Darwin's text and displaced Darwin's strategic intentions. Second, we could explain Campbell's shift as a consequence of greater immersion in the performative context, the "cultural grammar" (Campbell, 1986), or the language of practice. On this account, Campbell's reading strategy changed as his exposure to related cultural practices led to a rethinking of the relationship between Darwin's text and those varied practices. By recontextualizing Darwin's text, Campbell discovered previously unnoticed elements of its textual dynamic that led, in turn, to further reconceptualization of "what was going on" in the text (for example, Campbell's 1990 turn to Garver's work on prudence as a way of explaining the play between innovation and tradition in the text).

It may not be possible to ascribe with complete accuracy one of these accounts as the source of Campbell's interpretive shift. But a final account of Campbell's shift is not my principal objective. I introduce these two accounts to illustrate what I believe are two rival, but not mutually exclusive, approaches to critical and interpretive innovation in rhetorical studies. For the most part, our critical practices and our critical pedagogy privilege the first account of change sketched above. Innovation in rhetorical criticism tends to follow from the introduction of new theoretical, conceptual, or methodological perspectives or models. Phenomenology, hermeneutics, symbolic interactionism, structuralism, dramatism, deconstruction—these are just a few of the theoretical or conceptual systems that have inspired rhetorical critics over the last few decades. And as critics have incorporated these perspectives into their critical practices, critical pedagogy has followed suit and fashioned methods for the advanced training of rhetoric critics.

It is, I believe, impossible to modify disciplinary practices through pronouncements "from above." Disciplinary practices change "from below." The disciplinary practices of rhetorical criticism will change through alterations in the dominant models of critical pedagogy. My discussion of thickening critical practice through attention to performative traditions suggests certain shifts in the way the discipline trains rhetoric critics. Consistent with recent work in literary theory (Mailloux, 1989), I think less attention needs to be given to theoretical or conceptual perspectives or methods and more attention needs to be devoted to performative contexts and traditions in critical pedagogy. Learning *how* to read texts in context needs to be emphasized in our pedagogical practices and not left for critics to discover on their own. This approach is not a form of "theory bashing" but rather a reversal of the dominant theory-practice relationship. Rhetorical reconstruction aims, in Gaonkar's (1989) terms, "to reconfigure the relationship between rhetorical theory and critical practice rather than simply 'marginalize' theory" (270). The project of "thickening . . . concepts through grounded critical readings" (270) cannot proceed, however, without an adequate contextual "ground" and a more detailed and nuanced sense of how that ground functions to enable and constrain textual practice. This sense cannot be developed in the abstract but only through the concrete engagement of texts and performative traditions. Critical pedagogy that emphasizes performative traditions as a crucial mode of contextualization prepares students to study the play of languages, voices, structures, and conventions in the text's field of action. As the example of Campbell (and others) illustrates, greater attention to the rich interplay of text and performative context helps thicken critical practice and invites, not inhibits, conceptual elaboration and refinement. By emphasizing performative traditions in critical pedagogy, we not only prepare students to enter the disciplinary conversation but we enrich that conversation as well.[19]

NOTES

1. Gaonkar correctly identifies one of the central burdens in current rhetorical criticism but, mistakenly I believe, suggests that this problem is unique to the discipline. Given his attention to disciplinary anxieties, Gaonkar fails to note the prevalence of recuperative gestures in critical and historical inquiry. Any effort to reread a text in a way that violates its dominant interpretive history requires some form of recuperation that will establish the need for, and wisdom of, the rereading. For example, Furtwangler's (1984) rereading of *The Federalist Papers* as an instance of "political literature" and not political theory is based on the recuperation of *form* as a central element of the text. Similarly, LaCapra's (1983) desire to reread key texts in recent intellectual history as "dialogized," rather than read them as mere "documents," is based on a more elaborate recuperative strategy that tries to rethink the relationship between texts and context. Rhetorical recuperation needs to be understood within this larger configuration of interpretive practice.

2. Gaonkar echoes Mohrmann's (1980) observation regarding the persistence of the classical vocabulary: "so we find the familiar steed rocking in a comfortable paddock" (268).

3. Gaonkar appears to accept Black's (1978) reading of Aristotle's *Rhetoric* as a "narrow" instrumental handbook (262). He acknowledges (78

n. 3) but then defers Beiner's (1983) quest to reopen the debate on Aristotle. "What is not so clear," Beiner writes, "is whether he [Aristotle] merely understood it [rhetoric] as the necessarily imperfect medium within which political life is conducted, or whether he also saw it as a positive expression of the mediated quality of social life. . . . What remains open to question is whether his *Rhetoric* was merely a handbook for the instrumental employment of this medium or whether it pointed toward an affirmation of the medium itself" (95–96). Twentieth-century rhetorical studies in the United States affirms LaCapra's (1983) observation that "a discipline may constitute itself in part through reductive readings of its important texts—readings that are contested by the 'founding' texts themselves in significant ways. These readings render the texts less multifaceted and perhaps less critical but more operational for organized research" (60). A recuperation of the (repressed) constitutive aspects of classical rhetoric might help negotiate the instrumental/intertextual impasse Gaonkar describes in his essay.

4. Gaonkar's use of the term *autonomy* is an effort to escape the radically situated nature of rhetorical discourse promoted by the dominant tradition of rhetorical studies. But autonomy, at least the kind discussed in certain schools of aesthetics, is problematic given Gaonkar's account of the operation of "structures that govern human agency" (52). The conceptual challenge, then, is to rethink the text/context relationship as something other than radical situatedness or radical autonomy.

5. The position I want to describe is not, I contend, "a simple reversal of the process of production" (33). The sense of reconstructive analysis I outline in the latter portion of the essay has certain affinities to the position William Keith develops in his essay in this volume.

6. Leff (in Leff and Sachs, 1990) notes the "radical particularism" of the neo-Aristotelian tradition (253). Leff struggles in this essay, as I struggle in this project, to articulate a mode of contextualization that is capable of acknowledging "the situated character of rhetorical discourse" (255) without falling prey to "a singleminded concentration on particulars" that "collapse[s] the context into the text" (256). What Leff doesn't do, and what I attempt here, is to engage the situational recuperation of rhetoric directly.

7. It is worth noting that Bitzer rejects an organic analogy in his account of the rhetorical situation: "Finally, I do not mean that a rhetorical discourse must be embedded in historic context in the sense that a living tree must be rooted in soil. A tree does not obtain its character-as-tree from the soil, but rhetorical discourse . . . does obtain its character-as-rhetorical from the situation which generates it" (3).

8. My reconstruction of the contrasting prefigurations of context draws from and extends upon Burke's (1969) discussion of modes of placement and the paradox of substance. Specifically, Wichelns oscillates between "placement" (contextual definition) and "derivation" (ancestral definition).

9. Black (1978) uses Wrage's study to illustrate some of the limitations of neo-Aristotelian criticism. Black contrasts Wrage's historical reconstruction with aesthetic re-creation that seeks to comprehend the work "in and for itself" (52). A rhetorical version of critical re-creation, Black suggests, emphasizes the identification of "rhetorical technique" as a central concern of the critic (56–57). I discuss Black's reading of Wrage in my own analysis of Clay's 1850 performance (Jasinski, 1995), where the emphasis is on situating Clay within a performative tradition of conflicting idioms of prudence. Leff (in Leff and Sachs, 1990) suggests that Black anticipates (and perhaps shapes) the direction of subsequent critical scholarship in his shift away from neo-Aristotelian particularism and movement toward recurring "formal structures" (255). This movement, as Leff notes, evades the question of rethinking the particular.

10. Nichols's position in this passage is similar to that adopted by Black in his discussion of Chapman's "Coatesville Address," a discussion motivated to a large extent by the problems Black locates in Nichols' practical mode of contextualization. Black (1978) writes: "The context of the Coatesville Address is less a specific place than a culture" (84).

11. I say "apparently" because, as I try to show in the next section of the essay, the relationship between context and purpose is more complicated than it looks at first glance.

12. There is some irony in McGee's (1990) fragmentation strategy since the situated recuperation of rhetoric prefigures it as fragmentary.

13. LaCapra (1983) summarizes the limitations of instrumentalism or intentionalism in the following terms: "By presenting the text solely as an 'embodied' or realized 'intentionality,' it prevents one from formulating as an explicit problem the question of the relationship between intentions, insofar as they can be plausibly reconstructed, and what the text may be argued to do or disclose. This relationship may involve multiple forms of tension, including self-contestation. Not only may the intention not fill out the text in a coherent or unified way; the intention or intentions of the author may be uncertain or radically ambivalent" (36).

14. I think this is also true of Black's approach to the question How can the critic respond to a speech that is "doctrinally archaic?" By advocating that the critic attend to the conventionalization of technique or the way discourse molds "an audience's sensibilities to language" (56), Black moves beyond the constraints of occasion and audience by inadvertently shifting his critical presuppositions from instrumental to constitutive.

15. A version of this problem exists in early American history in the quest to locate the "paradigm" or single language of politics in the revolutionary and founding periods.

16. Hogan's (1989) study of the "National Conference of Catholic Bishops Pastoral Letter on War and Peace" helps to illustrate further the problems of the particularist position. Hogan, correctly in my view, responds to a previous reading of the bishops' text (Goldzwig and Cheney, 1984) as "revolutionary" by recontextualizing the text within the institutional practices of the Roman Catholic Church. But Hogan in effect hypervalorizes this context: it becomes *the* context in which the text is to be read. Explicitly invoking Black's use of the particular, Hogan writes: "But as a rhetorical document, the pastoral letter is best interpreted within its own 'particular world,' and that world is generally religious and specifically Catholic. . . . In the religious context, the pastoral letter is not at all a radical statement. On the contrary, it thwarted an attempt to overturn the Church's theological and political tradition" (411). The critical question is whether the text's context is as singular and stable as Hogan's statement indicates.

17. Leff's discussion of "hermeneutic rhetoric" (this volume) moves in a different direction, one that I think is compatible with my emphasis on performative traditions.

18. There is, I think, a certain anxiety built into this kind of critical program. The anxiety is over the sufficiency of the level of reconstructive analysis. That is, what constitutes an adequate account of how traditions, or performative context generally, "actually function" in a text? Should the analysis remain at a thematic level (topics addressed), a structural level (figurative and argumentative forms), a linguistic level (idioms and voices), or perhaps a syntactic level? In my view no conceptual or methodological gesture can remove this anxiety; critics have to negotiate this dilemma in and through their critical labor.

19. My position in this final paragraph owes much to comments made to me many years ago by Tom Goodnight. Needless to say, it's taken me awhile to appreciate Goodnight's wisdom.

REFERENCES

Baird, A. C., and Thonssen, L. (1947). Methodology in the criticism of public address. *Quarterly Journal of Speech, 33*, 134–138.

Bakhtin, M. M. (1981). *The dialogic imagination.* C. Emerson and M. Holquist (Trans.). Austin: University of Texas Press.

Beiner, R. (1983). *Political judgment.* Chicago: Chicago University Press.

Bercovitch, S. (1978). *The American jeremiad.* Madison: University of Wisconsin Press.

Bineham, J. L. (1995). The hermeneutic medium. *Philosophy and Rhetoric, 28*, 1–16.

Bitzer, L. F. (1968). The rhetorical situation. *Philosophy and Rhetoric, 1*, 1–14.

Black, E. (1978). *Rhetorical criticism: A study in method*. Madison: University of Wisconsin Press. Orig. pub. 1965.

Burke, K. (1945/1969). *A grammar of motives*. Berkeley: University of California Press.

Campbell, J. A. (1986). Scientific revolution and the grammar of culture: The case of Darwin's *Origins. Quarterly Journal of Speech, 72*, 351–376.

——— . (1990). On the way to the *Origin:* Darwin's evolutionary insight and its rhetorical transformation. *The Van Zelst lecture in communication*. Northwestern University School of Speech, Evanston, Il.

Farr, J. (1988). Conceptual change and constitutional innovation. In T. Ball and J. G. A. Pocock (eds.), *Conceptual change and the constitution*, 13–34. Lawrence: University Press of Kansas.

Fliegelman, J. (1993). *Declaring independence: Jefferson, natural language, and the culture of performance*. Stanford: Stanford University Press.

Forgie, G. B. (1979). *Patricide in the house divided: A psychological interpretation of Lincoln and his age*. New York: W. W. Norton.

Foucault, M. (1982). The subject and power. In H. L. Dreyfus and P. Rabinow (Eds.), *Michel Foucault: Beyond structuralism and hermeneutics*, 208–226. Chicago: University of Chicago Press.

Furtwangler, A. (1984). *The authority of Publius: A reading of the Federalist papers*. Ithaca: Cornell University Press.

Gaonkar, D. P. (1989). The oratorical text: The enigma of arrival. In M. C. Leff and and F. J. Kauffeld (Eds.), *Texts in context: Critical dialogues on significant episodes in American political rhetoric*. Davis, CA: Hermagoras.

Gaonkar, D. P. (1990). Object and method in rhetorical criticism: From Wichelns to Leff and McGee. *Western Journal of Speech Communication, 54*, 290–316.

Giddens, A. (1979). *Central problems in social theory: Action, structure and contradiction in social analysis*. Berkeley: University of California Press.

Goldzwig, S., and Cheney, G. (1984). The U.S. Catholic bishops on nuclear arms: Corporate advocacy, role redefinition, and rhetorical adaptation. *Central States Speech Journal, 35*, 8–23.

Hariman, R. (1989). Time and the reconstitution of gradualism in King's address: A response to Cox. In M. C. Leff and F. J. Kauffeld (Eds.), *Texts in context*, 205–217. Davis, CA: Hermagoras.

Hogan, J. M. (1989). Managing dissent in the Catholic church: A reinterpretation of the pastoral letter on war and peace. *Quarterly Journal of Speech, 75,* 400–415.

Hudson, H. H. (1923). The field of rhetoric. *Quarterly Journal of Speech Education, 9,* 167–180.

Jasinski, J. (1995). The forms and limits of prudence in Henry Clay's (1850) defense of the compromise measures. *Quarterly Journal of Speech, 81,* 454–478.

Jasinski, J. (in press). Rearticulating history through epideictic discourse: Frederick Douglass's "The Meaning of the Fourth of July to the Negro." In T. W. Benson (Ed.), *Rhetoric and political culture in nineteenth-century America.* East Lansing: Michigan State University Press.

LaCapra, D. (1983). *Rethinking intellectual history: Texts, contexts, language.* Ithaca: Cornell University Press.

Leff, M. (1992). Things made by words: Reflections on textual criticism. *Quarterly Journal of Speech, 78,* 223–231.

——— . (1993). The idea of rhetoric as interpretive practice: A humanist's response to Gaonkar. *Southern Communication Journal, 58,* 296–300.

Leff, M. C., and Mohrmann, G. P. (1974). Lincoln at Cooper Union: A rhetorical analysis of the text. *Quarterly Journal of Speech, 60,* 346–358.

Leff, M., and Sachs, A. (1990). Words the most like things: Iconicity and the rhetorical text. *Western Journal of Speech Communication, 54,* 252–273.

Lucas, S. E. (1981). The schism in rhetorical scholarship. *Quarterly Journal of Speech, 67,* 1–20.

——— . (1988). The renaissance of American public address: Text and context in rhetorical criticism. *Quarterly Journal of Speech, 74,* 241–260.

——— . (1989). Justifying America: The Declaration of Independence as a rhetorical document. In T. W. Benson (Ed.), *American rhetoric: Context and criticism,* 67–130. Carbondale: Southern Illinois University Press.

Mailloux, S. (1989). *Rhetorical power.* Ithaca: Cornell University Press.

McGee, M. C. (1990). Text, context, and the fragmentation of contemporary culture. *Western Journal of Speech Communication, 54,* 274–289.

Mohrmann, G. P. (1980). Elegy in a critical grave-yard. *Western Journal of Speech Communication, 44,* 265–274.

Montrose, L. A. (1989). Professing the Renaissance: The poetics and politics of culture. In H. A. Veeser (Ed.), *The new historicism,* 15–36. New York: Routledge.

Nichols, M. H. (1954). Lincoln's First Inaugural. In W. M. Parrish and M. Hochmuth [Nichols] (Eds.), *American speeches,* 21–71. New York: Longmans, Green.

———. (1955). The criticism of rhetoric. In M. Hochmuth [Nichols] (Ed.), *A history and criticism of American public address,* vol. 3, 1–23. New York: Longmans, Green.

Perelman, C., and Olbrechts-Tyteca, L. (1969). *The new rhetoric: A treatise on argumentation.* J. Wilkinson and P. Weaver (Trans.). Notre Dame: University of Notre Dame Press.

Pocock, J. G. A. (1987). The concept of language and the *metier d'historien:* Some considerations on practice. In A. Pagden (Ed.), *The languages of political theory in early-modern Europe,* 19–38. Cambridge: Cambridge University Press.

Warner, M. (1990). *The letters of the republic: Publication and the public sphere in eighteenth-century America.* Cambridge: Harvard University Press.

Warnick, B. (1992). Leff in context: What is the critic's role? *Quarterly Journal of Speech, 78,* 232–37.

Wichelns, H. A. (1962). The literary criticism of oratory. In A. M. Drummond (Ed.), *Studies in rhetoric and public speaking in honor of James Albert Winans,* 181–216. New York: Russell and Russell. Orig. pub. 1925.

Wrage, E. J. (1943). Henry Clay. In W. N. Brigance (Ed.), *A history and criticism of American public address,* vol. 2, 603–638. New York: McGraw-Hill.

CHAPTER 9

ENGINEERING RHETORIC

William M. Keith

INTRODUCTION

In a recent essay, John Lyne (1993) has raised somewhat indirectly a fundamental question for rhetorical criticism in its mainstream tradition. Most rhetorical criticism has tended to be what Dilip Gaonkar calls "functionalist," in that it comprehends a piece of discourse as strategic, and attempts to assess its functional excellences or lack thereof (e.g., Did it persuade? Were the appeals appropriate to the audience? etc.) In analyzing Stephen Gould and Richard Lewontin's "The Spandrels of San Marco," Lyne notes an interesting parallel between their argument about evolutionary theory and rhetorical theory. Gould and Lewontin want to rein in the totalizing tendency of evolutionists to hold that every discernable feature of an organism must be a result of selection—and therefore functional, on the assumption that natural selection "selects for" functional biological features and "selects out" nonadaptive, nonfunctional ones.

Gould and Lewontin's central analogical example is the architecture of the cathedral of St. Mark in Venice. A "spandrel" is the wall shape/space created by the intersection of two ceiling vaults; while it is superbly decorated in St. Mark's, it is not a space "put there intentionally" to be painted. Rather, it is a structural by-product of the vaults' architecture (they have to be a certain shape to hold up the ceiling), and to ask about the "function" of spandrels per se would be nonsense. Gould and Lewontin suggest that many of the features an organism displays are constrained by structure, rather than environmental adaptation. For example, humans will never routinely be nine feet tall, because our skeletal and circulatory systems are inadequate to support this size; the very possibility is constrained by the overall structure.[1] Gould and Lewontin's strategy is to mock the ever more elaborate and outrageous stories evolutionists must weave to find the adaptive significance in an organism's every detail. Lyne notes in passing that the same kind of questions can be raised about rhetorical criticism. When critics attend to certain features of the discourse, how can they be sure that they are not attending to "rhetorical spandrels," discursive elements that are not the result of design or the constraints of rhetorical selection and adaptation, but simply the traces or by-products of larger structures?

Not only does this question admit of no easy answer, it cuts much deeper than the surface "How do you know which things count?" form would suggest (cf. Gaonkar, 1990). This question actually points to the contrast between two critical traditions, the rhetorical and the structuralist. The rhetorical tradition, typically with its eye on the political orator, has emphasized adaptation and function, while the structuralist tradition—from Marx, to Lévi-Strauss, to Lukas and Goldmann, Gramsci and Foucault—has emphasized how larger social-cultural structures determine the possibilities for individual speakers. In the first tradition (which Gaonkar calls the "Aristotelian ideology" and "the inventional strategy" of reading), speakers are the origin of meaning, adapting their words to their audiences and purposes. In the second tradition, the speaker is merely the point of articulation, where the macrostructures of culture and society, held in place through a system of signs and rationalizations that give the illusion of individual choice, hegemonically constrain the choices of speakers, who cannot "adapt" what they do not control. Gaonkar brings this structuralist perspective to bear on the rhetorical tradition, issuing a challenge not unlike Gould and Lewontin's: Now that we understand so well the power of structures to control discursive possibilities, isn't it an act of critical false consciousness (if not self-delusion) to continue closely reading texts, weaving fabulous stories of their adaptive brilliance or perversity—as if speakers could simply *choose* all that, as if intentional persuasion still made sense? It is particularly important that Gaonkar pose this question, and that he receive an answer, because so many in the community of rhetorical theorists and critics have wanted to graft rhetoric to structuralist theories, without apparently appreciating the contradiction involved (Biesecker [1989] has discussed this problem as well). If we held that rhetoric consists in the macroconstraints on the production of discourse, Gaonkar is quite right to point out that we must simultaneously give up a connection to the "rhetorical tradition," particularly the Aristotelian one, since it simply cannot accommodate such a perspective. The crushing blow from his argument is that, on the level of disciplinary politics, recognizing structuralist perspectives seems to put rhetoric out of business; without a connection to The Tradition (whatever one takes that to be), "rhetoric" becomes little more than a convenient but empty term to be filled with the latest (post-)structuralist theories.

Should we give up the game so easily? Does acknowledging the truths in a structuralist perspective require us to abandon the strategic rhetoric that has comprised the historical tradition? This essay, while acknowledging the justice of much of Gaonkar's critique, attempts to establish a place for functionalist readings of discourse, maintaining that while the problematic character of functionalist criticism is *intrinsic to rhetoric*, it is still a vital tradition worth preserving, especially when the cost is merely a critical pluralism.

ASKING THE RIGHT QUESTIONS

Gaonkar's essay (this volume) accomplishes two main tasks. First, it problematizes rhetoric as a hermeneutic/critical theory. Since its theoretical vocabulary is derived from production, it is not naturally a critical vocabulary; the five canons were a guide to producing, not interpreting, discourse. Given the nature of producing discourse, we would expect to see a "thin" vocabulary; teaching communication is a shallow heuristic activity, not a deep algorithmic one, and does not require a ramified theory, but rather a series of rules of thumb. Second, Gaonkar connects this problematic to the larger disciplinary narrative of repression and recognition; we have *compensated* for the thinness of vocabulary by telling a tale of repression (repression by philosophers is why rhetoric is so hard to find) and recognition/ recovery (so we have to actively seek rhetoric out, whether in theories or artifacts). Thus the underdetermination of artifacts by rhetorical theories is explained by repression rather than by the theories' failure to strongly enough specify their objects—it's not that rhetorical theory is vague, but that we've been conditioned not to see things rhetorically. So one expects there will be a certain amount of work necessary to overcome our repressed awareness of rhetoric and reveal the rhetorical quality of artifacts (e g , in popular culture) and authors (Kuhn, Foucault, or Latour as rhetorical theorists). The subsequent pervasiveness of rhetoric is attributable to our enhanced recognition of its existence ("It was really there, all along!") rather than to the "thinness" and excessive flexibility of rhetorical theory that allows it to be read into nearly anything ("Here is a formula for reading anything as rhetoric . . .").

The basic problem, which Gaonkar identifies on both the theoretical and disciplinary level, is this:

What does rhetoric contribute *distinctively* as a theory of language and communication?

This is a problem because in order to thicken up rhetorical theory, deepening the formula by which rhetoric is identified (with the possible exception of Burke, whose mode of theory construction is akin to collage), other (i.e., not from "the tradition") material always gets added in, and the distinctiveness of rhetoric can then be attributed to these theoretical additions. As Gaonkar shows so patiently, Gross and Prelli in particular seem to end up, respectively, as a literary critic and a sociologist. The term *rhetorical* becomes a placeholder without substantial meaning, a gear in the critical machine that turns nothing and is turned by nothing.[2] There are lots of theories of language, meaning, text, interpretation—why should rhetorical theory command anyone's attention? McCloskey wants to find solace in the classical tradition, but that option recedes in the distance between the handbook tradition and the goal of a globalized metadiscourse. Campbell seconds Gaonkar's analysis by admitting the connection between productive theories and thin critical theories; he likes the flexibility inherent in the thin rhetorical theory, and thus its affinity to *phronesis* and production. But even by valorizing what Gaonkar criticizes, he may be settling much too quickly; what we're after might go much deeper than that.

My diagnosis is that the same problem, a kind of reflexive invisibility, actually emerges on *three* levels: rhetoric appears to be invisible at the level of the text, the theory—and the discipline. My thesis is that this situation follows from the very nature of rhetoric, rather than theorists' fumbling attempts to bring rhetoric to light. A stipulation: Let rhetorical theory be those explanations that answer the question:

1. Why do people say the things they do?

This is a fairly natural account, I think: It transposes a productive, handbook tradition:

2. What should someone say *here*?

into a hermeneutic stance:

3. Why did someone say *that here*?

and of course, one does not need to think that the third question's answer literally reconstructs the answer to the first, a position Gaonkar criticizes as a "romantic hermeneutics." This account accords with much of what's taught in textbooks about rhetoric, much of the tradition, etc.

In essence, it turns questions about rhetoric into questions about strategy and language. This is the Aristotelian ideology, which Gaonkar sees at the root of failed attempts to make rhetoric a universal hermeneutic. Gaonkar claims that, *pace* Campbell, a vocabulary of production derived from Aristotle is insufficient to the task, and thus is always supplemented/supplanted by other theories. So in answering the above question, rhetoric appears in the guise of some other theory (Kuhn, deconstruction, etc.) and then, according to the recognition strategy, says that other theory is "really" a rhetorical theory. Even as rhetoric aspires to unmask the other discourses it analyzes, it seems to unmask itself in various guises—or does it?

The key here is the notion of strategy and its relation to a hermeneutic stance. *The difficulties in reconstructing discourse as strategic are not accidental, but intrinsic.* Briefly, it should be noted that the Aristotelian ideology *is* inconsistent with most structuralist, poststructuralist, and deconstructive accounts of language. Quite simply, these accounts claim that (1) meaning in texts derives from their place within a larger symbol/meaning system, not from the author's (strategic) intentions, as the Aristotelian ideology seems to imply; and (2) that there is always more meaning (and strategy?) in a text than "what the author put in," so audiences are not constrained by the author's intention, which may be irrelevant to the political and cultural structures that guide their understanding. Without denying either the cogency of these accounts or their analysis of the Aristotelian ideology, I will contest (below) the degree to which they exclude or nullify Aristotelian approaches.

LA RHETORIQUE S'EFFACÉE

The basic difficulty can be approached several ways. To begin, consider a chestnut from The Tradition and the public speaking course: The best persuasion conceals itself. Making strategy apparent in discourse generally causes the strategy to fail. This doesn't seem to be particularly variable within Western cultures, since it seems to have been taken as a truism from classical times to the present. The reason is something like this: The audience is likely to be persuaded if they perceive the rhetor as sharing, to an extent, their interests. If this convergence actually obtained, no strategizing would be necessary, and the (longed-for-by-Habermas) condition of "true communication" would be realized—the true "lover" of the *Phaedrus*. To the extent that strategy makes an appearance, audience members may suspect a divergence of interests and thus be wary about the persuasion. Of course, through rhetorical ineptitude one could mistakenly present an actual confluence of interests as an apparent divergence, spoiling chances for persuasion. So even guilelessness, perhaps, requires strategy. Disingenuousness is thus the natural condition of human communication; persuasion aims at its own transparency.

Rhetorical readings seek the *presence* of strategy in a text; but if rhetoric conceals itself, then *such readers should expect not to find it*. If it is the nature of rhetoric that it continually effaces itself, then rhetorical theories are likely to be odd creatures indeed. Consider the French verb *effacer*: it means not only "to turn away from" (physically, spatially), but "to hide, obscure, conceal, remove, or erase." These multiple senses capture the present point, since within a text strategy recedes from view even as it becomes paramount. (And note that both rhetorical theory, and the discipline strategically claiming that theory, recede just as quickly.) And *effacer* can be a reflexive verb; we might say that *la rhetorique s'effacée*, rhetoric effaces itself. Texts appear to cry out "I'm just representing reality,"or "I'm just expressing the thoughts of my author"; we may recognise the distortion here—yet the pull of these siren songs gets stronger as they are more nearly false to the rhetorical nature of the text.

I am not the first to note these characteristics of rhetoric. In *The Electronic Word* (1993), Richard Lanham argues that there are two ways of approaching a text: "looking *at*" the text (attending to forms of language and expression, the nuances of expression, the design of a page) and "looking *though*" the text (attending to its "real" content, while all else is irrelevant). For Lanham, rhetoric is a "bi-stable" mode of perception that simultaneously keeps these contradictory kinds of reading in view. Lanham writes:

> Rhetoric as a theory has proved so exasperating and unsatisfactory precisely because it oscillated from one world view [the philosopher's] to the other [the rhetorician's]. . . . Rhetoric's central decorum enshrined this bi-stable oscillation: the great art of art was the art of hiding art, but you had better start out with some art to hide. (110–111)

Lanham claims that this "root self-contradiction" is unproblematic, as long as it remains grounded:

> [It] causes trouble only when you take it out of time. *In* time, as a perpetual oscillation, it works fine. Generations of thinkers have bemused themselves, as we do today, by taking the oscillation out of time, stopping it to point out how immiscible the two ingredients are, how moral and formal judgments can never mix. (111)

Lanham's suggestions are striking and sensible, but he concedes the basic point: we cannot expect rhetoric to hold still as a stable object of theorizing; it will always prescind from the kind of treatment that rhetorical theorists want—need—to give it.

If rhetoric is not manifest within a text, then rhetorical interpretation or reading is fraught with difficulties. In fact, one would expect it to have just those problems Gaonkar describes. The ephemerality of textual strategy would preclude a "thick" theoretical vocabulary: To what textual features would such a vocabulary attach itself? The range of such a interpretive approach would be promiscuously wide: Since it seeks what is not present, this non-presence can be found anywhere!

In addition, the structuralist objection—that there will be more to a text than its strategy (occluded to begin with)—has considerable force. Strategy (and tactics) assume *control*: that one can control features of the text or talk—and so the audience's understanding—for certain purposes. But control is exactly what is difficult; control of language or meaning is at best elusive, and doesn't seem to extend reliably through language to others. So one begins rhetorical criticism knowing that much of what can be found in the discourse was not "under control," and in making a reconstruction the critic must decide what parts were controlled, introducing a variability that runs against the commonsensical aim of such criticism. Why would anyone think that language allows control? Where does this enter into rhetoric? Is rhetoric the "power of language?"

DIGRESSION ON MAGIC

Jacqueline de Romilly (1973) usefully unpacks some fourth-century Greek relationships between magic and rhetoric. These are not trivial. Aristotle's claim that rhetoric is a *tékhnē* has to be seen as a repudiation of a magical tradition (the mystical power of the *logos* and so forth) which is so abhorrent to Plato, including all the contents of Derrida's Pharmacy: magic, drugs, potions, spells, writing, etc. To the Greeks of that time, a host of practical and moral issues turned on the difference between magic and strategy.

But both approaches, the magical and logistical, are strategic: Aristotle's tékhnē is supposed to give one control of tactics, while a magical approach holds the power of rhetoric is invisibly implicit in the *logos*. But exactly how are these different—has anything really been explained in a move from the magical to the rational? What, we might ask, is the practical difference between:

4. If I say these words, under these circumstances, *they will be persuaded,* which results in particular actions on their part.

and

5. If I say these words, under these circumstances, *they will be under a spell,* which results in particular actions on their part.

Not much, apparently. The difference lies in the *locus of persuasive agency* in each case. In the case of magic it is something mysterious; in the case of rhetoric, each rhetorical theory is distinctive in the place to which it assigns the active principle of rhetoric. According to Connors (1986), pre-Socratic Greeks generally did think that the *logos* had a kind of magical power. De Romilly suggests that Aristotle's approach to strategy (rhetoric as tékhnē) transfers the magical agency of the *logos* into the rationality shared by speaker and audience,[3] and so his account is basically a theory of argument. In Burke's account, identification, guilt, and redemption are made to due the duty of rationality, but the element of agency is still there.

Another way to understand the problem about control involves a comparison between the portions of the discourse that are "always already inscribed" with meaning, and those that the rhetor "controlled" or "intended." Can we make sense of this difference? (The problem formulated by Lyne reemerges here.) Is the line between them stable or endlessly de/re/constructed? The answer to the first question is probably "Not in general, but only in specific cases" (thin theory, again); the answer to the second question has to acknowledge instability. Different readings, at different times, for different purposes will draw this line in a different place (repression and recognition, again).

I assume that a strategic account of rhetoric has failed if it cannot distinguish rhetoric from magic. Yet that problem still haunts rhetorical theory, even if implicitly. Why can't rhetoric seem to escape these problems? Is it, as Gaonkar suggests, that it clings to a failed strategy for transforming a productive tradition into a hermeneutic theory? One has wonder whether any other strategy would do better, or if there is something exceptional about rhetorical theory, something that sets it apart, intrinsically, from the hermeneutic tradition to which Gaonkar compares it.

THE DISAPPEARANCE OF RHETORIC

The invisibility of rhetoric is exactly accounted for by rhetoric's focus on strategy, which accounts for the disciplinary problem of repression/recognition. Rhetoric appears to have no subject matter because the actual subject matter (strategy) is never present in the object of analysis. No wonder it looks like pulling a rabbit out of a hat when the rhetorical theorist suddenly makes rhetoric appear in this or that cultural location, in science, or art, or film, or even politics. We have to come to see rhetorical readings as a choice, one way of understanding a text; Lanham's perpetual oscillation unfortunately entails that one part of the oscillation, the rhetorical part, might be long suppressed.

Aristotle solves this problem (on the productive end, going from theory to product) through a trick of generalization: Rhetoric is the skill of discerning possibly persuasive arguments περὶ ἕκαστον (peri hekaston), in each case or subject matter. Now, suddenly, rhetoric is a *general* skill that one "brings to" a subject matter. It will be applied differently in each case, so there's no need to specify the theory in advance. Thinness has great advantages in productive theories. But going the other direction, from product to theory/criticism, is more difficult. "Wait—was rhetoric used in creating the text before me? Which are the skill-produced parts of this discourse?" Scholars of rhetoric find themselves in the uncomfortable position of claiming to see rhetoric where others don't, and then claiming that the rhetoric is there precisely because it doesn't appear to be!

Nostalgia for public address won't help, as is argued in Brummett's (1991) criticism of what he calls "rhetorical nostalgia" (56 ff.). Identifying strategy was not *actually* easier when the objects of analysis did not extend beyond platform and legislative speeches; even though these are self-consciously designed as rhetorical, their really interesting rhetorical aspects (i.e., as reflections of a culture) may not have resulted from the composition process as the writers understood it.

Thus we are left with a problem: What kind of hermeneutic theory is appropriate for rhetoric, given its intrinsically occult (literally: hidden) status? How can we say anything interesting about strategy, if that is to be our contribution? A general rhetorical hermeneutic is possible, but only insofar, I claim, as it recognizes the problems just discussed. Failure to take account of them will only lead one back on paths already trod.

ENGINEERING RHETORIC

My account will parallel one about engineering: as an activity, a theory, a discipline. Engineering is a productive discipline, in ways similar to rhetoric as a productive discipline. In fact, engineering might encompass the *design arts*: How do you make things that work a certain way, for a certain purposes, within various (social, cultural, psychological, economic, physical, etc.) constraints? Examples could include architecture, mechanical/chemical/electrical engineering, printing, urban planning, etc. Rhetoric, then, may be concerned with design of language for purposes both individual and social. And a rhetorical hermeneutics would be concerned with identifying and understanding such designs.

What are the conditions I will place on such an account?

1. Open-textured: no sharp edges; includes shifting borders and practical contexts
2. Not totalizing: never claiming to tell the whole story
3. Pragmatic, not realist

What are the parallels between rhetoric and engineering? First, engineers don't in general need to make theory or generate knowledge (though these may be by-products of their efforts); they can coexist with a good deal of "thinness." They make things that "work," based on their understanding of other things that "work," where "working" is defined for a particular practical context only. So, to simplify somewhat, the perception that engineering is a subbranch of physics or chemistry is inaccurate; engineers don't have to claim to be discovering knowledge, reality, or anything like that. They claim to make things that work in a given situation and given purpose; they are *techn*icians in the etymological sense. (Consider the term *engineered*, and what it signifies about an artifact.)

Engineers can get along without grand theory (physics); historically, many practical solutions are discovered long before anyone understands theoretically how or why they can work. (Construction—How *did* they build that darn Sphinx?—and pharmacology are two examples.) This account is of engineering broadly conceived, and challenges the picture "from blackboard, to lab, to engineer, to realization," which is really an account of how universities are organized, not how engineering has to proceed. While engineers have techniques, they have no privileged method, or route to knowledge. (Of course, physicists may not either, but they are heavily invested in the *claim* that they do.) Instead, engineers make things, often based on old things that worked in similar situations with similar purposes. (*Ad hoc* would not be an insult in this context, as it always is in science and theory.)

So knowledge in engineering consists in understanding a wide range of these cases and being able to apply them in new cases (the element of tékhnē). Of course this element may be present in every field, profession, or activity, but it is not possible to disguise it in rhetoric because of the situatedness of the critical objects; this is Leff's (1989) point about the "habitation of rhetoric in the particular," which we might rephrase as the disappearance of rhetoric into the particular. Aristotle's definition of *rhetoric* (1355b) can be read as a renunciation of grand theory, as an acknowledgment that rhetoric is a training for the capacity or skill of seeing and understanding communication situations in a particular way, neither requiring a theory nor demanding a precise payoff in results. Part of rhetoric's parallel to engineering is thus exhibited in its history of thick manuals and thin theoretical tomes.

Two points stand out here. First, reversing Aristotle's account (to produce rhetoric-as-hermeneutic) is difficult, since the deeper the theory, the farther it is from practice. This means that without some kind of intervention, handbook rhetoric converted to rhetoric-as-hermeneutic will result in a strikingly thin theory. Second, much depends on what one takes the "possibly persuasive" (τὸ ἐνδεχόμενον πιθανόν, *to endekhomenon pithanon*) in Aristotle's definition to mean. Liddell and Scott (1983) give the definition of ἐνδεχόμενον as equivalent to the Latin *suscipere* ("acknowledge, recognize"), and (of things) *to admit, allow of*; impersonally, *it may be, it is possible that*; they also note *by every possible means*. The elements of means and ends are clearly present, and lead us to a fundamental question: What is the space of possibilities here?

This question is crucial, since it is precisely this space of possibilities that a rhetorical hermeneutic must use to open up a text to a rhetorical reading. If the space is too small, rhetoric will be rarely found, as before the twentieth century it was rarely recognized outside politics and law. As Black (1978) showed, the space of possibilities for Aristotle is more restricted than critics assumed; rhetorical practice for Aristotle operates out of a set of possibilities that includes commonly accepted arguments directed toward audiences that sit in judgment at one of three structured, institutionally sanctioned situations, the judicial, the deliberative, and the epideictic. (1358a–b) So, while the *form* of Aristotle's definition has considerable appeal, Gaonkar is right (as was Black) to argue that the *content* of Aristotle cannot support a rhetorical theory. But if the space of possibility is too large, then rhetoric will be trivially a part of every text, every utterance, every human interaction, and Gaonkar argues that this situation is no better.

My account of the scope of rhetorical theory requires the notion of *reverse engineering*, a term widely used in production/manufacturing, and even in neuroscience research (artificial intelligence is the attempt to "reverse engineer" the human brain [Arbib and Robinson, 1990]). Confronted with an artifact (often a competitor's product), an engineer might have the job of making something "like it" or that "works like it." She would thus have to understand how it works, and how it was made, and attempt to duplicate the process. (How *do* they get the lead into the pencil? See Petroski, 1989.) Without focusing on the industrial espionage part of the story, we can see that something intellectually very interesting happens during the engineer's attempt to understand the artifact. She has to take her understanding of the processes by which such things can be constructed, including the known constraints of time, efficiency, physical possibility, etc, and in essence *interpret* the artifact as an outcome of an intelligible process; "intelligibility" here means a sense that some sort of vaguely rational means-ends thinking went into designing the thing. This is precisely the kind of thinking that the engineer could understand and therefore reconstruct. (This is the "rationality" issue Black [1978] emphasizes.)

To digress for a moment, one expects that at this point structuralists and those of like mind (such as Foucaldians) will object to the excessive *rationalism* of this account of intentional creation and design—Are people really so strategic? Could they intend to be? But I find such objections somewhat, well, disingenuous. Yes, this account suggests that for certain purposes it makes sense or is helpful to reconstruct discourse strategically. But to hold that the structures of meaning are beyond the control of any individual speaker's intentions commits one only to *a different location* for the rationality or structure in one's account. Theory, after all, is somehow a structured explanation of something. Foucault's epistemes, for example, are awfully well structured and rational, and we might raise the same questions about them—Could they really be so structured and pervasive as to discipline our thinking across the culture? (Willard, 1996, questions this.) I am dubious about arguments to the effect that the rationality/structure which explains discourse is *really* in these metadiscursive objects, and other accounts are just wrong (i.e., the claim that "the structure of discourse couldn't be made intelligible as strategy").[4] The continuity between strategy and metastructure is a stick that can be grasped at either end.

An engineer typically looks at means and ends in terms of a set of constraints on each. Constraints on the means include materials and processes available, and typically involves a interlocking system: If you make *this* part heavier, then you must make *that* part stronger to hold it, and then when the first part gets hot it will stay hot longer and so needs a heat damping device, etc. Constraints on the ends include the suitability of the final product to its use, the cost-effectiveness of producing it, its durability, its relationship to similar products, its salability, etc. The assumption of rationality comes in relating the features of the product (under a certain description) to the various constraints on means and ends, and there are typically many ways to do this, to "satisfy" the constraints. In addition, these vocabularies are not fixed (they may be quite situation-specific), and neither is the description of the objects' properties; there is enormous flexibility, even with material objects, in reconstructing them. While in some cases this process of reconstruction seems quite transparent, that may be an effect of familiarity. In fact, there is an underlying *indeterminacy* to the process:

- *Which* aspects of the object in question were "engineered" in the first place?
- Doesn't the artifact's status as engineered obtain *only* under a certain description of it?
- Isn't the reconstruction of the engineering process always underdetermined by the features of the artifact? (I.e., there are always more engineering explanations than the object can eliminate through inspection.)

A well-designed object (for its specific context) tends to conceal its artifactuality, its designedness. Well-designed things call out to the user "I am natural," "There's no other way I could be made," "Form is just following function here." But these are masks for the design issues addressed by the engineer of the thing (consciously or not).

When the use is most obvious, the design is best hidden; a truly fine handle needs no label, since it seems to invite one's hand.[5] To the extent that one has "to figure out how to use" something it shows bad design; good design (like the Macintosh user interface), disappears into the object, and is "natural."[6] This makes the reengineering task considerably harder, since the features of the object one might most want to reproduce (i.e., those that make it effective) will be the most difficult to see.

To appreciate these points, consider a case distant in cultural and scientific time, which will mirror the issues Lyne raised. The megaliths at Stonehenge are clearly human products; someone put them there. (This is an important interpretive first decision; in the case of archeological "burial" grounds it is not always obvious that they *are* burial grounds, since the bones may simply lie wherever people died.) In reverse engineering the megaliths, an engineer would first have to decide which features of them were "engineered" in the first place—which features are *design* features. But since we don't know what they were used for, it's hard to tell. The stones were quarried and transported a considerable distance to the site—so much we can reconstruct from the geology. We might also make good guesses about how they were transported. But why this stone, and not that which was locally available? Is that a (religious, social, practical) design feature of the megaliths? Why the shapes? Were these the most convenient size to transport, or do the various sizes and shapes have another purpose? Why the lintel stones? Each upright stone is buried to a certain (common) depth. This depth keeps it upright—but a greater or lesser depth would have served as well. Is there a design significance to the depth? The placement of the stones in circles has involved endless speculation. We should note what such speculation involves: It requires constructing a story (a rationale) in which people with certain means and purposes brought about the artifact (as understood under a particular description). All of this reverse engineering talk involves setting the artifact within a certain human context, even though other accounts of it are possible, and perhaps equally "true."

Thus the "engineered/just-came-that-way" and "designed/natural" distinctions are as unstable for engineering as the intentional/accidental distinction for discourse. Control is also an issue in engineering; to say that a feature has been engineered in implies that this feature was under the control of the designer, and of course depends on the description of the thing. (Children tend to think that the bronze statues which decorate public spaces are intended to be green—and sometimes they are.) Of course, engineers successfully reverse engineer things all the time, so neither of these instabilities is an insurmountable obstacle to their hermeneutic practice. They don't need to be for rhetoric, either.

IMPLICATIONS

Rhetorical hermeneutics as reverse engineering must be positioned as a critical practice. My account involves bumping the engineering metaphor up to the metadiscourse level and being equally pragmatic: rhetoric is one among many possible (re)descriptions of discourse, and choosing a description depends *not* on what is "really true" about discourse, but on the successful engagement of specific problems. Redescribing discourse in strategic terms is one such possible redescription, and does not invalidate others. Here is where the practical traditions of rhetoric become important; reverse engineering involves a practical hermeneutic, of means and ends, as does the production of rhetorical discourse.

But we shouldn't mistake the means of production, so to speak, for the nature of rhetoric. It is the role of the rhetorical tradition to comprehend the institutions within which people understand themselves as doing strategic communication, and to explain, extend, and teach such strategy. Sproule (1988) has commented on the "new forms of rhetoric," and claims that the critical tradition must change to adapt to these. But that claim overstates the case because it entrenches the view that the institutional/situational conditions of communication (oratory vs. public relations as the primary rhetorical form) determine the nature of rhetoric or rhetorical criticism. From the perspective offered here, we could say that rhetoric has not changed, only the nature of *what* is engineered and *why*.

What would mean in practice to reverse engineer discourse? It would entail, first, giving up most of the psychologizing critics do about speakers. Except in special cases, one simply cannot read off the literal, psychological, intentional process from a text; Gaonkar is right that one cannot simply reverse the production process in criticism. More importantly, we have to give up thinking there is any reason to care about speakers' intentions in the first place. Rhetorical critics, if these suggestions are taken seriously, *will view texts as sets of strategic responses to the constraints that obtain for them,* without making the leap from redescription-as-strategy to redescription-as-reconstruction of psychologically real intentions. The engineer looking at an ancient machine or artifact may well be able to explain some things about it as design features, meeting constraints of which the makers couldn't have been aware; the critic may well know more than the speaker could know about how a given text worked out against its relevant constraints. We are forced to ponder the megaliths at Stonehenge without any knowledge of why or how they were built; still, given an understanding of the constraints faced by the builders (how far the stones had to be carried without mechanical power, how they could be quarried, how they were set into their holes, etc.), we can reconstruct the various possibilities involved in doing that kind of construction; a contemporary engineer could say, "Well, of course they had to use this kind of stone, since with the tools they had the other available kinds of stone could not have been worked." This goes beyond what the builders of Stonehenge might have known (consciously or unconsciously), but it is no less an explanation for all that. Rhetorical critics are interesting precisely because they are adept at seeing multifarious constraints on speakers and texts: the audience, the ideational context, the relevant genre, previous discourse, cultural givens, and many others. Reconstructing how a text "does what it does" while responding (or not) to these constraints is perfectly possible without invoking the reality of the speaker's intentions, and this understanding can feed back into the intentional practice of other speakers—and that the nature of the constraints is debatable is yet another valuable part of the critical process. "Seeing the possibly persuasive" becomes a matter of having analyzed and understood enough situations to be able to give an account of the constraints in the current one, the range of solutions for those constraints, and how a text does or doesn't embody them.

Another way to see the dispensibility of intentions for a critical practice employing a production-derived vocabulary is that there is no reason at all why the *critical vocabulary* should be commensurate with the *vocabulary available to the creator(s)* of a message. The methods used to unpack the rhetorical event will in almost all cases be more complex and ramified than the methods used to create it. This has never troubled anyone before; critics have long deployed Aristotelian vocabulary (ethos, logos, pathos, etc.) on speeches whose authors knew little of it. It is precisely through the exploitation of this gap between the intentions of the "speaker" and the actuality of the text that rhetorical critics can do something interesting and sophisticated—if all the design features were self-evident, what would be left to say?

The second thing which rhetoric would have to give up is any sense of totalizing power as *the* account or theory of discourse. When rhetoric loses its pretensions to being the objective science of discourse and meaning (leaving those pretensions, maybe, to others), it accepts certain burdens, just as any normative, socially situated inquiry must. A rhetorical reading is one among others, making critics accountable for giving such readings. The first two sections tried to establish that texts don't "demand" to be read rhetorically; quite the opposite. So a question looms over the enterprise: Why? Mountain-climbing answers ("Because it's there!") won't do, and neither will claims that the text in question is "really" rhetorical. Scientists have long defended their immunity from accountability by such appeals to the connection between their enterprise and reality, but rhetorical critics know better.

Scholars have lately begun to question the distinction between the inside and outside of science. Traditionally, the inside of science consisted in the logical methods of experiment and proof, while everything else, especially the psychological characteristics of scientists and the social character of science, was outside of science. This strategy effectively isolated science from social criticism; scientists could respond to criticism by saying, "That's not my problem; I just do *science*." The deconstruction of this distinction makes science irrevocably social, and connects every part of science to social concerns. Just as the loss of the inside/outside distinction in science makes the social present in every part of science, so rhetorical criticism cannot evade its social context.

Engineering itself is intimately tied to the social: What is it that people want or need to be made—and why? Engineering has been defined by R. S. Kirby as "the art of the practical applications of scientific and empirical knowledge to the design and production or accomplishment of various sorts of constructive projects, machines, and materials of use or value to man" (1990:2). He goes on to adumbrate the relationship of engineering to society by quoting Hardy Cross:

> It is customary to think of engineering as a part of a trilogy, pure science, applied science and engineering. It needs emphasis that this trilogy is only one of a triad of trilogies into which engineering fits. The first is pure science, applied science, engineering; the second is economic theory, finance and engineering; and the third is social relations, industrial relations, engineering. Many engineering problems are as closely allied to social problems as they are to pure science.

These connections and responsibilities must control the progress of engineering, not illusions about science transcending social concerns. Engineers in practice may not always ask "Why make this—to what good end?" but the question is always there (even though it is usually constructed out of existence by positivist traditions in science). In addition, the history of engineering shows that engineering achievements were/are intimately bound up with social/cultural aims and values (Kirby, 1990:19)

In short, the burden of making rhetoric visible involves, in part, taking responsibility for a *reason* to make it visible. Marxist critics have long done this; the success of much literary theory can, I think, be traced to this. But many rhetorical (and perhaps literary) critics still wish to be "scientists" (scholars) of discourse, discovering answers about what discourse "really" is: it is really semiotic, or overburdened with meaning, or fixed by political forces, or speaker's intentions, or whatever. The search for the "right" answer, unfortunately, will go on. But rhetorical critics make bad scientists because they are engineers by trade. Theories of rhetoric slide into triviality unless properly restrained, due to the self-effacing nature of rhetoric. If there is no theoretical ground for restraint, then let it be provided by a social/political/practical context of reading.

CONCLUSION

Now, how does all this come together—self-effacement, engineering, and the status of rhetoric? As demonstrated by the argument on self-effacement, rhetoric intrinsically has a reflexive quality, which makes things difficult for those who want to show that rhetoric is a substantive discipline. McKeon-style claims about rhetoric as the intersection of everything else *sound* good, but they may not work out very neatly: If the globalization of rhetoric were taken seriously, we would no longer be able to claim (as McCloskey does so openly) that "everything is *really* rhetoric." This claim for many seems at once intuitive, and necessary to the discipline, but the problems with it are embedded in the terms *real* and *everything*.

Claiming that everything is really rhetoric brings on a kind of paradox, one familiar to sociologists of knowledge as the problem of *reflexivity* (Ashmore, 1989; Latour, 1987; Woolgar, 1988). What's needed in this context is the honest sense of reflexivity which is practiced by Latour and Woolgar. Woolgar realizes that as a sociologist describing science he cannot simply say "Everything is really social," because the statement presupposes the very contrast—between the real and the social—that it is supposed to deny! McCloskey, and too many others, are in much the same position. If they were to follow their commitment to rhetoric all the way through, they would see that it would *necessitate* an analysis of the rhetoric of Rhetoric—which is precisely what Gaonkar has done. (That can be said without conceding that it is the only possible account of the rhetoric of Rhetoric.)

The second problem is that one doesn't need the absolute generality of rhetoric to forestall positivists and others. One can show (as we have seen over and over) that any given instance of science is rhetorical without having to hold that there is nothing at all which not rhetorical. Suppose we posit a natural world "out there," acting as if there is an independent reality (this is what Arthur Fine [1986, 1991] calls the "natural ontological attitude"), a reality which doesn't respond to persuasion (things don't fall up, people can't flap their arms and fly, etc.) Does this threaten our ability to show, in each particular case, that scientific practice is rhetorical? Not at all. One can even admit that this world, in many roles, plays a part in the persuasions of scientists. This is just Latour's view: that material objects get their meaning and reality from the roles they play in various epistemic economies (as do human agents), but they are not constituted exclusively by those roles and thus are no less "real" (in the usual sense) for all that. And by admitting the contrasting conceptual territory, one gives bite to the notion of rhetoric. This is what makes Bokeno's criterion for rhetorical theory ("a conception of rhetoric which is smaller than the conception of human conceptual activity") cited by Gaonkar a sensible one.

What I have been arguing in this essay is, in a sense, a sort of antirealist account of discourse theory: There isn't a "real" truth about discourse, there are simply many descriptions of the ways it works. Against Gaonkar, I want to say that there is a version of "intentionalist" rhetoric which, under the right description, is extremely useful and important (even if opposing descriptions, ones which highlight the macrosocial features of discourse, can be useful and important in other contexts). Against McCloskey, I hold that under any description rhetoric still can have some specificity, and that analyzing the rhetoric of Rhetoric is going to be a key to understanding its multiple roles and descriptions, since it continually effaces itself.

Many commentators have cited Edwin Black's *Rhetorical Criticism*, and with good reason: I think we are just now beginning to address the problems he framed. Brushing aside his dated descriptions of science, we can understand Black's argument in his first chapter to be something like this: A discursive practice, be it rhetoric or science, deserves our respect only to the extent that it can be *held accountable* in some way.[7] Black takes it that the ways in which scientific claims are held accountable is well understood. But more importantly, he sets out the standard for rhetorical theory: A critical discourse must be capable of accountability (or what Gaonkar, in a most unfortunate word choice, calls "falsification"); that is, there has to be a means (a rhetoric?) for contesting claims that are made—and probably more than one means. In trivially global discourse, such as some versions of Freudianism or Marxism, accountability seems lacking, since every contestation leads directly back into a confirmation of the theory (see Frederick Crews's lucid work—1994a, 1994b, 1995—on the implications of Freudian theory for therapeutic practice to see how corrosive this problem can be). Rhetoric, despite its global hermeneutic status, despite its natural effacement, should not suffer this fate; rhetorical criticism is too important not be accountable. Black set the stage, and Gaonkar has pointed us to the tasks that remain.

NOTES

1. My example. In *Freaks* (1978), Leslie Fiedler notes that "the medical records of Giants taller than eight feet are particularly appalling. . . . [While] true, or 'genetic' Giants can compete mentally and physically with the acutest of normals . . . [these healthy individuals] seldom exceed seven foot six, and never reach eight feet, much less nine" (106).

2. Cf. Ludwig Wittgenstein, *Philosophical Investigations*, sections 270–271. As Wittgenstein liked to point out, a term invested with complete generality loses its conceptual power because it fails to make any kind of distinction; it becomes a kind of gesture without function.

3. The notions of *judgment (krisis)* and *judge (krites)* are relevant here; see Black's *Rhetorical Criticism*, ch. 4. Rhetoric is exactly that discourse directed to an audience attempting to make a reasonable judgment. Cf. Aristotle, *Rhetoric*, 1358a–b.

4. It is in this sense, perhaps, that Derrida is actually a poststructuralist, since he refuses to admit the final stability of any rationalized account of discourse.

5. And, of course, all these remarks about naturalness assume that it is heavily context-dependent; what seems natural to one set of people at a certain place and time may certain not seem so in other contexts—or to other hands.

6. Certainly enough familiarity and investment of effort will render bad design "natural" to users, as the history of certain software products

shows. But this point doesn't tell against the original naturalness of design or lack thereof, since a lack of naturalness is all too evident to new users.

7. The relevant passage is:

A critical statement is, in some sense, verifiable. A critical statement, even a critical judgment, is one for which reasons can be given, reasons that may gain the agreement of rational people. . . . Neither the physicist nor the critic should expect their inference or their findings to be accepted on faith. Both carry the burden of proving their claims, and that proof must be of a sort that is accessible to others as proof. (7–8)

REFERENCES

Arbib, M., and Robinson, J. (1990). Natural and artificial parallel computation. In M. Arbib and J. Robinson (Eds.), *Natural and artificial parallel computation*. Cambridge: MIT Press.

Aristotle. (1991). *Aristotle's* Rhetoric: *A theory of civil discourse*. G. Kennedy (Trans.). Oxford: Oxford University Press.

Ashmore, M. (1989). *The reflexive thesis: Wrighting the sociology of scientific knowledge*. Chicago: Chicago UniversityPress.

Biesecker, B. A. (1989). Rethinking the rhetorical situation from within a thematic of différance. *Philosophy and Rhetoric, 22,* 110–130.

Black, E. (1965/1978). *Rhetorical criticism: A study in method*. Madison: University of Wisconsin Press.

Brummett, B. (1991). *Rhetorical dimensions of popular culture*. Tuscaloosa: University of Alabama Press.

Connors, R. (1986). Greek rhetoric and the transition to orality. *Philosophy and Rhetoric, 19,* 38–65.

Crews, F. (1994a, 17 Nov.). The revenge of the repressed, part I. *New York Review of Books,* 54–60.

———. (1994b, 1 Dec.).The revenge of the repressed, part II. *New York Review of Books,* 49–58.

———, (1995, 23 March) Exchange and commentary on "The revenge of the repressed." *New York Review of Books,* 65–66.

de Romilly, J. (1975). *Magic and rhetoric in ancient Greece*. Cambridge: Harvard University Press.

Fiedler, L. (1978). *Freaks: Myths and images of the secret self*. New York: Simon and Schuster.

Fine, A. (1986). And not anti-realism either. In A. Fine, *The shaky game*, 136–150. Chicago: Chicago University Press.

———. (1991). Unnatural attitudes: Realist and instrumentalist attachments to science. *Mind, 95,* 149–179.

Gaonkar, D. (1990). Object and method in rhetorical criticism: From Wichelns to Leff and McGee. *Western Journal of Speech Communication, 54,* 290–316.

Kirby, R. S. (1990). *Engineering in history.* 2nd edition. New York: Dover.

Lanham, R. (1993). *The electronic word.* Chicago: Chicago University Press.

Latour, B. (1987). *Science in action.* Cambridge: Harvard University Press.

Leff, M. (1987). The habitation of rhetoric. In J. W. Wenzel (Ed.), *Argument and critical practice.* Annadale, VA: Speech Communication Association, 1–11.

Liddell, H. G., and Scott, R. (1983). *Lexicon.* (Abridged ed.) Oxford: Oxford University Press. Orig. pub. 1871.

Lyne, J. (1993) Angels in the architecture. In J. Selzer (Ed.), *Understanding scientific prose.* Madison: University of Wisconsin Press.

Petroski, H. (1989). *The pencil: A history of design and circumstance.* New York: Knopf.

Sproule, J. (1988). The new managerial rhetoric and the old criticism. *Quarterly Journal of Speech, 74,* 468–486.

Willard, C. A. (1996). *Liberalism and the problem of knowledge: A theory of rhetoric for modern democracy.* Chicago: University of Chicago Press.

Wittgenstein, L. (1958). *Philosophical investigations.* London: Basil Blackwell.

Woolgar, S. (1988). *Knowledge and reflexivity.* London: Sage.

CHAPTER 10

FROM *TEKHNE* TO TECHNIQUE: RHETORIC AS A DESIGN ART

David S. Kaufer

In his pathbreaking papers on rhetoric, Dilip Gaonkar (1990; this volume) brings to our attention the following dilemma: We understand rhetoric as (horn 1) a set of clearly demarcated (as in ancient times) yet thin and diffuse production practices with no native hermeneutic. Rhetoric on this horn is more a way of acting in the world for limited and local ends than in comprehending those actions from rich and enduring interpretive frameworks. Or we understand rhetoric as (horn 2) subsumable within a specific hermeneutic practice (dramatism, Whig Liberalism, Marxism, feminism), leaving rhetoric with no enclosed or demarcated hermeneutic identity of its own. On this second horn, rhetoric is a pervasive, but nonetheless parasitic, way of understanding the world of symbolic action.

Horn 1 is appealing to classicists who like their definitions of rhetoric narrow and carefully circumscribed. Horn 2 is appealing to modernists who want to establish a close relationship between rhetoric and the newer arts and sciences of interpretation.

Gaonkar's dilemma turns on the metaphoric contrasts of *thin* and *thick*, *classical* and *modern*, *production* and *reception*. Classical rhetoric is thin and production-oriented. Modern rhetoric is thick and reception-oriented. Classicists have sought to blunt the edge of Gaonkar's dilemma by arguing that classical rhetoric is not as thin, diffuse, and production centered as it might seem. Modernists have taken Gaonkar's dilemma as justification for preferring the more modern renderings of rhetoric to the classical ones, as a way of understanding complex social events more than list-like guidelines for effective public speech. Others have responded to Gaonkar with positions that fall somewhere between these poles.

Gaonkar's dilemma provides a professional litmus test for any rhetorician about what the content of rhetoric is and how it is to be studied. In this essay, I use Gaonkar's dilemma as a way of teasing out a middle ground. I suggest that the horns are symptomatic of rhetoric's original misclassification as a mundane practical art. Classifying rhetoric as a lowly practical art makes it seem vulnerably thin, open for "rehabilitation" as a hermeneutic art. The modern horn of Gaonkar's dilemma arises as a natural response and correction to the classical horn. As an alternative to this response and counter, I suggest rhetoric is more profitably understood as a design art. The rest of this paper fills out the claim about design as a solution to Gaonkar's dilemma, returning at the end to the dilemma itself.

If my association with rhetoric as a member of the family of design arts has merit, then it goes some way toward explaining both why Gaonkar's dilemma has bite and how it can be addressed. Traditionally, Platonists have rejected rhetoric for its imprecision, its sense of praxis with no foundation in a structured art or *techne*. Rhetoric comes to be identified with a practical art in the lowest sense of that term, far too thin, eclectic, and opportunistic to support a systematic hermeneutic. Rhetorical theorists who fight against Platonism often do so out of a sense of indignation as much as out of a sense of understanding the charge being made. The charge being made is that rhetoric does not live up to the internal standards of coherence of a true techne, a true art of design, where praxis is carefully regulated by techne, where a theory of reception is closely monitored and informed by a theory of production.

METHODOLOGICAL APPROACH

Before I flesh out my claim relating rhetoric and design, let me say something about the approach I'll be taking that opens the issue of rhetoric's status as a practical vs. design art in the first place. To the question *What is rhetoric?* one can offer many possible answers. One can give historical answers—It's the body of knowledge Plato criticized and Aristotle taught. One can give stipulative definitions— It's the adaptation of people to ideas and vice versa (Bryant, 1953). One can give exemplary descriptions—It's what Clinton did last night when he promised a middle class tax cut without offering specifics. These types of answers are familiar to rhetorical theorists and critics and I needn't say more about them. The kind of answer I am interested in here comes out of a branch of thought known as *complexity theory*. Complexity theory is the study of the minimal complexity needed to describe a system, either as it exists in the abstract or for some specific application or purpose. A complexity analysis has either a strong or weak relationship to a psychological model of mind. In a strong relationship, a complexity analysis is a psychological theory. In a weak relationship, it provides an analysis of the shape and interactivity of detail that any psychologically real model must accommodate.

Chomsky applied complexity theory (strongly he thought, but weakly in the minds of others) to natural languages when he asked of a language like English, What is the minimal complexity required to describe the grammar of English? Complexity theory can be put in formal, mathematical terms. Chomsky did just this in *Syntactic Structures* (1957) when he showed that the expressive power of one type of formal grammar (phrase-structure grammars) was too simple, and thus insufficiently complex, to explain the grammar of English. As students of Chomsky know, Chomsky settled upon transformational grammars as having the minimal complexity required to characterize all and only the sentences of English.

Complexity theory is not limited to formal mathematics, however. One can apply complexity theory to verbal theories, as a way of testing whether a theory of interest includes all the vocabulary that is needed to render intelligible the elements in the universe of discourse it stakes as relevant. The logical positivists of the 1930s proposed the principle of *verification*, which made the meaning of a scientific statement its mode of verification. A verbal complexity analysis revealed that this statement could not itself be a statement *of* positivism, was beyond the expressive scope of positivist semantics, because the statement itself, having no independent mode of verification, had no inherent meaningfulness in positivist doctrine. In this case, critics of positivism found that the spirit of the doctrine could not be stuffed into the strict letter of its formulation.

To apply a complexity analysis to a body of knowledge is to assume that the knowledge under scrutiny has enough internal complexity to make exploring the minimal complexity of its interior worthwhile. Rhetoric has traditionally been cast as the very antithesis of such knowledge. Its parts are seen to fall into relatively inert, nonhierarchical, and independent entries across various taxonomical lists. A body of knowledge seemingly shaped like a list distributed over multiple categories is a *least likely* candidate for a complexity analysis. This is the stereotypical perception of rhetoric's internal shape, I want to suggest. It is a shape that has linked rhetoric with a practical art of superficial "how to" knowledge, that makes rhetoric seem the poorest of candidates for a complexity analysis, and that causes rhetoric's internal complexity to seem like such a nonissue that we never think to ask how *minimally* complex rhetorical knowledge can possibly be. In rhetorical theory, a complexity analysis seeks to develop an explanatory framework that accounts for a significant portion of the observed results of a rhetorical artifact with minimal conceptual complexity. It is essentially the application of Occam's Razor, a basic launching point for the sciences, to rhetorical theorizing. A way to falsify and improve upon an account (and I do think rhetorical accounts should be falsified and improved upon) would be to show that a rhetorical analysis can be treated with comparable coverage and explanatory power but more simplicity.

RHETORIC AS PRACTICAL VERSUS DESIGN ART

My argument is that rhetoric has been historically mistaken for a practical art when it is better understood as an art of design. It is at this juncture useful to acknowledge those who have sought to ennoble rhetoric as a liberal art rising above the mundane practical. To a few acquainted with rhetoric as a body of knowledge associated with liberalism and practiced by the likes of Demosthenes, Cicero, Edmund Burke, and Daniel Webster, rhetoric since the Greeks has been an important calling. Along with logic and grammar, rhetoric formed the trivium of education in medieval Europe; until the middle of the nineteenth century, it remained an unchallenged cornerstone of a liberal arts curriculum in American universities; and, to this day, students of the rhetorical tradition recognize rhetoric as an art fundamental to a free society, especially in times and places where democracy and open forums of expression are prized.

Still, the appropriateness of rhetoric among the liberal arts of history, philosophy, and literature has remained suspect. The high-minded universals of the humanities have seemed products of leisurely breeding and random curiosity more than tactical action and meeting deadlines. It has been difficult to reconcile the dignified universals of the humanities with the interestedness, practicality, and localness of rhetorical design. The universal values taught in Quintillian's school of rhetoric ("the good man skilled in speaking") notwithstanding, for example, the rhetorician seeks to exploit a single situation for utilitarian advantage. The humanities were charted to give their practitioners a wise and reflective soul, not an edge.

Despite the high-mindedness with which it is often justified, rhetoric is more widely treated as a practical art of the mundane, both in classical and modern incarnations. The mundane practical arts are those forms of production whose successful execution depends on a person merely setting the goal to do or make something. Working a typewriter or a cash register is a practical art because having the desire to learn it is, for the average adult with a high school education, the dominant predictor for attaining the learning. In a practical art, the effect of an action is pretty much circumscribed by its goal, and so we can specify most of what the effect will be when we can specify the goal. In the practical arts, a theory of the agent's motivation and intention dominates a theory of effects; since the techniques are presumed efficacious ("hit this key to get the subtotal"), it's only important to know what someone is *trying* to do. The handbook tradition of rhetoric, one aimed at novice learners, is often couched in a simple "how to" style that gives rhetoric the appearance of a practical art.

Architecture and engineering are, in fact, prototypical design arts. In prototypical design arts, an artifact is planned; externalized at intermediate phases in the form of sketches, blueprints, models, mock-ups, thumbnails, or storyboards; and, eventually, cast into finished form. The coevolution of intention and artifact is considered so vastly difficult and detailed that slippage is not only necessary but expected. The effects being judged are vastly more intricate and complex than the designer's most general goals, *making the conditions of reception part of the environment needed to refine the theory of production*. Unlike a practical art, which need not "mature" because production theory need not answer to the dynamic input of reception, a design art is thought to increase in sophistication and complexity as result of the contexts of reception continuing to inform and differentiate aspects of production theory and vice versa.

The design arts are typically associated with "high" art, that is, arts dependent on the intricate interplay between the goals, strategies, and tactics of the designer on the one hand, and the logic of the material artifact that is shaped or caused to evolve as a consequence of the designer's effect upon it. Plenty of not-so-great musicians, one imagines, share the basic intentions of the great ones. Plenty of nonmusical instrument-makers share with musicians the logic of the instrument's capacity to make sound. Only the exemplary musician, presumably, can interleave the logic of the intentional world with the physical capacities of the instrument. In the fine arts generally, the logic of intentionality and the logic of the artifact are brought together and allowed to coevolve on what appears to be, to the nonexpert, a seamless course.

Complexity, delicacy, fragility, and slippage in the coevolution of intentionality and artifact—and the consequent explosion of possibilities—form the central perception of what makes an art "fine."

The emergent artifact in a fine art is demeaned when the principal
adjective applied to it is (merely) "practical"—even if the artifact, say
a bridge, a building, or a corporate logo, is expressly designed for
and put to practical use! In the design arts, "merely practical" is an
incomplete, if not insulting, descriptor of the emergent artifact
because intentionality and usability are only isolated components of
the design story. While only a trained judge may be able to detect and
recover intricate details of the coevolution, even laypersons can
appreciate that a coevolution has taken place, and that what now
appears in the finished product of a seamless technique grew, originally, out of large and formidable seams. The perception of these
seams and the artist's ability to conceal them gracefully is what
allows us to appreciate the fineness of a fine art. Yet, for various
reasons that I consider below, it is much more elusive to perceive,
and so appreciate, these seams in rhetorical design. And as a consequence of missing these seams, we tend to categorize rhetoric as a
practical more than a design art.

Art descends into the "merely" practical when the realization
of intentionality seems unremarkable. A laid-off worker needs
money, applies for a job as a cashier at a fast-food store, and learns to
work a cash register. Working a cash register has no daunting learning curve, seems no big deal. Yet it is connected in an intimate way
to making money, the original goal. Because the realization of the
goal seems not terribly far ahead or far removed from the goal itself,
the goal and its realization seem related as a practical art.

Similar considerations lower rhetoric into the well of practical
art. A speaker wants to be persuasive, stands on a soapbox, and begins
to deliver rhetoric. Everything is done with the issuance of words.
The intentionality of the speaker arguably begins in (internal, unvo-
calized) words and the delivery finishes off in the same medium. No
expensive apparatus, external instrumentation, or elaborate set-up is
required. Only words are required, a medium available to humans
without effort after a few months of life. In a practical art, the seams
separating intentionality from artifact appear insignificant. And in
an art like rhetoric, where it is words all the way down, the seams are
particularly invisible. Seamedness is starkly visible in prototypical
design arts, yet barely visible, if not invisible, in rhetorical design.

TOPICAL SYSTEMS VERSUS MODULAR DESIGN

The modularity of design environments is an obvious first principle; yet it seems an exotic assumption for rhetorical design. Why?

The answer seems to be that design problems *solved implicitly* seldom require *explicit representation*. This has been the case with rhetoric's modularity. Were the need for modularity as practically pressing in rhetoric as it is, say, for software engineering, it is likely that the handbooks would have taught speech writing in much the way programming texts now teach software design. But the rhetorical tradition found ways of teaching rhetoric that allowed students to visit different modules of design without having to know that they were doing so.

In his authoritative translation of Aristotle's *Rhetoric*, George Kennedy (1991:320) defines (*koina*) *topos* as a

> mental "place" where an argument can be found or the argument itself . . . a form or strategy of argument usable in demonstrating propositions on any subject; to be distinguished from an *idion*, which is a proposition specific to some body of knowledge.

Topics refer at once to a container (a place) and to the objects contained (a form or strategy of argument). They refer at once to a process (demonstrating) and to the results of applying the process (the propositions demonstrated). Propositions are always about some specific knowledge, yet the rhetorical topics are described as resisting an "aboutness" relationship to such knowledge. When they are about a particular body of knowledge, they are *idion* or special topics, knowledge unrelated to rhetoric. Aristotle specifically distinguishes between special topics, those that reside within the specialized disciplines, and rhetorical, or common (*koinoi*), topics.

These robust patterns hold their shape across these modules. A pattern which can mnemonically help induce an argumentative plan from a memory of events can also help induce some anticipated tactical advantages over an opponent and, further, can help develop specific patterns of language to hold the moment with an audience. One and the same verbal gestalt can be mnemonically useful, in sum, for helping a speaker form an argument, turn the tables, and manufacture language to anchor the audience's drifting attention to the weight of the moment.

The meaning of *topos* was similarly diffuse. To speak of the topics was, at one and the same time, to speak of events warehoused in long-term memory; to speak of actualizing these events as plans in real-time interaction; to speak of indexing these plans to monitor one's leverage; to speak of the verbatim memory required to recall who said what, when, and the effect of these verbal actions on the state of leverage across the whole of the interaction; and, not least, to speak of the complex linguistic choices determining what is actually said—the material reality of rhetoric.

The topoi are inherently diffuse because they are verbal gestalts with no single module or environment of application. Some concepts have a diffuse reference and can only be understood precisely if understood in that way, and the topics of classical rhetoric are a case in point. With illustrative examples from the Lincoln-Douglas debates, table 10.1 characterizes two of Aristotle's twenty-eight koinoi topoi (often called the "enthymeme topics") as patterns holding their shape across argument plans, relational tactics, and linguistic events. This table offers as a kind of demonstration proof that when we ask what a topic was supposed do for Aristotle and other classical rhetoricians, it seems to simultaneously establish

TABLE 10.1
Analysis of Sample Enthymeme Topics

Topical Pattern	Plan	Tactic	Event
Precedent	Show that the argument of self descends from a chain of events carrying positive principles.	Reverse leverage by showing that history smiles on the self's argument more than that of the opponent.	Both Douglas and Lincoln trace their argument to the "sacred principles of the founding fathers."
Correlatives	Show, through correlative slots, that argument of opponent is missing crucial information or contradictory.	Reverse leverage by showing correlatives that expose the opponent's argument as having less force.	Lincoln: Douglas endorses freedom to choose slavery in the territories. Every choice implies the slot of chooser. But who gets to choose and when? Any answer smokes out Douglas as having no clear position.

internal coherence for an argument (as a plan), leverage for a speaker (as a tactic), and a linguistic stream of variable and opposing information (as language events). To speak of the topics that inform rhetorical design is to speak of the refinement of information at all these sites.

Consider, for example, the case of the pattern "precedent" in the first row of table 10.1. As a plan, a precedent is an abstract structure that represents events linked to common principles that are being carried forward into time. As a tactic, a speaker might invoke such an abstract structure against one offered by an opponent. Used tactically, the abstract representation of history offered in a precedent structure becomes a weapon for showing that history can take sides in a dispute. As an event, precedent structures, constructed at the plan level, instigated at the tactical level, must still be implemented in the moment-to-moment production of language. Thus, abstract and complex precedent structures get implemented with the production of local words and phrases like "the founding fathers maintained that . . ."

If this analysis has merit, we can begin to appreciate the difficulty of characterizing rhetorical knowledge in any single way. The temptation is to localize such knowledge within a single module—as a long-term event memory, as plans, as tactics, or as linguistic knowledge. For a practical art of rhetoric, the genius of the topics is to allow speakers, through simple verbal gestalts, to move fluidly and tacitly across the modules of rhetorical design without requiring a technical understanding of the individual modules through which they are moving. This allows perfection of the craft with a minimal technical understanding of the art. For an art of rhetoric as design, however, it is not enough to rely on mnemonic gestalts to assure that the different modules will be visited for the purposes of able performance. We must investigate each of the modules of design on its own terms, as part of a systemic understanding.

Rhetorical knowledge, being referentially diffuse, gets stigmatized as imprecise and is then reduced to discrete knowledge bundles. Plans become the province of psychology; tactics, the province of political science and management; events, the province of linguistics. Each discipline has become very successful in its own right. Rhetorical knowledge, the knowledge applied in rhetorical design, is the link between them. If we are to make rhetoric precise, we must accept rhetorical knowledge as the relationships obtaining across diffuse realms and we must then go on to understand these realms well enough to be able to say useful things about their interconnections. Otherwise, we are in danger of doing what so many post-

Enlightenment thinkers end up doing when they decline to investigate rhetoric with the lament that rhetoric is not physics: saying
nothing about rhetoric at all.

THE SYMMETRY OF PRODUCTION AND
RECEPTION IN RHETORICAL DESIGN

To look into rhetoric's minimal complexity is to ask how minimally complex must the system of the rhetor's productive choice be
to account for the range of what the speaker can by saying by design.

To clarify things a bit, let me make two distinctions. I distinguish interpretation and interpretation-by-design. Interpretation-by-
design is interpreting what is uttered against the contrastive set of
alternative choices that could have been uttered and weren't. I also
distinguish interpreting and tracking an interpretation. The capacity
to track an interpretation is a speaker or hearer's ability to account
for all the things that an utterance can mean, or indicate, *by design*
in the context of utterance. Tracking an interpretation is thus the
process by which the class of utterances that fall within the speaker's
interpretation by design is enumerated. To track the speaker's interpretations is to search through the speaker's utterance as an interpretation-by-design.

The reciprocity between production and reception in acts of
rhetoric is not captured in explicit speech act theories of communication where intention and meaning are overt. The reciprocity
between rhetorical production and reception can involve intentions
and meanings that are covert, below the surface, not fully available
even to the speaker's consciousness at the time of utterance. A
politician who says "There is no mechanism for lowering taxes"
may simply perceive himself or herself as saying that "As far as I see
it, taxes won't be lowered." But the politician has also said or at
least indicated, *by design*, much more than that. For example, the
politician has, arguably, also indicated, by design, that "I am not
open to persuasion on this matter." To make this argument, one
can offer an alternative rendering—what could have been said but
wasn't—that would have blocked the indication. Such an alternative
would be, "I haven't yet heard a good reason to lower taxes." Because
such an alternative production was possible and not used, we learn
something about the design choice of the speaker, something about
the speaker's system of production.

At the same time, the reciprocity between speaker and hearer
on the speaker's interpretation-by-design is a far more restricted

notion than the potential "anything goes" of unconstrained interpretation. Interpreting a speaker, the province of hermeneutics, is far
less constrained than interpretation-by-design, the province of
rhetoric. The politician above, through his or her utterance, can also
be interpreted as committing to "tax-and-spend liberalism." But this
last interpretation cannot be demonstrated as part of the speaker's
interpretation-by-design because it cannot be *rescinded through an
alternative rendering of the speaker's productive choice.* We can't
block this interpretation by systematically manipulating the choice
points within the speaker's utterance. Interpretation always tells us
about the receiver; often tells us about the speaker; but usually does
not tell us much about the speaker's space of productive choice.
Interpretation-by-design is the way we conventionally account for
this space of a speaker's productive choice.

   At first blush, it may seem that my distinction between interpretation and interpretation-by-design resonates with Hirsch's distinction between meaning and significance in *Validity in Interpretation* (1967). For Hirsch, meaning is the horizon of signification
warranted within the intentionality of the writer; significance is the
horizon warranted within the purposes of the reader. These horizons entail information that is not in the conscious intention of the
speaker or reader at the point of utterance or reception. In this sense,
they are similar to interpretation-by-design, which also involves
more information than is in the speaker's conscious state at the
time of production. However, unlike Hirsch's distinction, which
draws the boundary between the writer's horizon of meaning and
the reader's, my notion of interpretation-by-design draws the boundary between the set of all relatively paraphrasable things that it was
warrantable for the speaker to have said, and the particular element
from that set that was chosen. I don't know a great deal about how to
characterize this distinction further; yet we rely on it all the time
when we draw "meaning" from seeming paraphrases of what a
speaker or writer said that were not uttered. A theory of rhetoric as
design needs to explore how we learn to make competent inferences
about interpretation-by-design and how these inferences inform production habits.

Untangling Hidden Complexities in Aristotle's Modes of Proof

   To illustrate the value of complexity analysis in rhetorical studies, let us see how such an approach can open up some hidden inter-

dependencies in Aristotle's three modes of rhetorical proof: *logos*, *ethos*, and *pathos*. From the standpoint of Aristotle's theory, these modes form a natural class of proof. They are closely related species of a common genus. The members of the class differ only in the place where the proof is understood to reside. In logos, the proof is in the speech itself. In ethos, it resides in the speaker. In pathos, in the audience. These distinction seems simple enough until we try to classify specific cases. Take the following utterance:

1. I am a senator.

This utterance has persuasive force through the conventional meanings of the words. The words identify the speaker as belonging to a class that is judged knowledgeable and competent to persuade. Logos must surely play in role in the kind of proof exemplified by the utterance. The utterance also indicates the qualifications that one must have in order to enjoy the entitlement of the category role "senator." In this sense, the utterance persuades through ethos. Moreover, the utterance may easily induce in hearers positive emotions (esteem, admiration, pride) that facilitate persuasion. In this sense, the utterance also exemplifies proof by pathos.

Now there is nothing itself untoward about collapsing three modes of proof on a single utterance. There is no a priori reason to enforce a one-to-one correspondence between modes of proofs and the utterances that can exemplify them. However, there is something unsettling about the thinness of the story we have to tell about what qualifies an utterance as exemplifying one or another kind of proof.

Our stories are thin, I suggest, because they have thus failed to capture the very complex design space in which these modes of proof are in fact composed. If logos is proof in the words, then how can an utterance issued to persuade not exemplify it? To make logos a meaningful target for design, we need to distinguish words from portable words. Words come and go in immediate contexts and few survive intact, much less verbatim, into future contexts. Portable words, however, do survive intact and so have a power that can outlast the context of their immediate production. To have both durability and predictability, a rhetor must aim for portable words, words and meanings that will reside in the memories and ongoing interactions of audiences for future action. We are a long way from an adequate theory of the interaction among language, memory, and the reach of language (through memory and repetition) across contexts. Sometimes the reach and influence of language across contexts has— at least in part—a linguistic source. There may be something remarkable about the words themselves, their sound, rhythm, meter, weight. Sometimes however the reach and influence of language may have its source in the ideas—the reasoning, and line of argument—that undergird the words, while the words themselves change from one context to the next. I don't have a great deal more to say here about the subtleties of language/context interactions. My point is that a theory of logos from a design standpoint minimally requires a theory of this interaction.

Ethos is another mode of proof, but the environment for its design is qualitatively different from the environment of logos. Rather than a theory of language/context interactions, ethos relies on a theory of language/public entitlement interaction. What can I say to entitle myself to say or do things to enhance persuasion? Unless one lives in an illiterate community, going to school is not an entitlement with public visibility. Being first in one's class is a more conventional entitlement. Most cultural conditions ("having had chicken pox") are not entitlements. But there are few cultural conditions that can't function as entitlements in some favored context. A nine-year-old can cite "having had chicken pox" as an ethical argument for attending a party with kids who have been exposed to chicken pox. Without a representation of how entitlements work in one's culture, or how contexts can elevate conditions into entitlements, one can't compose (or comprehend) ethical proofs. From a practical standpoint, logos and ethos are closely related elements of rhetorical proof. From a design standpoint, they are worlds apart in how speakers and receivers think through and recover their meaning. Another world opens up for pathos. Pathos is the complex interaction of language and the system of emotions.

Aristotle and ancient rhetoricians in general were no doubt aware of these vastly different realms behind the Aristotelian modes of proof. But the impulse of classical rhetoric, rooted in praxis, was to elide these differences and compress them in the service of practicality. To be fair, the "impulse" may have been more an artifact of the loose and fragmented writings that have survived from the classical period; or perhaps more an artifact of the inclinations of the modern-day speech teachers who drew from classical rhetoric for classroom practice. A design art, in any case, evolves through expansion and reconciliation rather than elision and compression. Because it must serve argument and action, design knowledge, like practical knowledge, must be reconciled and routed to practical ends. But the reconciliation must overcome the resistance of expansion. Expansion is the first stop in design knowledge, used to reflect the complexity of the choices involved in what is being designed.

The rhythm of expansion and reconciliation makes it easier to see deep commonalities between entities that seem superficially unrelated; and large conceptual schisms between entities that seem superficially paired. It also makes it easier to keep like to like in the design environment and to keep unlikes apart. For example, from the standpoint of design, we see that ethos can span vastly different rhetorical goals and can determine even the willingness to engage in public discourse. Compare (1) reproduced below, with (2), a statement of Lincoln's during the Freeport debate when he begged the audience for time to put on his spectacles:

1. I am a senator.
2. I am no longer a younger man.

Utterance 1 indicates a clear instance of ethos as public discourse. The speaker utters an entitlement that is meant to enhance credibility. Utterance 2 is a bit of ethos in which a speaker (Lincoln) appeals to his humanness by acknowledging and then deferring the expectation of entering into public discourse. We expect leaders to be Rhodes scholars and senators in order to be entitled for public discourse. But once they are there, we allow them humanness as an entitlement, signaling that they have managed to keep their feet on the ground with the common folk. Both occurrences exemplify ethos, but from very different rhetorical goals and a very different environment of productive conditions. In the first case, the speaker wants to use a public role entitlement to seem an exceptional case. In the second case, the speaker shuns a public entitlement to fit into the norm.

Public/private distinctions are thus vital in accommodating huge variations in how ethos is produced and recognized. But we also require the same distinction at the level of individual words to explain how subtle shadings of rhetorical meaning are produced and perceived. Take the following utterances:

3. He is a conscientious public servant.
4. I don't blame Lincoln [for his failed policies]. He is conscientious.

The first utterance uses the word *conscientious* to modify a term understood to reside in a public setting (*public servant*). The second utterance, spoken by Douglas at Ottawa, uses the same word to descriptively contrast the person, Lincoln, with his failed policies in the public realm. In the first case, *conscientious* imports its positive connotations to the public sphere term. In the second case, the positive connotations of *conscientious* are blocked. *Conscientious* becomes a descriptor of private praise meant to damn a ineffectual public figure. The context for producing and perceiving these shadings of the same word is incredibly complex, requiring an understanding of how features of a single word can transfer or fail to transfer from private to public realms.

Yet a third place where the private/public distinction surfaces in contexts of production and reception is the conspiracy argument. The conspiracy argument could not be designed nor perceived were it not possible to envision private ends being furthered under the cover of a public trust. Utterances 5 and 6 below can't possibly be a conspiracy charge because they capture the lofty 5 or the lowly 6 doing above board things; conspirators must work for goals that betray the public trust but without public visibility or accountability. Utterances 7 and 8 come closer to this pattern, but 7 carries it more than 8. Conspirators must be high enough on a hierarchy to be given a public trust as a prerequisite to betrayal.

5. The senators are conspiring to promote freedom.
6. The hoodlums are conspiring to promote freedom.
7. The senators are conspiring to promote communism.
8. The hoodlums are conspiring to promote communism.

An Architecture of Rhetorical Design

In the previous sections we have considered only a few of the implications of viewing rhetoric as a design art. For the past few years, Brian Butler, a scholar of information systems and organizational design, and I have been working on a complexity analysis of rhetoric. Figure 10.1 illustrates the architecture we have been working with to date. We have sought to understand the minimal structure and interactivity that is required to capture many of the interesting regularities one unearths when studying specimens of naturally occurring rhetoric. Our aim has been to develop weak theory, theory that does not capture a cognitive theory of how rhetoric is designed but that captures important regularities about the shape and detail that a mental theory must explain.

As a test for our analysis, we have chosen the Lincoln-Douglas debates because of their richness, the expertise of both advocates, the status of the debates as an ongoing series of rhetorical events, and the fact that the adversaries had well-known positions and were available to respond to one another. Getting a handle on the complexity

FIGURE 10.1
The Structure of Goals in Rhetorical Design

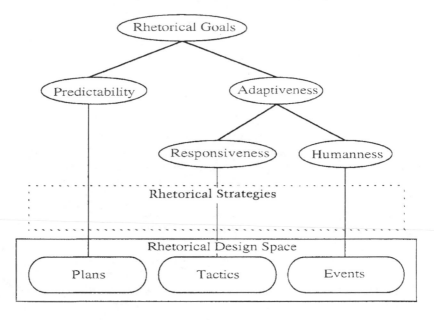

at issue in the Lincoln-Douglas debates is hardly getting a handle on the whole of rhetoric. But our general bias is inductive, believing that our general knowledge of rhetoric means little if it doesn't allow us to explain even one specimen of rhetoric in depth. Only time will tell if complexity analyses performed across many instances of rhetoric can be reconciled into coherent theories. In the remainder of this section we will focus on elaborating the detail of the architecture of rhetorical design and understanding how it can be applied to investigate various aspects of the Lincoln-Douglas debates.

THE STRUCTURE OF THE ARCHITECTURE

The model of rhetorical design consists of two main parts, the rhetor's internal and external environment. Within the rhetor's internal environment are the components of the design process, including the rhetor's general knowledge, goals, rhetorical strategies, and the rhetorical design space. Each of these components plays an important role in determining the outcome of the rhetorical design process. It is these components that interact to create intricate works of public discourse.

The external environment captures the various significant characteristics of the rhetorical situation, such as the audience and opponent. It also provides an external memory, a permanent storage space, for the intermediate products (e.g., outlines, notes, drafts) of the rhetor's internal environment as well as permanent storage for the physical signs (i.e., the words) that literally make up the final artifact, the rhetor's product-in-process.

In the following paragraphs I review the goals that enable a rhetor to manage and evaluate the rhetorical design process. I then consider how the design space is broken down into *Plans, Tactics,* and *Events,* each providing a different perspective on the rhetorical design space.

Goals of Rhetorical Design

The primary goals of rhetorical design are predictability and adaptiveness. The rhetor needs to present a message that insists on some constants over time and space. The rhetor must strike the audience as "standing firm" in positions that both preceded and will outlast the immediate rhetorical situation. In this way, the rhetor fulfills the goals of predictability. Rhetors rely on the Plans module in the design space to demonstrate their predictability.

However, predictability needs to be supplemented by the goal of adaptiveness. It is adaptiveness, in the form of the subgoals of responsiveness (to the opponent) and humanness (with the audience), which demonstrates a rhetor's awareness of the rhetorical environment. Without responsiveness to outside interrogation, a message's predictability can seem inert and inflexible. Without humanness, a message's predictability and responsiveness to the opponent can still fail to connect to the everyday reality of the audience. The rhetor relies on the Tactics module to demonstrate the responsiveness of his or her position to outside scrutiny and the Events module to achieve humanness goals. Figure 10.2 overviews the structure of goals in rhetorical design.

THE RHETORICAL DESIGN SPACE

The rhetorical design space is essentially the rhetor's blackboard, the space of internal activity in which the rhetor's knowledge of the issue (not discussed here), under the supervision of rhetorical goals, gets assembled into seamless rhetorical artifacts. Although rhetorical artifacts look relatively seamless once com-

FIGURE 10.2
An Architecture of Rhetorical Design

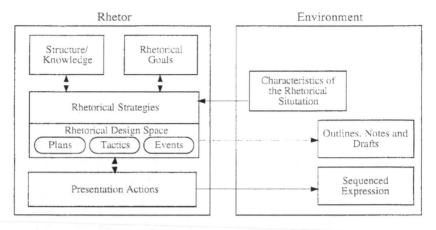

pleted, they originate from sharply defined seams or modules. We call these modules Plans, Tactics, and Events.

The Plans, Tactics, and Events modules suppose worlds with starkly contrastive, even contradictory, assumptions. In table 10.2, we summarize each module along four dimensions (the rows). These dimensions are the relevant goals of each module, the viewpoint toward the world it adopts, the significant elements that compose information in the module, and the various actions that indicate progress made in the module.

Relevant Goals

The Plans module is used to situate the speaker in a historical world, looking back to the past and extending into the future. In this module, the speaker presents himself or herself as a projectile of predictiveness, standing for constants that are not dislocated by time and place and moving them from the past to the future in the present decision-context. The Tactics module oversees the speaker's participation in the debate, insuring that the speaker can defend assertions of predictability through responsiveness to the opponent. The Events module is responsible for making the speaker seem like a full-blooded human being, a live presence that is time- and place-bound.

Viewpoint

The Plans module presupposes a world of principled forces that move ideological history in right (precedent) or wrong (counter-

TABLE 10.2
Plans, Tactics, and Events Modules Summarized

Module	Plans	Tactics	Events
Relevant Goals	Predictability— Win the battle of history by moving it in the right direction.	Predictability and responsiveness—Win the immediate conflict with the opponent.	Humanness— Win the moment with the audience by identifying with its everyday reality.
Viewpoint	The social world is constructed in precedent time. History is a branching line splintering the here and now of the audience into precedent and counterprecedent directions.	Discourse as a weapon of offensive and defense leverage that can maintain or threaten the opponent's face.	Discourse as a social bond creating moments in which language sharing can also be appreciated as culture-sharing.
Significant Elements	Groups, entitled individuals	Speaker, opponent, offense, defensive blocks, face	Words, phrases, verbatim memory, cultural/linguistic memory
Design Actions	Construct	Face-maintaining arguments (Offensive and Defensive), face-threatening arguments	Transparent actions, simple diversions, reflective diversions

precedent) directions. The ancient rhetoricians began with the idea that rhetoric involves a contest with an opponent. They associated rhetoric with the level of oppositional tactics. They saw the rhetorician as contesting worlds more than constructing the worlds they contested.

The Tactics module presupposes a very different world. It assumes a world of gaming between a speaker and opponents in a contest for the hearts and minds of an audience. The inert historical mechanics inherited from the Plans module become, within the

Tactics module, a framework for the dynamic game with the opponent. What are taken as inert, impersonal forces in the Plans module become dueling narratives in the Tactical view, as each speaker tries to claim a privileged vantage from which to recount the past and its bearing on the present context of decision.

In the Tactics module, the basic idea is that of dueling arguers, each trying to win by putting forth his or her own position and blocking the opponent's. Tactical arguments can be understood along two dimensions: orientation and face. Orientation refers to whether the speaker is in an offensive (advance) or defensive (block) posture. Face refers to whether the speaker seeks to maintain the opponent's face or threaten it. A speaker who agrees to duel, on the offense or defense, typically maintains the face of the opponent. In contrast, a speaker threatens face by sheathing the sword and complaining about the quality of the opposition. Threatening face, thus, is often coincident with the suspension of an offensive or defensive orientation

One of the key differences between Lincoln and Douglas is their preference for tactical actions. Lincoln, who prefers to play defense, is a master at blocking his opponent's plans. Douglas is an able offensive debater but weak on defense. He is good at reasserting his own position but bad at blocking anything of value Lincoln has to say. He responds to many opportunities for defense merely by threatening Lincoln's face. Thus, against many of Lincoln's more devastating attacks, rather than defend himself Douglas questions the quality of the attack.

The Events module presupposes a much less impersonal world than the Plans module and a much less hostile world than the Tactics module. It assumes a world of face-to-face interaction. The basic impulses of that interaction are cooperative, not competitive. The events module focuses the similarities that bind individuals together, not in some abstract sense of common destiny but in a concrete sense of sharing a language and, by implication, a culture. For the most part, the Events module arranges the rhetorical design space into communication with a language agreed upon (if only for comprehension) even by the opponent. It helps, in other words, to prepare the privately constructed rhetorical design space for public presentation. In the process, the Events module can also be used to establish deeper affinities between the speaker and the audience. Certain discourse events, recognizable in confessions, asides, diversions, irony, wit, humor, and the emotions, can create moments of mutual recognition between a speaker and the audience, moments with little purpose beyond sparking the audience's recognition that the everyday world of the speaker is, from the audience's first-person-singular vantage, also "my" world, the world "I" care about and want to keep intact, long before the ideological winds stir over it and long after they have died down.

Significant Elements

Within the Plans module, chronological time is merely an index of precedent time, the point at which new events on the horizon are, or have been, lined up with the right or wrong forces of history. There are no ordinary individuals doing ordinary things. All individuals who partake in plans are entitled by groups to change history. There are no mundane individuals involved in contest, conflict, opposition, controversy, emotions, or humor. There is only a cold mechanics directing how the historical world is to be viewed. It is the individuals in historically entitled category affiliations (e.g., "founding fathers," "Republicans," "Democrats") and authorized as agents with respect to "public" events (i.e., events associated with principles whose applicability extends across time and space) that are the focus of this module. All events are test cases, pregnant with incipient principles, that have either been aligned with historical forces or are awaiting such alignment. From the perspective of the Plans module, rhetoric is understood to be an occasion for deciding how the mechanics of the past apply to the present.

The Tactics module introduces an important consideration that social anthropologists call "face" (Goffman, 1959; Brown and Levinson, 1987). Individuals in the tactical world are implicated in a live contest through face-to-face, print, or electronic connection. More than the strict contents of their offensive and defensive moves can be questioned or countered. The speaker can also threaten the opponent's face, his or her advertised capacity to compete in a public forum. Among other things, this capacity includes the opponent's basic knowledge of the subject, and his or her preparation, credentials, good will, and motives. In the Plans module, by way of contrast, individuals are always effaced by their group affiliation and entitlement. Groups sponsor, if not directly instigate, a direction for history that is never contested. Face in the Plans module never arises as an issue. Working from the Tactics module, the speaker can decide to play offense or defense—both of which, working from the assumption that the opponent is a qualified public agent, maintain the face of the opponent—or decide to threaten the opponent's face, issuing a direct challenge to the opponent's fitness to share the platform. The elements of the Events module are the words and memories that link language to cultural cohesion. The Events module is used to chunk Plans and Tactics into linguistic events. Only through the language can the speaker create humor and emotion.

Design Actions

The basic actions of the Plans module are constructive inasmuch as a speaker uses this module to build the historical world that is to be contested.

The Tactics module opens the way for actions that are beyond the expressive capacities of the Plans module—the ability to play defense or offense. Playing defense, the speaker seeks to take leverage away from the opponent's plans. The speaker on defense produces information to show the inadequate, incomplete, contradictory, self-interested, and self-aggrandizing tendencies in forces that, within the Plans module, are looked upon as inviolable and impersonal laws of the past. The design actions based on the Events module depend on whether the speaker intends the audience to look transparently through the language, to the meanings invoked; or at the language itself (a distinction make popular by Lanham [1983]), diverting the audience from the normal assumption that the language transparently "carries" the message without being an overt part of it.

Some diverting actions overturn the audience's expectation that the speaker is engaged in public discourse, discourse constructed from the Plan module. Such diversions occur in language associated with confessionals, anecdotes, tales, yarns, sayings, and other earthy forms of expression that strike a linguistic contrast with the high-minded, formal, and abstract registers of public expression. Other more complex diverts occur in the reflexive tropes in which public discourse seems both achieved and undermined in a single linguistic stroke. Reflective diversions, like irony, wit, and humor, focus the audience on the nature of the language as an important part of the rhetorical design. In all of these Event-based designs the language is being used as a rhetorical tool rather than simply playing the role of a neutral communication device.

Rhetorical Strategy

The final component in our architecture is rhetorical strategy. In many ways, this is the nerve center of rhetorical design, orchestrating the knowledge and design actions to produce rhetorical designs that meet the appropriate goals. If the goal is to be predictable, though not excessively responsive or human, a reasonable strategy is to focus on the Plans module and less on Tactics and

Events. If the focal goal is to be responsive to the opponent, the Tactics module must be weighted more highly than others. Likewise, if the goal is to demonstrate one's humanity, the Events module should be the dominant strategic focus. In most rhetorical design contexts, the rhetorical goals are themselves complex interactions and so require a complex activation of these modules. Considering the situation, audience, opponent, and many other factors, the rhetor must choose his or her rhetorical strategy. It is these choices that in many ways control the look and feel of a speaker's rhetorical design.

Before closing this discussion of architecture, let me take stock and consider from a different angle why I relate rhetoric to design. In classical rhetoric, rhetors were understood to need to impose their own lens on the flow of the external situation, a lens called a "stasis." A stasis was a "place" in the issue where the rhetor could train his or her focus and plan the generation of discourse—the journalist's *who, what, how, when, where* but applied to conflict situations. Points of stasis, in other words, were the mental targets at which a speaker aimed public utterance.

My take on rhetoric is different. I propose that the main external reference point "out there" for speakers is a moving mental construct called the "here and now" of the audience. Rhetoric is not the application of language to define external situations. It is rather the application of language to bring a world, a cast of characters, and a contest to the listener's here and now. The speaker's job is to have the audience associate the near future with the historical world that contains the characters and contest that best fits the speaker's interests as he or she understands them. But this is a world that must be carefully designed to adjust the audience to the speaker's purpose and vice versa. To design it, the speaker must rely on a battery of tools taken from the toolkit of rhetorical design. Some of these tools supply the goals about what to do. Others supply the symbolic bricks and mortar out of which historical worlds are built. Still others are the offensive and defensive maneuvers through which the alternative designs of opponents are discredited. And others still are the linguistic events that impose social categories on the conceptual design so that it can be public and recorded.

Classical theory did not emphasize the malleability of the social world and the rhetor's power to shape and reshape it. Rhetors do not simply submit utterances to a social world around them. Such acts of submission, literally and figuratively, describe the culturally impotent, not the rhetor. Rhetors rather design the social world around them and bring it to the here and now, a new orientation to rhetoric made famous by the British social psychologist

Michael Billig (1987, 1990). This, perhaps, is the most important reason why it is more illuminating to think of rhetoric as a design art. The rhetor is an architect of the social world. Aristotle spoke of different kinds of rhetoric as focusing on the past (judicial), present (encomium), and future (policy) respectively. But in constructing the social world, the rhetor must design the here and now to accommodate every horizon of time. He or she must be timeless enough to retrofit the audience to its historical past, timely enough to anticipate its future, and well enough timed to give it pleasure in the now.

LINCOLN AND DOUGLAS AS DESIGNERS

How do Lincoln and Douglas go about their business as designers of rhetoric? Everything I have said so far means little if we cannot finally use it to get a more detailed understanding of the environment in which rhetoric is produced and perceived in naturally occurring contexts.

Plan Design

Douglas came to the debates believing that slavery was a red herring to the real issue of national growth and expansion. Insofar as the antislavery Republicans threatened to filibuster on issues of expansion until the question of slavery was addressed, Douglas had to address slavery as an exigence from within his own narrative of American history. In the debates, he outlines how the founders had no moral qualms with slavery, how they held slaves themselves, and how the issue needed to be handled at the level of the state or local territory. Slavery was not, nor should be, according to Douglas, a national issue.

Lincoln, the leader of the Illinois Republicans, came to the debates believing that the country would be torn apart if the slavery question was left unaddressed. So he had to address the exigence of slavery from within his own precedent narrative. According to that narrative, the founders may have held slaves but were aware of the dire moral consequences of doing so. They knew they could not eliminate it in one generation. But they hoped to contain it and eventually eliminate it over the long term by legally excluding it from the new territories.

Precedent narratives themselves interact with another plan structure, organizational authority. Organizational authority involves a speaker's backing in a constituent group. A speaker's authority to anchor himself or herself in a precedent narrative usually depends upon belonging to a group that anchors itself in this history. Throughout the debates, Douglas derives his precedent narrative from the political authority of the Jeffersonian Democrats and the old-line Whigs. Lincoln derives his from the newly founded Republicans.

Organizational authority has its limits, however. Many Illinois Republicans were abolitionists, but abolition was a losing position in the debates of 1858, which both candidates directed to the voters of central Illinois. For this reason, Lincoln had to disavow certain aspects of Republican thinking without compromising his allegiance to the Republicans. Many Illinois Democrats were Buchananites, sympathetic to the South, and interested in extending slavery. Yet this southern position was also a losing position to the voters of central Illinois, meaning that Douglas had to disavow aspects of Democratic thinking without unduly alienating Democrats.

In another plan structure, what Butler and I call the "public confessional," a speaker goes on the public record for or against the party platform, but then "confesses" that, in his or her heart, he or she respectfully dissents from these public statements. Both Lincoln and Douglas use public confessionals to withdraw from the full implications of their party affiliations without sacrificing their organizational authority.

Another plan structure is the conspiracy. Throughout the debates, Lincoln and Douglas attack one another with conspiracy plans. To Douglas, Lincoln has sought to advance abolition under the name of Republicanism. To Lincoln, Douglas has sought to advance the extension of slavery under the name of popular sovereignty.

History is another plan structure. This consists of events drawn from the past that are used to fill in detail for its own sake; or as an adjunct to another plan structure, such as precedent narratives, organizational authority, the public confessional, or conspiracy. Lincoln and Douglas draw from many archived and hypothetical events in American history to fill in their plans for rhetoric.

Yet another plan structure is the principle plan. This structure furnishes norms like "slavery is evil" or "slavery is permissible." Principle plans are needed to bring into sharp relief the underlying norms and values that cause precedent narratives to function as they do. Unlike a history plan, which furnishes events from the past with no normative basis, precedent narratives contain events with norms at their base, with "lessons" to teach about the past that are supposed to carry over into future planning. Principle plans are needed to expound in detail the norms that underlie one's precedent narratives. For example, in the later debates at Galesburg, Quincy, and Alton, Lincoln goes into great detail about the moral evil of slavery. Only by understanding Lincoln's ethical principles against slavery can an audience understand the normative basis of his or her precedent narrative.

A final plan is venue. Venue is a plan to show standing. Why am I, the speaker, entitled to speak or even care about the issue at hand? Venue occupies an important place in the Lincoln-Douglas debates. Douglas believes that slavery is an issue to be settled only through local politics. Lincoln believes it to be a national issue, and thus one senatorial candidates need to address.

Plans are used to build the historical world and to project a future from the normative basis of the past. They are also used to pin down alternative norms and the worlds they generate. These positive worlds and discredited alternatives are all part of one story, however. It is the speaker's story of historical mechanics, the way the world simply "works." Were there no live opponents in the world, rhetorical design would be plan-driven more than anything else. Speakers would offer their historical mechanics to audiences and audiences would accept them. Rhetoric would have more the design of Homeric poetry than the more complex interactive (i.e., Plans-Tactics-Events) Aristotle implicitly understood it to have.

The world is full of live opponents, however, opponents who seek to interrupt our stories from outside our design. This means that, as designers, rhetoricians need to anticipate having their stories interrupted. They need to anticipate where their narratives are likely to be most vulnerable, most called into question. And they need to plan supporting actions for these vulnerable parts that are not, strictly speaking, part of the story but part of patching it up under the stress of interruption. These considerations introduce tactics into rhetorical design. Many rhetorical theorists collapse rhetoric into the theory of argument. But within a theory of rhetorical design, argument is a tactical action that is taken only when a speaker's description of the world is interrupted and the speaker resorts to argument in order to overcome the interruption and to resume the telling.

Tactical Design

Because of the physical proximity of opponents in a debate context, the Lincoln-Douglas debates offer a direct look at a speaker's tactical maneuvering with a live opponent. At the tactical level, speakers can play positive offense, negative offense, or defense with an opponent.

Positive offense is played when a speaker seeks to bring his or her plan structures to bear in discourse with an opponent. Speakers articulates their precedent narratives, organizational hierarchies, confessionals, conspiracies, histories, and principles that are consistent with their view of the way the world works. Although speakers invoke the Tactics module when they expect to be interrupted, they play positive offense in order to put as much of their whole positions on the table as possible prior to interruption. Speakers play positive offense in order to control the terms of the contest. In a debate context, positive offense is associated with first affirmative openings. Similarly, in the Lincoln-Douglas debates, the opening of each debate is the time when each speaker has the best opportunity to play positive offense. A look at the debates reveals that Douglas controls the terms of the early debates while Lincoln asserts more control in the later debates. This observation corresponds closely to the way the speakers play positive offense in their respective openings. In the early debates, Douglas's openings dominate and Lincoln must backpedal by showing how Douglas's description of the world falls short. But in the later debates, especially Quincy, Lincoln's opening puts Douglas on the offense and Douglas must backpedal within the terms of Lincoln's historical mechanics.

Negative offense comes into play when a speaker leads with his or her negative characterizations of the opponent's worldview. Negative offense becomes relevant for tactical design when a speaker anticipates or has already suffered interruption from the opponent and wants to discredit the interruption. Speakers accomplish this by characterizing the opponent's contribution in the terms of their own stories.

We must distinguish a speaker's negative characterizations of the opponent's world and the opponent's own characterization of that world. The former is played out by depicting the opponent in the alien territory of the speaker's words. The latter is played out by allowing the opponent to depict himself or herself in words of his or her own choosing. Both Douglas and Lincoln are adept in negative offense. Both are skilled in recounting worlds where the other is doing harm. In Douglas's world, Lincoln is ruining the country on behalf of abolition. In Lincoln's world, Douglas is ruining the country on behalf of proslavery interests.

Defense at the tactical level arises when a speaker takes on the opponent *on the turf of* the opponent. The speaker stalks the opponent within the words laid out by the opponent. Speakers playing offense against one another, positive or negative, are likely to talk past one another, because there is no common metalanguage within which to standardize their conflicting stories. However, speakers who turn to defense are more likely to home in on common issues because defense is a gesture to search within the terms of the other for a resolution. Defensive play is at the root of what many rhetoricians have lauded as adaptiveness in argument because it encourages arguers to search within the opponent's terms for common ground. Henry Johnstone called such defensive play in argument "ad hominem validity" and he associated this tactical maneuvering with the distinctiveness of philosophical argument. Wayne Booth associated defensive play with the willingness to engage in a "meeting of minds" with an opponent, the noblest form of communication when conflicting values are at stake.

The value of defensive play is that is allows a speaker to block aspects of an opponent's story in a manner that can persuade the opponent (or at least a fair-minded member of the audience). An axiom of rhetoric is that a speaker is more likely to make headway with an opponent by respecting the terms of the opponent. Designing a defense at the tactical level is an implementation of this axiom.

What is distinctive about Lincoln-Douglas is the huge gap between the speakers when it comes to the capacity or interest in designing a tactical defense. A boxscore of the tactical maneuvering in the debates would look something like the following: Of the two debaters, Douglas is the superior in the design of a positive offense. Readers of the debate know more about Douglas's historical mechanics than they know about Lincoln's. The speakers are about even in negative offense. Readers know about as much of Lincoln's sins within Douglas's account as they know about Douglas's sins within Lincoln's. But there is no contest when it comes to defensive play. Lincoln is a superb defensive tactician. He has no fear taking on Douglas within Douglas's own terms. This makes his responses to Douglas more credible and gives them a power to block Douglas's worldview when they work as intended. Douglas, on the other hand, barely plays any defense throughout the debates. He addresses Lincoln only from the vantage of his own stories, where Lincoln is a safe stereotype, easy to refute. He misses many opportunities to score points against Lincoln by playing a negative offense when he could have played defense. This singular difference in design at the tactical level says much about why Lincoln is revered by rhetoricians and why Douglas's style reminds so many rhetorical theorists of what political discourse has become.

The Plans module allows a speaker to represent the flow of historical time outside of the temporal boundaries of the immediate rhetorical situation. It represents time as a series of spatial intervals with a known plot and outcome that is waiting to unfold. The Tactics module represents time as a series of unfolding turns between the speaker and an opponent within the rhetorical situation. Plans span millennia, centuries, decades, months of revealed history. Tactics span years, months, weeks, days, minutes of strategic interaction and posturing against an opponent. Neither Plans nor Tactics captures the moment-by-moment interaction with an audience. This is the time frame of events in rhetorical design.

Event Design

The Events module monitors the moment-by-moment interaction of the speaker with the audience at whom the message is aimed. Events monitor the implementation of plans and tactics into linguistic utterances. They are required to transform plans and tactics from the internal representations of speakers into a public language that can affect the internal representations of audiences and opponents. The Event module also monitors the adaptation of plans and tactics for specific audiences. Lincoln maintains and generates internally consistent plan structures across the debates. So does Douglas. But Douglas's plans are implemented in different ways from northern to southern Illinois. In the north, "abolitionists" tend to be his primary target. In the south, "northerners" become more the target. The plans do not change in their basic structure, but the place in which they are generated does exert an influence on the specific content of the event generated.

The Event module also determines whether an expression of an event is realized as a declarative, or whether it is realized as interactive, as a query, denial, challenge, bid, trap, promise, threat, concession, disclaimer, or some other nondeclarative speech act. In an interactive speech act, the event expressed awaits a response from the audience for closure. Events also monitor the construction of emotional states, as a speaker cannot arouse (or at least control with precision) emotions in an audience without completing *the expression* that conveys the emotion. The concepts "blacks" and "free territories" do not by themselves scare Illinois audiences. But when Douglas formulates them into the conceivable event of the blacks settling the free territories, he means precisely to scare them.

Finally, the Events module oversees a speaker's use of diversions, the effort of the speaker to wink at the audience as a human being detached from the role of public speaker. Such diverts are manifested in the phenomena of wit, humor, and irony. While plans and tactics satisfy predictability goals, and make a speaker seem predictable in the public sphere, the use of diverts satisfies humanness goals, and makes a speaker seem human and likable. Just as Lincoln's defensive play is in marked contrast to Douglas's lack of it, his use of diverts—wit, irony, humor—stands in marked contrast to Douglas's straightforward sincerity. By the end of the debates, we know a great deal about the historical world Douglas wants us to occupy, but much less about how a real person, including Douglas, could occupy it. In contrast, we may know a bit less about Lincoln's public world, but are more disposed to believe that it is a world that we can comfortably inhabit with a bit of humor and laughter.

GAONKAR'S DILEMMA REVISITED

The first horn of Gaonkar's dilemma depends upon rhetorical theorist's failing to comprehend the charge that rhetoric does not live up to the internal standards of coherence of a true techne, a true art of design, where praxis is carefully regulated techne, where a theory of reception is closely monitored and informed by a theory of production. Rather than seek *demonstrations* that rhetoric qualifies as an art of design, no less than architecture or engineering, rhetorical theorists more often seek arguments to show why the practical art is useful, why it deserves a better reputation than it suffers. Gaonkar's dilemma should help rhetorical theorists understand why standard gestures to "rehabilitate" the practical art don't work. For as long as rhetoric remains the (from modern standards, unsystematized) art of production the ancients knew it to be, our efforts to comprehend natural acts of rhetoric within a systematic hermeneutic will always leave rhetoric behind. Our theories of rhetoric won't be comprehensive enough to understand rhetoric. This sad state has given rise to Gaonkar's second horn. To understand rhetoric, modern interpreters have left rhetoric behind. The second horn corrects the instability of the first, but at a huge cost of its own.

We can think our way out of the dilemma, I suggest, by enriching our production theories of rhetoric so that they accommodate a theory of reception as well. But this insistence is one and the same with the insistence on exploring rhetoric as a bona fide member of the family of design arts. Arts of design, like engineering and architecture, build in an immanent sense of critique and reception. Critical theory is understood as part and parcel of the theory of production. Better designs are made from learning how to "read" previous ones. Production theory and hermeneutics are not separate arts but different aspects of the same creative impulse. Classifying rhetoric as a practical art has divided the creative impulse, depriving rhetoric of a native hermeneutic. Gaonkar was astute enough to recognize that this split has left rhetoric not only in a deprived but an unstable state; and even more astute to have fashioned this instability into the horns of a dilemma. Understanding rhetoric as an art of design repairs this instability, and shows us how to find our way out of the fascinating puzzle he has put before us.

REFERENCES

Aristotle. (1991). *Aristotle on rhetoric: A theory of civic discourse.* G. A. Kennedy (Trans.). New York: Oxford University Press.

Billig, M. (1987). *Arguing and thinking.* New York: Cambridge University Press.

———. (1990). *Ideology and opinions.* Beverly Hills: Sage.

Booth, W. (1974). *A rhetoric of irony.* Chicago: University of Chicago Press.

Brown, P., and Levinson, S. C. (1987). *Politeness: Some universals in language usage.* Cambridge: Cambridge University Press.

Bryant, D. (1953). Rhetoric: Its function and its scope. *Quarterly Journal of Speech, 39,* 401–424.

Chomsky, N. (1957). *Syntactic structures.* The Hague: Mouton.

Gaonkar, D. (1990). Rhetoric and its double: Reflections on the rhetorical turn in the human sciences. In H. W. Simons (Ed.), *The rhetorical turn,* 341–366. Chicago: University of Chicago Press.

Goffman, Erving. (1959). *The presentation of self in everyday life.* Garden City, NJ: Doubleday Anchor.

Hirsch, E.D. (1967). *Validity in interpretation.* New Haven: Yale University Press.

Kaufer, D., and Butler, B. (1996). *Rhetoric and the arts of design.* Hillsdale, NJ: Lawrence Erlbaum.

Johannsen, R. W. (Ed.). (1965). *The Lincoln-Douglas debates*. New York: Oxford University Press.

Johnstone, H. W., Jr. (1959) *Philosophy and argument*. State College: Pennsylvania State University Press.

Lanham, R. (1983). *Literacy and the survival of humanism*. New Haven: Yale University Press.

CHAPTER 11

"RHETORIC OF SCIENCE": DOUBLE THE TROUBLE?

Steve Fuller

The very idea of *rhetoric of science* has a grating quality; it seems to be an important point of friction between scientific and humanistic paradigms. But we need to ask what the friction tells us about rhetoric—and about science. Dilip Gaonkar focuses primarily on the ambiguous, if not downright amorphous, status of *rhetoric* in the rhetoric of science: Does rhetoric add anything distinctive to, say, related efforts in the sociology of scientific knowledge? The specter of Scylla and Charybdis frames Gaonkar's answer. The more that rhetoric of science looks like classical rhetoric, the less exciting its interpretations seem. (This is the case against Prelli.) Yet, the more that rhetoric of science strays from classical sources, and the more provocative its readings become, the more interchangeable its methods seem with those used by sociologists and critical theorists. (This is the case against Gross.) Gaonkar never formally traces the elusiveness of rhetoric in these projects to rhetoric's inability to capture the distinctive character of scientific discourse, but he does allude to this line of thinking, and not altogether unfavorably. It is the historical purism that Gaonkar identifies most closely with the work of Brian Vickers, Thomas Farrell, and Michael Leff. In framing my own remarks, I too wish to indulge in a bit of historical purism, but this time about the science end, which fares no better than the rhetoric end of rhetoric of science.

Historical purists perform the very important role of reminding us that a word like *rhetoric* (and its cognates) may linger in our discourse long after the contexts in which it makes sense to use it have passed. To purist ears, the discourse of the rhetoric of science sounds like a curious sort of gibberish: Its speakers say "rhetoric" but they must mean something else—but what exactly? Leff, in particular, has functioned as an ombudsman for classical rhetoricians amidst those rhetoricians of science—most of them, in fact—who would stretch the meaning of rhetoric to cover technical writings anonymously disseminated across large heterogeneous audiences whose readings are informed by incommensurable expectations and motivations (Leff, 1987). Where in this swarm of discourse (wonders Leff) are the common values, topics, and exigencies, which in the Greek city-state were reinforced by a common place, a forum, where speakers engaged each other face-to-face? To pose the question bluntly: Where is the rhetoric in a field whose authors think of themselves as primarily contributing to an archive rather than to a conversation?

This is an eminently fair question. However, I diverge from Leff and other purists in thinking that the implied answer (there is no rhetoric in the archives) cuts just as much against the science in rhetoric of science as against the rhetoric. Those (like Leff, at times) who long for the forum of an Athens past often contrast this public space for rhetoric with the babble of contemporary academic disciplines. Implicit also is a contrast in politics between the participatory democracy operative in the forum and the colonization of everyday life practiced by jargon-toting experts. But to someone trained in the philosophy of science such as myself, these contrasts fail to pick out what it is about science that has captivated the philosophical imagination since the eighteenth century, namely, its supposedly exemplary status as the open society, the very model of public debate and democratic governance in the modern era, one which promises to incorporate all of humanity, typically through a process of citizen education. This is, of course, the project of the Enlightenment, whose representatives have formed the core of the liberal tradition: Mill, Dewey, Popper.

Does the Open Society Need Special Education? Sophistic versus Isocratean Rhetorics of Science

It is no coincidence that the three philosophers just mentioned were prominent in both political theory and philosophy of science. In fact, social and political theorists have more explicitly appealed to the emancipatory powers of science than philosophers of science proper. The former group of theorists portray the cultural relativist as the advocate of the closed society, in contrast to the open society advocated by scientific-rationalist philosophers (Wilson, 1970; Hollis and Lukes, 1982; both drawing on Popper, 1945). This philosophical sensibility seeped into the primitive sociological theories of sci-

ence constructed in the Second World War. In particular, Merton
(1942) represented science as perhaps the only sphere in modern
society where the principles of participatory democracy may actually
apply. Without denying that many Enlightenment thinkers have
contributed to antirhetoric rhetoric, nevertheless these are also the
thinkers who argued that, because of its participatory character and
its uniformly critical yet reasoned attitudes toward knowledge
claims, experimental science was the first practice to realize fully the
promise of the Athenian polis (Zilsel, 1945). Contrary to what the
rhetorical purists claim, then, science would seem to be an eminent
site for the practice (and study) of rhetoric.

However, the purity of free and open inquiry is quickly diluted,
once we turn to the fine print of these Enlightenment tracts. When
science is said to be universally accessible, does that mean the *practice* or the *products* of science? In other words, is the goal of Enlightenment to incorporate everyone as contentious contributors to scientific discourse or as compliant consumers of science-based
technologies? The latter option comes closer to the answer in both
cases. Knowledge can be universally distributed, yet its production
remain concentrated in the hands of the relative few. In that case,
through education and other forms of epistemic consumption, people
can peacefully participate in social transformations brought about by
scientific and technical innovation. Indeed, an important sense in
which democracy was supposed to mark progress in the art of government over authoritarian regimes of the past was that it rendered
people capable of administering their own submission, thereby
avoiding the need for regular shows of force. Thus, the tradition in
rhetoric originating with Isocrates has promoted a form of citizen
education in which people are taught to recognize, and hence vol-
untarily defer to, superior judgment when they run across it.

It would be a mistake to see the influence of Isocrates as confined to the education of like-minded aristocrats—or, more precisely,
to think that the nature of citizen education is so different when
we move from aristocratic to democratic contexts. Consider the case
of John Stuart Mill. We often forget that when *On Liberty* was first
published, Mill was widely perceived as a closet elitist precisely
because he made education a necessary condition for full participation in public life. His now celebrated defense of minority rights
emerged from a concern that the great unwashed might not give
geniuses their due (Spitz, 1975). From Mill's Isocratean standpoint,
access to the public forum had become so eased by the mid–nineteenth century—given the extension of suffrage to all adult males—
that a democracy of the masses might only recognize force as a com-

mon source of authority. Among Mill's predecessors, Thomas Hobbes was probably most cognizant, yet also most accepting, of this point. In a world where everyone is allowed to argue claims as he or she sees fit, there will be no natural point of agreement. The imposition of closure on dispute thus becomes a political necessity, but one without any pretense to having resolved the dispute in question. As Shapin and Schaffer (1985) document, Hobbes originally raised this point in opposition to restricting entry into the Royal Society to mutually recognized experts in the craft of experiment, among whom (it was argued) agreement could be easily reached as to the nature and significance of empirical findings. For Hobbes, what Robert Boyle and his allies wanted to pass off as their superior epistemic insight, or credibility as witnesses to nature, reflected nothing more than the mundane fact that similarly conditioned people will see things in similar ways. In this context, epistemology is the velvet glove that hides the iron fist.

According to the conventional wisdom, Boyle won and Hobbes lost. However, a more exact portrayal of the situation may be to say that Boyle and Hobbes have split the difference in the modern academy. (Here I draw on Fuller, 1994a.) If we take the craft of writing for professional journals as our benchmark, we see that the natural sciences exhibit Isocratean tendencies that Boyle would have appreciated. Early in their professional training, students learn how to write for the journals in which they will publish. They do not submit an article for editorial scrutiny until they already believe that its chances of acceptance are high. Such mastery at self-censorship accounts for why natural science journals seem to maintain high standards despite having very high acceptance rates. At the level of the editorial forum, the natural sciences seem quite democratic, as most journals apply the same standards of critical judgment to the work submitted, no matter the source. But a latter-day Hobbes would quickly observe that authors and editors converge so easily only because those who submit to such journals have been pre- and self-selected so as to minimize the possibility that a substantial divergence of opinion would ever reach the forum. In contrast, professional training in the social sciences is less focused on journal writing, largely because there is less agreement over which journals one should write for. Consequently, editors of social science journals must often discipline and reject in public the sorts of utterances that would have been deleted by the prudent natural science author prior to submission. This leaves the overall impression that the low acceptance rates in social science journals is due just as much to a divergence of standards as to a surfeit of poorly crafted articles. Under such circumstances, it is natural to interpret editorial decisions as exercises of political rather than epistemic authority, which in turn spurs the proliferation of alternative journals where rejected authors can find editorial solace. Nevertheless, for all its fractiousness, the Hobbesian would argue that the social sciences at least enjoy the virtue of being open-faced in its dealings.

Following John Poulakos (1989), we can see these two images of science democratized, the Boylean natural sciences and the Hobbesian social sciences, as reflections of two ancient models of rhetorical practice, the Isocratean and the Sophistic. The former conceives of rhetoric as hegemonic, the latter as dynastic, but both terms need to be understood in their original Greek setting. In an Athens repeatedly torn by strife, Isocrates saw rhetoric as a consensus-building practice that sublimates baser forms of disagreements into considered speech that can help resolve public disputes. A distinctive feature of his pedagogy was that students would write down and memorize their speeches before delivering them, which would give them time to refine impulsive thoughts by incorporating them into a common body of discourse. One is here reminded of the many drafts a scientific article undergoes from its conception as a write-up of lab work to a finished piece that occupies a specific place in the scientific literature (Knorr-Cetina, 1981). This hegemonic approach was designed to remedy the excesses that supposedly resulted from Sophistic rhetorical pedagogy, which stressed minimal preparation prior to oral delivery. Here students were instructed on how to shift the burden of proof on their interlocutors by arguing that the novelty of the speech situation removed any advantage that past wisdom might otherwise be thought to have. Thus, one aims to displace, rather than harmonize with, the opponent by offering new words for new times. The rapid succession and stormy coexistence of fashions in the social sciences testify to the continuing relevance of Sophistic pedagogy—for better or worse.

For better, says Paul Feyerabend (1978), and I largely agree, insofar as Sophistic aspirations undermine science's crypto-elitism (Fuller, 1994b). Philosophers of science have been ill-served by not having historical purists of their own to remind them that the idyllic image of science as an intimately open society is long gone—if it ever existed at all. In fact, if Shapin and Schaffer are to be believed, what is typically regarded as the "birth of modern science" marked the open society's fall from epistemic grace, and since then things have gotten progressively worse. In his own way, Feyerabend steps into the purist's shoes when he argues that Big Science is no longer a vehicle for inquiry, now that the fates of competing research programs are tied to the allocation of scarce resources whose collection and maintenance form an increasing share of the coercive power exerted by the state. Who would want to entertain, let alone test, a theory which if true would displace thousands of technicians, whose skills were honed on laboratory technology costing millions of dollars? If, as Popper and much of the philosophical tradition (including Feyerabend) believe, conjectures and refutations constitute the lifeblood of inquiry, and the incentive to conjecture and refute is now discouraged for political and economic reasons, then inquiry proper may be said to have come to an end (Fuller, 1994b). Big Science may be a multinational corporation or a high-grade public works project, but either way it has outgrown its function as an epistemic enterprise. Feyerabend's anarchistic remedy for this situation is, of course, to disestablish the state as the quickest way of reducing science to a size that enables critical inquiry to flourish. While Feyerabend clearly endorses a conception of scientific discourse that is robustly rhetorical (that is, in a way that a purist could love), he also believes that institutionalized science undermines such a conception and hence deserves itself to be undermined. Here is probably the strongest argument for science shifting back from an Isocratean to a Sophistic rhetoric.

Does the culture of contestation enliven or trivialize knowledge claims? Who should offer guidance—the Sophists or Isocrates? And what does the answer tell us about the nature of scientific knowledge? As has been suggested so far, while virtually every philosopher has endorsed some version of the idea that criticism is the lifeblood of epistemic growth, most philosophers (not to mention scientists) recoil from the promiscuous pursuit of criticism. The officially expressed fear is that inchoate or controversial research programs may be prematurely terminated for their failure to answer criticisms at the time they are lodged. And even if the criticisms miss their target, they may leave enough doubts to make it that much harder for the targeted program to develop. Moreover, if the activity of lodging criticisms is itself too highly valued, then inquirers will lose all incentive to develop their own knowledge claims beyond a certain point. For these reasons, philosophers have tried to come up with ways of protecting certain kinds of knowledge claims from immediate attack. Sometimes they appeal to logic, sometimes to history, and increasingly to expertise, but the net effect is to defer the critic's access to the forum.

At a practical level, this attitude wreaks havoc on the scholarly refereeing system. Genuinely probing referee's reports often go unheeded (let alone unappreciated) because scholarly authors are encouraged to work out their arguments with such thoroughness prior to submission that they are psychologically ill-disposed to any response that would have them rethink major portions of their position. In this way, the whole point of criticism is routinely defeated. Small wonder that the natural sciences have succeeded by taking the Isocratean route of avoiding contestation altogether!

The rhetorical intuitions informing scholarship's love-hate relationship with criticism are worth examining. In part, criticism is loathed because it is seen as playing a destructive rather than a creative role in thought: At most, it is seen as a selection mechanism. Philosophers prefer theories that are reasonably developed before being subjected to criticism, while they regard theories that receive most of their elaboration in the face of criticism as having been ill-conceived or ad hoc—this despite striking historical cases to the contrary (e.g., Darwin's *The Origin of Species*, only half of which remained intact after its first dozen years of publication). A rhetorician would start to suspect that a big part of the mystique of science lies in its dialectical encounters being portrayed as do-or-die struggles that occur relatively rarely because of the magnitude of the stakes, which is reflected in the degree to which a theory must be developed before being brought to the forum. Conversely, respect for science may conceivably diminish if too many of its knowledge claims are too frequently contested. We will probably be in a position to test this hypothesis shortly, given the following set of trends: the increasing use of conflicting scientific experts in court cases, the proliferation of electronic networks whose debates cut across more respectable academic forums, and the privatization of knowledge as intellectual property (see Ezrahi, 1990; Fuller 1994c). This moment in history reminds me of the mythical origins of rhetoric in the overthrow of tyranny and the emergence of conflicting property claims, the resolution of which requires a new kind of skill. However, it will be a while before it is recognized as such. In the interim it remains an open question just how rhetorically scientists treat texts.

WILL THE REAL MASTER RHETORICIAN PLEASE STAND UP: DARWIN OR CAMPBELL?

Let me now issue the following Feyerabendian challenge to the rhetoric of science in its current form: (When) do readers engage scientific texts as rhetorical episodes, that is, as if the author were publicly addressing them with the purpose of moving them to act one way or another? By simply taking for granted that readers engage texts rhetorically, the rhetorician of science appears to be naively passing off a normative theory of how scientific texts should be read, as though it were already implicitly applied by some actual readers whose interpretive processes the rhetorician then wants to capture. Of course, it is the rhetorician's prerogative to interpret a scientific text in a way that will interest his or her own readers. And so, even if (as I suspect) no one in nineteenth-century Britain ever read Darwin's texts with, say, John Angus Campbell's (1987) rhetorical archness, Campbell may nevertheless be teaching some valuable lessons in persuasion for aspiring rhetors in his own audience.

However, much of the rhetoric that supports the rhetoric of science portrays the field not simply as another of branch of prescriptive criticism, but as a distinctly empirical enterprise that traces the reception of a text by diverse audiences in a variety of settings, which together articulate the processes alternatively identified as the transmission, circulation, or distribution of knowledge. As Gaonkar himself stresses, whatever else such words may imply about affinities with Foucault or sociology, they are meant to mark a departure from the humanistic tendency to articulate the ideal reader, one who not only knows everything that could be known at the time about his or her own discursive situation but who also enjoys the leisure of applying that knowledge to a comprehensive understanding of the author's meaning. However, this phantom reader still lurks in the practice of the rhetoricians of science who figure in Gaonkar's critique. I will briefly dwell on Campbell's celebrated reading of Darwin to illustrate my point.

Campbell (1987:72–73) calls Darwin a master rhetorician for his ability to make his rhetoric seem unimportant or at best incidental to his scientific point, and to persuade his professional peers because his narrative was governed by the conventions of Baconian induction and quasi-positivist standards of proof. Campbell offers ample evidence, drawn from notebooks and correspondence, to show that Darwin did, indeed, deliberately cloak his frankly speculative opinions concerning natural selection in this philosophically respectable idiom. Unfortunately, Campbell does not pursue the empirical question of whether Darwin's strategy actually worked: Were Darwin's readers persuaded that he was methodologically warranted in deriving the theory of natural selection from the natural historical record? If we consider the British response to *Origin of Species* in its first decade of publication, the answer would have to be a resounding *no*. In fact, Darwin's staunchest supporter, Thomas Henry Huxley, found the patently noninductive character of natural selection to be the biggest strike against Darwin's account, *especially* given that Darwin was trying to court inductivists. However, contrary to Campbell's suggestion, the British scientific community was not uniformly inductivist. But the more speculatively oriented philosophers of science (e.g., William Whewell), who countenanced causal mechanisms that transcended, or qualitatively differed, from the inductive record, also tended to be creationists of one sort or another and therefore hostile to Darwin. In fact, the clearly perceived methodological inadequacies of Darwin's theory became the rallying point for the anti-Darwinism that dominated the scientific community for the next seven decades (see Ellegard, 1990, esp. chapter 9).

Clearly, Darwin succeeded in some sense; otherwise, his work would not have the significance that it enjoys today. But Campbell's sympathetic reading of Darwin's intentions does not bring us much closer to understanding that success. At this point, however, some rhetoricians (following Aristotle, *Rhetoric* 1355b, 1.1.14) will object that success is irrelevant to the evaluation of rhetorical practice. The relevant analogy here is between, on the one hand, a doctor's competence and a patient's fate and, on the other, a rhetor's craft and the audience's reception of the rhetor's speech. Just as we don't judge a doctor incompetent because her patient dies, neither should we judge the rhetor unskilled simply because the audience fails to respond appropriately. Now, it must be said that this line of reasoning is bound to be compelling in a defeatist political culture, as Athens was under Alexandrian rule. Speaking decorously regardless of whether the speech can make a difference, which Aristotle advises, is like living with dignity in the face of a terminal illness.

Methodologically speaking, Aristotle's analogy is compelling just so long as there are separate traditions for evaluating a text as sheer performance and as a transformation of the speech situation. However, this presupposes a comparative method that is, for the most part, lacking in most recent studies in the rhetoric of science. Instead, we find studies of, say, Darwin's *Origin*, a solitary text of proven historical significance, from which the rhetorician then infers that something about the way it was constructed a century and a half ago accounts for its continuing significance today. By contrast, comparative studies of reception ask why was one text used in ways that significantly restructured debate in some domain of inquiry, whereas another text—ostensibly vying for the same span of collective attention—failed to do so, or rather, had some other effect. For example, in Fuller 1993 (126–133) I attempt to explain why a text by Alfred Marshall rather than by Graham Wallas succeeded in founding a science of politics in Britain at the turn of the century, even though the former author was an economist and the latter a political practitioner and theorist. Indeed, as sheer performance, Wallas's sprightly *Human Nature in Politics* outshone Marshall's textbookish *Principles of Economics* in the public sphere. Clearly, this was not the whole story. Yet, a rigorous textualist blessed with Campbell's humanist sensibility should be able to show that, read with sufficient care, *either* text *could* have had the desired impact on its audience. All the more mysterious, then, why only *one* did.

Moreover, the tendency to reduce reception to performative virtues accounts for the following spurious question that is often posed by Darwin scholars (e.g., Kitcher, 1991): Why did Darwin's critics fail to appreciate the cogency of his arguments for natural selection? The answers typically given turn on claims about the biases or incapacities of Darwin's readers, as well as corresponding claims about Darwin's own depth and foresight (or perhaps his text's unparalleled richness). Yet, the appropriateness of this question rests on several simple but historically unwarranted assumptions about Darwin's rhetorical situation: (1) that Darwin's critics were obliged to read *Origin* as closely as the humanist does now; (2) that the primary cognitive interest of Darwin's critics was to evaluate Darwin's claims; (3) that the criticisms made of Darwin should be taken as primarily addressed to Darwin and his followers.

These three assumptions underwrite a book-club model of scientific rhetoric—as if one should think of *Origin*'s reception as an event focused on the text itself. It would be better to think of *Origin* as having been thrown into the middle of many ongoing debates, subject to the vicissitudes of several parties trying to get whatever mileage they can out of what the book says. In that case, the rhetorically interesting feature of *Origin* is its ability to restructure the debates in which it so variously figured; for even as Darwin's opponents contested the specific doctrine of natural selection, they typically adopted enough of *Origin*'s language to presume that some version of the general doctrine of evolution was true (Ellegard, 1990:1–3). Thus, in the thirty years following the first edition of *Origin*, one can witness a subtle but real shift in the burden of proof from evolutionists to creationists. This process can be explained in terms of the associations that disputants were able to make between *Origin*'s language and their own concerns. And such explanations can be offered without the rhetorician of science having to impute a spurious psychology to either Darwin or his readers.

More generally, the obliqueness of Campbell's interpretive strategy to his announced objective makes me wonder whether the reception of a scientific text is best analyzed as an instance of persuasion in any strict sense. After all, scientific texts typically do not include injunctions to act, or even think, in a certain way. Of course, they may be shown to have contributed to changes in thought and action, but rarely with the decisiveness or immediacy associated with the clear cases of persuasion one finds in the analysis of public address. Instead, a major scientific text serves as a sustained focus of attention, whereby various interest groups develop stakes in promoting particular interpretations of the text, which then allows those groups to contest their differences in a relatively systematic fashion. (It was in this sense that Newton's *Principia Mathematica* was paradigmatic: See Fuller, 1988:216–221.) Thus, Darwin succeeded in getting most of the scientific and broader intellectual communities to think that it was integral to their own interests to take a stand on the theses propounded in his book. His text set the terms in which to debate the most important cultural issues of the second half of the nineteenth century. But this accomplishment—however significant and ripe for rhetorical analysis it may be—must be seen against the fact that most knowledgeable people remained *unpersuaded* by Darwin's central claims for many years after the publication of *Origin*.

Is it rhetorically possible to write a book today that would have an impact on the conduct of scientific inquiry comparable to that of Newton's *Principia Mathematica* or Darwin's *Origin of Species*? And if not, what does that tell us about the nature of revolutionary change in science? To cast these questions as ones of *rhetoric* is to challenge certain tacit assumptions common to most science studies practitioners. Two quite different reasons are routinely offered for why, in recent times, there have been no books as influential as Newton's or Darwin's. One reason is simply that geniuses of the calibre of Newton and Darwin are extremely rare occurrences. The other is that the relevant set of sciences have not yet developed sufficiently to enable the possibility of a Newton- or Darwin-like synthesis. I propose a third reason for consideration: No one with the interest, energy, and skill to forge such a synthesis knows how to write in a way that would simultaneously address all the audiences whose cooperation would be necessary for turning that synthesis into a new paradigm for normal science. Or, in the case of Newton, whose formidable mathematical style had the potential to alienate readers, anyone with the ability to make that style more accessible.

Newton and Darwin flourished at two ends of a period in European history when access to written materials was sufficiently widespread that scientific authors could presume that readers came to their texts with a prior understanding of certain natural phenomena upon which the authors could then build their cases. This understanding typically resulted from readers having relatively easy access to more elementary works on a topic. Thus, authors did not need to recapitulate the entire domain of natural history before proceeding to their own contribution (Eisenstein, 1979). However, the spread of the printed word had not yet reached the point of serving the highly differentiated and mutually unintelligible communities of readers that we have today. Indeed, popular beliefs presented in the right way could make substantial inroads into scientific thought. For example, in the mid–nineteenth century, evolution was a popular but scientifically suspect explanation for organic change, which Darwin then proceeded to rehabilitate with a vengeance in *Origin*. All this changed with the increased specialization of the scholarly community, but the intense pace at which it has occurred—something to which a rhetorician would be sensitive—must take into account the role of commercial publishing, whose interests have probably been the ones best served by the replacement of synthetic tomes with specialized academic journals (Horowitz, 1986).

WHY RHETORIC FAILS TO EXPLAIN:
BIG SCIENCE AS MASS COMMUNICATIONS

By harboring a residual notion of the ideal reader, Campbell and his compatriots in the rhetoric of science have failed to take to heart the simple idea that reading is a culturally variable process. It is not enough to show, say, that Darwin's readers understood his text one way, whereas todays readers understand it another. In either case, the rhetorician of science is likely to imagine a leisured and learned reader genuinely interested in what the author has to say. Yet, this image may well be false to the historical record: How much time and effort did people give to reading, and with what other social practices was it associated (see Rose, 1992; Graff, 1987)? These questions acquire a special significance in the case of scientists, whose reading habits have become increasingly and self-consciously strategic as the dimensions of their enterprise have expanded. Indeed, failure to fully grasp a text's meaning rarely suffices as grounds for not using the text to support one's own work (see Fuller, 1988:134–135). The sheer volume of texts is the crudest indicator here, but a potentially more important, albeit subtler, measure is the pace at which the frontier of research advances. The harder the science, the more research specialties resemble fads in their life cycles (De Mey, 1982, esp. chapters 7–9). (In the softer sciences, research specialties have long half-lives, so that it is never clear when they definitively go out of fashion.) Not surprisingly, scientific texts acquire many of the qualities of consumer goods, including their rapid disposability and planned obsolescence.

Of course, the endless supply of citation classics announced by the Institute for Scientific Information demonstrates that some very few scientific texts continue exert a disproportionate amount of impact over a field, at least in the course of a generation. A citation classic is an article that has been frequently cited by other articles in a field on a regular basis, over about a ten- or twenty-year period. The vanishingly small percentage of published articles that fall into this category is symptomatic of the highly stratified character of science, whereby very few researchers capture an entire field's attention. Merton (1973) originally called this "the Matthew Effect," which he took as evidence for science's spontaneous ability to maintain quality control. More recent students of the sociology of scientific knowledge have been less impressed, arguing that when the bulk of a field's practitioners routinely goes unread, it means that an enormous amount of talent is being wasted (Turner and Chubin, 1976). However, there is little evidence to suggest that such impact is the result of people having read the citation classic with the sort of critical engagement that would satisfy the rhetorician of science.

In fact, a Lazarsfeld-style multistep-flow model of mass communication may better explain the reception of scientific texts than the rhetorician's paradigm of public address (see De Mey 1982:139). Ever since Francis Bacon invented the term, *invisible colleges* have dominated scientific reception. An invisible college is a network of opinion leaders, typically the directors of the major research teams, who collectively determine the place (if any) that a text will occupy in the ongoing disciplinary narrative. The other members of the team then stereotype their reading of the text in the appropriate way, ignoring whatever else may be contained. Scientific authors have responded to this treatment of their texts by increasingly indulging in boilerplate writing, the composition of easily moveable modules of text that are sure to prove useful to readers with a variety of research interests. This strategy has even been built into twentieth-century scientific style manuals (Bazerman 1987).

When mass communication researchers began thinking in terms of flows and effects in the 1940s, emphasis was placed on either *gatekeepers*, who centrally controlled the flow of information, or *opinion leaders*, who determined the influence it had on local audiences. In either case, a clear distinction was drawn between active and passive parties to the communicative act. However, the plethora of broadcasters, audiences, and modes of response for any

given medium have increasingly cast doubts on the wisdom of envis-
aging the flows and effects as moving in any overall direction (Chaffee and Hochheimer, 1982). Ironically, there is reason to think that
these reservations may apply *less* to the natural sciences. Whereas in
the case of television, the identities of broadcasters and influential
viewers are clearly differentiated, and the ways in which viewers
can react to what they see are quite multifarious, neither condition
holds for a fully autonomous natural science. Indeed, what marks a
science as autonomous is precisely that there is only one canonical
way to respond to the information one receives, namely, to broadcast
through the very same channels (i.e., to publish in the journals one
reads), the information flows of which are controlled by a group of
editorial gatekeepers whose members significantly overlap with the
opinion leaders who influence how the broadcasts are received.

A good way to see this point is as a remark about the institutionalization of the first of Merton's (1942) four norms of scientific
practice, universalism. According to the norm, scientific inquiry is,
in principle, accessible to everyone, regardless of the differences that
may otherwise separate people. In practice, however, what is meant
is the access one has to overwhelmingly anglophone publication
outlets in the United States and the United Kingdom. Although
ethnographic studies have shown that scientists attach meanings to
seemingly neutral terms in ways that are specific to the scientists'
cultural origins, nevertheless these meanings do not extend from
the informal to formal communications (e.g., Raj, 1988). In fact, it is
through this typically deliberate process of self-editing that scientists
from around the world are able to contribute to a universal discourse.

CONCLUSION: FOR A NORMATIVE RHETORIC OF SCIENCE

While I follow rhetoricians of science in believing that the best
way to understand texts is in terms of what happens once they get
into the hands of readers, I deny, on empirical grounds, that the best
way to understand what happens is in terms of the theory of reading
most closely associated with classical rhetoric and the humanistic
tradition. Indeed, I wonder whether anything more than humanist
hubris would lead rhetoricians to think that the reading and writing
practices that they value the most would be shared by the people
who are most highly valued as knowledge producers in our society.
Such hubris obscures the intriguing, and perhaps disturbing, fact
that the communication habits of the most highly touted knowledge producers resemble the habits of the typically much less

esteemed consumers of mass media. This unwitting commonality cries out for some sort of normative reorientation: Assuming that communicative media are essential to knowledge production, then either natural scientists are not as good as we thought—or television viewers are not as bad.

Upon encountering the brute character of scientific reading and writing practices, the die-hard textualist has three options. The first, common among rhetoricians of science of a literary bent, involves tacitly replacing the real readers with an ideal reader, someone knowledgeable about the science under discussion but who is, at the same time, blessed with a humanist's sense of interpretive care. This option invites the specious forms of historical understanding noted above.

A second option available to the textualist is to bite the bullet and admit that we all routinely misread each other's texts. Ever since deconstructionists redefined poetic and philosophical originality as the ability to provide strong misreadings of one's distinguished predecessors (Bloom, 1972), this view has held a certain attraction. At a more mundane level, historians interested in reconstructing a debate from original documents often unwittingly stumble upon this option, which, in their telling, may reduce a Manichaean struggle to a comedy of errors: The great minds would have realised they were not so far apart, had they bothered to read each other a little more closely. At this point, it becomes a complete mystery in what sense we can claim to have made epistemic progress. Indeed, if either natural or social scientists really expected their colleagues to read with the care lavished upon them by rhetoricians of science, we should find more frequent complaints about being misunderstood in the pages of academic journals along with more frequent appeals to the text of what one originally said. Artful and not so artful misunderstandings are easy to spot in virtually any scientific debate. Often they provide the best explanation of the debate itself. However, this has not led to increased employment for rhetorical critics ready to set the record straight on behalf of the aggrieved parties. On the contrary, when a scientific author claims to be misunderstood, the journal editor takes the complaint simply as a plea to let the current debate go another round. Few readers interpret the ensuing clarifications as instances of correcting error, which should make us wonder more generally about the appropriateness of regarding scientific communication as a vehicle for promoting something that might be called a common body of knowledge.

Enter the third option, which promises moderate relief from this epistemic predicament. It openly accepts that textualism is nothing more than a normative orientation toward scientific reading and writing practices. The claim would be, then, that science would be a better enterprise *if* scientists were to adopt the textual practices of humanists, but it would not be presumed that scientists are naturally inclined to do this. Such a claim could be grounded in a social theory—Habermas's (1981) theory of communicative action would be only one example—that takes the quality of language use to be an index of the quality of the human condition. Feyerabend would be a potential ally in this project.

Ironically, the failure of the rhetoric of science to decide whether it wants to be a descriptive or a prescriptive enterprise is reminiscent of the ambiguities surrounding the rational reconstructions that positivist philosophers of science have made of scientific theories. In order to demonstrate a grip on something real, philosophers have claimed to be *describing the logical structure* of theories. The highlighted turn of phrase conveys the impression that the logic is not imposed by the philosopher, but rather already inhabits the theories themselves, albeit so as to be invisible to all but the trained philosophical eye. For purposes of grounding a discipline, this descriptivist manner of speaking is probably more powerful than simply expressing a normative preference for rewriting theories in logical form. Likewise, if rhetoricians require a distinct domain of inquiry for their own legitimatory purposes, one can hardly blame them for conjuring up the specter of hidden tropes and Aristotelian moments in the texts they analyze. It is quite another matter, of course, to believe that anyone other than the rhetoricians in question ever finds these phantoms in the texts. I, for one, don't. I also don't believe that the rhetoric of science would be best served by staking out its own domain of inquiry. Instead, the field should be more straightforwardly in the business of reforming existing domains. Otherwise, I fear that the rhetoric of science may become a poor man's version of the philosophy of science, a field whose practitioners trade intuitions about the efficacy of devices rather than, say, the validity of arguments.

This tendency is already pronounced in Gross (1990, esp. the epilogue), who slides effortlessly between rhetorical and philosophical critique. For example, Gross's central argument for the purely rhetorical, motivational character of what philosophers call "scientific realism" rests more on the fact that scientists regularly assert more than their evidence warrants—a fact to which philosophers often appeal—than on the observed effects of realist appeals on scientific audiences. Consequently, Gross has been embroiled in a number of debates in which he has been forced to adopt the mantle of the philosophical relativist, and hence to reduce issues of rhetoric to refutations of realism (see McGuire and Melia, 1991).

For reasons that should be clear by now, I believe that most exercises in the rhetoric of science—certainly the ones critiqued by Gaonkar—are better regarded as prescriptions for how texts ought to be read than as descriptions of how they have actually been read. Granting this reinterpretation of their project, what rhetoricians of science now need are accounts of social life—equally normative—in which it would make sense to read texts with the sort of care that their own readings display. Moreover, if these are rhetorically effective accounts, audiences should be moved to try to make the world conform to them. Feyerabendian anarchism offers one such account of how science can be made safe for rhetoric, but it is hardly the only, let alone the most persuasive, account (see Fuller, 1993)

Luckily, scientists who practice the rhetoric of science for purposes of reforming their own fields are already alive to this issue (Nelson, McGill, and McCloskey, 1987). Rhetoricians of psychology (Billig, 1987; Danziger, 1990) and economics (Klamer, McCloskey, and Solow, 1989) are exemplary in their attempts to return to a more public space by deconstructing the linguistic barriers that currently restrict the range of people who can comfortably participate in their practices. Admittedly, these rhetoricians vary significantly over how radical the reforms need to be: Some treat their discipline's jargon as a relatively superficial accretion on practices that are largely accountable to the general public, while others seek a deeper diagnosis, one whose treatment would require a more complete overhaul, if not outright replacement, of the discipline. McCloskey (1985, 1990) and Mirowski (1986, 1989), respectively, epitomize the contrast in the discipline where the reformist impulse has been most striking, economics. In either case, we witness rhetoricians of science positioning themselves as rhetorical agents interested in not merely interpreting, but in actually changing the practices of their audiences.

ACKNOWLEDGEMENT

This is an expanded version of "Rhetoric of Science: A Doubly Vexed Expression," *Southern Communication Journal* 58 (1993): 306–311. I want to thank Bill Keith for pushing me to clarify my views about the history of rhetoric and the relevance of the mass communication literature to an understanding of contemporary Big Science.

REFERENCES

Bazerman, C. (1987). *Shaping written knowledge*. Madison: University of Wisconsin Press.

Billig, M. (1987). *Arguing and thinking*. Cambridge: Cambridge University Press.

Bloom, H. (1972). *The anxiety of influence*. Oxford: Oxford University Press.

Campbell, J. (1987). Charles Darwin: Rhetorician of science. In J. Nelson, A. Megill, and D. McCloskey (Eds.), *The rhetoric of the human sciences*, 69–86. Madison: University of Wisconsin Press.

Chaffee, S., and Hochheimer, J. (1982). The beginnings of political communication research in the United States: Origins of the limited effects model. In E. Rogers and F. Balle (Eds.), *The media revolution in America and western Europe*, 263–283. Norwood, NJ: Ablex Publishers.

Danziger, K. (1990). *The construction of the subject*. Cambridge: Cambridge University Press.

De Mey, M. (1982). *The cognitive paradigm*. Dordrecht: Reidel.

Eisenstein, E. (1979). *The printing press as an agent of change*. Cambridge: Cambridge University Press.

Ellegard, A. (1990). *Darwin and the general reader*. Chicago: University of Chicago Press.

Ezrahi, Y. (1990). *The descent of icarus*. Cambridge: Harvard University Press.

Feyerabend, P. (1978). *Science in a free society*. London: Verso.

Fuller, S. (1988). *Social epistemology*. Bloomington: Indiana University Press.

———. (1993). *Philosophy, rhetoric and the end of knowledge: The coming of science and technology studies*. Madison: University of Wisconsin Press.

———. (1994a). Social psychology of scientific knowledge: Another strong programme.In W. Shadish and S. Fuller (Eds.), *Social Psychology of Science*, 162–178. New York: Guilford.

———. (1994b). The sphere of critical thinking in a post-epistemic world. *Informal Logic, 16*, 39–54.

———. (1994c). Why post-industrial society never came.*Academe, 80*, 22–28.

Graff, H. (1987). *The legacies of literacy.* Bloomington: Indiana University Press.

Gross, A. (1990). *The rhetoric of science.* Cambridge: Harvard University Press.

Habermas, J. (1981). *The theory of communicative action.* Boston: Beacon.

Hollis, M., and Lukes, S. (Eds.). (1982). *Rationality and relativism.* Cambridge: MIT Press.

Horowitz, I. (1986). *Communicating ideas.* Oxford: Oxford University Press.

Kitcher, P. (1991). Persuasion. In M. Pera and W. Shea (Eds.), *Persuading science: The art of scientific rhetoric,* 3–28. Canton, MA: Science History Publications.

Klamer, A., McCloskey, D., and Solow, R. (Eds.). (1989). *The consequences of economic rhetoric.* Cambridge: Cambridge University Press.

Knorr-Cetina, K. (1981). *The manufacture of knowledge.* Oxford: Pergamon.

Leff, M. (1987). Modern sophistic and the unity of rhetoric. In J. Nelson, A. Megill, and D. McCloskey (Eds.), *The rhetoric of the human sciences,* 19–37. Madison: University of Wisconsin Press.

McCloskey, D. (1985). *The rhetoric of economics.* Madison: University of Wisconsin Press.

———. (1990). *If you're so smart . . .* Chicago: University of Chicago Press.

McGuire, J., and Melia, T. (1991). The rhetoric of the radical rhetoric of science. *Rhetorica, 9,* 301–316.

Merton, R. (1942). Science and technology in a democratic order. *Journal of Legal and Political Sociology, 1,* 115–126.

———. (1973). *Sociology of science.* Chicago: University of Chicago Press.

Mirowski, P. (1986). *Against mechanism.* Totowa: Rowman and Littlefield.

———. (1989). *More heat than light.* Cambridge: Cambridge University Press.

Nelson, J., Megill, A., and McCloskey, D. (Eds.). (1987). *The rhetoric of the human sciences.* Madison: University of Wisconsin Press.

Popper, K. (1945). *The open society and its enemies.* New York: Harper and Row.

Poulakos, J. (1989). Early changes in rhetorical practice and understanding from the Sophists to Isocrates. *La Rhetorique de Texte, 8/9,* 307–324.

Raj, K. (1988). Images of knowledge, social organization, and attitudes in an Indian physics department. *Science in Context, 2,* 317–339.

Rose, J. (1992). Rereading the English common reader: A preface to a history of   audiences. *Journal of the History of Ideas, 53,* 47–70.

Shapin, S., and Schaffer, S. (1985). *Leviathan and the air-pump.* Princeton: Princeton University Press.

Spitz, D. (Ed.). (1975). *Critical edition of J. S. Mill's* On liberty.New York: Norton.

Turner, S., and Chubin, D. (1976). Another appraisal of Ortega, the Coles, and science policy: The Ecclesiastes hypothesis. *Social Science Information, 15,* 657–662.

Wilson, B. (Ed.). (1970). *Rationality.* Oxford: Blackwell.

Zilsel, E. (1945). The genesis of the concept of scientific progress. *Journal of the History of Ideas, 6,* 35–50.

CHAPTER 12

THE RHETORICAL CRITIC
AND THE INVISIBLE POLIS

Andrew King

THE ARGUMENT

How can we fashion a political rhetoric for the postmodern interregnum and beyond? While a rhetorical aesthetic or utopian rhetorical theory may flourish in any age, genuine political rhetoric cannot. I assert that political rhetoric requires a *polis*, a community anchored in physical space, engaged in daily problems of survival and socialization, and enforcing limits on the behavior of its citizens. I will argue that political rhetoric is constantly born anew during the formation of new communities and extinguished by their devolution or death. Political rhetoric, I assert, is the characteristic product of the great waves of community formation in the West: the city-state of the Greco Roman era, the Renaissance free-labor city, and the modern nation-state. All other political rhetorics are so-called only as a nominal courtesy, through metaphoric extension. Despite the postmodern era's lip service to the local and the particular, this is an era characterized by global technology and profound skepticism. In such an epoch, what becomes of a community's "ability to set limits, define boundaries, trace ancestries when all that is really solid does melt into thin air?" (Wark, 1994:221). In short, there will be no lack of discourse, but not a grounded civic discourse rooted in that many-sided, multi-roled creature, the citizen. A brilliant rhetorical theorist, Dilip Gaonkar, has characterized classical rhetoric as "retrograde," but what he really means is that it has lost (temporarily) the center of gravity (community) and the locus of a social role (citizen) that gave it vitality and relevance. The lack of community is also the cause of the problems that Steve Fuller, one of Gaonkar's critics, points to. What we need are not new Platonic guardians—Fuller's solution—but a return of the polis.

The loss of the citizen has coincided with the loss of the sense of place. And as civil society increasingly loses its material grounding, and individuals arrange their private media environments, community becomes a nostalgic metaphor. Civil discourse cannot be carried on by surrogates; a civil rhetoric is one in which the members of the community "contribute the content" (Schement and Curtis, 1995:120). In a dispersed and fragmented polity, one cannot construct a genuine political rhetoric. A metaphoric community begets an ersatz political discourse. It is not enough to say that technology is not really an independent force, or to say reassuringly that its presence results from human decisions and desires. To the contrary, many Americans already experience their technology-filled environments as deterministic forces and see themselves as limited power holders with choices that are those of consumers rather than of citizens.

Thus most revisions of political rhetoric begin with a restoration of the absent *polis* or with compensatory strategies to cope with partial technological determinism, fragmented knowledge, and information dependency and overload. This battle for cognitive coherence is a pale substitute for genuine civic participation in a finite community.

The first science fiction novel was not written until 1816. Its appearance expressed a consciousness of perceptible change. However, the ideal of progress (moral and material) was implicit at least since the Enlightenment. A few decades later, it became the central thesis of social philosophy, of which Auguste Comte's work is only a notable example (Comte, 1853). Comte was unique only in that he posited the spectre of constantly accelerating social change. It is clear that by the end of the eighteenth century, people were becoming mindful of the magnitude of change within a single human lifetime. Similarly, information "began to be perceived as a thing," a commodity that disempowered the old order, mobilized audiences dispersed in time and space, and separated knowledge from its old anchorage in folk experience and within particular life spheres (Schement and Curtis, 1995, esp. 4–5).

Dictionaries, encyclopedias, bureaucratic files, and printing may not seem remarkable to the twentieth century, but they represented an unprecedented cultural change. Under their agency the new community (the nation-state) was solidified at the expense of the old civic republic. The study of words, syntax, and the various attempts to prune and design language for specialists and merchants at the expense of folk roots foreshadowed the impoverished social epistemology of our day, an epistemology that posits the construction of reality through language (Schement and Curtis, 1995, esp. 4–7). This is the kind of epistemology that could only arise among a generation of scholars whose roots are overwhelmingly urban and whose life experience is filtered through electronic media and paper. It is the late rotten bloom of the abstract society.

Information-as-commodity is an idea that rapidly burst its early Marxist parameters; it has emerged as the sounding shibboleth of the global economic order. As such it stands in sharp contrast to the humble rhetoric of the polis, with its heavy reliance on orality and local knowledge. The organic community that echoes through Pericles's funeral oration is almost incomprehensible to the university-trained rhetorician of our day; its appeals to produce more children and to savagely repress one's envy are as far from our consciousness as Thomas Hardy's "starlit Stonehenge."

So what is the case for a meaningful political rhetoric at the end of the twentieth century? Gaonkar, it would seem, despairs of a globalized rhetoric ever being restrained enough to permit a full theory of political rhetoric. His critique seems to undermine the possibility that rhetoric could do for a modern polis what it did for classical ones. He shows that the attempts within a globalized theory to extend the rhetoric of the polis into science seem bound to fail. Unfortunately, he may be right, since science is absolutely central to post-Enlightenment society, and the resources of civic humanism, in the guise of rhetoric, are inadequate to it. Some lessons from history will tell the tale. Permit me briefly to compare two ambitious attempts to restore civic rhetoric in the post-Enlightenment setting of the invisible polis. The first attempt is an early one by Auguste Comte, the founder of sociology, while the other is by Steve Fuller, the brilliant polymath and founder of the journal *Social Epistemology*. Fuller's most recent work, *Philosophy, Rhetoric, and the End of Knowledge: The Coming of Science and Technology Studies*, sets forth a utopian view.

Comte lived during an axial period. The world of the Old Regime and the Western Free Labor City had been swept away, while the world of the nation-state had been born in a cataclysm that had convulsed Europe. Comte faced unique problems and attempted to solve them. Conscious that the new world had been born by ripping apart the old one, Comte contemplated the nation-state, a deliberate creation of a new mercantile class armed with a revisionist history. Like many intellectuals of the ancient world (and the modern one), he had suffered a status dilemma. The new world had disempowered the old nobility and provided vast social, economic, and cultural mobility to others. Millions of people were leaving the ancient peasant communities of Europe. From Scotland to Austria, they steamed into the burgeoning industrial cities. As Comte watched the disinherited peasantry stream into the new cities of the continent, leaving behind their rural culture and the social control mechanisms of the village, he thought he saw a grander version of the old Paris mob rising in every city of Europe, the coming of the mass-man, a creature with the morality of an alley cat and the intelligence of a spinal dog. Unlike the revolutionary bourgeois, he could not look backward to an idealized version of the polis. By Comte's day it had become clear that a chasm separated the nation from earlier community forms and a reaction against classicism had set in. Unable to secure patronage from the new business classes, the artistic community developed an aesthetic that ridiculed ideals of hard work, discipline, and rationality. Their alienation threatened to spread to Comte's colleagues, the French intellectuals. Our contemporary utopian, Steve Fuller, confronts a culture whose individual members increasingly construct private spheres of meaning, designing an environment from their particular arrangements of a mix of radios, television sets, video recorders, disk players, computers, papers, magazines, books, and rental films.

Even the most sanguine media researchers despair over the creation of an informed citizenry from such a rich but fragmented mixture. They note that one cannot predict which information will be rejected and which retained, how the information will be used or even what will be seen as useful. In short, even the quality of similar experiences is unpredictable. As a result they are ready to see the agenda-setting attempts of the old mass media as salubrious. The fear of dissensus dampens the zeal of the global villagers who once hoped that the new electronic tribalism would foster a hunger for orality and direct debate on questions of value and policy. The folk will now suffer the same sense of homelessness as the world-weary intellectuals of the past three hundred years.

In *Philosophy, Rhetoric, and the End of Knowledge*, Fuller argues that "information," not knowledge, has become an item of value for economic exchange, for a secondary sort of social interconnectedness, and for the wise management of the planet. His resolutely secular vision (although his occasional gratuitous ridicule of conventional religious beliefs suggests that he sees them as dangerous because of the unfortunate tendency of ordinary folk to still be interested in ultimate questions) will not allow him to call his new Science and Technology Studies (STS) samurai a "priesthood," but they are warriors, all the same. They will penetrate the true philosopher's stone—the riddle of the production of knowledge. And possessing that talisman they will broker the production and consumption of new innovation in a way that respects the limits of the planet's resources and the aspirations of ordinary people. Scientists will have to give up their presumptuous rivalry with God and their wasteful search for the God-particle in favor of the service of a totally secular society managed by boundary-spanning discussion leaders who can move across different domains of thought. The new priesthood will foster the interconnectedness missing in an increasingly fragmented world.

COMTE AND FULLER: TWO PATHS TO TECHNOCRACY AND TECHNO-CIVIC RHETORIC

The renewal of interest in Auguste Comte signals the beginning of a period of reaction which resembles the period of romantic reaction during the early nineteenth century. Then, as now, irrevocable economic and political changes were being consolidated and new technologies were altering the human landscape completely. The nation-state, newspapers, encyclopedias, bureaucracies, a vast expansion of books, the rise of factories, and the vast expansion of canals in northern Europe may seem puny to us, but they represented unprecedented changes in Comte's world. Amid the chaos of post-Napoleonic France, Comte provided a conservative answer for a country reeling from the excesses of the French Revolution. With incredible daring he brought together the new spirit of empiricism and the reactionary organicism of Edmund Burke. Under Comte's dedicated direction, a new set of guardians would command the new science and politics so that the teeth could be pulled from the threatening specters of mass democracy and socialism. Like Steve Fuller, the banner-carrier for the new discipline of Science and Technology Studies, Comte wished to make knowledge production a publically visible and highly self-conscious act. Comte had a political agenda that would create the syntax and the rhetoric for the benign uses of the new science. Furthermore it would remove the teeth from socialism and blunt the momentum toward mass democracy. His utopia would contain persons so rich in material, moral, and social wealth that they would transcend greed. Again, like Steve Fuller, Comte would politicize knowledge so that scientific discovery could be framed by moral and political considerations instead of the farcically empty opportunism and careerism of scientists or manufacturers. "Discovery" would not proceed in isolation from communal interests. Comte dreamed of a new caste, a scientific priesthood that would heal the breech between empirical knowledge and normative wisdom.

It was a dream grander than that even of the late Richard McKeon, who found in Greco-Roman rhetoric a unifying architectonic for all of humane study and for the sciences as well. Students of McKeon will recall that in unifying the circle of humane study with a single method, the master believed that he was laying the groundwork for a global rhetoric that would bridge warring cultures by eroding their boundaries and uniting their people. But while McKeon's conception was grounded in his earlier classical studies of Roman imperial integration, Comte's vision was more Platonic in its sense of a single community formula and the propagation of a unifying educational system and ideology. Comte dreamed of a community in which consent was engineered by techno-priests, with himself as the Pontif, the great bridge. And even as Plato despaired of the limits of the dominant community form of *his* time (the *polis*), Comte feared the distinctive community formation of his time, the nation-state. He saw that the new birthing (often in revolution or some other cataclysmic event) had destroyed many of the old social controls, local cultures, and regional loyalties. He feared the middle-class bearers of the revolutionary heritage, bourgeois merchants and factory owners, whose specialized production and divisions of labor weakened communal identification and encouraged massification. *Gemeinschaft* had been replaced by *Gesellschaft*. The organic French village of Comte's youth, with its emphasis on primary relationships, was being swept away. In Paris, London, and Berlin, Comte believed, people were being reduced to mere "factors," or as his sociologist progeny would say, reduced to "roles" or edited down to "functions."

In the meantime the information revolution has made capitalism global. An ever wider but shallower set of relationships—between educator and student, between employer and employee, between buyer and seller—is in the offing. Factories and people are still relatively permanent, but most other production resources can be moved to other sites. The astonishing mobility of economic resources has left local communities and even whole states and regions with no purchase on their own destiny. Increasingly fragmented resources and information leave the individual with an idiosyncratic and skeptical view of the world. Fuller sees a displacement of the community that is more complete than the destruction of the Old Regime that so distressed Comte. The liquidation of civic culture has created massive psychic dislocation and powerlessness.

Both postmodern scholars and the dominant corporate business culture seem to agree that there is no place for the individual voice. Comte believed that capitalism, the national state, and modern science advanced in opposition to the medieval institutions they replaced. Capitalism and nationalism are full-blown social systems that either reorganized or liquidated traditional institutions and culture. By the late eighteenth century, the nation-state—an artificial inorganic community produced by a rationally calculated consent—provided an environment for social reform and the triumph of science. The French Revolution was the crucible for the consolidation of the national state. It spawned the idea of an entire nation in arms (a universal conscript army) and patriotism (membership in a community conscious of a common fate). The so-called romantic reaction following the Enlightenment was characterized by a compensatory interest in local custom, folk myth, ethnic uniqueness, and the occult. Against the homogenizing and unifying exercises of the State, the unique, the personal, and the local achieved luminous value and mystical status, and in this context Comte emerged as an privotal figure. A founder of sociology, he provided a synthesis of traditionally sanctioned hierarchy and the dynamism of scientific research. His program was to defeat scientific reformers (socialists) and Jacobin revolutionaries while conserving what he saw as the benefits to be gained from a constantly accelerating science.

Comte, like Steve Fuller, saw a great political and moral crisis arising out of intellectual anarchy, with no tidy barrier between the dislocated theory and disorganized practice in politics. The rift between the value horizons of ordinary people and the systematic instrumentalism of institutional science is as great in Fuller's mind as the rift between scientific social reformers and the deposed aristocracy was in Comte's day. But Fuller is not blinded by the innocence of conventional thinkers who see the information society as a sharp break from the old industrial order. He finds the information society to be an organic outgrowth of the old society, an extension that was implicit from the beginning of the industrial revolution (Schement and Curtis, 1995, esp. 25–28). The scientific spirit that Comte so passionately admired was anchored in radical reform groups, while the social discipline he sought was the property of nostalgic writers, members of the ruined aristocracy, and those polemical painters, such as Theophile Gautier (and writers like Baudelaire), who had taken over aristocratic dress and customs. Compared to the patronage of the monarch and nobility, little succor from the new bourgeois class was forthcoming. There is, finally, something corporate, something hollow in Comte even when he attains the summit of passion. Small wonder we find in Comte's overheated prose a feeling of being ungrounded, of playing the poseur, of never failing to hit the false note. Comte himself was torn between the magnetic poles of decorously ordered hierarchy and the world-transforming dynamism of science. This conflict resounded throughout his intellectual life. For example, Comte's huge admiration for the caste system of India was vitiated by his contempt for their lack of technological progressiveness. He felt that the Indians of the period of patrimonial-state formation had achieved social order at too great a cost; their bargain represented love without knowledge. On the other hand, the Jacobin reformers of the French revolution had exhibited a daring experimentalism, but their programs lacked the stabilizing virtues of veneration, benevolence and loyalty. Even as they reformed the community they destroyed the basis of its cohesion. They had left too many corpses, and when they had finished devouring others had turned and rent each other.

Granted, Comte's relationship to rhetorical theory is not readily apparent. The writers of the post-Napoleonic generation were affected by the unfavorable revolutionary assessment of the study of rhetoric; to them it represented the fundamental style note of the bad old days, an apparatus in the service of the Old Regime. The study of rhetoric had been denounced by the leaders of the French Revolution as a stumbling block in the way of truth. And despite their admiration of Cicero as a republican martyr and their own status as practicing rhetors, they could not endorse the formal recognition of an art that had been the apex of aristocratic education. It was condemned as a puerile art that allowed one to make a letter sound wiser than it was, and permitted the rogue to simulate the philosopher (Perelman, 1969, esp. vi). Comte's six-volume work *Cours de philosphie positive* does not use the word. On the other hand, he speaks of the kind of discourse that must prevail, who will speak, and the correct sort of messages that will be dinned into the ears of the young. He also speaks of the restoration of the conditions necessary for a genuine community, and these are, of course, the very conditions that make rhetoric possible. He argues that the basic maxims of social order (ideo-topoi) must be restored through an elaborate and controlled socialization. What Richard Weaver used to refer to as the communal "order of goods" is to be instilled in the young as the very first task in the revivification of a moral order.

While such ideas as the basic need for governance, disciplined subordination, and loyalty to extended family were thought to be biological tendencies, Comte feared that they could be undermined by a strong and determined radical faction. Thus, at all times, a sociological priesthood would take care to inculcate basic ideas such as the human hunger for government, the superiority of hierarchy, and the progressive evolution of society to ever "higher" stages. Civic discourse of the Ciceronian variety (the orator-statesman engaged in freewheeling debate) was not to be encouraged, however. This republican discourse had been fit for the Roman Republic and the Renaissance city, but it had been surpassed. Like the militaristic and theological societies, it was appropriate to a stage of human development that had passed on the great wheel of time. It had been surpassed in the march of history. Comte's priests would be scientists, poets, doctors, and governors, and the breech between science and society would be healed. The dynamism of scientific advance would not be wholly lost, but it would be ambushed by conservatism and subordinated to its program of orderly and carefully managed change. Family values and large scale industrial enterprise would be fitted into a seamless web so that neither damaged the other. Thus did conservatism meet the challenge of social change.

Only a first-rate intellect was capable of executing this bizarre synthesis. The world at sixes and sevens appears in his electrically charged work *System of Positive Polity* (1853). Comte never permitted himself to read anything that caused psychic pain. He disciplined himself to exclude all disturbing thoughts from his consciousness and was able to design a system that controlled the most minute areas of daily life.

While Comte's unacknowledged "rhetoricians" practice the engineering of consent, Fuller's STS specialists (despite his pretense to broadening the debate by including subalterns and silenced people) will act as guardians by framing the technical issues in ordinary language. In a straightforward sense (very clearly articulated in his piece in this volume), Fuller sees himself as the true heir to the Enlightenment, able to bring the light of democracy to the dark recesses of corporate science. The selection and translation afforded by "STS practitioners" will mediate between the scientific researcher and the consumer in such a way that the consumer can take hold of his or her destiny. Lo, a ray of light appears in the cracks of the science establishment. Citizens will engage in dialogue through the medium of STS. Although Fuller clearly treats science as a special, and in many ways higher, order of knowledge, he would still have scientists shed any godlike stance. Then STS can let these pretenders know that the scales have fallen from our eyes at last, though we blink in the brightness of new possibilities of knowledge. The old ideal of science as a search for truth independent of merely institutional criteria—that is to say, an activity carried out by solitary thinking subjects—will be refuted. Finally corporate science will be unmasked and the interests of ordinary individuals, collectively, will prevail. The glorious dawn arrives.

Fuller, like McKeon, envisions a grand role for rhetoric. Like Comte, Fuller wishes to restore community, to pull down the intellectual barriers between people and their institutions. Like Habermas, he worries that the people have been marginalized in the arena of civic discourse and that the only voices heard are those of experts and elites. The people have been given only a subaltern voice; they do not enter public discourse at the planning and execution of social and technological innovation. But when the subaltern finally does find a voice, it is only through ventriloquism (Baumlin and Baumlin, 1994:77). The people enter the discussion only at a point when the consequences of policy become visible; and usually only in the event of obvious and painful failure is the voice of the people heard even then. By that point, their only remedy is a kind of calamity-howling ending in clumsy political acts of assertion. William Bailey, an Arizona-based commentator, has often asserted that the only political rhetoric that appears to be effective in the present community (where the only serious voices are corporate) is one of either utter submission or intellectual terrorism.

Of course all this talk of democracy is ingenuous; giving attention to rhetoric per se won't insure a democratic outcome. With STS framing the scientific agenda and articulating the choices, STSers are as firmly in control as Comte's priests. In fact, more firmly in control, because the levers of power are so very much greater and the power of STS will be invisible, legitimated behind a facade of public service and intellectual rigor. A new bureaucratization of knowledge production is underway. Fuller objects to the postmodern demise of the individual, but his solution is more of the same corporate knowledge production and ignores the enormous purchase that international corporations already have on government data and government resources. Where is the space for the individual? Where is the space for the citizen? Fuller presents himself as an innocent in presenting the STS shock troops as facilitators and democratizers who can open the discussion for mass participation. First of all, Fuller's criticism of postmodernism and his Enlightenment nostalgia are transparent. He assumes that science will always gravitate to power, but he assumes the power arrangements that began in the Great Depression and World War II will continue forever. But postmodernism and the electronic revolution have already begun to demassify power. Even as Fuller was completing his book it had become evident that the both globalism and regional folkism were moving into the identity vacuum created by the decline of the nation-state. Science has always gravitated toward power, and Big Science has gravitated increasingly toward the international corporations. Fuller's STS board, screening resources controlled by a national government, already seems quaint. The national states themselves are scrambling to survive by making their own knowledge resources and data banks increasingly available to global corporations.

While most utopias practice socialism, they cannot dispense with a priestly caste, a final layer of accountable persons to ensure all will be right. This fact alone should alert us that despite all the equalitarian rhetoric of these people, their secret lust is for power. Who elected STS to be our mediators and negotiators? Another darker side of priestly governance is apparent when Fuller notes that "friends of rhetoric tend to over-emphasize the community-building functions of well-chosen language, often harboring some fairly nostalgic (if not downright mythical) views about the degree of common ground that is achievable, or desirable between people" (1993:18). If these are not the words of the homeless intellectual they are at least not the sentiments of anyone who has participated in the life of a small southern or midwestern town. They suggest that the heart of Fuller's social epistemology may be old-fashioned American pragmatism. Nothing succeeds like success, and the consequences of an idea contain its true value. Thus, Fuller goes on to tell us that we do not need a high degree of consensus in order to act together, and that in our pluralistic democracies large policies can be conducted routinely on a basis of very minimal consensus. The worst interpretation is that Fuller finds that the actual practice of civic rhetoric is messy and time-consuming because real communities are about process rather than goals. Fuller wants to get on with agenda of building utopia. The more likely interpretation is that Fuller is a victim of academic head culture. As Kenneth Burke long preached, identification among people came from consubtantiality— not only in the sense of a sharing of substance, but in an acting together. People like me (an ever-shrinking minority) who grew up in small closely knit rural societies know that consensus is not achieved independently of action. People forge an identity through marrying, burying, and helping one another survive; small-town caring allows people to survive the ordinary disasters and the common unhappiness that characterizes all lives. And once people act in concert to prop up even the most nonsensical arrangements, they will support them with passion and fury. It is innocent to say that we can act together and keep our dissensus.

Another distressing point is Fuller's attack on the tolerance of the humanist tradition. It is similar to H. L. Mencken's vulgar explanation for religious tolerance in early America: Americans were tolerant for merely demographic reasons: first, because no one protestant denomination achieved numerical preponderance; and second, because the many unchurched formed a huge indigestible boulder of indifference. The humanists are angry because they have been impotent. They suffer from powerlessness and a failed program. Fuller's contempt is withering. He dismisses humanistic tolerance, pointing out that "the irony behind such magnanimity is that humanists started singing the praises of relativism and pluralism only after successive historical failures at gaining control over politicians, artists, publics and each other" (365). Like good academicians, Fuller and Comte are as one in their contempt for the climbing mercantile classes as powerful elites without moral authority. Yet in place of the appetite of the business class we are offered nothing less than the total politicization of ordinary life. Fuller is a man contemptuous of boundaries. Yet as John Locke instructs us, it is in the spaces between the spheres of authority that allow for human freedom and growth. Under Fuller's STS the spheres of social control, socialization, and mastery of nature would be united.

Finally, the success of Fuller's cadre (for all its talk of embracing an open future) depends upon certain power arrangements that are not likely to endure; and worse, the cadre is the bearer of an ideology that seems transparently self-serving. Power arrangements first. Fuller seems astonishingly oblivious to the enormous power of American business to set the research agenda. In fact, he hardly mentions business. Nor does he mention the great appendage of business, American advertising, the arena where the real practicing rhetoricians are. The massive subsidy of science which began in the 1940s and changed the shape of the humanities forever has nearly run its course. The shape of the university was altered as well, and the humanities consigned to the outermost margins of power. Yet all trends are ultimately reversed, and suddenly we think we hear its long withdrawing roar begin. When research monies come predominantly from seed and fertilizer companies (as they do already in land-grant universities), how will the STS mandarins intervene in the research enterprise? Similar dilemmas may emerge with subsidies from pharmaceutical companies, or the department of defense. Has Professor Fuller observed how tangled private and public research agendas became as early as the 1970s?

The federal government's Cold War investment in higher education devastated the humanities and social sciences. The federal government could not have marginalized the arts and humanities any more effectively had it conducted an organized campaign against them. The best students are identified early and they are steered into the sciences through counseling, subsidy, prizes and awards, career promises, and the active encouragement of their peers, parents, and teachers, who believe in the social utility and moral worth of science. This unorganized conspiracy is called "modern America." Fuller does not want to change these arrangements in any way. He and his samurai just want to be the humanists and social scientists who get in on them.

RHETORIC AND THE POLIS

The responsible political rhetoric that Comte envisioned and Fuller hopes for may continue to elude us. This is because a political rhetoric makes no sense apart from the idea of community. I assert that the "problem" of rhetoric is the problem of its missing community. Like the discourse theorists who need so badly to assert the primacy of linguistic reality, most modern rhetorical theorists struggle on with an impoverished idea of community. Thus they all must develop a sort of community substitute, such as "public knowledge" or "universal audience" or "elites" or "culture"—pale substitutes for the old concept of the "citizen," the many-sided individual who served as both rhetor and audience in earlier communities. Many modern theorists argue for pluralistic rhetorics or purely syntactic rhetorics or ideal typical rhetorics, which is all very well as far as it goes. Once they begin to talk about civic discourse, however, they are confronted with the postmodern problem, the missing polis. Postmodernism, the name for decentering and the worship of the local, is only another name for broken community and the consequent fragmenting of traditional civic discourse.

A brief excursion backward will illuminate political rhetoric's limits. *Rhetoric* is a historical term, not a living presence. Its real flowering occurred during the great waves of community formation, at the edge of civilization, not in its center. Rhetoric flourishes during the times when new problems must be faced and new opportunities are made available to individuals, such as in the Greek *polis*, the Renaissance free city, and the republican period of the nation-state. At other times, rhetoric has a kind of twilight-life, its ghostly lineaments hanging about like reminders of a glorious but impotent past.

Greek civilization went through three periods: the Heroic (1800–900 B.C.), the Hellenistic (900–300 B.C.), and the Hellenic

(300 B.C.–A.D. 200). The first period was that of kingship; the second period was the high period of the polis, the autonomous city-state. The third period occurred when Macedonian kings and then Roman imperials leveled the city walls and turned city-states into administrative subunits of the Empire. It is generally agreed that the city-state evolved when aristocrats broke the trading monopoly of the kings. Gradually the new community came to be based on the concept of the "citizen," the fundamental social role in the polis. The many-sided citizen included lawyers, administrators, judges, soldiers. The polis was the unique community of the ancient world. Despite the pleas by the great Isocrates, the Greek world was not able to construct a more comprehensive, national identity. The amateurism of the population and the intense inter-civic rivalry gave the polis its dawn quality of intellectual ferment.

The conditions of the city-state were especially favorable to the development of rhetoric. It was a politically divided age in which city-states were engaged in constant conflict. The rhetorician occupied a special place; political discourse became the site where the tensions of the society—between the governed and the governors, between aristocrat and commoner, between soldier and merchant—were worked out.

The Sophists, whose creative genius greatly enriched that of the local citizenry, were usually themselves full citizens of other states. They were social dynamite for the polis, of course. As wandering exiles they had to live by their wits and so served as teachers, ambassadors, military experts, counselors, and founders of schools. They had seen a variety of customs and laws and were not shy about making social comparisons. They questioned the Greek taboos against incest by citing the example of incestuous Egyptian monarchs. Their relativism angered the local citizens, but it also created a space in which a new spirit of amateurism and inquiry could flower. Their stock-in-trade was the teaching of rhetoric, itself a challenge to the canonization of traditional thought. Appeals were not made to institutional criteria but had to be grounded in the daily experience of ordinary people. And since rhetoric argues on both sides of a proposition, in operation it was at least partially subversive of folk wisdom.

With the reduction of the city-state to an administrative unit after the death of Alexander in 322 B.C., the lot of the intellectual seemed to improve. Athens became an administrative subunit of the Macedonian Empire. The loss of self-government, however, also meant the loss of a number of the old citizen-skills. The polymaths—Plato, Aristotle, and Socrates—and the rhetoricians were no longer needed in a time of empire. The intellectual became a library specialist at Alexandria, a counselor, or a member of the literati, and the optimism of the polis gave way to the return of doctrines of despair, resignation, or the cultivation of small pleasures against a background of imperial consolidation and individual powerlessness.

My point here is that one cannot expect a healthy political rhetoric without a polis. It had a flowering in the second and first centuries A.D. under another city-state, republican Rome. The epideictic and ceremonial rhetoric that emerged after the triumph of Augustus was not unlike the ceremonial and festival rhetoric that arose after the decline of the Greek polis. The Second Sophistic differed from the first in that its political content was either concealed or harmless. A recrudescence of rhetoric occurred during the Renaissance city-state and another during the so-called Roman period of the nation-states in the late eighteenth and early nineteenth centuries.

The flowering of genuine political discourse belongs to community formation, not to community maintenance. During the formation of the unique free-labor city of the Renaissance, for example, there was a perceived inadequacy of institutional procedures and a failure of canonized thought. In the revival of cities (first in Italy and then throughout Europe), new problems arose for which there was no institutional formula. For the first time in a thousand years, Renaissance cities needed to master problems of large-scale water supply, of massive foreign trade, of self-governing civic assemblies. A large space for innovation had thus been created, since the formation of new communities opens intellectual and social space—and thus new linguistic space. People are rewarded for moving into the unknown. But as community forms harden or lose their capacity for innovation, formal institutional criteria replace the free play of minds.

As Gaonkar has begun, I will continue: a revisionist view of the discipline's history is in order. When the Burkean hordes breeched the walls and were joined by their movement study and New Critical allies, the unity of Speech Communication was splintered. When these new scholars struck down the Aristotelian canon in the 1960s, they arrived with an impoverished view of the self. Despite Burke's long engagement with radical politics, his "I" was merely a domiciled version of the social "they." The dominant Burkeans had mostly contempt for the concept of the citizen that had so energized the work of pioneers in the field of Speech Communication, such as Everett Lee Hunt, H. L. Ewbank, and the young Barnet Baskerville, who were populists in the best sense. While grossly stigmatizing what was an essentially Ciceronian rhetoric as a search for limited crowd effects or for the promotion of farcically empty individual careerism, the new scholars substituted a pale and cerebral end for rhetoric, the creation of meaning. Can attaining meaning (through "identification") become a fertile ground for a politics that puts rhetoric at its center?

Probably not; we cannot have a civil rhetoric without a ground for that rhetoric. Gaonkar's complaint about the disjuncture between classical rhetorical theory and contemporary discourse rings distressingly true, but he might have the story backwards. One gets the impression he thinks that in pointing out the disjunction he has argued that rhetoricians should foreswear their allegiance to classical vocabulary and join those who know how language and politics are connected—*not* through the individual. This is merely another version of the Burkean problem: Insisting that all the politics are already really there in the theories of meaning won't wash if the assertion is made in the face of an utterly disempowering political system. The two distinctive community formations of Western Civilization—the city and the nation—are both in disarray. Thus we have only memories and echoes of a true political rhetoric. The dominant voice of our time is a corporate voice, international, unaccountable, and inescapable; its attendant rhetoric will not become the discourse of the polis through clever reinterpretation or effort. Like Huck and Tom, we may have to start dreaming about lighting out for the territories.

REFERENCES

Baumlin, J. T., and Baumlin, T. F. (Eds). (1994). *Ethos: New essays in rhetorical and critical theory.* Dallas: Southern Methodist University Press.

Comte, A. (1853). *The positive philosophy.* Freely translated and condensed by Harriet Martineau from 6 volumes to 4. London: J. Chapman.

Fuller, S. (1993). *Philosophy, rhetoric, and the end of knowledge: The coming of science and technology studies.* Madison: University of Wisconsin Press.

Perelman, C., and Obrechts-Tyteca, L. (1969). *The new rhetoric: A treatise on argumentation.* John Wilkinson and Purcell Weaver (Trans.). Notre Dame: University of Notre Dame Press.

Schement, J., and Curtis, T. (1995). *Tendencies and tensions of the information age: The production and distribution of information in the United States.* New Brunswick: Transaction.

Wark, M. (1994). *Virtual geography: Living with global and media events.* Bloomington: University of Indiana Press.

PART IV

Reflections/Refractions

CHAPTER 13

AN ELLIPTICAL POSTSCRIPT

Thomas B. Farrell

Having followed these proceedings at something of a distance, occasionally entering the discussion to tweak one position or another, I think I have a pretty good idea of why Gaonkar's project has been so disconcerting. The point may be seen rather indirectly by remembering that the conventions that inform our myriad of discourse practices—conversation, lectures, scholarly writing, *Gesellschaft* transactions, bargaining and negotiation, phone sex, or whatever—are all counterfactual, contrary to the facts of our communication. We *perform* our sincerity, disclosure, truth-telling, and act as if we expect these things from others, even as we (or at least most of us) none too secretly "know" that it is a groundless expectation at best. Our communicative "work" is never pure. And this is never more obvious that when we purport to stand outside it, so as to explain it impartially to ourselves. Yet I suspect that part of what "polite" or decorous communication consists in is the tacit agreement not to notice this.

A little illustration can help show what happens when attention or conscious reflection is focused on this "tacit" agreement. A close friend of mine has an unsettling habit of calling attention to distinctive features of others' communicative behavior. For instance, if my friend Bob (an intense Little League coach) goes on and on describing an ancient Little League game in microscopic detail, this close friend of mine will listen for a while and then say, "Gee, Bob, do you have this same phenomenal pattern of recollection in other aspects of your life, say—your job?" This snappy interruption is annoying, and not only because it shifts topics. It also does two other, more subtle things. It forces reflection upon one's own rules and styles of communicating, rules and styles one may not even fully grasp. And it intrudes a devious little asymmetry into the conversation by decoding another's communicative style, rather than replying to the content. Now were Bob so inclined, he could raise the stakes further by replying, "Do you characteristically force communication to a metalevel?" In principle, this sort of trumping could go on indefinitely.

My little allegory, once explained, shows itself to be an example of this technique, as well as an attempted clue to the puzzle outlined in these pages. What Gaonkar has done, not only in the essay in this volume, but in several other places, is (with tour de force relish) to decode the counterfactual conventions informing the critical practices of rhetoric and its traditions. If this be injury (which I doubt), there is also vague insult added to the mix. Gaonkar does this for virtually no motivational reason other than an intrigue with the texts themselves. He might just as well be Gorgias of old, disposing "the folly of allegation," and for his "own delectation" (1986:57). When we are brought face to face with our insufficiencies in light of our tacit conventions, several options are available to us. We can scatter like thieves and cover our tracks. We can perk up like the guy in the old after-shave commercial, slap our cheek, and say, "Thanks, I needed that!" We can get defensive, mad as hell, and decide not to take it any more. Or, and this exhausts my intuitive options, we can try to take reflection to another level. This last option brings us full circle on the aforementioned problem of discourse about discourse. But ever since the invention of the history of ideas and the philosophy of science, this is one thing academic disciplines have collectively done. Let's say the rhetoric of science is, at least in part, about the way rhetoric operates within the texts and practices of science. Gaonkar's essay is about limit conditions and strains on rhetorical criticism that become apparent within the rhetoric of science. This book is a collection of essays about that essay, and its accompanying controversy. This little postscript is about those essays along with a few related issues. With each reflective foray we press inquiry, while also raising nagging legitimation questions about humanistic inquiry generally. What I wish to contribute to the proceedings includes:

First, my own sense of the "about"—the question Foucault once launched as the "what's really going on here?" question (Foucault, 1987).

Second, a tentative retracing of the rather different sense of "science" as it has been rhetoricized in these pages. If there is an overall moral to my reflections, it is that, in some respect, everyone in this controversy is correct. Of course, only someone with my remarkably comprehensive metahorizon of interpretation could have been able to grasp this (thus, this is the penultimate essay).

Third, an attempt to reposition limit conditions for the vocabulary in which this discussion/controversy has been broached. Central to this attempt is a renewal of plural sense of what "rhetoric" is and does, as a supplement for its more monological understanding.

WHAT'S IT ALL ABOUT?

The earliest idea of "science" informing the rhetoric-of-science project is, I think, given to us by the version of the Enlightenment most of us encountered in graduate school and in mainstream histories of ideas. It is, of course, the unifying method of scientific inquiry broadly conceived and then optimistically applied everywhere. Isaiah Berlin offers up these postulates, along with a knowing wink at their presumption: "that human nature is the same in all times and places, that universal goals, true ends, and effective means, are at least in principle discoverable; that the methods similar to those of Newtonian science, which had proved so successful in bringing to light the regularities of inanimate nature, should be discovered and applied in the fields of morals, politics, economics, and in the sphere of human relationships in general, thus eradicating vice and suffering and what Helvetius termed 'interested error' " (Berlin, 1980:1).[1]

My point, in turning to this larger sense of the "about," is not only that there is more than one sense of "science." It is the very important point that *this* sense of science, this "heavenly city of the eighteenth century" (Becker, 1959), is the sense of science that eroded and finally marginalized and dismissed rhetoric. How this happened is a long and complex story, too long and complex for these pages. We might note the delicious irony, as Lloyd Bitzer recently has, that the simultaneous motivations behind the Enlightenment were, in equal proportion, to advance "Philosophical Reason" and prop up conventional religion (Bitzer, 1995). What is most pertinent to these reflections is that Enlightenment reason wreaked havoc upon rhetoric by *trying to explain rhetoric.* The provisional result is that purportedly "scientific" theories of vivacity and vehemence, and the sublime, not only eroded permeable boundaries among arts, crafts, and other intellectual pursuits, but also (being hopelessly dated and eventually implausible) came to meet with precisely the sort of skepticism they deserved. So-called scientized philosophy survived, and still does, through its mystification of intellectual progress generally. Rhetoric lacked the vocabulary and institutional legitimacy to respond to this lethal accommodation. Elocution was not long in following.

This is a selective history, to be sure. But it has a little moral. There is a sense in which the rhetoric of science is a two-centuries'-late intellectual retribution for crimes against the "harlot of the arts." This also may help to explain the mixed reception of bemused curiosity and indifference affected by many onlookers, like the smug bourgeoisie of Victorian London, when confronted with the serial killer's victims; they are apt to murmur, "But they were, after all, streetwalkers." In framing the history this way, however, I am also implying something suggested by my title: that there are multiple senses of "science," just as there are multiple senses of "rhetoric." I say this because it seems to me that more than a trace of "straw man" may be found in the convenient version of science-as-Enlightenment-reason-devolved-into-philosophy-of-science-positivism. Had rhetoric the will, the vocabulary, the zealous advocates of its cause, it could easily have laid waste to the subject-centered dualism invoked to ground patriarchal Enlightenment culture.

Indeed, one is hard pressed to escape the entwinement of the figurative and the noetic in any Westernized comprehension of "knowing," as the *siècle de lumière* demonstrates. As James Edie has noted:

> On the basis of Professor Snell's studies we can conclude that one of the primary, if not *the* primary epistemological metaphor requires us to think of thinking as a kind of *seeing*. The metaphor of "intellectual sight" lies beneath a vast area of our Western epistemological vocabulary: *eidos, eidetic, idea, ideation, intuition, theory, theorize,* and the whole cluster of more directly "optical" expressions such as *reflect, speculate, focus, view, inspect, introspect, insight, outlook, perspective,* and so on. It no doubt also accounts for the frequency with which we use the metaphor of light or illumination (and words connected with these phenomena) to discuss the process of thought, since in order to *see*, men must have light. It is extremely doubtful whether the metaphor of light or the conception of the intellect as a *lumen naturale* will ever by discarded. (1976:174)

Discarded? Perhaps not. But deconstructed? Definitely. Insightful attention has been devoted to the myriad ways in which foundational texts in optics, biology, evolution, and cosmology employ stylistic figures and rhetorical devices to position skeptical audiences in the "light" of novel worldviews or scientific "theories." At root, any new scientific theory is a *speculation*, and would have to be

rhetorical in at least this thick, figurative sense. Then there is the tit-
illation of the visual, the erotically charged delight, as David Freedberg has shown, of seeing, in a new way, something usually hidden
(1989, ch. 15). It was, after all, Francis Bacon who described the
progress of the new science as man's progressive seduction and con-
quest of a feminized nature. Susan Wells (1995) has brilliantly captured the allegorical properties of cosmological science in her new
book *Sweet Reason*. And then there is the whole mystification of science itself, the gasping of outrage that could be heard in the wake of
Feyerabend's *Against Method*. For all the erratic proclivities of sciences and scientists, there seemed some nagging noetic faith that
there were referents out there somewhere, that science was going to
get to the "bottom of things." One wonders if the century has wit-
nessed a more clever rhetorical invention than the "synthetic *a priori*" (Kripke, 1976).

It is, I think, this residual (though very much waning) positivism that seems to foreground many of the issues raised in this
collection. Gaonkar himself worries (I *think* he is worrying) about
whether science itself doesn't just end up being a huge simulacrum,
with rhetoric its "placebo." I think the answer is: "It depends."
There are many sorts of so-called science. Some, such as women's
medicine, ecology, are avowedly rhetorical in precisely the sense
that Gaonkar labels "thin." Then there are theoretical physics,
applied technology, social and biological engineering. For the former, there quite literally may never be referents, and for the latter,
there may be nagging civic questions of life quality, human responsibility, and the like. Then there are rhetorical charades, like "Star
Wars," the Strategic Defense Initiative of the U.S. military in the late
1980s. This is rhetoric in the bad sophistical sense, making "the
worse case appear to be the better." Gaonkar's essay invited the various practitioners of the rhetoric of science to mull over their own
construals of "rhetoric," to the extent that these influenced the sorts
of criticism they might conduct. While I cannot go into the subject
with the depth it deserves, I hope I have said enough to suggest that
the rhetoric-of-science project might usefully reflect upon its own
construals of science as interpretive "subject."

But Gaonkar is quite correct in inviting closer attention to
unstated construals of the rhetorical that guide, or inhibit, our
appraisal of discourse. Nearly a quarter century ago, rhetoricians
decided to prioritize the neglected rhetorical "canon" of invention as
central to our disciplinary pursuits. In our mad dash toward beefing
up this newly awakened topic, few of us paid any heed to Michael
Polanyi's cautionary note. The note was that there can be no system

of rules, no *method* sufficiently complex as to determine the genuinely "new"; as he wrote of Poincaré, no genuine discovery may be
reversible (1958:123). A bit of energy spent reflecting on this topic
might have goaded us to explore further the allegorical connections
among rhetoric, craft, aesthetics, and design (as several current participants now seem headed). Instead, many of us were emboldened to
wade where we didn't belong: into the murky waters of bad philosophy.

Just as the revival of rhetorical invention begat the "rhetoric is
epistemic" movement, I believe it would not be off the mark to suggest that the latter development sparked interest in the rhetoric of science. And here I must confess some small complicity of my own. In
some of my early work, I tried to make a dialectical distinction
between the specialized world of the technical, where prediction and
control rules, and the more permeable, action-centered world of the
social, where at least my wish would be to have rhetoric rule (Farrell,
1976). It was and is a false distinction; but its intent was to steer
rhetoric into the controversies and issues of civic life. Simultaneously, I weighed in against the "everything is rhetorical" partisans
(what Gaonkar would call the "globalized" position) as having "no
interpretive subject." Fifteen years of rhetoric of science later, we
certainly do have an interpretive subject: the myriad sense and lim-
itless nuances of "science." My dare has been accepted. But the question Gaonkar rightly asks has not: What has happened to rhetoric?

PROBLEMATIZING SCIENCE

As Kaufer correctly notices and Leff correctly resists, Gaonkar's
project confronts two generations of rhetoric-of-science scholars
with something of a double bind: *either* they restrict rhetoric to an
identifiable, productionist "place" in cultural life, where its "thin"
vocabulary will be serviceable (though irrelevant); *or* they globalize
rhetoric, where rhetorical interpretation gains breadth, at the cost of
its identity. Rhetoric of science, for Gaonkar, is a prolonged bad
example of trying to have it "both ways." While Gaonkar's essay is
not exactly suffused with interpretive charity or largesse of spirit, I
would stop short of Gross's judgment that Gaonkar is offering a
"destructive criticism." Let us instead characterize it as "depreciative criticism." If appreciative criticism is value-added criticism,
depreciative criticism is value-depleting criticism.

Dilip Gaonkar's work is also a prime example of what I
described earlier as delegitimating, metacommunicative critique—I

understand your code, I saw what you did, I know what you're doing. Moreover, I'm going to tell all of your friends. The danger in this sort of thing is that it can deteriorate into what is on display in the McCloskey response: naked, defensive hostility, discussion that ends discussion. The very strangeness of the McCloskey response I would take to be evidence of my larger point about scholarly delegitimation. Gaonkar devotes exactly zero attention to McCloskey's influential work, and McCloskey takes no real heat, just a cold shoulder. Yet McCloskey is incensed on a personal level. He does "in jokes," ad hominem argument, personal invective, and some astonishing tough-guy talk, the equivalent of snapping towels in the locker room. Why? Well, I would guess that the metacommunicative "spread" of Gaonkar's project is broad enough to place in question McCloskey's own important work, even if only by implication; so McCloskey is outraged "vicariously."

Fortunately or not, the other participants in this colloquy have their decorum felicity conditions on properly. Gross understandably takes issue with the more sweeping of Gaonkar's claims about his own criticism, namely that it is Aristotelian in name only. Indeed, it seems more than a little old-fashioned to expect the more traditional vocabulary listing of *ethos, logos, pathos*, the list of enthymemes, and so forth. The ideologizing of agency may be a more serious matter. If this be a sin, I plead guilty and without apologia. Gross and surely the later Campbell seem less guilty of the charge. Campbell adroitly discerns the same subject-centeredness in Gaonkar's work, however much Gaonkar tries to dance around the evidence. But if I may be permitted an editorial aside: So what? Agency seems, like Kundera's "borders" and Raymond Williams's "conventions," inevitable. At the same time as positivists and poststructuralists of every stripe have been trying to expunge any trace of normativity from human "nature," earth was being named "Planet of the Year" by *Time* magazine in 1989. We humans have become "human resources," even as the earth has become our mother. It is a very interesting question where "agency" is located in the cosmologies of abstract physics and the so-called life sciences. The animation of conduct-centered civic rhetoric may indeed give way to animations of seduction and reluctant disclosure. In any case, there is no evidence in these pages that the search for and interest in "agency" has evoked criticism that is "thin" or "dry."

Both Leff and Miller provide helpful repositionings of Gaonkar's terminology. Miller offers the important corrective that Aristotle's *Rhetoric* was nowhere nearly as productionist as Gaonkar claims.

Leff notes the dialogic relationship between production and reception, something Gaonkar also overlooks. The discussion becomes a bit complicated by the fact that several of the participants have what seem to be productionist agendas of their own where both rhetoric and science are concerned. Here I am thinking of Keith and Kaufer, with their engineering and design rhetorics, and, to a lesser extent, Fuller's historicizing of science as production and King's ruminations on the invisible *polis*. Certainly one response to Gaonkar would be to concede this point, but then argue that science essentially is production, so this is the proper way it should be "read." Nobody exactly does this because, I think, nobody fully believes this. And it would be conceding too much. From a production-centered vision of rhetoric (a one-sided accentuation of tradition), most histories would come to King's conclusion: The public is gone. The polis is invisible. But such totalization misses the many places where public discourse of a sort does flourish, just as it accepts too readily a misreading of rhetorical tradition. And, quite ironically, it manages to miss the fact that many of the great controversies of our time are essentially public controversies about science—nuclear power, AIDs research, toxic waste disposal, etc. As a member of several PIRGs (Public Interest Research Groups) myself, I wonder about the factuality of such sweeping pronouncements. To use Gaonkar's vocabulary in ways he probably would not, at least portions of *this* rhetoric of science are contestable.

But there is a potentially more radical point about Gaonkar's vocabulary than any of the commentators make. Gaonkar's use of this vocabulary, coming as it does from the late Enlightenment, seems deeply ironic. (Marxism, after all, promised to be offering us— guess what?—a science.) But at least where the study of rhetoric is concerned, there is something more troubling than mere irony. The false disjunction of production and consumption has simply exhausted its usefulness. In fact, the terminology could itself be part of the problem. If we think of the rhetorical audience as a kind of gigantic digestive tract, or demographic market (these seem the primary resonances of the figure), then it shouldn't be terribly surprising to find that our normatively enhanced construct, the *public*, is dead.

From the point of view of rhetorical traditions, or at least the Aristotelian rhetorical tradition, rhetoric is not reducible to either production or consumption. Rather, it is in that enigmatic space Leff alludes to: the reciprocal middle. Rhetoric is neither a product, nor a sort of receivership. It is a praxis. And what is in the middle of this praxis is precisely what is missing from all the production/consumption paradigms, whenever they stumble over something in the world of the "common." I refer to the sense of what Aune calls "mediation" (1994:46–49). This sense is all over Aristotle's *Rhetoric*, which would be incomprehensible without it. Deliberative rhetoric is the highest because, through our own interests, we persuade ourselves, and this is the most effective persuasion of all. It is even possible to explain Aristotle's own particular take on the interrelationship of rhetoric and science from this perspective. Science "persuades" and instructs, too, he acknowledges, but primarily in terms of the principles and propositions of its own subject matter. Only rhetoric presents us with an art for persuading over what is common to all. And when he is speculating about the nature of public business, Aristotle admonishes:

> But the more we try to make either dialectic or rhetoric not what they really are, practical faculties, but sciences, the more we shall inadvertently be destroying their true nature; for we shall be refashioning them and shall be passing into the region of science dealing with definite subjects rather than simply with words and forms of reasoning. (1358a.20–28, W. Rhys Roberts translation)

This is Gaonkar's dilemma in its original form: a classic Aristotelian call for critical distance.

More can and perhaps should be said about the nature of this "mediation" within rhetorical practice. In both the enthymeme, the example, in the cognitively centered reading of the emotions, what Aristotle prescribes is a sort of "social thinking," a thinking that is complicitous with regard to the positions, interests, "realities" of others. Bizarre as it may seem to place Foucault on this same page, one of his later essays seems to glimpse a similar sense in his (derivative) understanding of "agonism":

> The relationship between power and freedom's refusal to submit cannot, of course, be separated. The crucial problem of power is not that of voluntary servitude (how could we seek to be slaves?). At the very heart of the power relationship, and constantly provoking it, are the recalcitrance of the will and the intransigence of freedom. Rather than speaking of an essential freedom, it would be better to speak of "agonism"—of a relationship which is at the same time reciprocal incitation and struggle, less of a face-to-face confrontation which paralyzes both sides than a permanent provocation. (1984:428)

Broadly construed, this is the whole rubric of "influence" which rhetoric studies. It surely bumps up against, and even helps to illumine, what happens in more sedimented regimes we call disciplines of science. But, just as surely, rhetoric cannot live there.

The Perils of Rhetoric

Perhaps this last aphorism is part of Gaonkar's point as well. But if so, it is difficult to tell. In a brilliantly multitextured analysis, one of the most difficult things to locate is the trajectory of motive or "agenda." Of course, only "agents" have agendas. But although Dilip Gaonkar works extraordinarily hard to be inscrutable, I know numerous scholars and colleagues who will readily testify as to his embodied subjectivity. Perhaps a Burkean speculation about motive would be apropos.

Some evidence of how heavily "motivated" this entire project is comes from a marvelous bit of marginalizing that no one but Willard seemed to notice. Or perhaps, in the aforementioned spirit of interpretive charity, everyone has tacitly agreed not to notice it. As for me, I checked my interpretive charity at the door, and so I must divulge. Gaonkar casually informs us that Kenneth Burke is not an Aristotelian. This is the same Kenneth Burke who reconceptualized form, who developed a theory of "entelechy," who pronounced the inevitability of hierarchy, who devoted the first 130 pages of *The Rhetoric of Motives* to updating the rhetorical tradition of Aristotle. (Brilliantly, we hardly need add.) This is the same Kenneth Burke who claimed, throughout his long life, to be an Aristotelian, who had a life-long affiliation with the "New Criticism" school at the University of Chicago, whose best friend was Richard McKeon, the founder the Aristotelian Committee on Ideas and Methods. The question must arise: Why is it important that Kenneth Burke not be an Aristotelian? Well, if Kenneth Burke is an Aristotelian, then there is at least one proponent of the rhetorical tradition who is capable of doing "thick" readings of many texts, science among them. This cuts against Gaonkar's claims, so Burke is not an Aristotelian. This is done with a sleight of hand that would be Houdini proud: in a footnote, no less!

All this presents us with a tacit invitation to probe further. Earlier, I offered the less-than-humble observation that all the participants in this colloquy are partly right. That would even include McCloskey, who is right in the minimalist sense of being "authentic." Gaonkar's polemic yields further polemics, reminding us once more how perilously close enlightenment is to myth. The rhetoric of science raises, in the largest sense I can put into words, the daunting question of what "science" is for. It is as if we were all in a crowded cocktail party and someone posed Kant's third question: What may we hope for? I don't know the answer. But I know enough to predict acute discomfort all around the room.

Dilip Gaonkar reads the rhetoric of science literature with a suspicion that, I believe, masks a larger ambivalence. He has his hand on his wallet at all times. But there are clues. One of Gaonkar's early essays was called "The Enigma of Arrival." Read negatively, the rhetoric of science discussion is one further chapter in modernity's endless fascination with itself. And more than just about anyone whose work I know, Gaonkar views this fascination with deep ambivalence. On one hand, there is the hatred of modernity; and on the other, there is a sense of "theory," de Man notwithstanding, that is deeply indebted to modernity and all its discontents. One suspects that here is the origin of all the loose talk about loose conduct, "promiscuity." Dilip Gaonkar's little secret is not his complicity with postmodernity, but rather with re-modernity. It is his complicity with tradition.

This postscript titles itself elliptical. By that, I meant that there could be no "final word" on these discussions, just as there is not an imaginable limit to the trajectories of metacommunication. But having pronounced that everyone is this discussion is partly right about something, I would be remiss not to notice the sense in which Gaonkar is partly right too. He is partly right in insisting that there are borders, perhaps permeable borders, between the prototypes of rhetoric (when it is functionally identifiable in paradigmatic ways) and the traces of the rhetorical that abound and even flourish in unlikely places. The former sense is what I have made part of my own career project. Eugene Garver's recent— brilliant—work, *Aristotle's* Rhetoric: *An Art of Character*, is also devoted to crafting an identifiable prototype of the "rhetorical" that is open to multiple reinterpretations.The latter sense has helped the rhetoricians of science appreciate the *eros* lurking with our "dead certainties." Science will never be "civics." (For that matter, civics may never be "civics.") But the most insightful contemporary works in the rhetorical construction of science, work such as Evelyn Fox Keller's *Refiguring Life* (1995), and Nelkin and Lindee's *The DNA Mystique* (1995), present us with rich tensions within the fabric of "pure" Theory. As the best rhetorical readings do, these rediscoveries of the rhetorical do not delegitimate or level their subject, but rather add to our appreciative understanding.

They are to me hopeful signs, signs that we may one day be mature enough to understand that we will never grow up. They are also, as Keller reminds us (in a memorable phase of Sharon Traweek's), "border crossings." So are the readings in the collections, crossings of discipline, convention, occasionally even of taste. But such crossings are only possible because there are borders in the first place.

NOTE

1. This is, to be sure, a one-sided characterization of "the Enlightenment." Berlin had his own quite self-interested agenda driving his treatment of the *siècle de lumière*. He wished to place one understanding of science as a unifying rational method in opposition to countervailing forces—Vico, Bruno, and others—who brought imagination and wonderment into the picture.

REFERENCES

Aune, J. A. (1994). *Rhetoric and Marxism*. Boulder, CO: Westview.

Becker, C. (1959). *The heavenly city of the eighteenth-century philosophers*. New Haven: Yale University Press.

Berlin, I. (1980). *Against the current: Essays in the history of ideas*. New York: Viking.

Bitzer, L. (1995, 11 May). Religious and philosophical influences on the enlightenment. *The Van Zelst Lecture*, Northwestern University.

Edie, J. (1976). *Speaking and meaning: The phenomenology of language*. Bloomington: Indiana University Press.

Farrell, T. B. (1976). Knowledge, consensus and rhetorical theory. *Quarterly Journal of Speech, 62*, 1–14.

Foucault, M. (1984). The subject and power. In B. Wallis (Ed.), *Art after modernism: Rethinking representation*. New York: The New Museum of Contemporary Art.

———. (1987). What is an author? In V. Lambroupoulos and D. N. Miller, (Eds.), *Twentieth-century literary theory: An introductory anthology*. Albany: State University of New York Press.

Freedberg, D. (1989). *The power of images: Studies in the history and theory of response*. Chicago: University of Chicago Press.

Garver, E. (1994) *Aristotle's* Rhetoric: *An art of character.* Chicago: University of Chicago Press.

Gorgias. (1986). *Encomium to Helen.* Larue van Hook (Trans.). Loeb Classical Library edition. Cambridge: Harvard University Press.

Keller, E. F. (1995). *Refiguring life: Metaphors of twentieth-century biology.* New York: Columbia University Press.

Kripke, S. (1976). *Naming and necessity.* Cambridge: Harvard University Press.

Nelkin, D., and Lindee, S. (1995). *The DNA mystique: The gene as cultural icon.* New York: W. H. Freeman.

Polanyi, M. (1958). *Personal knowledge: Toward a post-critical philosophy.* Evanston: Harper and Row.

Wells, S. (1995). *Sweet reason.* Chicago: University of Chicago Press.

CHAPTER 14

CLOSE READINGS OF THE THIRD KIND: REPLY TO MY CRITICS

Dilip Parameshwar Gaonkar

INTRODUCTION

Two dominant reading strategies are discernible in the work associated with the so-called "rhetorical turn" in contemporary thought. The first reading strategy seeks to make the object of analysis intelligible in terms of its rhetoricity. This strategy can sometimes produce startling results, especially when it is applied to objects habitually regarded as free of rhetoric. But on the whole, its interpretive and critical procedures are predictable. It relies heavily on the equation between rhetoric and persuasion. Any discursively mediated object marked by addressivity and suasory motives is immediately apprehended as rhetorical. Since addressivity and suasory motive are ubiquitous features of many sets of objects, this strategy has a tendency to globalize rhetoric. However, the temptation to globalize results in dimensionalizing the object as rhetorical rather than making the object intelligible in terms of its rhetoricity. To identify the rhetorical dimension of an object is not necessarily to make it intelligible. An object can be dimensionalized in any number of ways—from grammar to economics. The priority of the rhetorical dimension (or its claim to critical attention) requires further accounting, if this reading strategy is to succeed.

The second reading strategy takes an object commonly or tacitly apprehended as rhetorical and seeks to unpack its rhetoricity by recourse to more precisely articulated theoretical constructs. Here one lets go of rhetoric as an explanatory master trope in order to recover it as an object of understanding. The global equations between rhetoric and persuasion, rhetoric and figuration, and rhetoric and addressivity give way to the "middle-level" theories and concepts, usually drawn from the classical tradition but refashioned to meet contemporary interpretive tasks.[1] This reading strategy recapitulates the essential tension of rhetoric, the "discourse producing machine" as Barthes (1988) calls it, by making visible its abstract rule-governed structure in contingent and locally unstable time-space events, be they texts or performances. Thus the "eventness" of rhetoric in all its specificity is made to disclose the abstract machine that inhabits it without ever being able to govern it.

One way to read my critique of the rhetoric of science project (hereafter referred to as RS) is that RS relies primarily on the first strategy. Such a reading strategy may be necessary and justified under a climate of opinion where the rhetoricity of a discursive formation is systematically denied. During the triumphal days of positivism and its immediate aftermath, it might have been sufficient (even heroic) for the proponents of RS to show how science is persuasive, figurative, and addressed in the most general sort of way. This sort of "consciousness raising" about the discourse practices of science, while not unimportant, cannot constitute the core of a scholarly project that aspires to represent rhetoric as an interpretive discipline. At present it seems absurd to insist that something is rhetorical in a general sort of way when rhetoric, propelled by the postmodern thought and style, is being invoked as a ubiquitous explanatory suture. The incessant invoking of rhetoric in theory, practice and critique alike calls for a conceptual ethnography of the term that seeks not so much to discipline its usage which is impossible, but to critically measure its hermeneutic resources and burdens, and thereby to obviate its lapse into ideology. My essay, "The Idea of Rhetoric in the Rhetoric of Science" (hereafter referred to as IRRS), is an attempt to do such a conceptual ethnography on a limited scale. Nothing more, nothing less.

ON THE RHETORIC OF RHETORIC

Three identifiable clusters of criticisms have surfaced against IRRS. Each of these roughly corresponds to the three main theses presented in my essay regarding the contemporary self-understanding of rhetoric.

The Politics of Repression and Recognition

The first set of criticisms challenge my claim that the rhetoric of science, "like so many other research projects based on a revived

interest in rhetoric, has stalled after a promising beginning." This
claim, irksome to some of my critics, simply means that RS has not
made substantial progress beyond showing that science is persuasive, figurative and addressed in a general sort of way. Aside from
wanting to deconstruct the phrase "a general sort of way," my critics
are likely to respond to the above reformulation by saying that I am
playing with yet another set of binary oppositions that does not
square with critical practice, and that the second strategy is as much
in play as the first in the RS literature. There is some truth to this
rejoinder. Almost all of RS literature, especially the recent works of
Campbell, Gross, and Lyne, will attest to some interplay between
the two strategies. But the interplay tends to be asymmetrical. The
economy of critical practices is such that the proponents of RS are
prone to show that something is rhetorical by drawing attention to
how it partakes in global processes such as persuasion, figuration,
and addressivity rather than showing how those processes congeal to
produce a localized field of semiosis that can be explicated only by
recourse to regionally grounded theories and concepts such as decorum, prudence, performativity, self-fashioning, construction of textual authority, argument fields, etc. The two strategies differ in orientation. The second strategy pulls the critic into the interstices of
discourse and makes her come to grips with regional variations in
rhetoricity, whilst the first strategy abstracts outward towards intentionality and contextuality and calibrates the two in such a manner
that the "discourse object" (conceived as text or practice) is deferred.
This deferral occurs at the very moment when one is postulating
the centrality of the text. This is one of the puzzling features of John
Campbell's early essays on Darwin's *The Origin of Species*. Within
our disciplinary community, Campbell is routinely singled out as a
critic who has dedicated himself to reading a single canonical text.
Campbell himself playfully speaks of his devotion to the *Origin* as a
textual version of monogamy. And yet in his early essays spanning
more than a decade, the text remains buried. Why?

In *IRRS*, I argue that Campbell's commitment to the model of
intentional persuasion leads to the deferral of the text. On this point
there is some confusion. While I have serious reservations about the
usefulness of the intentionalist model of persuasion in deciphering
institutionally driven discursive formations such as science, I do
not summarily dismiss it (neither the traditional version found in
early Campbell nor the intentionless "reverse engineering" model
proposed by Keith in this volume). My minimal claim is that the
intentionalist strategy in rhetorical criticism, including RS, as practiced within our discipline has led to a deferral of the text. I posit it

as a conjunctural fact, not as a causal hypothesis. I do not make the maximalist claim, ascribed to me by my critics, that the intention-alist model of persuasion when combined with historical contextu-alization (neo-Aristotelian criticism being an example of such com-bination) *necessarily* leads to the deferral of the text.

But the conjunctural fact remains. The early Campbell is not an isolated case, but a paradigm case of a pattern which extends well beyond RS. The deferral of the text, when that deferral is not even compensated by the foregrounding of "practice" à la Foucault, seri-ously compromises the prospect of RS as it has compromised other critical projects in rhetorical studies.

This is not an unnoticed problem. As early as 1957, Redding puzzled over the question as to why our critics habitually retreat before the text (1957:100). Since the beginning of the 1980s, Leff has been recounting and refining a diagnostic narrative on the state of rhetorical criticism in which "the deferral of the text" features as the central theme (1980;1986; 1987; Leff and Procario, 1985). The defer-ral is frequently explained, by Leff and others, as a consequence either of a faulty methodology (as in the case of the neo-Aristotelian old guard) or of excessive theoreticism (as in the case of critical plu-ralists who became and remain dominant after the collapse of the neo-Aristotelian criticism). In an earlier essay, "Object and Method in Rhetorical Criticism" (1990), I have offered an alternative expla-nation based on what I call the "transparency thesis."

Before I discuss the transparency thesis, it should be noted that I did offer in *IRRS* a hypothesis as to why the RS project might have stalled:

> There are two possible explanations as to why the RS project has stalled: first, it has misread science; second, it has misap-propriated (not in the normative sense) rhetoric. While I am not qualified to pursue the first explanation, I am interested in entertaining the second for the light it might shed on the predicament facing not only RS but every other proposed con-temporary extension of rhetoric into the zone of interdisci-plinarity.

It is instructive that many of my critics refuse to seriously entertain the possibility that one might have an inadequate grasp of rhetoric. While the proponents of RS habitually demonstrate their mastery of the relevant terrain of science they are examining, the mastery of rhetoric is taken for granted. The suggestion that they may be oper-ating with an inappropriate idea of rhetoric seems preposterous. This testifies to the persistent prejudice, shared by many a friend and foe alike, that understanding rhetoric is a matter of common sense and that its conceptual structure is simple, transparent and unchanging.

The "transparency thesis" attempts to link the conjunctural fact of "the deferral of the text" with the postulate that the conceptual structure of rhetoric is transparent. Briefly, my argument proceeds as follows: Wichelns's founding essay, "The Literary Criticism of Oratory" (1925), set in motion a particular dialectic between object and method in rhetorical criticism. The neo-Aristotelian critics who sought to follow what they took to be Wichelns's methodological injunctions, allegedly derived from Aristotle's *Rhetoric*, created a critical corpus (now seen as flawed) in which the method came to master the object. My reading of Wichelns's essay shows that the method ascribed to him actually originates in the way he prefigures the privileged object of rhetorical criticism, oratory—as concerned with neither permanence nor beauty, but effect, and as bound to "occasion and audience." Under that prefiguration, the oratorical text is viewed as the transparent space where the rhetor's strategic design and contextual exigencies intersect. Jasinski, in the essay included in this volume, extends my reading of Wichelns by arguing that there are actually two competing conceptions of context in Wichelns's essay: a hyperparticularized version signaled by the word *occasion* and an enlarged version signaled by the word *society*. Jasinski further notes that under the instrumental-intentionalist reading strategy, even as one pays homage to the enlarged version of context, the hyperparticularized version is made to do all the interpretive work. This happens not only with Wichelns and his neo-Aristotelian followers like Nichols, but also with their critics like Wrage, Black, and Leff. At any rate, once the text is seen as the manifestation of the rhetor's strategic consciousness as it engages a hyperparticularized context, the text becomes a docile and transparent effect of that mediation. One has simply to go through a set of procedures, and the text meekly yields its secret, namely, the rhetor's purposive design.

There is also a second version of the "transparency thesis," in which the critic actually privileges the text rather than elements external to it. In the so-called "history of ideas" approach to public discourse, Wrage (1947) privileges the "ideational content" of oratory. Wrage distinguishes between "monumental works" and "fugitive literature," of which oratory is an important species. Intellectual historians study the former to trace the influence of ideas from one major thinker to the next. To the rhetorical critic, Wrage assigns the task of reading the latter to discover and assess "those ideas which find expression in the market place" (1947: 453). Now that the oratorical text is conceived as a key discursive space for mapping the struggle of ideas as they vie for cultural recognition, one would think it would command a modicum of autonomy and dense reading. Not so in the functionalist imagination of Wrage: "Public address does not exist for its own sake . . . its value is instrumental. . . . It is a vehicle for the conveyance of ideas" (453). For Wrage, the speech text has no intrinsic interest. A speech is merely a document for deciphering the configuration of ideas struggling to shape the public mind and sensibility. Wrage frequently refers to oratory as a "mirror." The oratorical text is not the central locus in the struggle of ideas, but a "mirror" that reflects the struggle taking place somewhere else. Wrage does not appear to be interested in the mode of articulation and textualization of the struggle of ideas manifested in the oration itself. Orations are fugitive spaces only fleetingly inhabited by the true protagonists in Wrage's scheme—the ideas themselves. Barnet Baskerville, Wrage's student, under the spell of the transparency thesis, relieves the rhetorical critic from her interpretive task: "Speeches are seldom abstruse or esoteric (as poems and novels sometimes are). A speech by its very nature is, or should be, immediately comprehensible; hence the interpretive function of the critic is seldom paramount" (1953:1–2).

Thus the oratorical text is made twice transparent. From the etic perspective, it is a transparent space where the rhetor's strategic design is disclosed. From the emic perspective, it is a transparent medium for transporting ideas.[2] To this twofold transparency, all one needs to add is a reading practice which views the global processes of persuasion, figuration, practical reason and addressivity as sufficient signs of rhetoricity, and one is near the end of the text as text. Without textual friction, criticism cannot illuminate.

To what extent is the "transparency thesis" (that has lead to the deferral of the text in public address criticism) also operative in RS? Each of the three practitioners of RS discussed in *IRRS*—Campbell, Gross and Prelli—adheres to the transparency thesis to varying degrees.

Prelli presents a clear instance. His proposed method of "topical invention"—consisting of a threefold characterization of rhetorical ends, a sixteen-fold *stasis* grid for analyzing issues, and a list of twenty-two possible and recurrent lines of arguments (*topoi*)—is far too schematic to map the interplay of rhetoric and resistance in the text. Armed with such an elaborate method one can, as Prelli does, make any argument-driven text (and that includes science) transparent by recasting it within a preconceived matrix of descriptive-normative categories.

As for Campbell, I have shown how his early essays, composed under the influence of an intentionalist reading strategy, refigure the *Origin* (with the design puzzle undone) as a transparent field of semiosis. In his later essays, Campbell reads the *Origin* by placing it in the intertextual space of notebooks, letters, and abandoned works, and thus depicts a two-decade-long itinerary of Darwin's evolutionary insight and its textual transformations in terms of a complex interweaving of rhetoric and resistance. At last, the *Origin* emerges from the shadow of the authorial design that governs it (much like the spirit governing the body).

Campbell, in his reply, concedes that the *Origin* is dwarfed in his early essays. But he regards that as an error of overemphasis, a failing in practical criticism, and not a consequence of his reliance on the intentionalist reading strategy. While acknowledging the correctness of some of my observations, Campbell rejects the theoretical rationale behind my critique of RS in general and of his work in particular. Since Campbell endorses Leff's critique of my position on the larger question of the relationship between rhetoric, hermeneutics and translation, I will address that topic later. Here I will attend to Campbell's defense of the intentionalist reading strategy. Campbell rejects my critique of that strategy because it involves a denial of human agency, which he regards as "extreme and possibly incoherent." This is incorrect. My case against the intentionalist reading strategy is not based on a radical rejection of agency. Let me reiterate what I said about agency in *IRRS*: First, a certain ideology of human agency is operative in rhetorical studies; and, that ideology underwrites the intentionalist reading strategy in rhetorical criticism. Second, Campbell's early essays show in a paradigmatic fashion how the intentionalist reading strategy can lead to the deferral of the text. Third, the privileging of the text is a taken-for-granted background assumption shared by many contemporary rhetorical critics, including Campbell and Gross. On the basis of these three propositions, I conclude that the deferral of the text, bound up with the intentionalist strategy, has been detrimental to rhetorical studies. This argument holds so long as one considers, to borrow Gross's phrase, "starring the text" pivotal to rhetorical criticism. To be sure, one can argue against the privileging of the text, as McGee, McKerrow, and the proponents of so-called "critical rhetoric" do. But the leading practitioners of RS within Speech Communication (and also the two prominent RS critics from Rhetoric and Composition—Charles Bazerman and Greg Myers) routinely gesture towards the centrality of the text.

This deferring of the text while gesturing towards its centrality suggests the presence of a resistance that should command critical attention. Campbell has to show how an intentionalist reading strategy rooted in the ideology of human agency can obviate the deferral of the text. Whether I affirm or deny agency is irrelevant in considering this problem. This is not to pretend that I am wholly agnostic about the question of human agency. I am, indeed, skeptical about the utility of a critical strategy based on the ideology of human agency. My skepticism is rooted not only in a taste for certain theories that tend to dissolve the question of agency in light of larger structures such as language, economy, and the unconscious, but also in a judgment that bears the imprint of prudence rather than dogma. Experience and intuition urge a conviction that under present conditions, reading public discourse in terms of individual human agency is unlikely procure much insight, especially when that discourse is institutionally driven, as in the case of science. As for my taste for theories that displace the question of agency, let me say the following: At one point, Campbell advises that I expand the circle of my acquaintances and learn how highly rhetoric is esteemed "from theology to law to literature to classics to philosophy." Yet another list of friends of rhetoric! Perhaps I should return the favor and urge Campbell attend to the august company he elects to keep. It is Ricoeur, the great Christian humanist of our time, who while reading Freud has this epiphany: "It must be said of the subject . . . what the Gospel says of the soul: to be saved, it must be lost" (1974, 20). Polemics aside, here we are on the outskirts of a larger question.

For so very long, rhetorical studies, especially its critical wing, has been committed to some version of the philosophy of the subject. That rhetoric, so public an art, so deeply implicated in the conduct of practical reason on the communal stage, should be measured in the language of intentions, calculations, and accountability comes as no surprise. But to insist on individual consciousness and its contents as the originary site of public discourse (including the discourse of science), when that discourse is produced and populated with significations within a matrix of technologies—literary, social, and material—that elude the reach and the imprint of the subject, is surely to cripple the critical enterprise before it gets off the ground. However deeply one may desire to reterritorialize the abandoned space of a now discredited subject-centered reason with an other-oriented practical reason as indicated by Campbell's positive references to Garver's work on "prudence," the vexatious fact remains that rhetoric, conceived primarily as a transaction by and between discrete individuals, cannot unlock the grammar of massive social formations such as "modern science" that are propelled by "system imperatives." It is a grim irony, barely softened by nostalgia, that one aspires to transport the deliberative model of *polis* to science when the *polis* stands in disrepair. There is deliberation in science, but as Garver himself would argue (alas, he too is a "little rhetoric" person), deliberation in science is not constitutive of *praxis* as it is in politics.

Gross presents a more complex case. He is committed to "starring the text." Most of his case studies do, in fact, take discrete scientific texts as the primary object of analysis. Gross, unlike Campbell, is not critically preoccupied with a single discursive formation. Theory driven, he wanders from text to text. Nor is Gross committed to a single theory as he draws his interpretive hypothesis from diverse conceptual sources, from Propp to Habermas. Further, he makes no effort to integrate those conceptual materials within the neo-Aristotelian approach he recommends. What illuminates his readings is the friction between the text and a specific interpretive hypothesis he fashions to read that text. For that reason, I ventured the following claim in *IRRS*: "Gross's neo-Aristotelianism is a phantom, it does not exist." Gross disagrees. He insists that the rhetorical signature of his reading is to be found in his theoretical commitment to neo-Aristotelianism. For me, that signature is illegible. According to Gross, I am unable to see the neo-Aristotelian signature in his work because I am pledged to a rather "pedantic" criterion as to what constitutes a rhetorical reading, namely, the active use of rhetorical lexicon. This is not an accurate reading of my position.

In *IRRS*, I am explicitly concerned with Plato's problematic regarding the specificity of the rhetorical. For anyone who aspires to theorize critical practice, as I do, that problematic poses the following question: What is the signature of a rhetorical reading? I don't expect a quick and easy answer. Nor do I believe that an answer can be posited aprioristically. It has to be sought in the work of practical critics. For that reason, I have elected to examine a relatively bounded critical formation such as RS and to focus within that formation on the work of critics like Campbell and Gross. As for the deployment of rhetorical lexicon, I don't regard it as a necessary, let alone a sufficient, indicator of rhetorical reading. In *IRRS*, I explicitly note that Campbell's early essays and most of Gross's essays are largely free of rhetorical lexicon and yet they are patently rhetorical readings. This raises the question: What makes their readings rhetorical in the absence of rhetorical lexicon?[3] In Campbell's case, what makes his readings rhetorical is his commitment to the model of intentional persuasion, and that commitment leads to the deferral of the text. In Gross's case, what makes his readings rhetorical is the thematics of textual authority: how does a given text construct (or fail to construct) its authority to enunciate scientific knowledge claims? Gross's methodological strategy of "starring the text" is well-suited for exploring his thematic interest in the "construction of textual authority." While exploring various forms and disguises of that authority in different scientific texts, ranging from Rheticus's *Narratio Prima* (1540) to Newton's *Opticks* (1730) to Watson and Crick's *The Double Helix* (1966), Gross eclectically draws interpretive hypotheses from a variety of theoretical sources. This sort of theoretical/critical pluralism, seemingly ratified by Burke's dictum that a critic should "use all that is there to use" in making the text intelligible, sometimes leads paradoxically to its deferral. In some of his essays, Gross, armed with a theoretically driven interpretive hypothesis, moves swiftly like a veritable hermeneutic warrior subduing the text and not allowing the play of rhetoric and resistance to surface. This is what happens when he reads Watson's *The Double Helix* as evincing the narrative patterns characteristic of fairy tales or when he reads the public controversy surrounding recombinant DNA as a social drama that unfolds in four stages identified by Victor Turner—the breach, crisis, redressive action, and reintegration. Thus, as I said in *IRRS*, "if there is a weakness to Gross's essays it is not because he does not use rhetorical vocabulary, but because he does not adequately 'star' the text." Despite that weakness, Gross is possibly the best reader of scientific texts in our discipline.

But Gross has a different reading of his own work. "An Aristotelian rhetoric of science," he writes, "is marked by ideological allegiances far deeper than any terminology." Here Gross invokes my own, much cited and contested, characterization of the ideology of human agency to show how his work conforms to its basic tenets:

> a view of the speaker as the seat of origin rather than a point of articulation, a view of strategy as identifiable under an intentional description, a view of discourse as constitutive of character and community, a view of audience positioned simultaneously as "spectator" and "participant," and a view of "ends" that binds speaker, strategy, discourse and audience in a web of purposive actions.[4]

Gross also strives to show, against my claim, that "a rhetoric centered on human agency is no bar to the understanding of science." Further, he contests my reading of his reading of *Narratio Prima*. In *IRRS*, I cite Gross's reading of *Narratio Prima* as an excellent illustration of intertextual reading as opposed to an intentionalist reading. Not so, says Gross. He tries to show how his reading of *Narratio*

Prima discloses the rhetorical action in terms of human agency.

Gross's reading of his own work is plausible but reductive. It hardly does justice to the complexity of his original reading of *Narratio Prima*. It appears that Gross is willing to impoverish his own critical practice in order to secure some space for human agency in the operations of "big" science against those, like Latour (another friend of rhetoric!), who would blithely reduce it to units that can be "shuffled like a pack of cards." Perhaps one could avoid such unpleasant elections by imagining and reading agency allegorically through its textual representations, as James Boyd White does so well, rather than reading it literally as emanating from a deliberating consciousness. However, Gross elects to be eclectic. While reviewing his essay on Darwin, Gross suggests, as Campbell does elsewhere, that the intertextual reading and the intentional reading are complementary. To illustrate that point, Gross cites an observation from that essay: "The significant distinction in argument between the *Notebooks* and the *Origin* lies in the contrast between what convinced Darwin and what Darwin thought would persuade his audience." This is a revealing passage. Here the chronological priority of the *Notebooks* over the *Origin* signals the priority of self-persuasion over persuasion directed at the other, and hence, the priority of the deliberating consciousness over its textual representations. Thus, Gross comes to "star" the text and defer it too.

Rhetoric As a Hermeneutic Metadiscourse

The second cluster of criticisms is directed at my characterization of contemporary rhetoric as a hermeneutic metadiscourse and the implications I adduce on the basis of that charactertization. In elaborating on that thesis, I make the following claims. First, there is a palpable difference between contemporary and classical views of rhetoric.: "We have reversed the priority the ancients accorded to rhetoric as a practical/productive activity over rhetoric as a critical/interpretive activity." Second, despite this shift in orientation contemporary rhetoric remains dependent for its theory and vocabulary on classical rhetoric, especially on a certain version of Aristotelian rhetoric. Third, this creates a conceptual disjuncture: an Aristotelian vocabulary initially generated in the course of "theorizing" about certain types of practical and productive activities delimited to the realm of appearance (that is, the "public sphere" as the Greeks understood it) is ill-equipped to serve as a critical vocabulary for interpreting cultural practices that cover the whole of human affairs, including science. To be precise, the current practical/productionist vocabulary derived from classical rhetoric is "thin,"and thus not sufficiently complex for the task of interpretation. Fourth, the task of translating a practical/productionist vocabulary into an interpretive vocabulary, already underway in the practical labors of rhetorical critics, is hampered by the ideology of human agency.

Each of these four claims has been challenged by several of my critics. Among other things, I have been criticized for overdrawing the difference between contemporary and classical views of rhetoric; for ignoring the hermeneutical dimension of classical rhetoric as illustrated, for instance, in the concept of *imitatio*, for operating with a faulty concept of interpretation and translation; for not recognizing that the "thinness" of rhetorical vocabulary is mediated by the complexity and continuity of rhetorical tradition; and for proposing an untenable concept of human agency. Since these objections have been voiced most effectively by Michael Leff, I will respond primarily to his essay in this section.

Let me begin by conceding that I have, indeed, overdrawn the distinction between classical and contemporary views and practices of rhetoric along the binary opposition between production and interpretation. Leff is quite correct in pointing out that the classical instruction in rhetoric, even though oriented primarily towards performance, involved an unavoidable hermeneutic component. On Leff's account, the doctrine of *imitatio* is the most obvious point of intersection "between the reading of texts and the production of persuasive discourse," and it frames and foregrounds a complex process that allows "historical texts to serve as resources for invention." Interpretation in rhetorical performance does not aspire to isolate and sacralize the meaning of a given text, but instead, reads that text as a pedagogical site for mastering the conventions and convictions of a community. This sort of hermeneutical rhetoric, as Leff prefers to call it, is quite different from the modern critical practice of elevating the preceptive lore to the status of theoretical principles that could be applied directly (and, alas, often mechanically) to both textual production and textual criticism. To press the contrast further, the doctrine of *imitatio* urges a holistic approach where the model, be it text or person, telegraphs a cultural tradition and economy within which the copyist must interpret to invent—and invent to interpret.

According to Leff, an exclusively "productionist" reading of classical rhetoric, especially of Aristotle, is an error characteristic of modernist appropriations of tradition in our discipline and not an intrinsic feature of the tradition itself:

> Modern rhetorical critics have concentrated on the technical
> lore as a free-standing system, and as a result they have left
> little space for considering how that lore might participate in a
> larger and more flexible program of language studies. And
> Gaonkar, because he begins with a strong unqualified binary
> opposition between production and interpretation, assumes the
> problem in applying classical rhetoric to interpretive work
> stems from the *essence* of classical rhetoric. He does not con-
> sider that the problem may reflect the way modern scholars
> *interpret* the tradition. (this volume, 96)

Leff thus suggests that I have committed the error I denounce. If
modern rhetorical critics erroneously essentialized classical rhetoric
as "productionist," I reinforce that error by denouncing it as therefore narrow and irrelevant for our time.

There is some truth to this critique. But the charge that I essen-
tialize the "classical tradition" as productionist is unwarranted. First
of all, my reading strategy mitigates against such an essencializa-
tion. In my reading, I explore how rhetoric, as a term and as a tradition, is imagined and deployed. I try to draw out the tensions
between those imaginings (theory) and deployments (practice). As
Leff acknowledges, I do take note of the difference between the
Ciceronian and the Aristotelian versions of the productionist
paradigm. Here, once again, I am interested in highlighting how
uneasy the coalition is between those two classical versions as they
are invoked and deployed in contemporary critical practice. At present, a critical struggle is underway. The Ciceronian version of
"hermeneutical rhetoric" is vying for preeminence against at least
three other contenders: the theoretically eclectic "critical plural-
ists," the postmodern proponents of "critical rhetoric," and the
reconstructed Aristotelians. In this unfolding critical struggle, the
most productive tension is to be found between the two traditional
rivals: the Ciceronians and the Aristotelians. Together these two
groups of scholars are trying to negotiate the postmodern challenge
by re-reading the classical tradition rather than distancing from it.
This task of rearticulating the tradition is discernible in the recent
writings of Beiner, Farrell, Garver, Hariman, Jasinski and Leff and it
is being carried out under the aegis of what one might call the "pru-
dence/decorum" paradigm. While I cannot here comment on the
promise of this new paradigm, it should suffice to note that despite
significant internal differences, as evident from the Ciceronian aesthetic stress on decorum that privileges composition and textuality
as opposed to the Aristotelian ethical stress on prudence that privi-

leges deliberation and practical reason, both versions are equally committed to upholding the ideology of human agency. Leff's account of *imitatio* leaves little doubt as to how central that ideology is to a "hermeneutically" inscribed compositional rhetoric. The same can be said about the different versions of "constitutively" motivated deliberative rhetoric found in the writings of Beiner, Farrell and Garver. My chief disagreement with the proponents of the "prudence/decorum" paradigm turns on the question of agency. Leff is well aware of that. "Gaonkar's central tenet," he writes, "[is] that the 'ideology of human agency' associated with classical rhetoric radically separates the older, humanistic paradigm from the contemporary, interpretive turn in rhetorical studies."

Here I am prepared to admit to the lesser charge of essentializing the contemporary receptions of the classical tradition in rhetoric. Whatever the classical tradition is in itself, the attempts to appropriate it in our discipline, from Wichelns and Hunt through Black and Bitzer to Leff and Farrell, spanning nearly eighty years, disclose a deep and abiding commitment to the ideology of human agency despite significant differences in their interpretive strategies. That commitment and its confinements are not accidental. In my judgment, any version of rhetoric so committed is disadvantaged in doing interpretive work with institutionally driven discursive formations such as modern science. (This partly accounts for Black and Bitzer's explicit rejection of the RS project). On this point, I am firm. Despite a serious effort to come to terms with certain structural features of contemporary society—the mass-mediated consumer culture, market driven economy, institutionalization of technoscience, and bureaucratically managed state—the recent innovations in the "prudence/decorum" paradigm continue to rely almost exclusively on a face-to-face model of persuasive discourse. This is evident from key norms and concepts such as "dialogue," "conversation," "ideal speech situation," and "performance" that are frequently invoked and elaborated. The proponents of the "prudence/decorum" paradigm, preoccupied as they are with the immediate pragmatics of agent-centered text-composition and deliberative performance, have not devised an adequate strategy for signalling the constitutive presence of larger historical/discursive formations within which a given text or performance is embedded. The contemporary critic needs a better understanding of the relationship between the public sphere, where rhetoric does its business of ideological integration, and social formations like the economy, technoscience and bureaucracy that are run on a non-dialogic, systemic logic. Even a renovated Ciceronian/Aristotelian theory of rhetoric, so long as it remains committed to the view of speaker/author as the origin of discourse, is severely handicapped in reading discursive formations of not only of modern science but also of modern polity. The explosive growth of printed-mediated civic prose over the last two centuries—legislative tracts, public commission reports, record of congressional debates, digests of motions and amendments, newspaper accounts, editorial comments, magazine articles—that accompany and sometimes overwhelm all our democratic procedures and practices may be viewed as the print counterpart of what Ian Hacking has called the "avalanche of numbers." That avalanche of the printed word, now augmented by radio "talk" and televisual image, has another effect. Its incessant production, its proliferating genres, its numbing technical detail, and the vastness of its self-perpetuating archive create a huge set of baffles between the core dramas of democratic procedure and the daily limitations of popular interest and competence. This is not to suggest that individual citizens no longer deliberate, discuss and make decisions, but that they do so as points of intersection, relay, and circulation in a complex web of discursive practices.

Finally, my views on the so-called "thinness" thesis and the related question regarding the translatability of the classical rhetorical lexicon (hereafter referred to as CRL) have generated considerable confusion, including the charge that I am a Popperian falsificationist. I am partly responsible for that confusion because I don't state clearly whether I regard CRL as intrinsically "thin," or whether I think it is deployed "thinly" by rhetorical critics in our discipline. Let me clarify my position by citing two passages from *IRRS*.

(1) By "thinness," I am referring to the abstract quality of the traditional vocabulary as illustrated, for instance, in the tripartite scheme of proofs (*ethos*, *pathos*, and *logos*) that enables one to find its presence in virtually any discursive practice. (33)

(2) Is it possible to translate effectively an Aristotelian vocabulary initially generated in the course of "theorizing" about certain types of practical (*praxis*) and productive (*poesis*) activities delimited to the realm of appearances (that is, "public sphere" as Greeks understood it) into a vocabulary for interpretive understanding of cultural practices that cover the whole of human affairs, including science? This question cannot be profitably addressed in an a priori fashion. It must be addressed in the historical context of our disciplinary practices. (30)

While the first passage leaves the impression that I regard CRL as intrinsically "thin," the second passage is clearly concerned with the challenge of deploying that lexicon in contemporary criticism and interpretation. Even in the first passage, my concern about "thinness" stems from how CRL, given its abstract quality, is likely to influence critical practice. At any rate, I don't consider CRL as intrinsically thin. "Thinness" is a relative concept. One could argue as Leff has, in what he playfully calls his "Third Dilippic" (1995), that CRL is the most "dense" vocabulary spawned by any of the verbal arts in the premodern times and possibly since. I concede that CRL is quite dense, but dense in certain ways. It is dense descriptively and taxonomically, especially suited for a "show and tell" pedagogy oriented towards composition and performance. It is also dense normatively in positing a stupefying set of rules based on general claims about human nature, social convention, and communicative strategy. Leff also argues that CRL is incredibly flexible in terms of applications. Historically, certain elements of CRL have "found their way into a variety of arts and disciplines largely or entirely unrelated to their original purpose." Thus, Leff concludes that CRL "can be reinterpreted and applied to new purposes," including interpretive criticism. Here again, I concede that CRL has a rich and complex history of applications. But, as Leff himself admits, it is largely a pedagogically driven history of how to compose and perform with words (and sometimes without words as in painting, architecture, and musicology). CRL bears the burden of that history as it struggles to reposition itself as a language of interpretation. Recourse to such a descriptive/normative vocabulary, however dense and flexible, can result in "thin" readings in practical criticism. In fact, "thin" readings are unavoidable if one views interpretation as a reverse of composition and such a view of interpretation is tacitly held by many who subscribe to the ideology of human agency.

My position on the translatability of CRL is quite clear. I am surprised to find that Leff and Miller (two of the most sympathetic and astute readers of *IRRS*) believe that I foreclose the possibility of translation of CRL from a "productionist" to an "interpretive" vocabulary. Do I need to affirm that translation is possible, when I take as my object of analysis the translative process itself?

(3) Keeping these challenges in sight, can we translate the current rhetorical lexicon? Once again, there is no point in soliciting a speculative answer. The translation is already underway. The practical critics are already struggling with the problem. It is only in their critical labor and struggles that one

can glimpse the translative process. The critic's blindness to the translative process that is underway in their work does not necessarily devalue the insight that they are transforming rhetoric in the course of illuminating some text or practice. (34)

Throughout *IRRS*, I refuse to give an a priori answer and I insist that "practical criticism" is the privileged site for studying the translative process. For that very reason, my theoretical essays on criticism draw their material from the work of practical critics like Black, Campbell, Gross, Leff, McGee, and Wichelns. While screening the translative process, I also identify certain modes of resistance, to which the practical critic tends to be blind, modes that block or retard translation. And I have argued that the ideology of human agency which underwrites the productionist/pedagogical deployment of CRL is most resistant to translation. On this point, there is a serious (perhaps unresolvable) disagreement between me and many of my critics—Campbell, Gross, Leff, and Miller.

I must, however, acknowledge a point made by Miller that the concept of translation, while pivotal to my argument, is left unexamined. Miller goes on to give a brief but instructive account of different ways of conceptualizing translation. Further, she claims that I view translation as "an unproblematic process of lexical matching" (a view of translation she also ascribes to Kuhn) which is untenable in interpretive criticism. While I concede that I have not been sufficiently reflexive in using the concept of "translation," I don't subscribe to the doctrine of "lexical matching." Nor do I subscribe to the "dialogic" (Gadamerean) view of "translation" Miller endorses. I have repeatedly stated that a meta-discursive vocabulary such as CRL is subject to translation only indirectly in practical criticism. Be that as it may, I am indebted to Miller for pressing me to think reflexively about translation.

The Globalization of Rhetoric

The third set of criticisms, voiced primarily by McCloskey and Willard, is directed at my account of the globalization of rhetoric in our time. Basically, I am criticized for opposing the globalization of rhetoric and for promoting a narrow and exclusive view of rhetoric as a civic art. This is a completely erroneous reading. I am neither for nor against globalization. I simply point out that globalization is an unavoidable consequence of the interpretive turn in contemporary rhetoric. That claim, if it is true, should be of concern to the "little rhetoricians" like Leff and Farrell rather than to the "big rhetoricians" like McCloskey and Willard. Paradoxically, it is the champions of "big rhetoric" who insist on positioning me as a "little rhetorician," while the proponents of "little rhetoric" either remain discreetly silent or concede my point in theory but discount it as inconsequential in practical criticism. It seems that the "little rhetoricians" are better at reading an adversary than the "big rhetoricians" are at reading one who is agnostic about the size of rhetoric. I suppose, as Farrell notes, indifference is more irksome than criticism in academic exchanges.

There are at least two modes of globalizing or degobalizing rhetoric: by definitional maneuver and by critical-interpretive practice. I am not particularly interested in the work of those who seek to globalize or deglobalize rhetoric primarily through definitional maneuvers and philosophical speculation. A majority of philosophically-driven essays in "rhetoric as epistemic," "rhetoric of inquiry" and RS belong to that category. Ernesto Grassi's speculative thesis about the origin of language, which posits the priority and universality of rhetorical/poetic speech over philosophical speech is a telling instance of the futility of this mode of globalization (1980). Similarly, Bitzer's deglobalizing claim that scientific discourse is not rhetorical because it does not need an "audience capable of mediating change" is an instance of unproductive definitional exclusion (1968). Critical practice, the heart of inquiry in the humanities, is neither enhanced nor defeated by such definitional extensions or exclusions.

On the other hand, I am intrigued with the work of those who seek (not always consciously) to globalize or deglobalize rhetoric through critical-interpretive practice. Critics within those two rival camps face certain challenges in realizing their theoretical and disciplinary goals. Those challenges can be addressed only indirectly while carrying out the immediate task of criticism.

The case for globalization cannot be effectively made by simply showing that a given discourse field, traditionally regarded as free of rhetoric, is saturated with general rhetorical processes such as addressivity, figuration, and suasory motive. The globalizing critic must generate in the course her criticism regionally specific rhetorical concepts and terms. For instance, the strategy of ascertaining the presence of metaphors in a given disciplinary discourse, say philosophy or economics, does not necessarily regionalize metaphorics. It does vindicate the obvious, an edifying disclosure perhaps for those still caught in the fog of positivism. (Willard thinks there are still a few too many of those.) In the case of philosophy, as with any other disciplinary formations, the question is no longer (perhaps never was) whether there is metaphor in the text of philosophy, but whether philosophy can sustain its constitutive claim to rigor by bridling the unruly play of tropes. Habermas says "yes" fearing that a "no" would herald an end to philosophy; Derrida says "no" fearing that an "yes" would foreclose the possibility of reading philosophy as a "kind of writing."[7] Derrida does not simply deny the possibility of "bridling" tropes. He shows how the very question of "bridling" tropes, with all its sutures and slippages, deflects attention from the fact that metaphor too is a philosophical concept, hence in Nietzschean terms a worn-out metaphor—that is, a metaphor of metaphor. The affinity between rhetoric and metaphor is no more secure than the opposition between concept and metaphor. Moreover, a metaphorics of philosophy is different from a metaphorics of biology or of economics. A global metaphorology, like a global rhetoric, is no more than a propaedeutic to a regionally differentiated study of discourse—its objects, its practices, and its formations.

Further, such a regionalization would require a synchronic as well as a diachronic account of how a given trope/concept functions within a disciplinary formation and/or across trans-disciplinary formations. Take, for instance, the notion of "objectivity." If one were to argue that objectivity within a disciplinary formation, say in historiography, functions primarily as a rhetorical/regulative practice rather than as a empirical/methodological practice, one would have to show how objectivity is rhetoricized by its differential positioning in relation to other historiographic practices within a general economy of investigation, validation and publication; and further how objectivity as a citable practice has been constituted over a period of time through contestation, occultation, and pragmatics.[8] The fact that objectivity is a polysemous trope/concept/practice does not necessarily mean that it is rhetorically motivated. Objectivity becomes rhetorical (or becomes readable as a rhetoric) only when a set of practices associated with it is mobilized and privileged in a specific way within the representational politics of a discipline.

Here, once again, I must emphasize that the regionalization of rhetoric is already underway in the work of critics like Bazerman, Campbell, Gross, Lyne, Miller, and Myers. But that work is being hampered, as I have argued both in *IRRS* and here, due to an unexamined commitment to a face-to-face dialogic model of rhetoric and the global vocabulary associated with it.

The proponents of deglobalized, "restrained" rhetoric who privilege civic discourse begin with a distinct advantage, because the received tradition, especially its Aristotelian version (despite a claim to universality) was *regionally* generated. CRL bears the imprint of its initial formulation in the public sphere. Thus, the task before the deglobalizing critic is to make a rhetorical reading of civic discourse relevant and valuable under the so-called postmodern condition. As I have indicated earlier, aside from my concerns regarding the continuing hold of the ideology of human agency, the critical work currently being done under the "prudence-decorum" paradigm has addressed that task in an admirable fashion.

Finally, a word is necessary about Garver's remarkable new reading of Aristotle's *Rhetoric* that presents a nuanced and carefully argued case for a"restricted" civic rhetoric (Garver, 1994). That case, to summarize briefly, is based on a series of binary oppositions— the internal good vs. the external good; guiding ends vs. given ends; illocutionary acts vs. perlocutionary effects; energeia vs. kinesis, etc.—that roughly characterize the two versions of rhetorical art, the civic and the professional. The former is restricted and constitutive, the latter is global and supplementary. Rhetoric as a civic art regards "persuasion as something that happens in a speech, not simply by means of speech" (1994:35). It has two ends, "the internal good of finding in each case the available means of persuasion, and the external good of successfully persuading" (44). The rhetoric as a global art is motivated exclusively by the external good of successful persuasion by means of speech. Further, Garver argues that rhetoric is fully realized only in the realm of practical discourse as represented by Aristotle's three genres: deliberative, forensic, and epideictic. Only within the folds of those three genres is persuasion praxis, something that is carried out for its own sake and something that is accomplished purely in the act of arguing. Outside of those genres, rhetoric is global but derivative. There are obviously many instances of rhetorical practice that do occur outside of practical/civic discourse, "as when a math teacher has to explain the mean value theorem to resistant students (54–55)." However, in a math lesson rhetoric is not constitutive, but supplementary. Garver also argues that "restricted rhetoric . . . should be dominant over universal rhetoric" (47).

Garver argues his case in such exquisite detail that deglobalizing critic would be tempted to to embrace his position. There is, however, a catch and it pertains to to the so-called "demise of the public" thesis so vigorously argued by modernists and post modernists alike. According to that thesis, the citizen today in a mass-mediated society is thoroughly privatized, and she relates to the polity abstractly through the internalization of of its laws and concretely through its various bureaucratic agencies. With the decline of active citizenry, civic rhetoric, because "it cannot be delegated," is severly impaired. Moreover, the constitutive power of civic rhetoric can no longer regulate the supplementary play of global rhetoric. While Garver does not endorse the "demise of the public" thesis, he is not exactly sanguine about our civic life:

> It could well be that today civic rhetoric is of such marginal importance that it cannot be central to other forms of rhetoric. In the history of rhetoric, when that happens, rhetoric becomes a universal art instead of a civic and practical one. Persuasion is no longer an energeia but a kinesis which aims at a goal outside of itself. . . . Under such circumstances, considerations that are marginal for Aristotle become central to rhetoric: *to prepon, kairos,* decorum, genius, *sprezzatura.* (48)

Are we at such a juncture? If we are, then we are required to study rhetoric as a "global supplement " with the same care with which Garver has examined rhetoric as a "civic art." Further, we have to ask whether the constitutive power of rhetoric, however restricted its domain, is already infected by the play of supplementarity. To read civic discourse at such a moment, one would need a different stratcgy.

CONCLUSION: A CLOSE READING OF THE THIRD KIND

The surface of the public text (of which the oratorical text is a paradigmatic species), like that of a clear pond, is translucent. Nothing seems to be hidden. To a certain point, one can discern with apparent ease the textual design that links the implied character with the imagined community by argument, affect, and ideology. The surface of the literary text, by contrast, is dense and opaque. It is muddied by figuration and resists easy comprehension. (This distinction between the public text and the literary text is inspired by, without being analogous to, Barthes' distinction between the "readerly" text and the "writerly" text.)

The critic is expected to negotiate the two types of texts differently. When faced with a literary text, the critic reads it so as to make what is opaque transparent. Here interpretation moves from complexity to simplicity. If we bracket for the moment deconstructionist interventions, the practice of literary hermeneutics is motivated, among other things, by a desire to make an opaque text legible and readable. There is a certain pleasure in unpacking a figurative composition, especially if that composition can be shown (as with the New Critics) to harbor an organic center, the foregrounding of which magically dispels opacity and confers lucidity. To be sure, what is opaque will remain opaque even after the critic has hermeneutically rendered it transparent. Transparency is but a fleeting moment in the dialectic of the opaque and the translucent.

The difference between the transparent and the translucent is notable. The latter implies partial transparency. According to the dictionary, *translucent* refers both to what is shining or glowing (hence, *luminous*) and what is readily perceptible (hence, *lucid*). The crossing of the luminous and the lucid creates an effect of "admitting and diffusing light so that objects beyond cannot be clearly distinguished." The surface of the public text is translucent in precisely this sense. It is readily perceptible and distracting. Its electric surface is easy and tempting to consume, but its glare deflects a close reading. In rhetorical hermeneutics, the public text is generally read either instrumentally or contextually. The instrumental reading maps the surface in terms of its strategic/purposive design; the contextual reading dissolves the surface in terms of constraints and possibilities. A close reading of the third kind (hereafter referred to as CRTK) that I am proposing here reads the surface as a layered and sedimented space, where the visible and the invisible are contiguous. Such a reading involves a double refusal. First, it refuses the readability that can be procured by erasing the text through recourse to extra-textual frames, as in the instrumental and contextual approaches. Second, it refuses the hermeneutic temptation of explaining the manifest surface in terms of a hidden base. In CRTK the base and the surface are relative constructs. The base of the text, like the bottom of a pond, is settled and sedimented. Just as the pond becomes unsettled and muddied in unseasonable weather, the text is unsettled under a certain kind of reading. In CRTK, unsettling the text is like stirring a pond with a stick. It is a calculated shot in the half-light. The critic has a hunch as to what she expects to stir up from the base of the text, but her critical probe/stick becomes (or appears) crooked the moment it enters the text. The critic, at best, has an uncertain grasp of the commotion she is causing through her interpretive probe in what was once a placid textual surface.

In CRTK, to extend the metaphor, the critic stirs the seemingly translucent pond/text till until it becomes muddy; then, she reads the sedimented particles that have surfaced from the base, identifying their character and formation, and their gradual return to the base. Thus, the critic reads the base only when the base is moving, and that movement is caused by reading itself. Here one must not assume that reading is necessarily in command of the text. While in social scientific research one worries about how one's measuring devices might distort the object being measured, in the humanities one has to worry about how one's critical probes might become estranged and vagrant by a mere contact with the object of analysis. No sooner does a putative interpretive hypothesis come in contact with the text, then that hypothesis (not the text) begins to undergo an involuntary metamorphosis. After the reading (or the storm), the surface of the text (or the pond) looks pretty much the way it did before, except for the resettled base that has a different topography. But after the reading one's interpretive hypothesis is no longer the same. It is lost in the text, absorbed by the resettled base, waiting to surface with the next reading, the next storm. In that manner, interpretive traditions come into being and persist through readings and receptions of the text.

CRTK, like all readings, is caught up in a dialectic between object and method. Its claim to proffer a cultural critique is rooted in the way it prefigures the object field. CRTK engages the public text as a cultural artifact rather than as a manifestation of a rhetor's strategic consciousness. It seeks to map the articulatory practices of a cultural conjuncture and not that of an authorial cunning. CRTK views public discourse as if it were a turnstile, with speaking subjects rapidly entering and exiting, bearing dead metaphors, usable traditions, fragmented arguments, recycled images, and worn emotions. In this mobile economy of public signs and affects, innovation is indistinguishable from bricolage and every attempt at individual voicing gets effaced by the imploding heteroglossia. Hence, CRTK searches the public text not to ascertain the authorial signature, but to map the condition of its existence, the mode of its dissemination, and the force of its articulation.

Finally, CRTK is a way of reading the transparent and the banal. The CRTK critic would not read the transparent, as Leff would, as an effect of self-effacing rhetorical artistry. Nor would the CRTK critic read the banal, as Jasinski would, as enhanced by its participation in a performative tradition. The CRTK critic would read the transparent and the banal for what they are and how they can be crossed. An ethics of reading, much discussed among the humanists of our time, to be credible in relation to public discourse, would have proceed from a disciplined recognition of the banality of the transparent and the transparency of the banal. Only then could one justifiably display that imposing public emotion, anger, at the decay of our public culture (Nussbaum, 1994, 402–438).

Till then a dream sequence from Terry Gilliam's film *Brazil*, which serves as an emblem for CRTK, should keep us in a holding pattern. The winged protagonist, Icarus-like, is flying through the clouds over a serene and bucolic landscape searching for an unseen beloved. The moment he spots the beloved, also flying through the clouds, the earth beneath suddenly opens and a city of skyscrapers erupts. The beloved, in a falling motion, recedes from view on the other side of the tall city. The protagonist awakes. In reality, the tall city is not buried, it is not hidden. It was always there, an unnoticed city, a purloined city. We live there.

NOTES

In composing this reply, I have profited from discussions and communications with a large number of students and colleagues, especially: Melissa Deem, Alan Gross, Robert Hariman, James Jasinksi, Christopher Kamrath, William Keith, Michael Leff, Daniel O'Keefe, and John Sloop.

1. For a discussion of "middle-level" theories, see Merton (1967).

2. For the distinction between "etic" and "emic" perspectives in rhetorical criticism, see Black (1980).

3. I regard the presence of a critical lexicon, rhetorical or any other, as an initial signal the text emits to set in motion a series of reading protocols regarding genre, tradition and interpretive community. Its presence does not guarantee a specific mode of reading, nor its absence exclude that mode of reading.

4. This is an intertextually charged passage. Aside from the texts from classical rhetoric, it refers to E. D. Hirsch (1967) on intention, to James Boyd White (1984) on character and community, Ronald Beiner (1983) on political judgment and prudence (a synthesis of Aristotle and Kant via Gadamer).

5. I have been criticized for the unfavorable comparison I draw between RS and SSK and its allies: "(T)he differences between RS and SSK (Sociology of Scientific Knowledge) are striking and instructive. Although both started roughly at the same time in the 70s, SSK has developed into a complex empirical research program that displays considerable internal variation in theory and methodology, while RS remains little more than an uncoordinated research initiative carried out by a handful of committed individuals" My claim above has been challenged on two grounds. First, I am not empirically justified in pronouncing that the RS project has stalled because my judgment is based on a severely truncated reading of the available scholarly literature on RS. Second, I am not justified in distinguishing between RS and SSK insofar as the latter constitutes an integral part of the rhetorical turn in the study of science. I can only offer a brief response to

these objections here. As to the first objection, my claim that RS is stalled is based on a fairly comprehensive reading of the relevant literature in Speech Communication. To do conceptual ethnography of the term rhetoric, by means of a "close" reading, it was necessary to concentrate on a determinate body of literature. In a monograph-length essay, it is simply not possible to cover all the relevant literature on RS except in a superficial manner. The question is whether the literature examined is representative. I believe it is. As to the second objection, I regard the proclivity to collapse the distinction between RS and SSS (SSK and its allies) as yet another instance of the politics of repression and recognition that serves as a perennial alibi for eliding the question of the specificity of rhetoric.

6. The charge that I am a Popperian falsificationist is based on the following passage in *IRRS*: "In its current form, rhetoric as a language of criticism is so thin and abstract that it is virtually invulnerable to falsification, and for that very reason it commands little sustained attention." To begin with, I do not subscribe to the doctrine of falsification. Anyone who reads the above sentence in the general context of my essay would not find the label tenable. I concede that it is an unfortunate word choice, especially in an essay on the rhetoric of science. I knew this well before *IRRS* was completed from John Campbell's response to an early first draft. I could have substituted the word "contestable" for "falsifiable," as I do in an endnote, without diluting my point. But Campbell had already composed some fine passages berating me for being a falsificationist. It would be ungentlemanly to switch a word in the midst of a polemic. Now I discover that an academic polemic is not cricket! There is, however, an element of confusion in my falsifiability/contestability criterion. As Willard (and Daniel O'Keefe in a personal communication) indicate, that the demand that a given vocabulary be falsifiable is not viable. In O'Keefe's words: "Asking that a *vocabulary* be falsifiable is a category mistake; only *claims* can be falsifiable, not vocabularies or categories. The appropriate test for a vocabulary is whether it gives rise to useful descriptions. . . . Perhaps, Gaonkar's statement about 'falsifiability' is simply a poorly-chosen way of complaining that rhetorical vocabulary has not yielded useful fruit." Indeed, it was a poorly-chosen word.

7. Habermas (1990); Rorty (1978-79); Derrida (1982).

8. For a discussion of the "implicit" rhetoric of objectivity in historiography, see Novick (1988).

REFERENCES

Barthes, R. (1988). The old rhetoric: An *aide-memoiré*. In *The semiological challenge*. R. Howard (trans). New York, NY: Hill and Wang.

Baskerville, B. (1953). The critical method in speech. *The Central States Speech Journal*, 4, 1–5.

Beiner, R. (1983). *Political Judgement*. Chicago, IL: University of Chicago Press.

Bitzer, L. (1968). The rhetorical situation. *Philosophy and Rhetoric, 1,* 1–14.

Black, E. (1980). A note on theory and practice in rhetorical criticism. *Western Journal of Speech Communication, 44,* 331–336.

Derrida, J. (1982). White mythology: metaphor in the text of philosophy. In *Margins of Philosophy*. Alan Bass (Trans). Chicago, IL: University of Chicago Press, 207–272.

Gaonkar, D. P. (1990). Object and method in rhetorical criticism: From Wichelns to Leff and McGee. *Western Speech Communication Journal, 54,* 290–316.

Garver, E. (1994). *Aristotle's* Rhetoric: *An art of character.* Chicago: University of Chicago Press.

Grassi, E. (1980). *Philosophy as rhetoric: The humanist tradition.* University Park, PA: The Pennsylvania State University Press.

Habermas, J. (1990). *The philosophical discourse of modernity.* F. G. Lawrence (Trans.). Cambridge, MA: MIT Press, 161–185.

Hirsch, E.D. Jr. (1967). *Validity in interpretation.* New Haven, CT: Yale University Press.

Leff, M. C. (1995). The third Dilippic. Paper presented as the meeting of Speech Communication Association, San Antonio, November, 1995.

———. (1987). The habitation of rhetoric. In *Argument and critical practices.* J. W. Wenzel (Ed.). Annandale, VA: SCA Publications, 1–8.

———. (1986). Textual criticism: The legacy of G. P. Mohrmann. *Quarterly Journal of Speech, 72,* 346–358.

———. (1980). Intepretation and the art of the rhetorical critic. *Western Journal of Speech Communication, 44,* 337–349.

Leff, M. C. and Procario, M. O. (1985). Rhetorical theory in speech communication. *Speech communication in the twentieth century.* T. W. Benson (Ed.). Carbondale, IL: Southern Illinois University Press, 3–27.

Merton, R. K. (1967). *On theoretical sociology: Five essays, old and new.* New York: Free Press.

Novick, P. (1988). *That noble dream: The "objectivity question" and the American historical profession.* New York, NY: Cambridge University Press.

Nussbaum, M. C. (1994). *The therapy of desire: Theory and practice in hellenistic ethics.* Princeton, NJ: Princeton University Press.

Redding, W. C. (1957). Extrinsic and intrinsic criticism. *Western Speech Communication Journal, 21,* 96–102.

Ricoeur, P. (1974). *The conflict of interpretations: Essays in hermeneutics.* D. Ihde (Ed.). Evanston, IL: Northwestern University Press.

Rorty, R. (1978–1979). Philosophy as a kind of writing: An essay on Derrida. *New Literary History, X,* 141–160.

White, J. B. (1984). *When words lose their meaning: The constitution and reconstitution of language, character and community.* Chicago, IL: Chicago University Press.

Wichelns, J. H. (1925). The literary criticism of public oratory. In *Studies in rhetoric and public speaking in honor of James A. Winans.* New York, NY: Century, 181–216.

Wrage, E. J. (1947). Public address: A study in social and intellectual history. *Quarterly Journal of Speech, 33,* 451–457.

CONTRIBUTORS

John Angus Campbell is Professor of Communication at the University of Memphis. Professor Campbell's numerous essays focus primarily on the rhetorical dimensions of Charles Darwin's campaign for evolution; two of these received the Speech Communication Association's Golden Anniversary Award. Professor Campbell serves on the editorial board of the *Quarterly Journal of Speech*, and has served on the boards of *Rhetorica* and the *Western Journal of Speech Communication*. In 1990 he was selected to be Van Zelst Professor of Communication at Northwestern University, and in 1993 received the Distinguished Teaching Award at the University of Washington. He is currently at work on a book entitled *Charles Darwin: A Rhetorical Biography*. acampell@msuvx2.memphis.edu

Dilip Parameshwar Gaonkar is an Associate Professor of Communication Studies at Northwestern University. He has published numerous influential essays on rhetorical theory and criticism, and has twice been honored with the Speech Communication Association's Golden Anniversary Award. He is an associate editor of the journal *Public Culture*, codirector of the Institute for Transcultural Studies at Chicago, and is currently at work on trans-cultural rhetorical studies. d-gaonkar@nwu.edu

Thomas Farrell is Professor of Communication Studies at Northwestern University. He has published widely on rhetorical theory and the criticism of popular and traditional texts, and has received the Winans-Wichelns Award for distinguished scholarship in rhetoric and public address in 1994, and the Charles Woolbert Award for research in 1990 from the Speech Communication Association. He recently published *The Norms of Rhetorical Culture* (Yale University Press, 1994). tbf402@nwu.edu

Steve Fuller is Professor of Sociology and Social Policy at the University of Durham, UK. He is the executive editor and founder of the journal *Social Epistemology*, and the author of three books, the most recent of which is *Philosophy, Rhetoric and the End of Knowledge: The Coming of Science and Technology Studies* (University of Wisconsin Press, 1993). He is completing two books, one on the epistemology of multiculturalism and the other on the origins and impacts of Thomas Kuhn's *The Structure of Scientific Revolutions*. steve.fuller@durham.ac.uk

Alan G. Gross is Professor of Rhetoric at the University of Minnesota. He has published widely on the rhetoric of science, including *The Rhetoric of Science* (Harvard University Press, 1990). He is currently at work on a history of the scientific article. agross@maroon.tc.umn.edu

James Jasinski is Assistant Professor in the Department of Speech Communication at the University of Illinois. His critical studies of American public discourse have appeared in the *Quarterly Journal of Speech*, and *Rhetoric Society Quarterly*. He received the Outstanding Scholarship Award for 1993 from the Public Address division of the Speech Communication Association. jasinski@vmd.cso.uiuc.edu

David Kaufer is Professor of Rhetoric and Head of the Department of English at Carnegie Mellon University. He is also codirector of an interdisciplinary masters program in Communication Planning and Design, run jointly by the Departments of English and Design in the College of Fine Arts. He is coauthor (with Kathleen Carley) of *Communication at a Distance: The Influence of Print on Socio-cultural Organization and Change* (Erlbaum, 1993). With Brian Butler, he has recently completed a new book (Erlbaum, 1996) which argues for rhetoric's appropriate placement in the family of design arts. kaufer@andrew.cmu.edu

William Keith is Assistant Professor in the Department of Communication at Oregon State University. His essays have appeared in *Argumentation, Social Epistemology*, and the *Southern Communication Journal*, among others. He has written on rhetorical theory, the rhetoric of science, argumentation theory, and the rhetoric of artificial intelligence. keithw@ucs.orst.edu

Andrew King is Professor and Chair of the Department of Speech Communication at Louisiana State University. He has authored three books, numerous articles, and is presently serving as editor of the *Southern Communication Journal*. Professor King's academic interests lie in the areas of communication and power, and nineteenth-century political discourse. aking@salvador.speech.lsu.edu

Michael Leff is Professor of Communication Studies at Northwestern University. A former editor of *Rhetorica: The Journal of the History of Rhetoric*, he has published widely on the topics of the history of rhetoric and rhetorical criticism. He has won two major awards for scholarship from the Speech Communication Association—the Winans-Wichelns Award and the Woolbert Award. With Winifred Horner, he is editor of *Rhetoric and Pedagogy: Its History, Theory and Practice. Studies in Honor of James J. Murphy* (LEA, in press). leff@merle.acus.nwu.edu

Deirdre McCloskey is John F. Murray Professor of Economics and Professor of History at the University of Iowa. She has written on British economic history, and in recent years on the literary element in economics. In this vein she has written, under the name Donald McCloskey, *The Rhetoric of Economics* (1985), *If You're So Smart: The Narrative of Economic Expertise* (1990), and *Knowledge and Persuasion in Economics* (1994). donald.mccloskey@uiowa.edu

Carolyn R. Miller is Professor of English at North Carolina State University. She has published on rhetorical theory and the rhetoric of science and technology in the *Quarterly Journal of Speech, Rhetorica, Argumentation,* and other journals, as well as in several essay collections. She is 1996–1998 president of the Rhetoric Society of America. crmiller@ncsu.edu

Charles Arthur Willard is Professor and Chair in the Department of Communication, University of Louisville. His books include *Argumentation and the Social Grounds of Knowledge* (Alabama UP, 1983), *A Theory of Argumentation* (Alabama UP, 1989), and *Liberalism and the Problem of Knowledge: A New Rhetoric for Modern Democracy* (Chicago UP, 1996). He is a founding codirector of the International Society for the Study of Argumentation, and has coedited four *Proceedings* for the Conference on Argumentation held at the University of Amsterdam. cawill01@ulkyvm.louisville.edu

SUBJECT INDEX

A

adaptation: differential, 132;
  imperfect, 131–2
agency, rhetorical, 12, 48, 53–4,
  56–7, 75, 92–4, 99, 115, 120–3,
  188–9, 196, 326, 336–7, 343
anger, 352
anxiety, disciplinary, 19, 195
argumentation, 74
argument field, 64
Aristotelian ideology. *See* ideology
  of human agency
arrangement, 142–4
audience, 9, 32, 43, 48, 50, 59–60,
  121, 130, 133, 142–4, 156, 198,
  207; universal, 311
autonomy, 219

B

bi-stability, 230

C

case studies, 41, 152
chiasmus, 203
citation classics, 291
close readings of the third kind
  (CRTK), 350–3
coarticulation, 47, 73, 75–6

Coatesville Address (Chapman),
  207
communication, mass, 290, 293;
  multi-step flow model, 291
communitarian strategy, 42–3, 68
community, 18–19, 43, 121, 144
constraints, 237–40
constructivism, 42, 61, 65
contestable readings/
  interpretations, 14, 62, 107, 139,
  145
context: functionalist account of,
  199; and rhetorical criticism, 15,
  196–218; and rhetorical theory,
  13, 199
control, 231–2, 238
conversation, 165–6
Cooper Union address (Lincoln),
  202–3
Cornell School, 30,
cultural grammar, 50, 53–4, 56, 58,
  132, 217

D

deconstruction, 12, 33, 124–6, 293
decorum (*see also* to prepon), 48,
  97, 332, 350
democracy, and science, 281, 283
Descent of Man, The (Darwin), 131
design (*see also* rhetoric, as design
  art): author's conscious, 196;

NAME INDEX

A

Althusser, L., 76
Aristotle, 17, 26–7, 30, 32, 48, 60, 75–6, 78, 91, 118, 131, 138–40, 157, 177, 182, 187–9, 231–2, 235–6, 257–9, 270, 325
Asad, T., 162–3
Ashmore, M., 102
Aspect, A., 148
Aune, J., 325

B

Bacon, F., 132, 291, 321
Bakhtin, M., 215
Baird, A. C., 200, 205
Barnes, B., 102
Barthes, R., 6, 26, 331, 350
Baskerville, B., 4–5, 313, 335
Baudrillard, J., 77
Bazerman, C., 80, 156, 336, 348
Becker, H., 151
Beiner, R., 342–3
Berlin, I., 319, 328
Bernstein, R., 168
Biesecker, B., 226
Billig, M., 108, 270
Bineham, J., 214
Bitzer, L., 2, 32, 79, 156, 219, 319, 343, 347

Black, E., 2, 8, 11, 50, 79, 94, 102, 108, 113, 156, 160, 205–8, 210, 220, 236, 243, 334, 343, 346
Bokeno, R., 45–8, 107, 109, 243
Booth, W., 3, 5, 270
Bowler, P., 131
Boyle, R., 107, 282
Brahe, T., 52
Brown, R.H., 152
Brummett, B., 233
Bryant, D., 32, 34–5, 57, 185, 248
Buchwald, J., 146
Burke, K., 28, 31, 38, 51, 55, 66, 71–3, 78, 116, 122, 178, 199, 219, 228, 232, 309, 313, 326
Butler, B., 261

C

Campbell, J., 11, 13–5, 18, 48–60, 64, 79–80, 91–2, 94–5, 106, 109–10, 121, 123, 128, 141, 157, 180, 181, 197, 212, 214, 216, 228–9, 285–8, 290, 323, 332–3, 335–8, 346, 348
Chomsky, N., 248
Cicero, 8, 27–8, 33, 48, 72–3, 78, 306
Clay, H., 200
Cohen, B., 63, 151
Collins, H., 41, 102–3, 180
Comte, A., 18–9, 300–8, 310–1